MOON

Pittsburgh

DAN ELDRIDGE

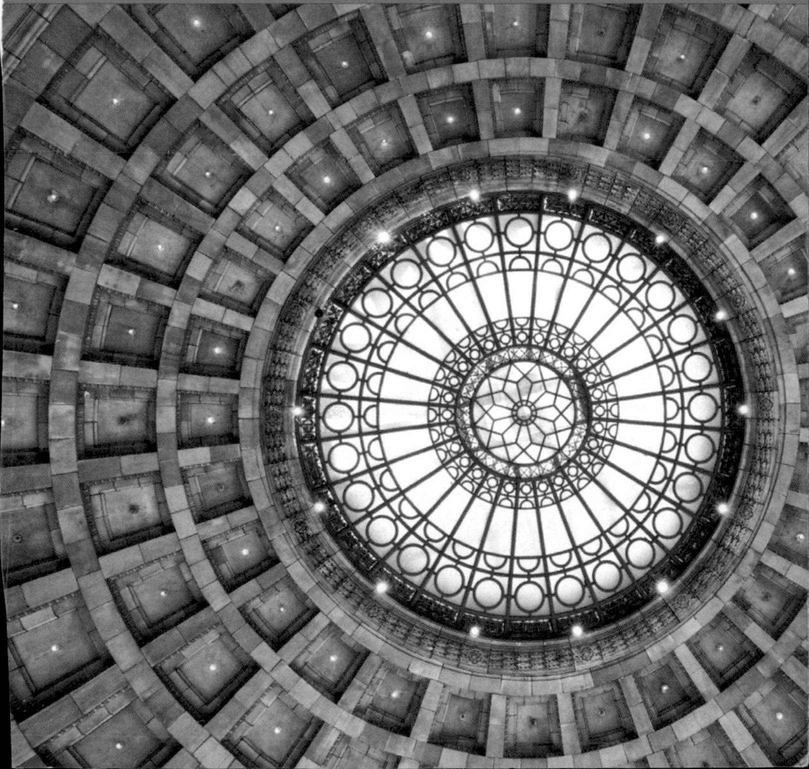

Contents

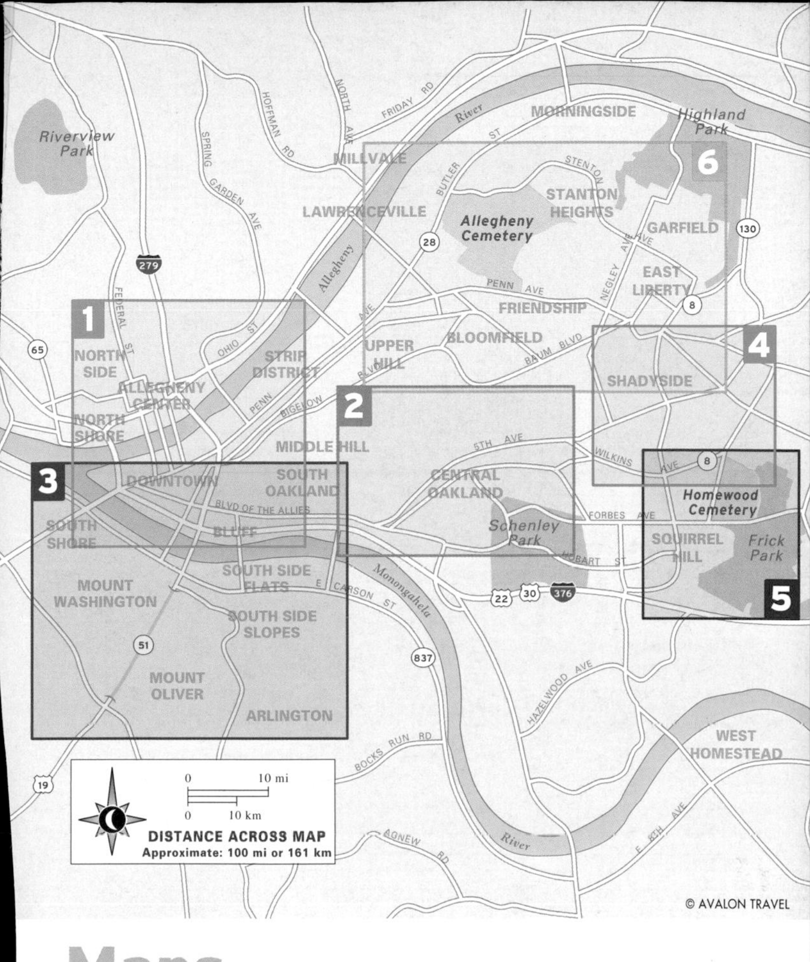

Riverview Park
MILLVALE
LAWRENCEVILLE
MORNINGSIDE
Highland Park
STANTON HEIGHTS
Allegheny Cemetery
GARFIELD
EAST LIBERTY
FRIENDSHIP
BLOOMFIELD
UPPER HILL
NORTH SIDE
ALLEGHENY CENTER
NORTH SHORE
STRIP DISTRICT
SHADYSIDE
MIDDLE HILL
CENTRAL OAKLAND
DOWNTOWN
SOUTH OAKLAND
BLUFF
SOUTH SHORE
Homewood Cemetery
Schenley Park
SQUIRREL HILL
Frick Park
SOUTH SIDE FLATS
MOUNT WASHINGTON
SOUTH SIDE SLOPES
MOUNT OLIVER
ARLINGTON
WEST HOMESTEAD
DISTANCE ACROSS MAP
Approximate: 100 mi or 161 km
© AVALON TRAVEL

Maps

MAP 1

Mattress Factory
Randyland
CENTRAL NORTHSIDE
House Poem and City of Asylum
ALLEGHENY GENERAL HOSPITAL
JACKSONIA ST
SAMPSONIA WY
PARKHURST ST
N TAYLOR AVE
CITRON WAY
E NORTH AVE
PENNSYLVANIA AVE
BUENA VISTA ST
MONTEREY ST
PALO ALTO ST
SHERMAN AVE
ARCH ST
ELOISE ST
W NORTH AVE
FEDERAL ST
JAMES ST
FORELAND
MIDDLE ST
Calvary United Methodist Church
National Aviary
NORTH COMMONS
ALLEGHENY CENTER
EAST OHIO ST
VIRGIN WAY
Children's Museum of Pittsburgh
BEECH AVE
DOUNTON WAY
WESTERN AVE
MAOLIS WAY
N LINCOLN AVE
BRIGHTON RD
ROPE WAY
WEST OHIO ST
RIDGE AVE
MERCHANT ST
WEST COMMONS
EAST COMMONS
SOUTH COMMONS
ALLEGHENY AVE
GALVESTON AVE
ALLEGHENY WEST
COMMUNITY COLLEGE OF ALLEGHENY COUNTY
65TH INFANTRY DIVISON MEMORIAL HWY
279
REEDSDALE ST
To Rivers Casino
Allegheny
ART ROONEY AVE
North Side
W GENERAL ROBINSON ST
SANDUSKY ST
The Andy Warhol Museum
Carnegie Science Center and Highmark SportsWorks
CHUCK NOLL WY
NORTH SHORE
Three Sisters Bridges
CARSON BRG
RACHEL
NORTH SHORE DR
ROBERTO CLEMENTE BDG
ANDY WARHOL BRG
FORT DUQUESNE BRIDGE
River
Allegheny
10TH ST BYP
FORT DUQUESNE BLVD
BARKERS PL
7TH ST
PENN AVE
Point State Park
CENTRAL BUSINESS DISTRICT
STANWIX ST
CECIL WAY
COMMONWEALTH PL
Gateway
LIBERTY AVE
Wood Street
Fort Pitt Museum
Monongahela River
PPG Place
Market Square
MARKET ST
5TH AVE
FORBES AVE
4TH AVE
376
Smithfield Street Bridge
SIGHTS
2 MATTRESS FACTORY
3 HOUSE POEM AND CITY OF ASYLUM
4 RANDYLAND
8 CALVARY UNITED METHODIST CHURCH
10 NATIONAL AVIARY
11 CHILDREN'S MUSEUM OF PITTSBURGH
14 PHOTO ANTIQUITIES MUSEUM
17 RIVERS CASINO
18 CARNEGIE SCIENCE CENTER AND HIGHMARK SPORTSWORKS
28 THE ANDY WARHOL MUSEUM
29 THREE SISTERS BRIDGES
30 POINT STATE PARK
31 FORT PITT MUSEUM
33 THE CULTURAL DISTRICT
42 PNC LEGACY PROJECT
57 TOONSEUM
59 AUGUST WILSON CENTER FOR AFRICAN AMERICAN CULTURE
63 MARKET SQUARE
64 PPG PLACE
69 SMITHFIELD STREET BRIDGE
71 ALLEGHENY COUNTY COURTHOUSE AND OLD JAIL
82 SENATOR JOHN HEINZ HISTORY CENTER
91 ST. PATRICK CHURCH
98 ST. STANISLAUS KOSTKA CHURCH
103 PITTSBURGH PUBLIC MARKET
105 WIGLE WHISKEY
RESTAURANTS
1 BUENA VISTA COFFEE
5 WILSON'S BAR-B-Q
7 EL BURRO
13 MAX'S ALLEGHENY TAVERN
16 PENN BREWERY
36 SIX PENN KITCHEN
38 BUTCHER AND THE RYE
39 HABITAT
45 MEAT & POTATOES
53 NINE ON NINE
55 SEVICHE
61 ORIGINAL FISH MARKET
62 ORIGINAL OYSTER HOUSE
66 TAVERN 245
67 PENN AVENUE FISH COMPANY
81 ELEVEN
83 SUSHI KIM
86 GAUCHO PARRILLA ARGENTINA
89 PRIMANTI BROTHERS
90 PRESTOGEORGE
93 KAYA
94 DELUCA'S RESTAURANT
96 PEACE, LOVE & LITTLE DONUTS
97 PAMELA'S DINER
99 LA PRIMA ESPRESSO COMPANY
102 BAR MARCO
106 KLAVON'S ICE CREAM PARLOR

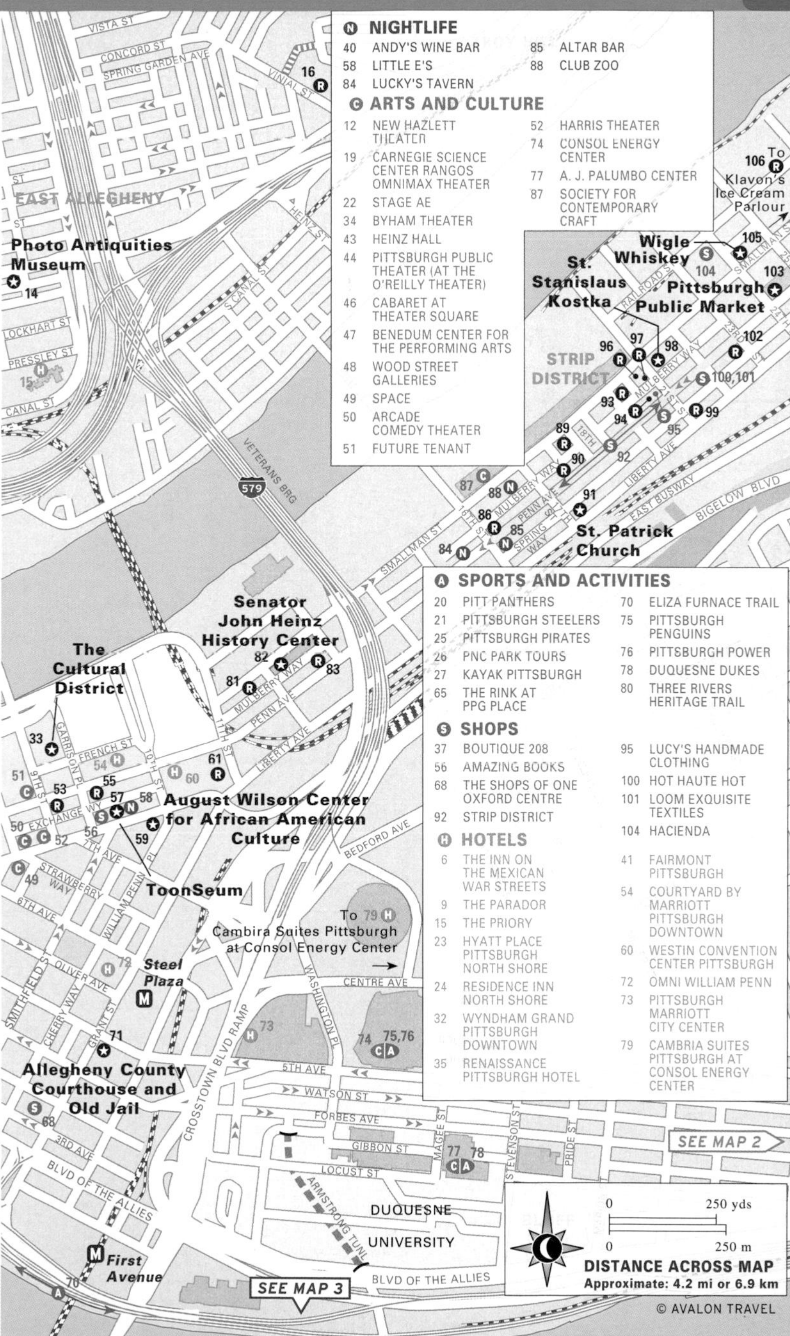
NIGHTLIFE
40 ANDY'S WINE BAR
58 LITTLE E'S
84 LUCKY'S TAVERN
85 ALTAR BAR
88 CLUB ZOO
ARTS AND CULTURE
12 NEW HAZLETT THEATER
19 CARNEGIE SCIENCE CENTER RANGOS OMNIMAX THEATER
22 STAGE AE
34 BYHAM THEATER
43 HEINZ HALL
44 PITTSBURGH PUBLIC THEATER (AT THE O'REILLY THEATER)
46 CABARET AT THEATER SQUARE
47 BENEDUM CENTER FOR THE PERFORMING ARTS
48 WOOD STREET GALLERIES
49 SPACE
50 ARCADE COMEDY THEATER
51 FUTURE TENANT
52 HARRIS THEATER
74 CONSOL ENERGY CENTER
77 A. J. PALUMBO CENTER
87 SOCIETY FOR CONTEMPORARY CRAFT
SPORTS AND ACTIVITIES
20 PITT PANTHERS
21 PITTSBURGH STEELERS
25 PITTSBURGH PIRATES
26 PNC PARK TOURS
27 KAYAK PITTSBURGH
65 THE RINK AT PPG PLACE
70 ELIZA FURNACE TRAIL
75 PITTSBURGH PENGUINS
76 PITTSBURGH POWER
78 DUQUESNE DUKES
80 THREE RIVERS HERITAGE TRAIL
SHOPS
37 BOUTIQUE 208
56 AMAZING BOOKS
68 THE SHOPS OF ONE OXFORD CENTRE
92 STRIP DISTRICT
95 LUCY'S HANDMADE CLOTHING
100 HOT HAUTE HOT
101 LOOM EXQUISITE TEXTILES
104 HACIENDA
HOTELS
6 THE INN ON THE MEXICAN WAR STREETS
9 THE PARADOR
15 THE PRIORY
23 HYATT PLACE PITTSBURGH NORTH SHORE
24 RESIDENCE INN NORTH SHORE
32 WYNDHAM GRAND PITTSBURGH DOWNTOWN
35 RENAISSANCE PITTSBURGH HOTEL
41 FAIRMONT PITTSBURGH
54 COURTYARD BY MARRIOTT PITTSBURGH DOWNTOWN
60 WESTIN CONVENTION CENTER PITTSBURGH
72 OMNI WILLIAM PENN
73 PITTSBURGH MARRIOTT CITY CENTER
79 CAMBRIA SUITES PITTSBURGH AT CONSOL ENERGY CENTER
EAST ALLEGHENY
Photo Antiquities Museum
STRIP DISTRICT
St. Stanislaus Kostka
Wigle Whiskey
Pittsburgh Public Market
To Klavon's Ice Cream Parlour
St. Patrick Church
Senator John Heinz History Center
The Cultural District
August Wilson Center for African American Culture
ToonSeum
To Cambira Suites Pittsburgh at Consol Energy Center
Steel Plaza
Allegheny County Courthouse and Old Jail
First Avenue
DUQUESNE UNIVERSITY
SEE MAP 2
SEE MAP 3
0 250 yds
0 250 m
DISTANCE ACROSS MAP
Approximate: 4.2 mi or 6.9 km
© AVALON TRAVEL

MAP 2

SEE MAP 6
West Penn Park
SMALLMAN ST
25TH ST
24TH ST
BIGELOW BLVD
BEDFORD DWELLINGS
WEBSTER AVE
WYLIE AVE
MIDDLE HILL
ELBA ST
CENTRE AVE
BRACKENRIDGE ST
UNIVERSITY OF PITTSBURGH
TERRACE VILLAGE
ALLEQUIPPA ST
DARRAGH ST
TERRACE ST
ECKSTEIN PL
OAK HILL DR
WEST OAKLAND
CHESTERFIELD RD
SEE MAP 1
CARLOW UNIVERSITY
5TH AVE
MAGEE-WOMEN'S HOSPITAL OF UPMC
CRAFT AVE
GALENA ST
HAMLET ST
JOE HAMMER SQ
LAWN ST
PENN LINCOLN PKWY
2ND AVE
TECHNOLOGY CENTER DR
Monongahela River
SIGHTS
7 SOLDIERS AND SAILORS MEMORIAL
9 ST. PAUL CATHEDRAL
10 RODEF SHALOM BIBLICAL BOTANICAL GARDEN
21 CARNEGIE MELLON UNIVERSITY
23 CARNEGIE MUSEUM OF NATURAL HISTORY
24 CARNEGIE MUSEUM OF ART
26 CATHEDRAL OF LEARNING
30 SCHENLEY PLAZA
47 PHIPPS CONSERVATORY AND BOTANICAL GARDENS
48 SCHENLEY PARK AND FLAGSTAFF HILL
RESTAURANTS
4 LEGUME
13 EAT UNIQUE
15 LULU'S NOODLES
16 LUCCA
17 ALI BABA
20 UNION GRILL
29 CONFLICT KITCHEN
31 HEMINGWAY'S
32 THE ORIGINAL HOT DOG SHOP
33 OISHII BENTO
35 SUSHI BOAT
36 FUEL AND FUDDLE
37 DAVE & ANDY'S
38 SPICE ISLAND TEA HOUSE
41 INDIA GARDEN
42 MAD MEX
NIGHTLIFE
3 AVA
11 KBOX KARAOKE HOUSE
34 PETER'S PUB
46 MINT HOOKAH BAR & LOUNGE
ARTS AND CULTURE
1 MELWOOD SCREENING ROOM
5 PETERSEN EVENTS CENTER
22 MILLER GALLERY AT CARNEGIE MELLON UNIVERSITY
25 CARNEGIE MUSIC HALL
27 CHARITY RANDALL THEATRE
43 PITTSBURGH PLAYHOUSE
SPORTS AND ACTIVITIES
6 PITT PANTHERS
49 SCHENLEY PARK
50 SCHENLEY PARK POOL
51 SCHENLEY PARK SKATING RINK
52 SCHENLEY PARK TENNIS COURTS
SHOPS
12 SNOW LION IMPORTS
14 IRISH DESIGN CENTER
18 PHANTOM OF THE ATTIC COMICS
19 CALIBAN BOOKSHOP
28 UNIVERSITY OF PITTSBURGH BOOK CENTER
39 IRON CITY BIKES
HOTELS
2 RESIDENCE INN PITTSBURGH UNIVERSITY/ MEDICAL CENTER
8 WYNDHAM PITTSBURGH UNIVERSITY CENTER
40 HILTON GARDEN INN PITTSBURGH UNIVERSITY PLACE
44 HAMPTON INN UNIVERSITY CENTER
45 QUALITY INN UNIVERSITY CENTER
©AVALON TRAVEL

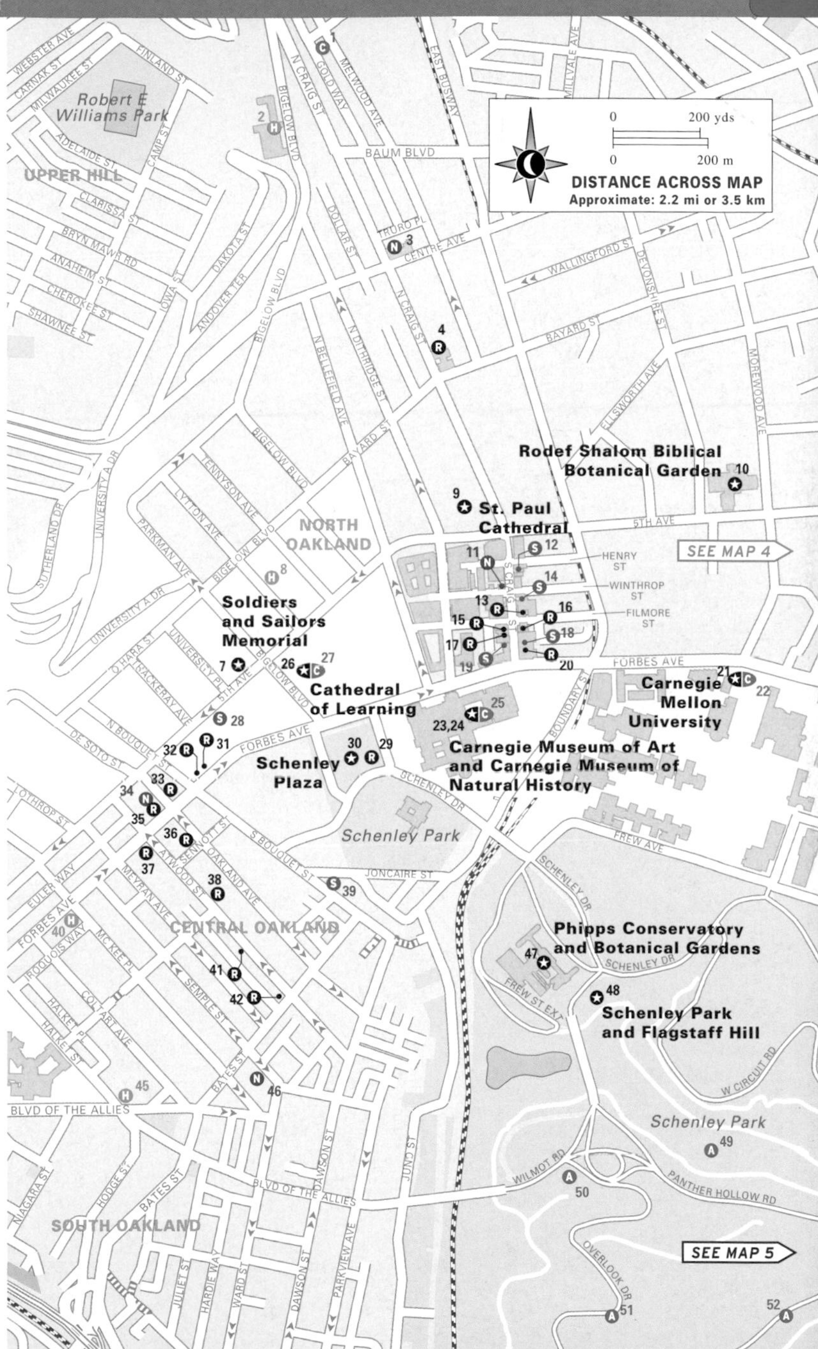
Robert E Williams Park
UPPER HILL
NORTH OAKLAND
CENTRAL OAKLAND
SOUTH OAKLAND
0
200 yds
0
200 m
DISTANCE ACROSS MAP
Approximate: 2.2 mi or 3.5 km
Rodef Shalom Biblical Botanical Garden
St. Paul Cathedral
Soldiers and Sailors Memorial
Cathedral of Learning
Schenley Plaza
Carnegie Mellon University
Carnegie Museum of Art and Carnegie Museum of Natural History
Schenley Park
Phipps Conservatory and Botanical Gardens
Schenley Park and Flagstaff Hill
SEE MAP 4
SEE MAP 5
WEBSTER AVE
CARNAK ST
MILWAUKEE ST
FINLAND ST
ADELAIDE ST
CAMP ST
CLARISSA ST
BRYN MAWR RD
ANAHEIM ST
CHEROKEE ST
SHAWNEE ST
DAKOTA ST
IOWA ST
ANDOVER TER
BIGELOW BLVD
N CRAIG ST
GOLD WAY
MELWOOD AVE
EAST BUSWAY
MILLVALE AVE
BAUM BLVD
TRURO PL
CENTRE AVE
DOLLAR ST
WALLINGFORD ST
DEVONSHIRE ST
BAYARD ST
N BELLEFIELD AVE
N DITHRIDGE ST
ELLSWORTH AVE
MOREWOOD AVE
TENNYSON AVE
LYTTON AVE
PARKMAN AVE
UNIVERSITY A DR
SUTHERLAND DR
5TH AVE
HENRY ST
WINTHROP ST
FILMORE ST
S CRAIG ST
FORBES AVE
BOUNDARY ST
O'HARA ST
THACKERAY AVE
UNIVERSITY PL
N BOUQUET ST
DE SOTO ST
LOTHROP ST
SCHENLEY DR
FREW AVE
S BOUQUET ST
JONCAIRE ST
SENNOTT ST
OAKLAND AVE
ATWOOD ST
MEYRAN AVE
EULER WAY
FORBES AVE
IROQUOIS WAY
MCKEE PL
SEMPLE ST
COLT ART AVE
HALKET PL
HALKET ST
BATES ST
BLVD OF THE ALLIES
FREW ST EXT
W CIRCUIT RD
WILMOT RD
PANTHER HOLLOW RD
OVERLOOK DR
NIAGARA ST
HODGE ST
JULIET ST
HARDIE WAY
WARD ST
DAWSON ST
PARKVIEW AVE
JUNO ST
1 2 3 4 7 8 9 10 11 12 13 14 15 16 17 18 19 20 21 22 23,24 25 26 27 28 29 30 31 32 33 34 35 36 37 38 39 40 41 42 45 46 47 48 49 50 51 52

MAP 3

SIGHTS

1 THE DUQUESNE INCLINE
6 GATEWAY CLIPPER FLEET
14 STATION SQUARE
15 THE MONONGAHELA INCLINE
75 SOUTH SIDE SLOPES

RESTAURANTS

2 MONTEREY BAY FISH GROTTO
3 GRANDVIEW SALOON & COAL HILL STEAKHOUSE
4 TIN ANGEL
5 LEMONT RESTAURANT
12 GRAND CONCOURSE
19 THE ZENITH
21 BIG DOG COFFEE
24 HOFBRÄUHAUS PITTSBURGH
28 BRIDGE TEN BRASSERIE
31 CAFE DU JOUR
34 YO RITA
41 BEEHIVE COFFEEHOUSE
45 PIZZA SOLA
52 DISH
53 NAKAMA JAPANESE STEAK HOUSE
54 CAMBOD-ICAN KITCHEN
56 THE MILK SHAKE FACTORY
58 FAT HEAD'S SALOON
70 IBIZA TAPAS AND WINE BAR
71 MALLORCA
73 DOUBLE WIDE GRILL

NIGHTLIFE

16 REDBEARD'S
17 WHIM
18 OVER THE BAR BICYCLE CAFÉ
33 JACK'S BAR
35 BAR 11
36 CLUB CAFÉ
38 THE SMILING MOOSE
39 DEE'S CAFÉ
40 ROWDY BUCK
47 LOCAL BAR + KITCHEN
48 SKYBAR
49 DIESEL
50 REX THEATRE
57 S BAR
60 PIPER'S PUB
61 VILLA SOUTHSIDE
62 SMOKIN' JOE'S
63 TIKI LOUNGE
66 ACACIA
68 LAVA LOUNGE

ARTS AND CULTURE

30 SILVER EYE CENTER FOR PHOTOGRAPHY
37 CITY THEATRE

SPORTS AND ACTIVITIES

7 PITTSBURGH PASSION
8 PITTSBURGH RIVERHOUNDS
10 JUST DUCKY TOURS
11 SEGWAY IN PARADISE
13 PITTSBURGH HISTORY AND LANDMARKS FOUNDATION TOURS
22 THE PITTSBURGH TOUR COMPANY DOUBLE DECKER TOURS
29 OLIVER BATH HOUSE
32 BREATHE YOGA STUDIO
55 GREEN GEARS PEDI CABS
64 RUGGERS PUB
65 ORMSBY POOL

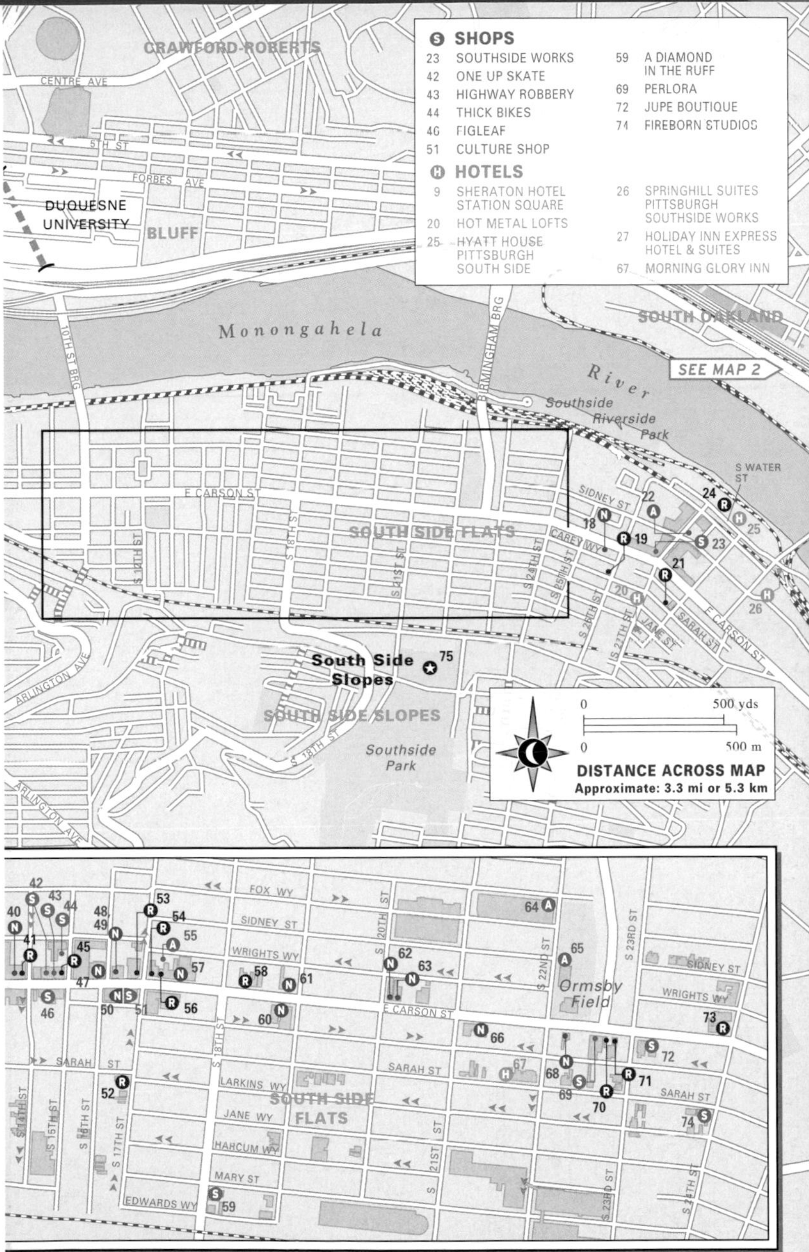
SHOPS
23 SOUTHSIDE WORKS
42 ONE UP SKATE
43 HIGHWAY ROBBERY
44 THICK BIKES
46 FIGLEAF
51 CULTURE SHOP
59 A DIAMOND IN THE RUFF
69 PERLORA
72 JUPE BOUTIQUE
74 FIREBORN STUDIOS
HOTELS
9 SHERATON HOTEL STATION SQUARE
20 HOT METAL LOFTS
25 HYATT HOUSE PITTSBURGH SOUTH SIDE
26 SPRINGHILL SUITES PITTSBURGH SOUTHSIDE WORKS
27 HOLIDAY INN EXPRESS HOTEL & SUITES
67 MORNING GLORY INN
CRAWFORD-ROBERTS
CENTRE AVE
5TH ST
FORBES AVE
DUQUESNE UNIVERSITY
BLUFF
Monongahela River
10TH ST BRG
BIRMINGHAM BRG
SOUTH OAKLAND
SEE MAP 2
Southside Riverside Park
S WATER ST
SIDNEY ST
CAREY WY
E CARSON ST
SOUTH SIDE FLATS
S 12TH ST
S 18TH ST
S 21ST ST
S 24TH ST
S 25TH ST
S 26TH ST
S 27TH ST
JANE ST
SARAH ST
South Side Slopes
SOUTH SIDE SLOPES
ARLINGTON AVE
S 18TH ST
Southside Park
0 500 yds
0 500 m
DISTANCE ACROSS MAP
Approximate: 3.3 mi or 5.3 km
FOX WY
SIDNEY ST
WRIGHTS WY
S 20TH ST
S 22ND ST
S 23RD ST
Ormsby Field
E CARSON ST
SARAH ST
LARKINS WY
JANE WY
HARCUM WY
MARY ST
EDWARDS WY
S 14TH ST
S 15TH ST
S 16TH ST
S 17TH ST
S 18TH ST
S 21ST ST
S 23RD ST
S 24TH ST
SOUTH SIDE FLATS
© AVALON TRAVEL

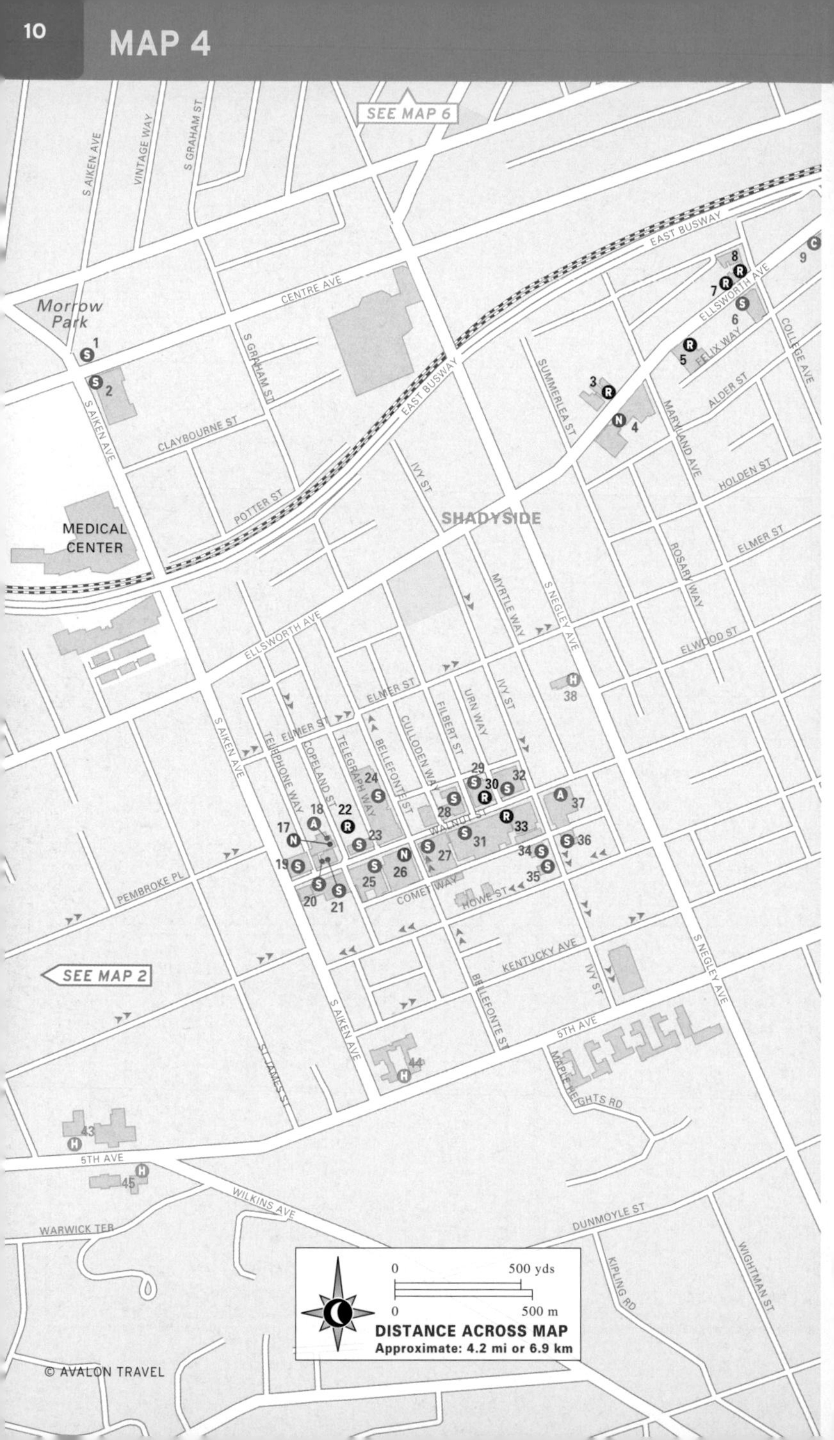
SEE MAP 6
S AIKEN AVE
VINTAGE WAY
S GRAHAM ST
EAST BUSWAY
CENTRE AVE
Morrow Park
S GRAHAM ST
ELLSWORTH AVE
FELIX WAY
COLLEGE AVE
SUMMERLEA ST
ALDER ST
MARYLAND AVE
CLAYBOURNE ST
IVY ST
HOLDEN ST
POTTER ST
SHADYSIDE
MEDICAL CENTER
ROSARY WAY
ELMER ST
MYRTLE WAY
S NEGLEY AVE
ELLSWORTH AVE
ELWOOD ST
ELMER ST
FILBERT ST
URN WAY
CULLODEN WAY
BELLEFONTE ST
TELEGRAPH WAY
COPELAND ST
TELEPHONE WAY
WALNUT ST
PEMBROKE PL
COMET WAY
HOWE ST
KENTUCKY AVE
SEE MAP 2
S AIKEN AVE
BELLEFONTE ST
5TH AVE
MAPLE HEIGHTS RD
ST JAMES ST
5TH AVE
WILKINS AVE
DUNMOYLE ST
WARWICK TER
KIPLING RD
WIGHTMAN ST
0 500 yds
0 500 m
DISTANCE ACROSS MAP
Approximate: 4.2 mi or 6.9 km

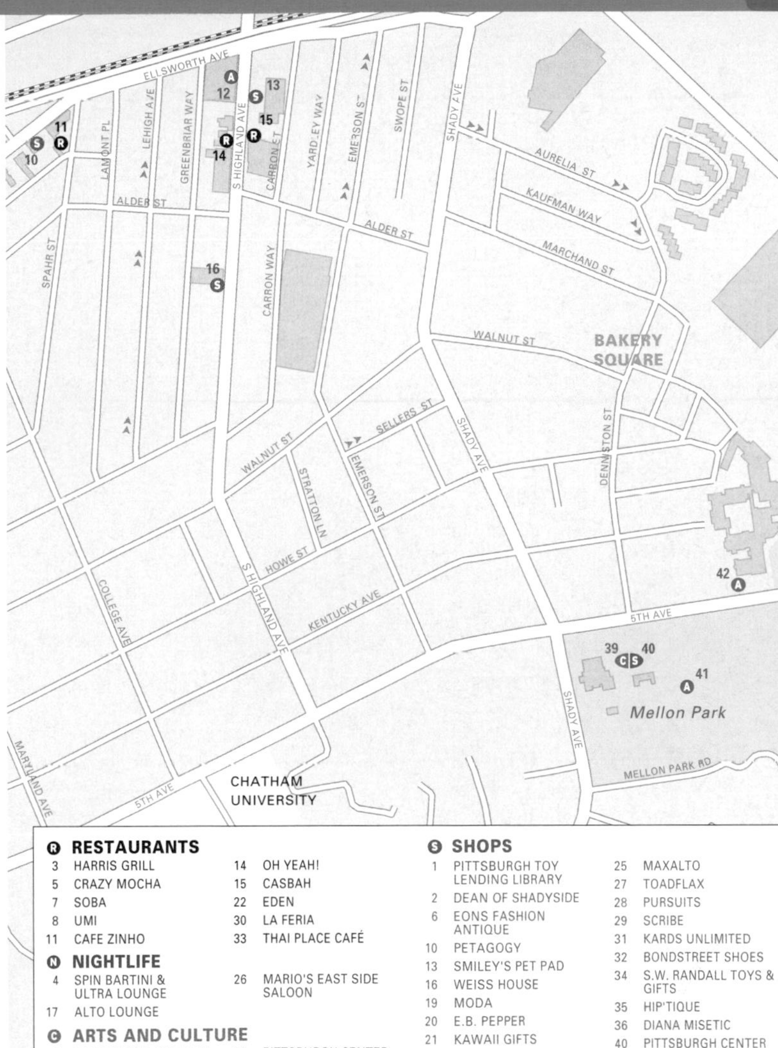

R RESTAURANTS

3 HARRIS GRILL
5 CRAZY MOCHA
7 SOBA
8 UMI
11 CAFE ZINHO
14 OH YEAH!
15 CASBAH
22 EDEN
30 LA FERIA
33 THAI PLACE CAFÉ

N NIGHTLIFE

4 SPIN BARTINI & ULTRA LOUNGE
17 ALTO LOUNGE
26 MARIO'S EAST SIDE SALOON

C ARTS AND CULTURE

9 MENDELSON GALLERY
39 PITTSBURGH CENTER FOR THE ARTS

A SPORTS AND ACTIVITIES

12 FITNESS FACTORY
18 AMAZING YOGA
37 X SHADYSIDE
41 MELLON PARK
42 MELLON PARK TENNIS CENTER

S SHOPS

1 PITTSBURGH TOY LENDING LIBRARY
2 DEAN OF SHADYSIDE
6 EONS FASHION ANTIQUE
10 PETAGOGY
13 SMILEY'S PET PAD
16 WEISS HOUSE
19 MODA
20 E.B. PEPPER
21 KAWAII GIFTS
23 THE PICKET FENCE
24 FOOTLOOSE
25 MAXALTO
27 TOADFLAX
28 PURSUITS
29 SCRIBE
31 KARDS UNLIMITED
32 BONDSTREET SHOES
34 S.W. RANDALL TOYS & GIFTS
35 HIP'TIQUE
36 DIANA MISETIC
40 PITTSBURGH CENTER FOR THE ARTS

H HOTELS

38 THE INN ON NEGLEY
43 MANSIONS ON FIFTH
44 SHADYSIDE INN ALL SUITES HOTEL
45 SUNNYLEDGE BOUTIQUE HOTEL

SEE MAP 5

MAP 5

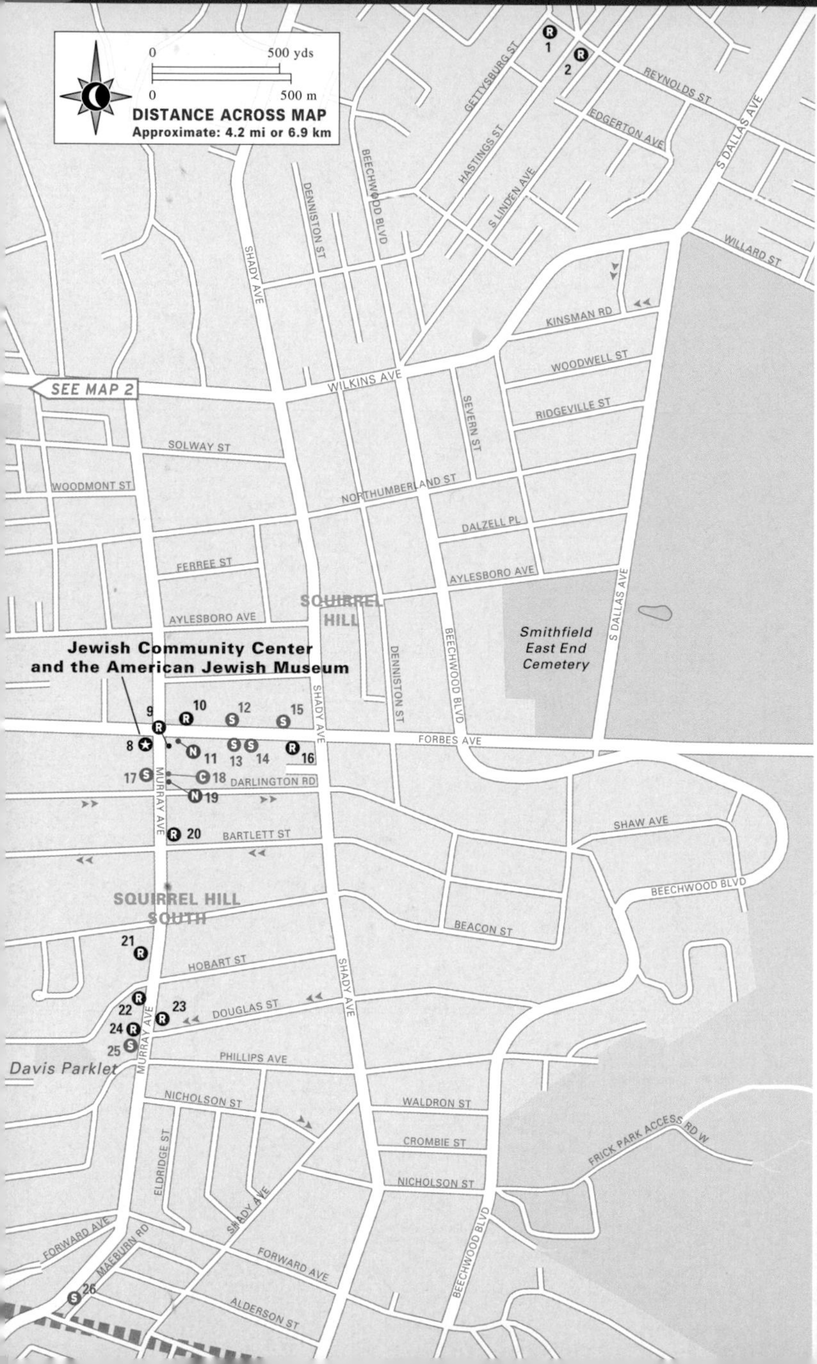

0 500 yds
0 500 m
DISTANCE ACROSS MAP
Approximate: 4.2 mi or 6.9 km

SEE MAP 2

Jewish Community Center and the American Jewish Museum

SQUIRREL HILL

SQUIRREL HILL SOUTH

Smithfield East End Cemetery

Davis Parklet

GETTYSBURG ST
HASTINGS ST
S LINDEN AVE
REYNOLDS ST
EDGERTON AVE
S DALLAS AVE
WILLARD ST
BEECHWOOD BLVD
DENNISTON ST
SHADY AVE
KINSMAN RD
WOODWELL ST
RIDGEVILLE ST
WILKINS AVE
SEVERN ST
SOLWAY ST
WOODMONT ST
NORTHUMBERLAND ST
DALZELL PL
FERREE ST
AYLESBORO AVE
FORBES AVE
DARLINGTON RD
MURRAY AVE
BARTLETT ST
SHAW AVE
BEACON ST
HOBART ST
DOUGLAS ST
PHILLIPS AVE
NICHOLSON ST
WALDRON ST
CROMBIE ST
ELDRIDGE ST
FRICK PARK ACCESS RD W
FORWARD AVE
MAEBURN RD
ALDERSON ST

1 2 8 9 10 11 12 13 14 15 16 17 18 19 20 21 22 23 24 25 26

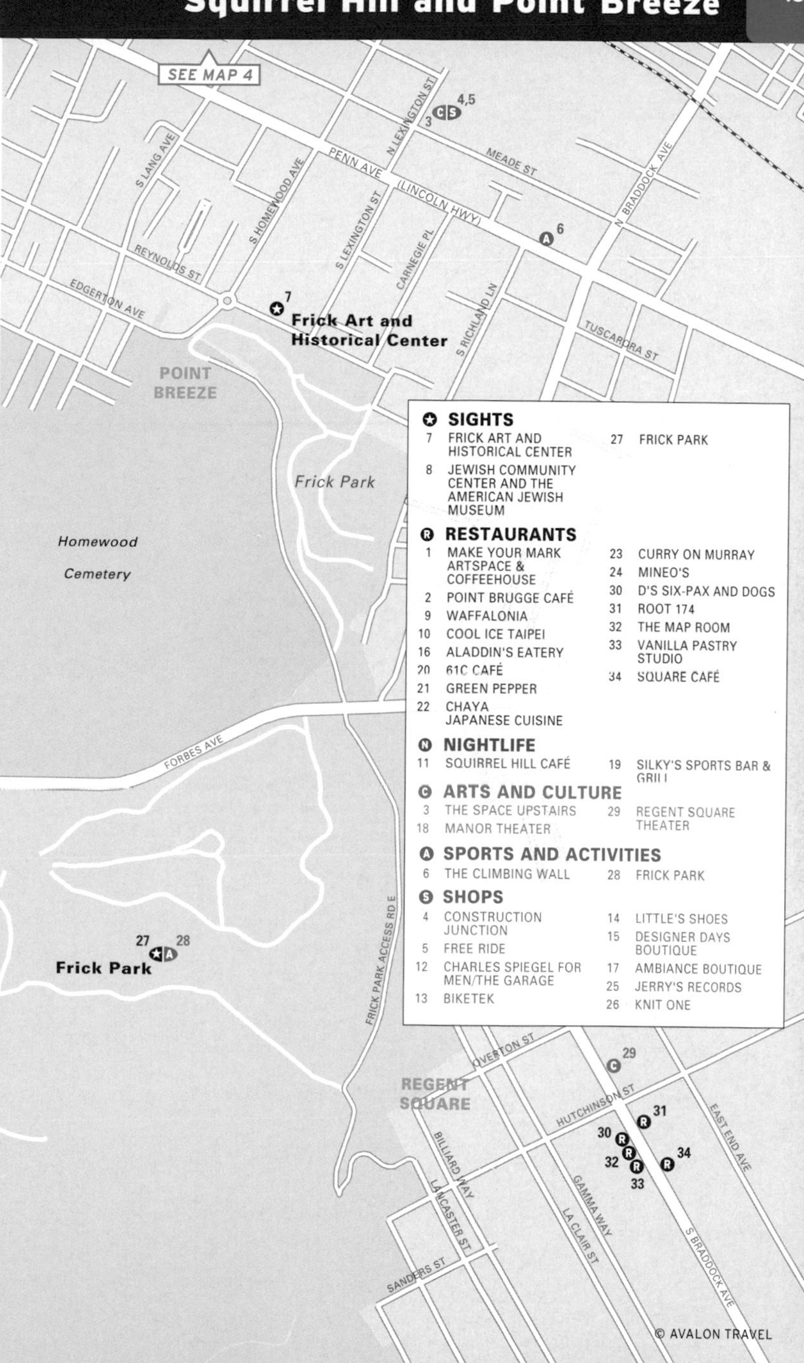

SIGHTS

7 FRICK ART AND HISTORICAL CENTER
8 JEWISH COMMUNITY CENTER AND THE AMERICAN JEWISH MUSEUM
27 FRICK PARK

RESTAURANTS

1 MAKE YOUR MARK ARTSPACE & COFFEEHOUSE
2 POINT BRUGGE CAFÉ
9 WAFFALONIA
10 COOL ICE TAIPEI
16 ALADDIN'S EATERY
20 61C CAFÉ
21 GREEN PEPPER
22 CHAYA JAPANESE CUISINE
23 CURRY ON MURRAY
24 MINEO'S
30 D'S SIX-PAX AND DOGS
31 ROOT 174
32 THE MAP ROOM
33 VANILLA PASTRY STUDIO
34 SQUARE CAFÉ

NIGHTLIFE

11 SQUIRREL HILL CAFÉ
19 SILKY'S SPORTS BAR & GRILL

ARTS AND CULTURE

3 THE SPACE UPSTAIRS
18 MANOR THEATER
29 REGENT SQUARE THEATER

SPORTS AND ACTIVITIES

6 THE CLIMBING WALL
28 FRICK PARK

SHOPS

4 CONSTRUCTION JUNCTION
5 FREE RIDE
12 CHARLES SPIEGEL FOR MEN/THE GARAGE
13 BIKETEK
14 LITTLE'S SHOES
15 DESIGNER DAYS BOUTIQUE
17 AMBIANCE BOUTIQUE
25 JERRY'S RECORDS
26 KNIT ONE

SIGHTS
10 ALLEGHENY CEMETERY
30 ARSENAL PARK
39 DOUGHBOY SQUARE
40 THE CLEMENTE MUSEUM
66 THE CENTER FOR POSTNATURAL HISTORY
78 PITTSBURGH ZOO AND PPG AQUARIUM

RESTAURANTS
3 CURE
11 LA GOURMANDINE
28 COCA CAFÉ
29 FRANKTUARY
33 ESPRESSO A MANO
36 TAMARI RESTAURANT AND LOUNGE
38 DOZEN BAKE SHOP
48 TRAM'S KITCHEN
50 TASTE OF INDIA
52 BLOOMFIELD BRIDGE TAVERN
54 DEL'S BAR & RISTORANTE DELPIZZO
58 TESSARO'S
59 THAI CUISINE
71 SPAK BROTHERS PIZZA
72 PEOPLE'S INDIAN RESTAURANT

SPORTS AND ACTIVITIES
8 KEYSTONE STATE WRESTLING
16 THREE RIVERS ROWING ASSOCIATION
19 ARSENAL LANES
42 WEST PENN SKATE PARK (POLISH HILL BOWL)
79 HIGHLAND PARK

SHOPS
2 UNIFAUN RECORDS
4 BLOOM ORGANIC SKINCARE PARLOR
5 WHO NEW?
9 16:62 DESIGN ZONE
13 MID-ATLANTIC MERCANTILE
17 720 RECORDS
18 GALLERY ON 43RD STREET
20 RATHER RIPPED RECORDS
22 HOUSE OF THE DEAD
23 WILDCARD

ARTS AND CULTURE
15 PAINT MONKEY
25 FE GALLERY
57 BOX HEART
69 THE IRMA FREEMAN CENTER FOR IMAGINATION
70 MOST WANTED FINE ART
73 PITTSBURGH GLASS CENTER
90 KELLY STRAYHORN THEATER

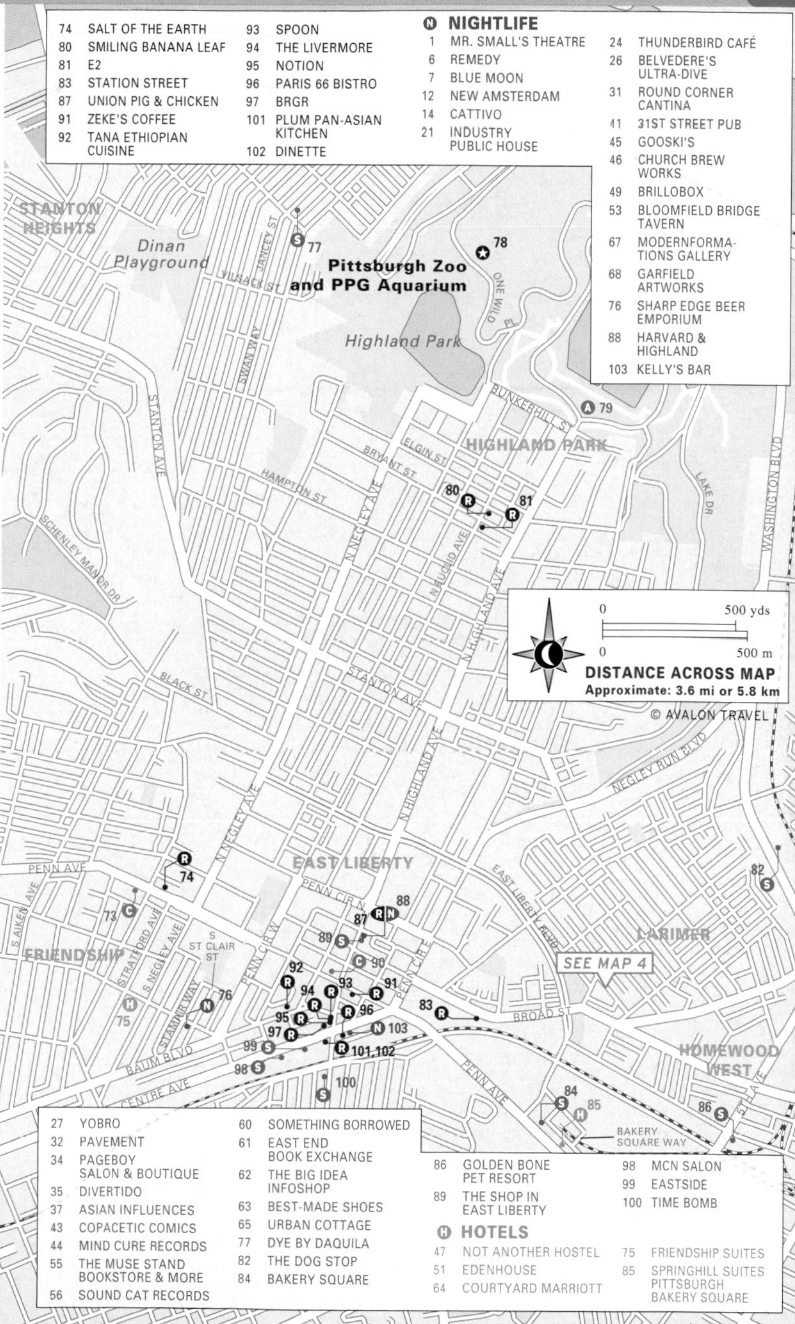
74 SALT OF THE EARTH
80 SMILING BANANA LEAF
81 E2
83 STATION STREET
87 UNION PIG & CHICKEN
91 ZEKE'S COFFEE
92 TANA ETHIOPIAN CUISINE
93 SPOON
94 THE LIVERMORE
95 NOTION
96 PARIS 66 BISTRO
97 BRGR
101 PLUM PAN-ASIAN KITCHEN
102 DINETTE
NIGHTLIFE
1 MR. SMALL'S THEATRE
6 REMEDY
7 BLUE MOON
12 NEW AMSTERDAM
14 CATTIVO
21 INDUSTRY PUBLIC HOUSE
24 THUNDERBIRD CAFÉ
26 BELVEDERE'S ULTRA-DIVE
31 ROUND CORNER CANTINA
41 31ST STREET PUB
45 GOOSKI'S
46 CHURCH BREW WORKS
49 BRILLOBOX
53 BLOOMFIELD BRIDGE TAVERN
67 MODERNFORMATIONS GALLERY
68 GARFIELD ARTWORKS
76 SHARP EDGE BEER EMPORIUM
88 HARVARD & HIGHLAND
103 KELLY'S BAR
STANTON HEIGHTS
Dinan Playground
Pittsburgh Zoo and PPG Aquarium
Highland Park
HIGHLAND PARK
EAST LIBERTY
FRIENDSHIP
LARIMER
HOMEWOOD WEST
SEE MAP 4
DISTANCE ACROSS MAP
Approximate: 3.6 mi or 5.8 km
0 500 yds
0 500 m
© AVALON TRAVEL
27 YOBRO
32 PAVEMENT
34 PAGEBOY SALON & BOUTIQUE
35 DIVERTIDO
37 ASIAN INFLUENCES
43 COPACETIC COMICS
44 MIND CURE RECORDS
55 THE MUSE STAND BOOKSTORE & MORE
56 SOUND CAT RECORDS
60 SOMETHING BORROWED
61 EAST END BOOK EXCHANGE
62 THE BIG IDEA INFOSHOP
63 BEST-MADE SHOES
65 URBAN COTTAGE
77 DYE BY DAQUILA
82 THE DOG STOP
84 BAKERY SQUARE
86 GOLDEN BONE PET RESORT
89 THE SHOP IN EAST LIBERTY
98 MCN SALON
99 EASTSIDE
100 TIME BOMB
HOTELS
47 NOT ANOTHER HOSTEL
51 EDENHOUSE
64 COURTYARD MARRIOTT
75 FRIENDSHIP SUITES
85 SPRINGHILL SUITES PITTSBURGH BAKERY SQUARE

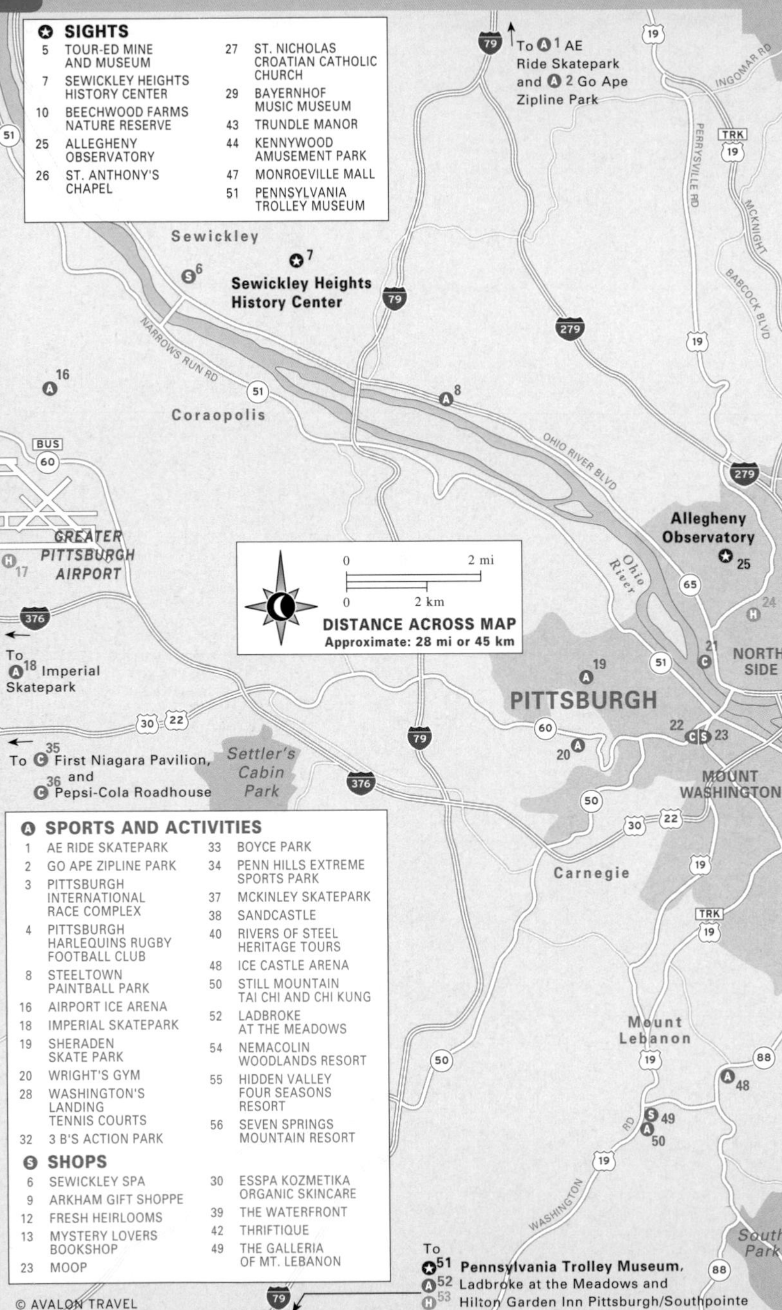

SIGHTS
5 TOUR-ED MINE AND MUSEUM
7 SEWICKLEY HEIGHTS HISTORY CENTER
10 BEECHWOOD FARMS NATURE RESERVE
25 ALLEGHENY OBSERVATORY
26 ST. ANTHONY'S CHAPEL
27 ST. NICHOLAS CROATIAN CATHOLIC CHURCH
29 BAYERNHOF MUSIC MUSEUM
43 TRUNDLE MANOR
44 KENNYWOOD AMUSEMENT PARK
47 MONROEVILLE MALL
51 PENNSYLVANIA TROLLEY MUSEUM
To 1 AE Ride Skatepark and 2 Go Ape Zipline Park
Sewickley
Sewickley Heights History Center
Coraopolis
NARROWS RUN RD
OHIO RIVER BLVD
INGOMAR RD
PERRYSVILLE RD
MCKNIGHT
BABCOCK BLVD
GREATER PITTSBURGH AIRPORT
Allegheny Observatory
Ohio River
0 2 mi
0 2 km
DISTANCE ACROSS MAP
Approximate: 28 mi or 45 km
To 18 Imperial Skatepark
NORTH SIDE
PITTSBURGH
MOUNT WASHINGTON
To 35 First Niagara Pavilion, and 36 Pepsi-Cola Roadhouse
Settler's Cabin Park
Carnegie
Mount Lebanon
WASHINGTON RD
South Park
To 51 Pennsylvania Trolley Museum, 52 Ladbroke at the Meadows and 53 Hilton Garden Inn Pittsburgh/Southpointe
SPORTS AND ACTIVITIES
1 AE RIDE SKATEPARK
2 GO APE ZIPLINE PARK
3 PITTSBURGH INTERNATIONAL RACE COMPLEX
4 PITTSBURGH HARLEQUINS RUGBY FOOTBALL CLUB
8 STEELTOWN PAINTBALL PARK
16 AIRPORT ICE ARENA
18 IMPERIAL SKATEPARK
19 SHERADEN SKATE PARK
20 WRIGHT'S GYM
28 WASHINGTON'S LANDING TENNIS COURTS
32 3 B'S ACTION PARK
33 BOYCE PARK
34 PENN HILLS EXTREME SPORTS PARK
37 MCKINLEY SKATEPARK
38 SANDCASTLE
40 RIVERS OF STEEL HERITAGE TOURS
48 ICE CASTLE ARENA
50 STILL MOUNTAIN TAI CHI AND CHI KUNG
52 LADBROKE AT THE MEADOWS
54 NEMACOLIN WOODLANDS RESORT
55 HIDDEN VALLEY FOUR SEASONS RESORT
56 SEVEN SPRINGS MOUNTAIN RESORT
SHOPS
6 SEWICKLEY SPA
9 ARKHAM GIFT SHOPPE
12 FRESH HEIRLOOMS
13 MYSTERY LOVERS BOOKSHOP
23 MOOP
30 ESSPA KOZMETIKA ORGANIC SKINCARE
39 THE WATERFRONT
42 THRIFTIQUE
49 THE GALLERIA OF MT. LEBANON

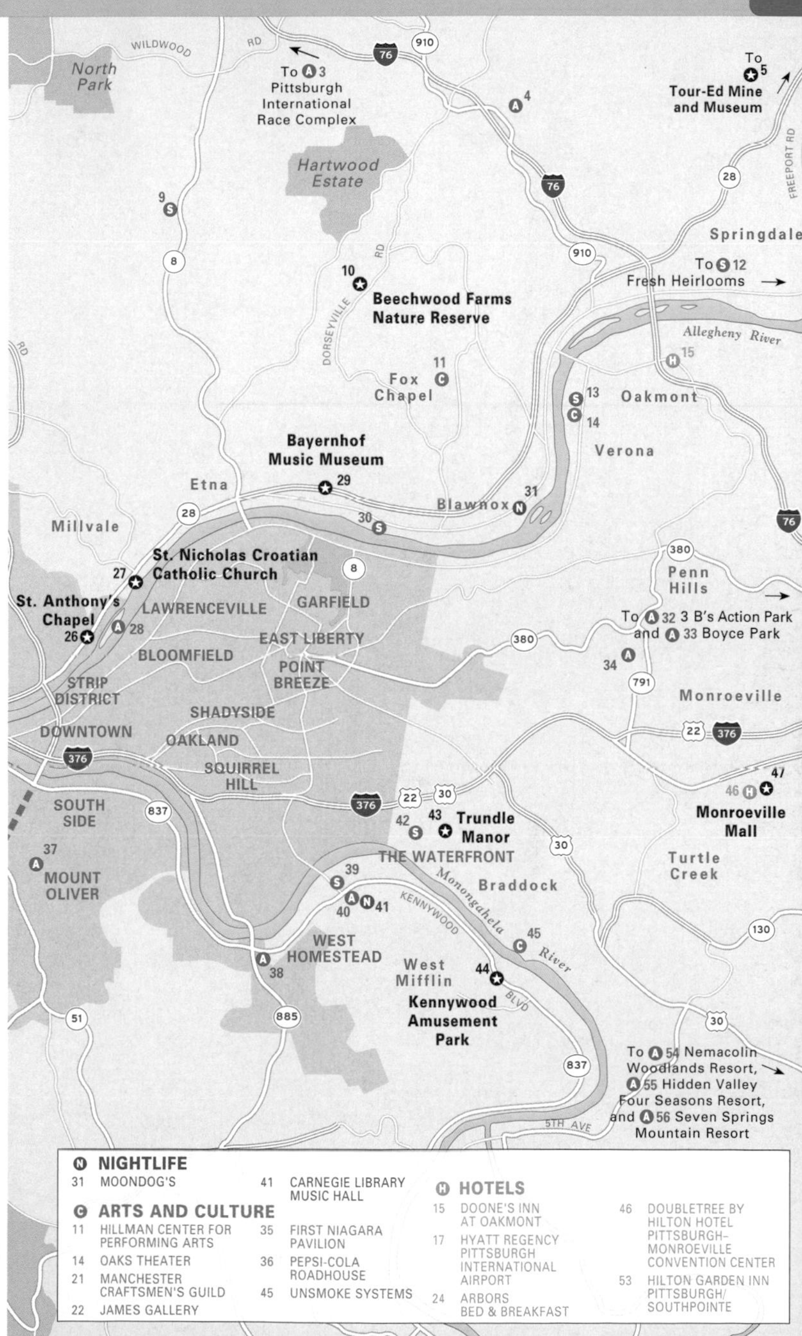

WILDWOOD RD
North Park
To A 3 Pittsburgh International Race Complex
76
910
A 4
To 5 Tour-Ed Mine and Museum
FREEPORT RD
28
Hartwood Estate
76
9 S
8
910
Springdale
To S 12 Fresh Heirlooms
10 Beechwood Farms Nature Reserve
DORSEYVILLE RD
Allegheny River
H 15
11 C Fox Chapel
S 13
C 14
Oakmont
Verona
RD
Bayernhof Music Museum
29
Etna
31
Blawnox N
28
30 S
76
Millvale
380
St. Nicholas Croatian Catholic Church
27
8
Penn Hills
St. Anthony's Chapel
26
A 28
LAWRENCEVILLE
GARFIELD
To A 32 3 B's Action Park and A 33 Boyce Park
EAST LIBERTY
380
BLOOMFIELD
34 A
POINT BREEZE
791
STRIP DISTRICT
Monroeville
SHADYSIDE
DOWNTOWN
22
376
OAKLAND
376
SQUIRREL HILL
47
22
30
46 H
SOUTH SIDE
837
376
Monroeville Mall
42 S
43 Trundle Manor
30
37 A
THE WATERFRONT
Turtle Creek
MOUNT OLIVER
39 S
Monongahela River
Braddock
A N 41
40
KENNYWOOD BLVD
130
45 C
WEST HOMESTEAD
A 38
West Mifflin
44
Kennywood Amusement Park
51
885
30
837
To A 54 Nemacolin Woodlands Resort, A 55 Hidden Valley Four Seasons Resort, and A 56 Seven Springs Mountain Resort
5TH AVE
N NIGHTLIFE
31 MOONDOG'S
41 CARNEGIE LIBRARY MUSIC HALL
C ARTS AND CULTURE
11 HILLMAN CENTER FOR PERFORMING ARTS
14 OAKS THEATER
21 MANCHESTER CRAFTSMEN'S GUILD
22 JAMES GALLERY
35 FIRST NIAGARA PAVILION
36 PEPSI-COLA ROADHOUSE
45 UNSMOKE SYSTEMS
H HOTELS
15 DOONE'S INN AT OAKMONT
17 HYATT REGENCY PITTSBURGH INTERNATIONAL AIRPORT
24 ARBORS BED & BREAKFAST
46 DOUBLETREE BY HILTON HOTEL PITTSBURGH–MONROEVILLE CONVENTION CENTER
53 HILTON GARDEN INN PITTSBURGH/ SOUTHPOINTE

DISCOVER Pittsburgh

Although the Steel City is world-renowned for its industrial past, almost no vestiges of that era remain today. At the beginning of the 21st century, Pittsburgh is nothing less than a remarkable model of Rustbelt Renewal. Visitors are often astonished to discover not only acres of green parkland and miles of biking and jogging trails, but also fresh air.

The renewed and revitalized Pittsburgh is about much more than just greener flora and healthier fauna. During your exploration of the city's distinct neighborhoods, you can expect to encounter contemporary art galleries, high-end eateries, and million-dollar sports stadiums.

The Carnegie Museum of Natural History is famous for its Dinosaurs in Their Time exhibit. The Andy Warhol Museum is a fascinating tribute to one of the city's most famous sons and the largest single-artist museum in the United States. And the city's historical funiculars, the Monongahela and the Duquesne Inclines, continue to shuttle tourists and local commuters up and down Mount Washington.

Whether it's ancient history or postmodern culture you've come to explore, you'll find what you're looking for in today's Pittsburgh. This is a city that honors its blue-collar history and yet keeps an eye on the future. It continues to be one of America's most tenacious and unusual urban landscapes.

Planning Your Trip

Where to Go

Downtown

Also known as the Golden Triangle, Pittsburgh's Downtown is where you'll find the Cultural District, which offers Broadway-style entertainment and the occasional concert. Downtown is also home to its fair share of highly regarded eateries, contemporary art galleries, and a few museums, the largest by far being the August Wilson Center for African American Culture. Following a massive renovation, the grandeur of Downtown's Point State Park has grown even more awe-inspiring. Downtown is also where you'll find the bus and train stations, the Welcome Pittsburgh visitors center, and probably your hotel.

Strip District

A formerly industrial area filled with warehouses and loft buildings, the Strip District plays two separate but important roles in the life of the city. During the day, the area is visited largely for its produce dealers and ethnic restaurants, which line the parallel thoroughfares of Penn Avenue and Smallman Street. But once night falls, clubgoers fill the district's bars and dance clubs in full force. Saturday morning is the time to see the Strip at its best.

North Side

Situated just across the Allegheny River from Downtown, the majority of the North Side's main attractions can be found in the area known as the North Shore, which is spread out alongside the river. The Pirates and the Steelers have been battling it out on their respective fields for years, although the North Shore is also home to the Andy Warhol Museum, the Carnegie Science Center, and Rivers Casino. Head a bit farther into the heart of the North Side to visit can't-miss attractions like the National Aviary, the Children's Museum of Pittsburgh, and the Mattress Factory.

Oakland

Sometimes referred to as Pennsylvania's third-largest "downtown," Oakland is the city's university district. Carnegie Mellon University and the University of Pittsburgh are the best known of Oakland's institutions of higher learning. The main branch of the Carnegie Library can be found here, along with the Carnegie Museums of Art and Natural History, behind which you'll find the urban playground

the National Aviary

of Schenley Park. Forbes Avenue, the neighborhood's main drag, is home to dozens of retail outlets, bars, and fast-food joints.

South Side

One of Pittsburgh's most eclectic and interesting areas, the South Side stretches along the Monongahela River from Station Square to SouthSide Works, a former steel mill turned shopping mall. East Carson Street, alternately referred to as Pittsburgh's Bourbon Street and the country's longest uninterrupted stretch of bars, runs the length of the district. Vintage clothing stores, art galleries, cafés, and ethnic eateries can also be found there.

Mount Washington

Sitting atop the city's South Side, Mount Washington exists in the mind of the average Pittsburgher for two reasons only: the breathtaking views along Grandview Avenue, which every visitor to the city should see, and the expensive eateries of Restaurant Row. Near to the Monongahela Incline, which ferries its passengers from Station Square to Mount Washington's peak, is the mini-commercial district of Shiloh Street.

Shadyside

Just east of Oakland, Shadyside is one of the city's most prestigious and image-conscious neighborhoods. Walnut Street forms the area's commercial core; you'll find both big-name and boutique shopping and a near-steady stream of pedestrian traffic. Running parallel to Walnut Street is Ellsworth Avenue, where many of Shadyside's better bars and restaurants can be found.

SouthSide Works

Squirrel Hill and Point Breeze

Home to one of the largest Jewish communities in the Mid-Atlantic region, Squirrel Hill begins at the eastern end of Carnegie Mellon University and is sandwiched comfortably between Schenley Park and Frick Park. Its two major thoroughfares, Forbes Avenue and Murray Avenue, offer grocers, movie theaters, synagogues, kosher eateries, and cafés.

On the opposite side of Frick Park, Point Breeze and the small district of Regent Square are Squirrel Hill's somewhat upscale neighbors to the east. Although largely residential, both areas have small commercial strips.

Bloomfield and Lawrenceville

Also known as Pittsburgh's Little Italy, the East End neighborhood of Bloomfield is a tightly knit residential community and a popular shopping district. Liberty Avenue, the neighborhood's heart and soul, is home to a charming medley of boutiques, cafés, grocery stores, and restaurants.

Lawrenceville, one of Pittsburgh's largest neighborhoods, stretches along the river from the Strip District to Morningside. A recent influx of artists and independent boutiques along the main drag of Butler Street has raised Lawrenceville's profile considerably.

East Liberty and Garfield

Formerly known only for their reputations as gang-inflicted danger zones, both East Liberty and Garfield have experienced major bouts of gentrification over the past decade. Garfield is notable primarily for the art galleries and cafés that run the length of its Penn

winter city lights

Avenue Arts Corridor, while East Liberty is home to a wide variety of popular bars, restaurants, and boutiques. East Liberty is also where you'll find the Bakery Square and EastSide retail complexes.

Greater Pittsburgh

The outlying suburbs and small towns of Greater Pittsburgh have much to offer the curious traveler, from the high-end retail district of Sewickley to the historical settlement of Old Economy Village. Other highlights include West Mifflin's Kennywood Amusement Park and the pioneering DIY arts community being built in Braddock.

When to Go

Choosing the perfect time to visit is really nothing more than a matter of personal inclination. When snow falls, the winter season (late December-early April) is absolutely gorgeous, yet the months of January and February can be unbearably cold; even native Pittsburghers tend to hibernate during this time of the year.

Pittsburgh's summers are often scorching hot and dripping with humidity, although this is also the season when the city comes alive with the most dynamism and excitement. What's more, a score of important festivals and events take place during the summer.

Spring and fall are both ideal seasons to visit Pittsburgh. Fall is especially lovely, complete with leaf-peeping opportunities and pleasant weather, with days that are cool but not cold and evenings that might best be described as light-jacket weather: sharp and brisk.

the Duquesne Incline

The Two-Day Best of Pittsburgh

Although a thorough exploration of Pittsburgh and its environs would require at least a week, the city is compact enough that its most important sights and activities can be experienced easily in two days. The following itinerary assumes a Saturday-morning arrival in Pittsburgh; with the exception of a visit to the Strip District, which is at its best on Saturday mornings, the following activities can easily be shuffled around at will.

Day 1

- Start your visit with an early-morning trip to the Strip District. Stop by Pamela's Diner for breakfast and then join the throngs of shoppers searching for kitschy souvenirs along Penn Avenue.

- Spend an hour or two at the Senator John Heinz History Center, and browse in the gift shop on your way out; you're unlikely to find a better selection of books about Pittsburgh anywhere else in the city. If the weather is cooperating, treat yourself to a trip up Mount Washington on the Duquesne Incline—there's a gift shop and small museum in the upper-level station—and then to one of the best views of the city along Grandview Avenue. The eastward walk along Grandview is one of the nicest strolls in town. Continue on for just under a mile, pausing to enjoy the view from the large lookout platforms, to reach the Monongahela Incline, which you can ride back down to street level. Upon reaching the bottom, you'll see Station Square just ahead—it's a perfect pit stop for

the Senator John Heinz History Center

coffee or lunch. Should you find yourself in the mood for fine dining, head to Station Square's historical Grand Concourse.

- Afterward, make your way down East Carson Street toward the South Side Flats for a bit of late-afternoon shopping.

- Head back to the heart of the South Side Flats and end your day with a nightcap. Rowdy Buck boasts a fun faux-Western theme (complete with lumberjack bartenders and DIY s'mores), or relax with a margarita on the rooftop deck at Local Bar + Kitchen, which also serves good pub grub.

Day 2

- Weekend brunch at trendy Bar Marco is a good way to start your day. But if you're only in the mood for a latte, wander over to Marty's Market instead and belly up to the outdoor coffee bar.

- When it's time to start moving again, take a long and leisurely stroll through Downtown and into Point State Park, stopping off at the ToonSeum or the PNC Legacy Project along the way. After you've seen the Point State Park fountain, use the pedestrian walkway on the Fort Duquesne Bridge to cross over the Allegheny River and into the section of the North Side known as the North Shore.

- Head to the nearby Andy Warhol Museum, the largest single-artist museum in the United States. The Warhol has a great gift shop and a surprisingly good basement café, a great choice for lunch.

- Next, head to the National Aviary in West Park, the only nonprofit bird

Fun and Cheap: Pittsburgh on a Budget

Center for PostNatural History

Operating on a shoestring budget? You've come to the right city. Budget living is practically a religion in some quarters of Pittsburgh, where a night on the town costs as little as $20, and a day exploring the urban jungle can be had for almost nothing at all. For both year-round and seasonal cheap-skate suggestions, visit www.livingpittsburgh.com.

SIGHTSEEING

For budget sightseeing, take a self-guided tour of the **Nationality Classrooms** inside Pitt's **Cathedral of Learning.** After exploring the nearby **Schenley Park,** stroll the length of the **Three Rivers Heritage Trail** on the North Shore, which has lately turned into something of an outdoor sculpture garden. And don't worry about public transit: As long as you stick to the four stops within the Golden Triangle itself and the two North Shore stops, rides on the city's light rail, known locally as the T, are always free.

FOOD

Due to its dead-broke student population, Oakland is replete with restaurants serving half-priced food after 11pm. Try **Fuel and Fuddle** for American pub grub, or **Mad Mex** for huge, toothsome burritos. And many of the food stalls in Oakland's **Schenley Plaza** are dirt cheap, yet of surprisingly high quality.

SHOPPING

For budget souvenir shopping, make the scene on **Penn Avenue** in the Strip District, where everything from fake Steelers T-shirts to Peruvian finger puppets is on offer. Parking in Downtown is free on Sundays.

THE ARTS

During summer, **free movies** are screened outdoors in seven different parks, including Schenley Park in Oakland and Grandview Park in Mount Washington. For movie listings and times, call **Cinema in the Park** (412/422-6426). **Mattress Factory** offers half-price admission on Tuesday, while admission to the **Andy Warhol Museum** is half off on Friday 5pm-10pm. Entrance to the **Center for PostNatural History** in Garfield is always free. **Unblurred,** the first Friday gallery crawl in the **Penn Avenue Arts Corridor,** is also free.

RECREATION

Kayak Pittsburgh offers fantastic ways to experience the city from a duck's-eye view; kayaks, canoes, and even hydrobikes and stand-up paddle boards can be rented for roughly $8-16 an hour. The **Pittsburgh History and Landmarks Foundation** offers scores of free walking tours, including one through Downtown's **Old Allegheny County Jail Museum;** click the "Tours & Events" tab at www.phlf.org for details.

gastropub Meat & Potatoes

zoo in the country. Before leaving the North Side, stop off at Rivers Casino to try your luck.

- Spend the rest of the afternoon exploring the Oakland neighborhood. Take a self-guided tour of the Nationality Classrooms in the Cathedral of Learning. If you need a quick bite to eat, head across the street to the lovely Schenley Plaza to see what's cooking at the Conflict Kitchen. If the sun is shining, visit Schenley Park and its Phipps Conservatory and Botanical Gardens.

- For dinner, head back into Downtown. Take a cab if the weather is chilly, or if you're still on the North Side, go by foot across one of the Three Sisters Bridges. Your dining destination is Meat & Potatoes, a gastropub that dishes out simple but excellent American fare and legendary Prohibition-era cocktails.

- After dinner, take in a show in the Cultural District. Pick up a free copy of the *Pittsburgh City Paper* to see what's going on. If nothing grabs your interest or you'd prefer a less expensive and more intimate entertainment option, head back to the South Side via taxi and stop in at Club Café, which usually offers two pop or folk concerts nightly. (Ask your cabbie to take the 10th Street Bridge from Downtown, which can also be crossed on foot.)

Phipps Conservatory

Bar Hop Like a Local

New Amsterdam

The Steel City doesn't call itself "a drinking town with a football problem" for no good reason: Most true-blue Pittsburghers genuinely love to drink. So if your aim is fitting in, you'll want to plan on regularly touring some of the city's finest taprooms and alehouses.

- Order a mai tai at the city's only Polynesian-themed bar, the **Tiki Lounge,** and then head down the street to its sister pub, the cavernous **Lava Lounge,** which seems to have been carved out of volcanic detritus.
- Head to Lawrenceville, where hipster outposts like **New Amsterdam, Brillobox,** and the **Round Corner Cantina** draw eclectic crowds on a nightly basis.
- The university district of Oakland is always good for a bit of late-night prowling. Wash down the big game with a microbrew at **Fuel and Fuddle,** or join the college kids for a mountain of French fries and a cheap six-pack at the **Original Hot Dog Shop.**
- Head to the **Sharp Edge Beer Emporium** in Friendship for happy hour; it's known as one of the finest Belgian beer bars in the country. If you're staying in Downtown, visit its sister pub, **Bistro 922 Penn,** which is popular with out-of-towners and the after-work crowd.
- Take a trip to Deutschland without ever leaving the city limits: The South Side's **Hofbräuhaus Pittsburgh** was modeled after an authentic Munich beer hall, while the North Side's **Penn Brewery** has authentic oompah music and some of the city's best beer, brewed right on the premises.
- **Church Brew Works** in Lawrenceville is not only a top-notch brewpub serving phenomenal wood-fired pizzas—it's also located inside an actual church.
- Traveling on two wheels? Lock your bike to a metal rack outside the South Side's **Over the Bar Bicycle Café,** which acts as something of a clubhouse for the city's hardcore bicycle obsessives.
- Looking for something a bit stiffer than beer? Pay a visit to **Wigle Whiskey** in the Strip District, which offers distillery tours and free samples of the goods. And thanks to a new state law, you can even buy a bottle here.

Sights

Look for ★ to find recommended sights.

HIGHLIGHTS

★ **Most Impressive Monument:** With its uniquely designed exterior and wide-ranging schedule of concerts, lectures, exhibits, and more, the **August Wilson Center for African American Culture** is the city's most promising and inspirational new cultural endeavor (page 33).

★ **Coolest Mini-Museum:** One of only three cartoon-art museums in the country, **ToonSeum** is a fascinating tribute to the art of cartooning (page 43).

★ **Best History Lesson:** The **Senator John Heinz History Center** documents the history, culture, and attendant struggles of the Southwestern Pennsylvania region. And while much of the museum is serious business, there's plenty to keep kids amused (page 44).

★ **Best Modern Art Museum:** Controversial, shocking, and endlessly entertaining, the North Side's **Andy Warhol Museum** is the largest official space dedicated to a single artist in the United States. The novelty-packed gift shop is practically a pop art museum in its own right (page 46).

★ **Most Intimate Animal Experience:** Thanks to its multimillion-dollar renovation, the North Side's **National Aviary** is more exciting, educational, and interactive than ever. Get up close and personal with all manner of feathered fowl and winged friends (page 53).

★ **Best Educational Museum:** Although Oakland's **Carnegie Museum of Natural History** is most famous for its Dinosaurs in Their Time exhibit, it's also home to a staggering array of both permanent and changing exhibits that educate visitors about the world and its many and varied inhabitants (page 57).

★ **Best Gothic Landmark:** The **Cathedral of Learning,** one of Pittsburgh's most beloved structures, is the second-tallest educational building in the world. Don't skip a visit to its multicultural classrooms (page 58).

★ **Best Way to Commune with Nature:** A peaceful, meditative urban oasis located in Schenley Park, the Victorian greenhouse known as the **Phipps Conservatory and Botanical Gardens** includes a 12,000-square-foot tropical forest wonderland (page 59).

★ **Best Mountainside Ride:** Pittsburgh's cable-powered **Duquesne and Monongahela Inclines** shuttle passengers back and forth between Mount Washington and the South Side. It's not a journey for the faint of heart (page 67).

★ **Most Historic Amusement Park:** One of the oldest operating amusement parks in the country, **Kennywood Amusement Park** features acres of thrill rides, an unmatched collection of wooden and steel coasters, and oodles of deep-fried junk food (page 79).

Before beginning your exploration of the hilly and often-circuitous city of Pittsburgh, consider this: Even locals enjoy joking about how easy it is to get hopelessly lost on the town's twisting and turning roads. The war correspondent Ernie Pyle probably explained it best in a 1937 column that appeared in the *Pittsburgh Press:* "Pittsburgh is undoubtedly the cockeyedest city in the United States," he wrote. "Physically, it is absolutely irrational. It must have been laid out by a mountain goat."

There's a perfectly good reason for all this, of course: Pittsburgh's topography consists largely of steep hills, deep valleys, and three proud rivers—the Allegheny, the Monongahela, and the Ohio—all of which weave their way in and out of Pittsburgh's multihued quilt of neighborhoods, creating chaos and confusion for motorists and pedestrians alike. But spend a day or two exploring the nearly vertical neighborhood of the South Side Slopes, or strolling the historical bridges that span the Allegheny and Monongahela Rivers, or breathing in the natural beauty of Schenley and Frick Parks, and decide for yourself if all the confusion isn't actually worth it. While Pittsburgh's sights and scenery may at first appear to be little more than a jumbled-together collection of industrial-era ephemera, a closer inspection reveals something much more uncommon: one of America's most charming small cities, which just happens to offer all the amenities of a major metropolitan town.

Which isn't to say that the Steel City's charms are intended to be any sort of a well-kept secret. On the contrary, since the early 1980s Pittsburgh has been consistently ranked as one of America's most livable towns. And much to the contentment of locals, who knew it all along, *National Geographic Traveler* magazine recently ranked Pittsburgh as one of its must-see, can't-miss international destinations of the year, alongside such exotic locales as Sri Lanka and Croatia.

In fact, it might make sense to think of poking around Pittsburgh as something akin to an urban scavenger hunt. It's true that finding what you're looking for won't always be easy. Getting from here to there may be even tougher still. But once you arrive, your reward will almost always be singularly unique.

Downtown

Map 1

ALLEGHENY COUNTY COURTHOUSE AND OLD JAIL

Designed in 1883 by the much-imitated architect Henry Hobson Richardson, the Allegheny County Courthouse, which was the third courthouse to be built in the county, is one of Downtown Pittsburgh's most recognizable and historical sights. The granite structure is virtually impossible to miss—just keep your eyes peeled for the truly ancient-looking block building that sticks out like a sore thumb (albeit a very attractive and smartly designed thumb) among Grant Street's more modern skyscrapers.

One of the building's most interesting features is its arching stone bridge, which locals frequently refer to as the **Bridge of Sighs.** This bridge connects the courthouse to the adjoining jail, which is no longer in operation. Yet during its time, convicts were simply transferred to the jail by means of the bridge following their courthouse sentencing. It's also worth noting that some of the old jail's individual granite blocks weighed more than five tons each. (The current jail, should you care to see it, is also in Downtown, at 950 2nd Ave., not far from the First Avenue T station.)

It is possible to enter the courthouse to look around, although you must pass through a metal detector first. A model of the entire courthouse complex is on display beneath glass on the second floor; also note the many rounded arches built into the courthouse's interior. Construction of the complex cost approximately $2.25 million, which was not a particularly small sum in the late 19th century.

Interestingly, the main building was designed with an interior courtyard at its center. Richardson considered this detail of his design to be particularly clever, as fresh air and light could then reach even the offices that weren't lucky enough to have street-facing windows. Today, the courthouse is a decent location for a midday picnic; anyone is welcome to join the nine-to-fivers who gather around the outdoor fountain in the courtyard. The Pittsburgh History and Landmarks Foundation occasionally leads free tours.

MAP 1: 436 Grant St., 412/350-4636; Mon.-Fri. 8:30am-4:30pm; free

★ AUGUST WILSON CENTER FOR AFRICAN AMERICAN CULTURE

For years, the August Wilson Center for African American Culture was a cultural center in name only. Since 2003, the group had been offering a wide-ranging schedule of educational and performance programs throughout the city—including dance, music, and spoken word—that celebrated the cultural advancements and achievements of all African Americans. But finally, after a number of financial false starts, the center's architecturally stunning and LEED-certified building on the edge of the city's Cultural District opened to the public in September 2009.

The center's mission involves "preserving, presenting, interpreting, celebrating, and shaping the art, culture, and history of African Americans in Western Pennsylvania and people of African descent throughout the world."

To that end, the center offers an impressively wide range of programming, events, and exhibitions. Live musical performances in the 486-seat theater range from jazz to hip-hop to experimental; lectures by African-American luminaries are regularly scheduled as well. The center is also home to an impressive collection of ongoing and changing exhibits that document and celebrate the African American experience throughout Western Pennsylvania and beyond.

The 65,000-square-foot center also sponsors a number of especially promising "cultivation" and family programs, during which members of the local African American community are encouraged to meet, mingle, and discuss the issues that most affect their populace today. Visit the center's website to stay current on its regularly changing schedule of programs and events.

MAP 1: 980 Liberty Ave., 412/258-2700, www.augustwilsoncenter.org; Tues.-Sat. 11am-6pm; free (special exhibitions on second floor $8 adult, $4 senior and student, $3 child)

THE CULTURAL DISTRICT

A 14-square-block area in the heart of the Golden Triangle, Pittsburgh's Cultural District encompasses 50 restaurants, nearly 100 retail establishments, and eight public parks. Yet none of those amenities have much to do with why tourists and locals alike flock here in droves on weekend afternoons and evenings. Instead, the expensively dressed crowds you'll spot clutching playbills in this compact region of Downtown come mostly to visit the area's four performing arts theaters. Each year, in fact, roughly 1,400

Pittsburgh: City of Firsts

When Pittsburgh bridge-builder George W. Ferris built his very first wheel—a Ferris wheel, for the 1893 Chicago World's Fair—he couldn't have possibly imagined that he'd given birth to a Steel City tradition of invention and innovation that continues today. A Latrobe-area pharmacist by the name of Dr. David Strickler, for instance, is responsible for creating the country's first banana split. That was way back in 1904. And Pittsburgh is also to blame for the now ubiquitous Big Mac—franchise owner Jim Delligatti debuted the sandwich at his Uniontown McDonald's store in 1967. Even the very first Internet emoticon, the smiley, was created by a Carnegie Mellon University computer scientist in 1980. Here's a look at a few other Pittsburgh famous firsts.

FIRST WORLD SERIES—1903

The Pirates were bested by the Boston Pilgrims in the eight-game series, four of which were played in a field not far from the current location of PNC Park.

FIRST MOTION PICTURE THEATER—1905

The Nickelodeon on Smithfield Street, Downtown, was the world's first theater devoted exclusively to the moving motion picture.

FIRST GAS STATION—1913

Gulf Refining Company built the country's first auto service station, which still sits in Friendship today. Look for it on Baum Boulevard.

FIRST COMMERCIAL RADIO STATION BROADCAST—1920

After first installing a radio transmitter in his Wilkinsburg garage, a Westinghouse engineer sent a KDKA signal from a location in East Pittsburgh. The station still transmits today.

FIRST BINGO GAME—EARLY 1920S

After creating the game and then taking it to carnivals nationwide in 1924, Pittsburgher Hugh J. Ward penned an official book of bingo rules in 1933.

POLIO VACCINE—1953

Dr. Jonas Salk and his staff developed the critical vaccine while at the University of Pittsburgh.

performances take place in the area—everything from chamber music and ballet performances to opera, drama, film screenings, and pop concerts.

Some of the district's most historically popular events are the concerts given by the Pittsburgh Symphony Orchestra at **Heinz Hall** (600 Penn Ave., 412/392-4900, www.pittsburghsymphony.org). The orchestra has long been noted by both stateside and international music critics as being one of the best orchestras in the country, and any visitor to Pittsburgh with the time and money would be wise to squeeze in a performance. In fact, merely sitting alone in an empty Heinz Hall could qualify as a cultural experience: The theater, which today has 2,261 seats, has a rather unique history.

The first structure to be built on the site was the St. Clair Hotel, which in 1880 changed its name to the Hotel Anderson. And although that hotel existed until 1927, during the end of the 19th century it was known for hosting mostly traveling theater companies, including Shakespearean actors.

The Anderson next became the Loews Penn Theater. One of the great American movie houses, the Penn Theater was known locally as the "Temple of the Cinema" and was considered the best and most ornate cinema between Chicago and New York City. But thanks in part to the invention of television, the theater was forced to close its doors in 1964. Slated to become a parking lot, the building was saved only by the intervention of the Pittsburgh Symphony itself, which at the time was performing in too-small halls in the university district of Oakland. Five years and $10 million later, construction was completed at the newly named Heinz Hall for the Performing Arts. An open-air Grand Plaza, complete with a small waterfall, was built adjacent to the hall in 1982. And then in 1995, the hall was given the gift of yet another facelift, during which it received a new orchestra shell, new wallpaper, paint, and carpeting, and new acoustical risers, among other improvements. The total cost: $6.5 million.

Of course, the Cultural District doesn't consist of simply old and historical structures. Modern architecture buffs in particular will want to pay a visit to the **O'Reilly Theater** (621 Penn Ave., 412/316-1600, www.pgharts.org/venues/oreilly.aspx), a $25 million state-of-the-art performance venue designed by the ultra-famous Michael Graves, who has since given up on buildings and today focuses almost entirely on product design.

The O'Reilly sits on the former site of the Lyceum Theater, a vaudeville house that was deemed unusable following a 1936 flood. The new structure, where the Pittsburgh Public Theater and touring stage actors perform, is especially notable for its unique thrust stage, which is surrounded by the audience on three sides. The effect is such that shows feel particularly intimate, sometimes uncomfortably so.

After observing the O'Reilly, followers of architect Michael Graves's work should examine the nearby **Agnes R. Katz Plaza,** which sits at the corner of Penn Avenue and 7th Street. Featuring possibly the most eclectic public sculptures in the Golden Triangle, the plaza is a striking example of Pittsburgh's ongoing bid to become a serious arts town. It's also rather tough to miss: Just look for the open square filled with a half dozen granite benches that resemble giant human eyes.

The plaza was a collaboration between artist Louise Bourgeois (who created the eyeball seats), landscape architect Daniel Urban Kiley (who designed the backless granite benches), and the aforementioned Michael Graves. The square's focal point is a 25-foot bronze fountain, also designed by Bourgeois.

But even those who couldn't care less about fine art and design will find much to like about the plaza. Not only is it perfect for people-watching, it's also a convenient place to take a break or meet friends in between theater- or restaurant-going.

Also notable in the Cultural District is the **Byham Theater** (101 6th Ave., 412/456-6666, www.pgharts.org/venues/byham.aspx), a structure built in 1903 that was originally known as the Gayety Theater. Like the Lyceum, the Gayety was a vaudeville house—one of the country's most well known, in fact. Although somewhat faded, a masterfully designed tile mosaic featuring what must have been the Gayety's logo can still be seen on the floor of the Byham's entry. Sometime in the 1930s, the Gayety became known as the Fulton, which soon after transformed into a movie house. The building didn't become known as the Byham until the mid-1990s.

The **Benedum Center for the Performing Arts** (719 Liberty Ave., 412/456-2600, www.pgharts.org/venues/benedum.aspx), however, holds a distinction entirely unique from the district's other venues: After a $43 million restoration by H. J. Heinz II (who restored the center to its former glory of 1928—it was then known as the Stanley Theater), the Benedum was added to the National Register of Historic Places.

Other venues in the Cultural District include the **August Wilson Center for African American Culture,** a massive museum and cultural center celebrating the artistic contributions of African Americans nationwide; **SPACE** (812 Liberty Ave., 412/325-7723, www.space-pittsburgh.org), a contemporary arts gallery; the **ToonSeum,** one of only three cartoon and comic art museums in the country; and the **Harris Theater** (809 Liberty Ave., 412/682-4111, www.pghfilmmakers.org), an independent cinema house where stage performances occasionally take place.

MAP 1: Bordered by Fort Duquesne Blvd., 10th St., Liberty Ave., and Stanwix St.; www.pgharts.org

FORT PITT MUSEUM

It's certainly fitting that the two-story, 12,000-square-foot Fort Pitt Museum is just a stone's throw from the confluence of Pittsburgh's three rivers. As the site of the French and Indian War, the Point, as the confluence is known, is also where the history of Pittsburgh itself first began being written. The museum uses dioramas and historical artifacts to tell the story of the war, the outcome of which was much more important than most Americans realize. (If Fort Pitt had ultimately fallen to the French, for instance, guess what language this guide would probably be written in?) Next door is an authentic blockhouse; it's the city's oldest building.

MAP 1: 101 Commonwealth Pl., Point State Park, 412/281-9285, www.heinzhistorycenter.org; daily 10am-5pm; $6 adult, $3 child (ages 6-17), $5 senior

clockwise from top left: PNC Legacy Project; ToonSeum; the August Wilson Center for African American Culture

MARKET SQUARE

Today, the relatively small area known as Market Square isn't much more than an open-air square-shaped block of restaurants and retail establishments with a small park at its center. What's more, the majority of the square's historical businesses have long since fled for the suburbs.

The good news, however, is that the once neglected and relatively unexciting Market Square has recently changed in a major way, thanks to a $5 million reconstruction process that officially kicked off in mid-August 2009. The crux of this seriously ambitious plan involved transforming Market Square into something of a European-style piazza, complete with a more pedestrian-friendly layout. Traffic, in other words, is no longer a part of the decidedly relaxing and carefree Market Square plan, which is now open only to pedestrians, who are free to lounge at the square's many outdoor tables and to take advantage of the free Wi-Fi access. Visit the Market Square website for news and updates about special events that occasionally take place.

The original market, designed by John Campbell in the late 1700s, was a covered and enclosed building generally referred to as the Diamond. It soon became the commercial center of the city. The buying and selling of foodstuffs took place there, and the city's courthouse, its jail, and its first newspaper, *The Pittsburgh Gazette,* were also housed inside.

Business continued as usual until the early 1900s, when a fire permanently destroyed the Diamond. A new market house was soon built in its place; it encompassed 11,000 square feet and reached all the way to the road now known as Forbes Avenue. Yet five days after Christmas in 1960, the final enclosed market house was demolished, due largely to unbearable overhead expenses.

Thankfully, a small number of the market's older businesses have been restored and may be visited. If you have the time to visit only one, make it the 140-year-old **Original Oyster House** (20 Market Sq., 412/566-7925, www.originaloysterhousepittsburgh.com, Mon.-Sat. 10am-10pm, Sun. 11am-7pm), a veritable Pittsburgh tradition offering enormous fish sandwiches and fried oysters. You might also try the much newer local legend known as **Primanti Brothers** (2 S. Market Pl., 412/261-1599, daily 10am-midnight, www.primantibros.com), where hearty meat sandwiches are served with French fries *inside.*

MAP 1: Bordered by Stanwix, Wood, 4th, and 5th Ave.; www.marketsquarepgh.com

PNC LEGACY PROJECT

It may not look like much from the outside, and the inside looks sort of like an odd contemporary art museum. But the PNC Legacy

Project is in fact a fantastic multimedia exhibit that celebrates Pittsburgh's history while honoring many of its most important visionaries, personalities, and entrepreneurs.

Part of the project's mission involves showcasing and celebrating the region's transformation. And if you spend enough time here, you'll definitely leave with a much better understanding of—and an appreciation for—what makes Pittsburgh the city it is today.

Pick up one of the handsets hanging from the ceiling to hear one of a series of oral histories from Pittsburgh's cultural and community leaders. Spend some time with the interactive video exhibit, which is filled to overflowing with historical images of nearly the entire Pittsburgh area in the mid-20th century.

As PNC explains it, the real purpose of the Legacy Project "is to honor, document, and preserve the history of its predecessor banks, their employees, and the communities they served." (Similar Legacy Projects exist in Washington, D.C.; Baltimore; Cleveland; Annapolis; Fredericksburg; and Rocky Mount, North Carolina.) This particular location does a fantastic job of achieving that goal. If you truly want to understand how the fabric and spirit of modern-day Pittsburgh came to be, passing an hour or so here is one of the best ways to do so.

MAP 1: Lantern Building, 600 Liberty Ave., 412/762-3380, www.pnclegacyproject.com; Mon.-Fri. 11am-3pm; free

POINT STATE PARK

It's easy enough to think of the triangle-shaped and recently renovated Point State Park which opened in the 1970s, as Pittsburgh's answer to Central Park: a grassy, seemingly secluded respite from the urban grind. But the 36-acre area, now used solely as a recreational park, has a bloody history of some national significance.

Originally known as Fort Pitt, this was the site of the French and Indian War, which was won by General John Forbes (and an army of 6,000) for the British Empire in 1758. The **Fort Pitt Museum** and its accompanying **Fort Pitt Blockhouse,** both inside the park, tell the story of this crucial epoch in American history. During your exploration of the park, look out for the 23 monuments and commemorative markers detailing spots of historical importance.

No interest in battlefield lore, however, is necessary to appreciate Point State Park's pivotal location at the axis of the city's three rivers: Not only do the Allegheny, the Monongahela, and the Ohio converge where the park begins, but a hidden "fourth river"—properly known as the Wisconsin Glacial Flow—streams lazily underneath them all. In fact, visitors who make their way to the westernmost tip of the park when its **fountain** is in operation will be able to view the fourth river themselves: That's it, shooting into a 30-foot-tall plume above the fountain's 200-foot-diameter concave bowl, in which children can often be seen frolicking. During the spring, summer, and fall, the fountain, which was dedicated in 1974, is in operation 7:30am-10pm, weather permitting.

The Point is also a place where Pittsburgh comes to play, especially during the summer months. It is also an outdoor concert venue, theater, and visual arts gallery during Pittsburgh's annual Three Rivers Arts Festival. In addition to the arts festival, the Three Rivers Regatta and the Fourth of July Fireworks take place here.

A lengthy and extensive multimillion-dollar renovation of Point State Park is finally coming to its conclusion. The park is now greener and more gorgeous than ever, with new amenities that include bike racks, better lighting, new park benches, and improved seating around the famous fountain. A new eatery offering snacks and light meals, **Cafe at the Point** (Mon.-Fri. 9am-4pm, Sat.-Sun. 11am-6pm), sits on an expanded terrazzo patio immediately off the city-side lawn, offering lovely views.

MAP 1: 101 Commonwealth Pl., 412/471-0235 (park), 412/281-9284 (museum), www.pointstatepark.com, www.dcnr.state.pa.us; daily sunrise-11pm; free

PPG PLACE

Completed in 1984 and designed by the legendarily influential architect Philip Johnson, PPG Place is easily the most noticeable and modern complex (some would say postmodern) within the confines of the Golden Triangle. Wander toward Downtown's Market Square to separately view the six structures of PPG Place, or simply look skyward as you approach: PPG's massive tower, covered in a reflective glass skin, rises skyward. At its top are jagged, "Glassy Gothic" spires with triangular and pointed tips. The remaining five buildings, while of a much smaller stature, are also covered in a glass skin and sport Gothic spires; in total, there are 231 spires in the complex.

Sometimes referred to as "the crown jewel of the Pittsburgh skyline," PPG Place is an unusual and somewhat bizarre series of edifices, to be sure, especially when compared to the immediate area's other corporate buildings, the majority of which are architecturally plain (except, of course, the few remaining historical structures, such as Henry Hobson Richardson's Allegheny County Courthouse).

So how exactly *did* the design for PPG Place come about? As critic Peter Blake put forth in the February 1984 issue of *Progressive Architecture:*

> If you are an architect asked to design a complex that will house the Corporate Headquarters of the Pittsburgh Plate Glass Company (plus other tenants), you will, obviously, design a glass building. The question is—what sort of glass building? And what sort of image will you try to project?

Blake goes on to suggest that Johnson might have designed something resembling one of Mies van der Rohe's sketches for skyscrapers in glass. But instead, Johnson chose to essentially create a miniature Rockefeller Center, complete with arcaded sidewalks that join all six buildings. Yet the complex also includes the magnificent, 13,000-square-foot Wintergarden, clearly a nod to the 17th-century gardens of Italy and France. And perhaps most exciting (and most interactive) for tourists are the 60- and 90-degree angles of glass that cover the facades of each face: Because of the way the plates of glass reflect upon each other, and upon the gritty scene of urban Pittsburgh surrounding them, the images appearing in the structure's reflections make for incredible photographs.

Should you grow tired after exploring the structure, simply drop into any of the adjoining cafés or descend to the ground floor of the complex, where a food court can be found.

A gingerbread house display and competition takes place each winter, which is also when the plaza between 3rd Avenue and 4th Avenue transforms into a popular ice-skating rink, **The Rink at PPG Place** (mid-Nov.-mid-Feb.; admission $8 adult, $7 senior and child, $3 skate rental).

MAP 1: 200 Three PPG Place, 412/434-1900 (events), 412/394-3641 (ice-skating rink), www.ppgplace.com

SMITHFIELD STREET BRIDGE

Anyone walking from Downtown Pittsburgh to Station Square, which sits on the opposite side of the Monongahela River, does so by strolling along one of the two footpaths of the Smithfield Street Bridge, a span often referred to locally as the "Kissing Fish Bridge" (view the bridge from afar and you'll understand the reference). Anyone interested in viewing a particularly striking Pittsburgh city skyline should give it a shot. As you cross, pause periodically along the way and observe the view in front of you, behind you, and even beneath you; a tugboat or even a coal barge might pass.

Constructed between the years 1881 and 1883, the Smithfield Street Bridge is actually the third such structure to exist on the site. The first, built in 1818, was the Monongahela Bridge, which was also the very first river crossing in Pittsburgh. Its construction put the city back only $102,000, although it was rendered unusable during the Great Fire of 1845.

The second bridge constructed on the site was designed by John Roebling, who also created both the Brooklyn Bridge and the span that was replaced by Pittsburgh's Roberto Clemente Bridge. Increasing loads of heavy traffic soon led to this second bridge's closure and then to the construction of the bridge we see today, which has been designated a Historic Landmark by the Department of the Interior, the American Society of Civil Engineers, and the Pittsburgh History and Landmarks Foundation.

Designed by Gustav Lindenthal—who was also responsible for the creation of Hell Gate Bridge, which connects Astoria, Queens, to Randalls Island in New York City—the Smithfield Street Bridge is a truss-style span over which streetcars once passed. But to create room for more traffic flow, that practice ended in the summer of 1985, and the streetcars were moved to the nearby Panhandle Bridge, which you'll cross today should you ride the T from any of Downtown's four streetcar stops to Station Square.

As you cross beneath the portals of the Smithfield Street Bridge on foot, pay close attention to the detailed lamps, as well as to small, intricate moldings representing the city's legendary industrial prowess.

MAP 1: Smithfield St. between Fort Pitt Blvd. and W. Carson St., www.pghbridges.com; free

THREE SISTERS BRIDGES

Although nearly all of Pittsburgh's Downtown spans are visually striking and historically significant, probably no trio of bridges means more to the city than those known collectively as the Three Sisters. And because all are identically designed and painted a rather striking shade of yellow known as Aztec gold, it's quite likely that these bridges are the first you'll notice when exploring the Golden Triangle. The Three Sisters are the only identical trio of side-by-side bridges in the world. They were also the very first self-anchored suspension spans built in the United States.

Today known as the **Roberto Clemente Bridge** (formerly the 6th Street Bridge, built in 1928), the **Andy Warhol Bridge** (formerly the 7th Street Bridge, built in 1926), and the **Rachel Carson Bridge** (formerly the 9th Street Bridge, built in 1927), all three bridges cross the Allegheny River to reach the North Side.

The Andy Warhol bridge was renamed on March 18, 2005. It earned its new name as part of a 10th anniversary celebration for the Andy Warhol Museum, which sits just steps from the north end of the bridge. The celebration for its renaming was, appropriately enough, probably the most Dionysian of the three. A number of the city's most left-of-center artists were in attendance, and students from a nearby performing arts high school gave a brief drama and dance show.

Perhaps even more interesting, though, is the Warhol Bridge's immediate neighbor to the west, the Roberto Clemente Bridge. The Roberto Clemente gained its new name on April 8, 1999, the day after a groundbreaking ceremony took place on the bridge's northern end for PNC Park, which became the new home of the

Pittsburgh baseball club two years later (Clemente was a legendary Pirate who played from 1955 until his death in a plane crash in 1972). The bridge's proudest moment probably came in 1928, the year it was erected. This was when the American Institute of Steel Construction named it the year's most beautiful steel bridge. And while each of the Three Sisters replaced a former bridge, the Roberto Clemente replaced a notable span built by the once-famous John Roebling, probably best known for creating New York City's Brooklyn Bridge.

The Rachel Carson Bridge was renamed on April 22, 2006, which was also Earth Day. It was quite an appropriate time for the renaming, as Carson was a pioneering environmentalist who authored the classic tome *Silent Spring* and remains known as one of Southwestern Pennsylvania's most influential natives. (Born in 1907, Carson was raised in Springdale at a site now known as the Rachel Carson Homestead, which is open to visitors.)

The renaming of the bridge happened largely due to the efforts of Esther Barazzone, the president of Chatham College, where Carson matriculated in the 1920s, when Chatham was still known as the Pennsylvania College for Women. Barazzone initially had her sights set on a statue of Carson, which would have been the city's first statue of a woman, but those plans were dashed due to Pittsburgh's financial problems.

MAP 1: Roberto Clemente Bridge, 6th St. between Federal St. and Fort Duquesne Blvd.; Andy Warhol Bridge, 7th St. between Sandusky St. and Fort Duquesne Blvd.; Rachel Carson Bridge, 9th St. between Anderson St. and Fort Duquesne Blvd.; www.pghbridges.com; free

★ TOONSEUM

As one of only three museums in the country dedicated exclusively to cartoon art (the other two are located in Manhattan and San Francisco), the ToonSeum is a fairly small gallery that nevertheless manages to pack in an incredible amount of original comic and cartoon art. It was formerly located in a small corner of the Children's Museum of Pittsburgh on the North Side, but the ToonSeum now resides in the city's downtown Cultural District, where its smartly curated exhibits change every couple of months. And because the museum's very mission involves promoting a deeper understanding of cartoon artists and their work, a wide range of original programming and hands-on educational workshops happen on a regular basis. The gift shop is worth a visit for its wonderful selection of comics, graphic novels, and cartoon-related ephemera.

MAP 1: 945 Liberty Ave., 412/232-0199, www.toonseum.org; Mon. and Wed.-Thurs. 10:30am-3:30pm; Fri. 10:30am-7pm, Sat. 10:30am-5pm, Sun. 11am-5pm; $6

Strip District

PITTSBURGH PUBLIC MARKET

Formerly located in the Produce Terminal Building on Smallman Street, the Pittsburgh Public Market recently relocated into a much larger and more welcoming nearby space. The Public Market has consistently been one of the city's most popular tourist attractions since it originally opened in 2010; it's also the first public market the city has seen in nearly five decades. Dozens of merchants and vendors offer everything from fresh fruit and veggies to wine, fine cheeses, handmade housewares and clothing, microbrewed beer, pasta, cookies, candies, and high-end deli products. Street artists and musicians are often spotted performing as well. And as the market continues to grow into its new space, there's no telling what or who you're likely to bump into.

MAP 1: 2401 Penn Ave., 412/281-4505, www.pittsburghpublicmarket.org; Wed.-Fri. and Sun. 10am-4pm, Sat. 9am-5pm

★ SENATOR JOHN HEINZ HISTORY CENTER

Certainly one of the city's most educational and culturally viable additions to the museum scene, the seven-story Heinz History Center acts as a nearly exhaustive record of Western Pennsylvania life and culture spanning more than 250 years. It is housed inside the former headquarters and warehouse of the Chautauqua Lake Ice Company.

Because so many exhibitions are hands-on and creatively curated, the museum is also enjoyable for children. Young visitors will find much to capture their attention in the **Western Pennsylvania Sports Museum,** which celebrates the achievements of area athletes and allows youngsters to play along. And on the museum's third floor is Discovery Place, a hands-on historical exhibit specifically designed for younger guests. Kids also love sitting in the driver's seat of the restored 1949 streetcar trolley, which is in the ground floor's Great Hall, where you'll find Kidsburgh, a small play area built above Reymer's Old-Fashioned Deli. And yet the History Center might best be described as a can't-miss attraction for folks of any age, assuming they carry even a passing interest in the development of the region and its people.

Although the museum opened its doors to the public in 1996, it didn't come into its full glory until late 2004, when a new wing affiliated with the Smithsonian Institution was completed. That process also established the center as the largest history museum in the state. Two recent additions to the Smithsonian wing are the aforementioned Sports Museum and the superbly curated Special

Collections Gallery, which takes an especially close look at the immigrant communities that flocked to Pittsburgh at the turn of the 20th century. You'll find artifacts used by the immigrant laborers, such as cigar-rolling supplies and tools that were used in the area's mines. There's also a life-size recreation of the inside of a typical laborer's home. Some of the more recent artifacts include the headgear and uniforms used by the steel miners of the 1970s; you'll also see an actual steel miner's locker, decorated in now-faded Pittsburgh Steelers stickers.

MAP 1: 1212 Smallman St., 412/454-6000, www.heinzhistorycenter.org; daily 10am-5pm; $15 adult, $6 student, $6 child (ages 6-17), free for children 5 and under, $13 senior

ST. PATRICK CHURCH AND ST. STANISLAUS KOSTKA CHURCH

The St. Patrick-St. Stanislaus Parish consists of two historical Catholic chapels of the same name, both in the heart of the tourist-friendly Strip District.

Known to area residents as "Old St. Patrick's," **St. Patrick Church** was Pittsburgh's very first Catholic parish. And while the church building itself wasn't constructed until 1936, the parish was founded way back in 1808 by a group of Irish immigrants. This most likely explains the structure's stone tower, built to resemble the towers of Irish monasteries in medieval times.

Today, St. Patrick's is probably best remembered by older generations of Pittsburghers because of Father James R. Cox, an astonishingly altruistic man who acted as the church's priest throughout the Great Depression. Among other good deeds, Cox helped the city's homeless and unemployed population construct a ragged but livable Shantytown along stretches of Liberty Avenue.

Old St. Patrick's also has something of a national reputation; it's one of the very few churches in the world to own a replica of the famous **Holy Stairs,** which represent the number of steps Jesus climbed on the day Pontius Pilate condemned him to death. Visitors may climb the 28 steps during normal church hours, except during the noon hour on Mondays and Thursdays, when Mass is held. Do keep in mind, however, that ascending the steps must be done on one's knees. (Walking *down* the steps is allowed.)

As for **St. Stanislaus Kostka,** it was consecrated in the summer of 1892 and was built using a blend of Romanesque and Baroque styles, with Byzantine influences. It can easily be spotted from blocks away, thanks to its front-facing **Great Rose Window,** which symbolizes God and the rays of the sun. In 2002, over $67,000 was spent to fully restore the window. The church is also home to a number of Munich-style stained glass windows; experts have proclaimed them to be some of the finest examples of their kind in the country. Especially impressive are the church's paintings, such as those found in the semi-dome over the main altar.

MAP 1: St. Patrick, 1711 Liberty Ave.; St. Stanislaus Kostka, 57 21st St.; 412/471-4767, www.saintsinthestrip.org; daily 8am-3:30pm (visit website for weekly Mass schedule); free

WIGLE WHISKEY

American whiskey, it could be argued, was actually born in Pittsburgh. And at this relatively young distillery, located in an industrial space, visitors will hear the history of the Whiskey Rebellion as seen from the viewpoint of Philip Wigle, the local man who unwittingly helped launch it. One-hour tours include a whiskey cocktail and a seated straight tasting; visitors will also learn how the various whiskeys distilled here are created. Children under 12 can't join the tour, but there is a gift shop of sorts on-site where Wigle beverages and other souvenirs can be purchased. Private tours for 12 or more people are $25 per person.

MAP 1: 2401 Smallman St., 412/224-2827, www.wiglewhiskey.com; Tues.-Sat. 10am-6pm, Sun. 10am-4pm; distillery tour $20

North Side

Map 1

★ THE ANDY WARHOL MUSEUM

As the country's largest museum dedicated to a single artist, the Andy Warhol Museum is a particularly unique feather in Pittsburgh's cap. To explore the building properly, start on the top floor; this is where temporary exhibitions are generally held. As you work your way slowly down, you'll encounter work both obscure (Jesus punching bags, oxidation paintings made of urine) and familiar (Campbell's soup cans, Brillo boxes). Definitely don't miss the Silver Clouds room, where aluminum balloons are kept afloat by fans. A theater that regularly screens films by and about Warhol and his entourage is on the ground level; in the basement sits a café and the city's only vintage photo booth. An archival collection housing thousands of pieces of Warhol's personal ephemera is also on-site.

MAP 1: 117 Sandusky St., 412/237-8300, www.warhol.org; Tues.-Thurs. and Sat.-Sun. 10am-5pm, Fri. 10am-10pm; $20 adult, $10 student, $10 child 3-18, half-price Fri. 5pm-10pm

CALVARY UNITED METHODIST CHURCH

Built in 1890 by residents of the North Side's so-called Millionaires Row, which can still be visited today in the **Allegheny West Historic District** (www.city.pittsburgh.pa.us/wt/html/allegheny_west.html),

clockwise from top left: Pittsburgh Public Market; Randyland; Senator John Heinz History Center

Andy Warhol's Pittsburgh

So you've come from far and wide to visit the Andy Warhol Museum, and now you'd like to discover some of the sites that transformed the shy Pittsburgh boy into a pop art superstar? The following suggestions, adapted from a tour that was once offered by the Greater Pittsburgh Convention and Visitors Bureau, will take you to a number of locations essential to young Andy's growth as an artist. For even more tips and ideas, visit the incredibly useful and comprehensive **Andy Warhol Family Album** at www.warhola.com.

Your first stop on the DIY Warhol Tour should absolutely be the **Warhola family home** in South Oakland, which still sits at 3252 Dawson Street. After falling into serous disrepair some years ago, the house was purchased by Andy's oldest brother, Paul, who is currently renovating the home. But don't expect much—just a typical row house with a collection of hedges. The Warholas were a family of especially modest means—Andy's father Andrei toiled as a construction worker during the Depression and was often without gainful employment.

If you're particularly adventurous, you could try to find **Andy's former elementary school,** which was alternately known as Holmes Elementary and Oakland Public School. It's somewhere near the corner of Dawson Street and Edith Place, very near to Andy's childhood home; it's also said to be on the National Register of Historic Places.

Another easy walk from the Warhola home is **Schenley High School** (4101 Bigelow Blvd.). Warhol was a student here, and this is also where some of his earlier artistic efforts first flourished. You might also consider visiting the home where Andy was born; it's at **73 Orr Street** in the Uptown neighborhood, which is also known as Soho.

In between Oakland and Squirrel Hill is the campus of **Carnegie Mellon University,** which was known as Carnegie Tech when Andy Warhol attended as a student in the department of painting and design.

Just south of Schenley Park is

Calvary United Methodist Church is probably best known for its stained-glass windows. Large and wonderfully gorgeous, the triple-lancet, Tiffany-produced windows are still considered the finest and most elaborately detailed examples of religious stained glass ever created by the company. Calvary's exterior is also notable: Many claim its set of gargoyles to be among the city's best.

Also interesting is the architecture of the Gothic-style church, which was constructed in the shape of a cross. The famous industrialist Charles Scaife, among scores of wealthy Pittsburgh merchants, was a member of the church's building committee. The uniquely curved pews, in fact, were constructed by the Joseph Horne Company, which sold dry goods in the city for decades.

Wrote Franklin Toker about Calvary United in *Pittsburgh: An Urban Portrait*: "Everything about the church inside and out is rich, textured, and above all, comfortable. To enter it is to intrude on a sumptuous private drawing room."

The **Allegheny Historic Preservation Society** is currently working

Greenfield and the Four Mile Run area, where you'll find **St. John Chrysostom Byzantine Catholic Church** (506 Saline St., www.sjcbcc.com). The church is where the Warhola family worshipped regularly; Andy was also baptized there. Visit the church's website for service schedules or, if you're so inclined, log onto the chapel's Church Cam, where you can watch the proceedings in real time. You'll find a link to the camera at www.warhol.org/figment, where you can also log onto a camera that shows a live feed of Warhol's gravesite.

Regarding that gravesite, you'll need a car to reach it. **St. John the Baptist Byzantine Catholic Cemetery** is in the South Hills neighborhood of Bethel Park, at the corner of Route 88 and Conner Road, and not far from South Hills Village Mall. Warhol is buried here next to his parents. The tombstone, located on a sloping hillside, is very modest and is sometimes decorated with a Campbell's soup can or two.

In the somewhat rough-and-tumble neighborhood of McKees Rocks is the **Holy Ghost Byzantine Catholic Church** (1437 Superior Ave.), where Warhol's funeral service took place.

Two of Andy Warhol's nephews, George and Marty Warhola, who both continue to live in Pittsburgh, are currently operating competing scrap metal businesses within three miles of each other on the North Side. Marty runs **Northside Scrap Metals, Inc.** (825 Pennsylvania Ave., www.northsidescrapmetals.com, formerly Paul Warhola Scrap Metals) and George owns **AJ Warhola Recycling Inc.** (203 Chesboro St.).

On March 18, 2005, with much fanfare, the 7th Street Bridge was renamed the **Andy Warhol Bridge.** Start on the Downtown end and walk across for a beautiful view of the city and the Allegheny River. Once you reach the North Side you'll be within spitting distance of the **Andy Warhol Museum** (117 Sandusky St., 412/237-8300, www.warhol.org) itself.

to preserve the sections of this historic landmark that have fallen into disrepair. To make a contribution, contact the AHPS at 412/323-1070.

MAP 1: 971 Beech Ave., 412/231-2007, www.calvarypgh.com; group tours given by appointment only; free

CARNEGIE SCIENCE CENTER AND HIGHMARK SPORTSWORKS

Filled with kid-friendly and hands-on exhibits, the Carnegie Science Center approaches an often-tedious subject with a rather honorable mission: "To [inspire] learning and curiosity by connecting science and technology with everyday life." In other words, gaining an understanding of the world in which we live can be a blast here, where permanent displays include the Kitchen Theater, which looks at science through the art of cooking, and SeaScape, a 2,000-square-foot aquarium. Visitors also flock to the Science Center for its four-story **Omnimax Theater,** as well as for its **Buhl**

Planetarium & Observatory, regarded as one of the world's most technologically sophisticated. (On Friday and Saturday nights, the planetarium plays host to a series of laser shows accompanied by classic rock soundtracks.) And docked in the Allegheny River just behind the Science Center is the World War II-era USS *Requin,* a Navy submarine that can be boarded and explored.

One of the center's newest attractions is Roboworld, known as the world's largest permanent robotics exhibition. And then there's the phenomenal **Highmark SportsWorks** facility, a wonderfully interactive experience where kids young and old are encouraged to learn about the mysterious workings of the body by engaging in physical activity. There are nearly 30 different interactive experiences, where visitors, for instance, can race a virtual Olympic sprinter, climb a 25-foot rock wall, or attempt to pitch a fastball. SportsWorks, in fact, is the very best sort of museum: It's practically a guaranteed good time.

MAP 1: 1 Allegheny Ave., 412/237-3400, www.carnegiesciencecenter.org; Sun.-Fri. 10am-5pm, Sat. 10am-7pm; $17.95 adult, $11.95 child (including Science Center exhibits, Highmark SportsWorks, planetarium shows, and USS *Requin;* Omnimax films and laser shows are extra)

CHILDREN'S MUSEUM OF PITTSBURGH

After a massive expansion project transformed the Children's Museum of Pittsburgh from a relatively insignificant structure into something of a youth-oriented educational town square, Pittsburgh now has bragging rights to one of the most pioneering and novel museums for kids in the country. Even better is the building's environmentally friendly focus: Designed and constructed with sustainable materials, the museum is an officially LEED-certified "green building." Now four times as large as the previous museum, with part of the building located in a disused U.S. Post Office and part in the former Buhl Planetarium, it holds 12 permanent exhibits, including a replica of the television world seen on PBS's *Mister Rogers' Neighborhood;* the Makeshop, a DIY maker space where kids and families can explore woodworking, circuitry, and sewing; and the fantastic Waterplay exhibit, where children can pump, move, channel, and dam various flows of water. (Bring bathing suits for this one!)

There is an excellent collection of interactive exhibits built around a philosophy quite similar to that of the Carnegie Science Museum: The house's official mantra is "Play with Real Stuff," and it means that by playing and experimenting, as opposed to simply looking and listening, kids will be more excited to learn about the world that surrounds them. For instance, the museum includes an art studio offering printmaking, paper-making, and painting. There's a garage where machinery and engines can be tinkered with. And definitely don't miss the Attic, with its oddly tilted Gravity Room, or the TapeScape, a massive indoor landscape made from 168 rolls of clear packing tape.

MAP 1: 10 Children's Way, Allegheny Square, 412/322-5058, www.pittsburghkids.org; daily 10am-5pm; $13 adult, $12 child and senior

HOUSE POEM AND CITY OF ASYLUM

The tiny wooden row house known as House Poem is owned by the Pittsburgh chapter of the international City of Asylum organization, which provides sanctuary to writers who have been persecuted in their own countries. The Chinese poet Huang Xiang was House Poem's first writer-in-residence, and he's also the person responsible for the striking Chinese characters that cover the home's facade, literally from the curb to the roof.

Wander down the small road toward **324 Sampsonia Way,** which houses the City of Asylum/Pittsburgh headquarters, and you'll stumble upon other unusually painted houses: 324 Sampsonia, for instance, was covered with a wrap-around mural featuring Pittsburgh cityscapes and traditional Burmese images when the Burmese writer Khet Mar and her husband, the painter Than Htay Muang, took up residence there.

Currently, the City of Asylum organization is in the process of constructing a literary center known as **Alphabet City** on the Garden Theater Block of West North Avenue, which is just a few blocks south of Sampsonia Way. Projected to open in the spring of 2014, the three ground-level storefronts of Alphabet City will house a bookstore, a recording/broadcast-enabled performance space, a restaurant, a free book-distribution program, and more.

MAP 1: 408 Sampsonia Way, 412/323-0278, www.cityofasylumpittsburgh.org; free

MATTRESS FACTORY

Not only is the Mattress Factory an internationally recognized organization that focuses singularly on installation art, but it also hosts a truly unique residency program. Over the past three decades, more than 250 artists have lived at the museum while creating new work. And while any given year sees a regular rotation of such new (and temporary) installations, the museum owns many permanent pieces as well. Some of the most stunning are James Turrell's odd and unsettling works of neon and light. Don't miss *Pleiades,* an entirely dark room where a presence of light may or may not appear. Another can't-miss is Yayoi Kusama's *Infinity Dots Mirrored Room;* entering it may just change your perspective on reality itself.

Admission is free for children under 6, and for CMU, Pitt, and

clockwise from top left: the National Aviary; the Andy Warhol Museum; Carnegie Science Center

Point Park students. Every Tuesday, the museum offers half-price admission (with the exception of group tours).

MAP 1: 500 Sampsonia Way, 412/231-3169, www.mattress.org; Tues.-Sat. 10am-5pm, Sun. 1pm-5pm; $15 adult, $10 student, $10 senior, half-price admission on Tues.

★ NATIONAL AVIARY

As home to more than 600 exotic birds of more than 200 species—many of them endangered—it's no wonder the National Aviary is known as one of the most important bird zoos in the country. Along with its extensive and many-hued flock, however, much of the aviary's deserved popularity is derived from the glass building's interior design: Visitors can choose to stroll through the two open rooms where birds fly freely among them, or they can venture into a more traditional viewing locale where birds and humans don't mix. (In these areas, a thin mesh-wire sheet is used to cage the creatures.) Yet completely unlike the traditional zoo environment, it is possible to literally get face-to-beak with a flamingo or a parrot. And while some visitors may find this setup surprising, or even frightening, young children often seem to mix quite naturally with the animals. What could possibly be a more exciting way to educate a preschooler or elementary school-age child about the wonders of the natural world?

Some of the many birds you may see include the bald eagle, the gray-winged trumpeter, the king vulture, the military macaw, the toco toucan, the African penguin, the speckled mousebird, and the white-crested laughing thrush. Feedings and various demonstrations take place throughout the day; visitors can even participate in the daily tropical forest and wetlands feedings of the truly glorious feathered fowl who call this special place home.

The aviary recently completed a massive, $17.5 million renovation and expansion, and new exhibitions have since been unveiled in the space, which is now LEED Silver certified and fully ADA accessible. The Helen M. Schmidt FliteZone Theater, for instance, is an indoor, 125-seat space where free-flight bird shows take place. Penguin Point, meanwhile, is the new home of the aviary's 16 African penguins; it offers up-close, 360-degree views of the flock.

MAP 1: Allegheny Commons West Park, 412/323-7235, www.aviary.org; daily 10am-5pm; $13 adult, $11 child, $12 senior (shows are $5 extra)

PHOTO ANTIQUITIES MUSEUM

A 2,500-square-foot museum dedicated to the preservation of historical photography, the Photo Antiquities Museum is decorated with a quaint Victorian interior and boasts an archive of more than 100,000 negatives and prints. Beginning with the very earliest days of photography, the collection spans not only images, of which roughly 3,000 are always on display, but also cameras and other photographic accessories. The era of the earliest daguerreotype (roughly 1839) is documented, as is every important photographic era, including the digital cameras of the 21st century. The relatively small museum has literally hundreds of historical photographs on display, and at the on-site gift shop, visitors can purchase reproductions—from 8 by 10 to mural-sized—of any of the museum's images. Lectures and tours are occasionally given by volunteers; call or visit the website for upcoming schedules.

MAP 1: 531 E. Ohio St., 412/231-7881, www.photoantiquities.org; Mon. and Wed.-Sat. 10am-4pm; $10 adult, $8 child, senior, and student

RANDYLAND

Although he claims not to be an artist, Pittsburgh native Randy Gilson has nevertheless spent more than 20 years transforming his three-story North Side home into what is commonly referred to as the most colorful building in the city. Indeed, stumbling across this improbably cheerful parcel of land, which sits smack-dab in the heart of the rough-and-tumble Central North Side, is certainly one of Pittsburgh's happiest surprises. The house itself is coated in shining-bright primary colors and covered in murals, vintage signs, and random tchotchkes of all sorts, including a handmade 3-D map of the North Side. Over the years, Gilson has also painstakingly applied his creative touch to a roughly 30-block area around his home, a process that has resulted in more than 800 Day-Glo street gardens and 50 vegetable gardens cropping up around the Mexican War Streets neighborhood.

But what exactly *is* Randyland? For the time being, at least, it's nothing more than a seriously unusual corner of Pittsburgh; there's nothing to buy, in other words, and nothing much to do. That is, unless you'd like to call Randyland home—Gilson is currently renting the space for $1,000 per month. Visit the website for details.

MAP 1: 1507 Arch St., 412/321-7776, www.visualvitamin.com; free

RIVERS CASINO

Located right on the shores of the Ohio River, roughly halfway between Heinz Field and the West End Bridge, the always-open, steel-and-glass-encased Rivers Casino has been home to a certain degree of controversy for a number of years now—long before its license to operate had even been granted by the city, in fact.

Its most vehement detractors, predictably enough, cited the many negative ramifications such a business would almost certainly stir up in an economically teetering city such as Pittsburgh: gambling addiction, growing levels of crime and prostitution, increased poverty. But despite the years of political hard-balling and liberal hand-wringing that preceded its arrival in August 2009, Rivers Casino is now a seemingly permanent addition to the North Shore's landscape. And what a truly enormous and world-class addition it is, reminiscent of the glamorous and higher-end mega-casinos that line the length of the Las Vegas strip.

The 120,000-square-foot gaming floor, for instance, features nearly 3,000 slot machines, and the covered parking lot has spaces for 3,800 visitors. There's also an outdoor amphitheater, a half dozen contemporary lounges and eateries, and a private club for high rollers. Special ventilation units clean and refresh the casino's air every 12 minutes, as smoking is allowed on parts of the gaming floor. Penny slots are abundant, and Pennsylvania's solitary $500 slot machine can be found here. And while table games were initially all electronically operated, that's since changed; visitors will find everything from craps and roulette to Pai Gow poker and mini baccarat, all staffed by actual dealers and croupiers. There's even a dedicated 30-table poker room.

There are, in fact, a number of casino anomalies: The gaming floor features a massive wall of windows, which offers a brilliant view of the Ohio River outside. And LCD TV screens, mostly featuring professional sports, are abundant. It appears as if Rivers will remain a permanent part of the Pittsburgh story. For the time being, at least, the casino is nothing if not a fascinating cultural addition to a city that has always been lacking in extravagances. Don't leave Pittsburgh without at least paying it a quick visit.

MAP 1: 777 Casino Dr., 412/231-7777, www.theriverscasino.com; daily 24 hours

Oakland

Map 2

CARNEGIE MELLON UNIVERSITY

After Scottish immigrant Andrew Carnegie made his fortune in the steel industry and then became one of the world's most famous philanthropists, he gave quite a bit back to the city of Pittsburgh, where buildings and institutions named after him seem nearly ubiquitous in some quarters.

Carnegie Mellon University was founded by Carnegie himself in 1900, who first dubbed it Carnegie Technical School; it later became known as the Carnegie Institute of Technology. Today, the university is considered a worldwide leader in the fields of robotics and computer engineering and, to a lesser extent, in fine arts and business administration.

To pay a visit to the campus, which is on Forbes Avenue just up the hill from the University of Pittsburgh, start by wandering the grassy, parklike expanse known as "the cut"; to its left sits the **University Student Center** (www.cmu.edu/university-center), where

The Ruins of Forbes Field

Long before the existence of PNC Park and even the historic Three Rivers Stadium—which was imploded and turned into a parking lot in 2001—the Pittsburgh Pirates baseball club battled its rivals at Forbes Field, a park in South Oakland. Not much remains of the old field, which saw its first match in 1909 and its last on June 28, 1970. Nonetheless, baseball history buffs may appreciate seeing the park's original home plate; it lies under a slightly foggy slab of plastic on the ground floor of the University of Pittsburgh's Wesley W. Posvar Hall, just outside the men's restroom. (Posvar itself sits next door to the Hillman Library, where employees at the checkout counter will be more than happy to provide you with a campus map.)

Even more exciting is the remaining portion of the right field wall, which sits just across the street from Posvar and stretches all the way to the building that houses that Katz Graduate School of Business. Even though the wall is slightly vine-covered, it's fairly easy to find: Just look for the hand-painted numbers indicating the distance in feet between the wall and home plate. And while you won't often find fans gathered around the historic artifact inside Posvar, hardcore Pirates obsessives do occasionally set up shop—complete with patio chairs and radios—alongside the old stadium wall. It's a rather moving sight to see the fans, most of them old-timers, sitting perfectly still with wool blankets over their legs and battered boomboxes atop their laps.

a convenience store, the student bookstore, a food court, and a café can be found. Once inside the Student Center, the **Information Desk** (412/268-2107, Sun.-Thurs. 8am-midnight, Fri.-Sat. 8am-2am), which is actually a walk-up window, should be your very first stop. The CMU student staffing the desk will respond to queries about where to go, what to see, and what to do while on campus. Detailed campus maps and handbills advertising upcoming events are available. To view an even wider collection of notices, such as flyers announcing upcoming rock concerts, cars for sale, and roommates wanted, ask the student to point you in the direction of the bulletin board down the hall.

In total, CMU has a collection of seven colleges and schools, and since the campus is relatively small and quite walkable, a stroll across the grounds shouldn't take much longer than a half hour.

Should you care to extend your stay, you might consider taking in a performance by the world-renowned **School of Drama** (www.drama.cmu.edu), which in 2013 was ranked as the world's fourth-best drama school by *The Hollywood Reporter.* Not only was CMU the first university in the country to offer academic drama degrees, but the majority of performances today receive high marks from local theater critics. Carnegie Mellon School of Drama graduates include Ted Danson, Holly Hunter, George Peppard, Blair Underwood, and Steven Bochco. Tickets can be purchased at the box office in the lobby of the **Purnell Center for the Arts** (412/268-2407, Mon.-Fri. noon-5pm generally, weekdays noon-5pm and 6:30pm-8pm when a performance takes place, and on weekends 90 minutes before curtain).

Visitors interested in computer technology might want to stroll the halls of Carnegie Mellon's **School of Computer Science** (www.cs.cmu.edu); its graduate program has been ranked the top such program in the country by *U.S. News & World Report*. The university's **Robotics Institute** (www.ri.cmu.edu) is also notable. Founded in 1979, it's the largest college research facility of its type in the United States, and its faculty, students, and the innovations of both frequently appear in the local and national press. Local author Lee Gutkind spent six years at the Robotics Institute in preparation for a book titled *Almost Human: Making Robots Think* (W.W. Norton & Company, 2009).

Any visitor to the Carnegie Mellon campus not particularly impressed by technological advancements should consider this: Beginning in 1937 with physics professor Clinton Davisson, 15 graduates or faculty members of Carnegie Mellon have had the very prestigious honor of being awarded the Nobel Prize.

MAP 2: 5000 Forbes Ave., 412/268-2000, www.cmu.edu; free

CARNEGIE MUSEUM OF ART

Pittsburgh's premiere museum of modern art, the Carnegie Museum of Art also maintains a noted collection of contemporary pieces, post-Impressionist paintings, late-19th-century American art, and both European and American decorative arts from the past 200 years. Paintings and furniture certainly aren't the entire story, however. There's also the Hall of Sculpture, filled with Greek and Roman reproductions (including a scaled-down Parthenon). The Hall of Architecture and the Heinz Architectural Center both see a good number of special exhibitions featuring modern masters. The acclaimed Carnegie International takes place every three years—it's Pittsburgh's version of the Whitney Biennial in New York City. The next show is scheduled to open in October 2016; if you can't make it, peruse the museum's Scaife Gallery, where Warhols, Pollacks, and de Koonings can be found.

MAP 2: 4400 Forbes Ave., 412/622-3131, www.cmoa.org; Tues.-Wed. and Fri.-Sat. 10am-5pm, Thurs. 10am-8pm, Sun. noon-5pm; $17.95 adult, $11.95 student and child 3-18, $14.95 senior

★ CARNEGIE MUSEUM OF NATURAL HISTORY

Located underneath the same roof as the affiliated Carnegie Museum of Art, the Carnegie Museum of Natural History is home to a wealth of scientific and environmental exhibitions, including the world-renowned Dinosaurs in Their Time exhibit. Some of the museum's other permanent displays include the Walton Hall of Ancient Egypt (mummies!); the Hall of African Wildlife, which is complete with stunning lifelike dioramas and jungle creatures; and the Botany Hall, where plant life can be contemplated. Area scientists and archaeologists work daily in the museum's on-site PaleoLab.

MAP 2: 4400 Forbes Ave., 412/622-3131, www.carnegiemnh.org; Tues.-Wed. and Fri.-Sat. 10am-5pm, Thurs. 10am-8pm, Sun. noon-5pm; $17.95 adult, $11.95 student and child 3-18, $14.95 senior

★ CATHEDRAL OF LEARNING

Aside from its hallowed status as one of the most majestic structures in the city, the Gothic Cathedral of Learning, which acts as the symbolic nucleus of the University of Pittsburgh campus, is also the second-tallest educational building in the world. (A structure at Moscow State University, in Russia, currently holds the title.)

Appropriately enough, the story of the cathedral's construction is substantially grandiose. In 1925, Chancellor John Bowman divulged his vision of a tower whose soaring-to-the-heavens architecture would send a subtle message to the varied citizens of Pittsburgh: namely, that a higher education could be considered just as essential and dignified as a higher power. Bowman enlisted a virtual army to raise the $10 million necessary to complete the project; during the Great Depression, when charitable contributions dried up, area schoolchildren took to kicking in a dime each to "buy a brick for Pitt."

The Cathedral of Learning was finally dedicated in 1937, and even today it cuts an impressive sight. A 42-story Indiana-limestone structure on the outside, the building's inside denotes a considerably more intimate feel. Filling a cavernous but churchly first floor is the 100-foot-wide-by-200-foot-long Commons Room; students can be found tapping on laptops and sipping coffee at its long wooden benches all hours of the day and night.

Running a ring around the first floor are the fabled **Nationality Classrooms** (412/624-6000, www.nationalityrooms.pitt.edu); collectively they are easily the building's most fascinating feature. Designed to represent specific periods from various nations of the world—including many whose citizens have created enclaves in Pittsburgh—both original and recreated accoutrements were joined together as each successive room was built.

Twenty-six rooms in all can be viewed independently or as part of a guided or taped tour, including a 10th-century Armenian classroom, a folk-style Norwegian classroom, and a Byzantine-era Romanian classroom. Take care not to miss the resplendent Damascus-style Syria-Lebanon room (which unfortunately can only be viewed through a glass partition) or the many rooms on the third floor, especially the Minka-style Japanese classroom and the Israeli and African Heritage classrooms. Guided tours and self-guided recorded tours take place year-round (Mon.-Sat. 9am-2:30pm, Sun. and holidays 11am-2:30pm). No tours are offered on Thanksgiving Day, December 24-26, or January 1. Tours are $4 for adults and $2 for children ages 8-18.

MAP 2: 4200 5th Ave., 412/624-4141, www.pitt.edu; free

★ PHIPPS CONSERVATORY AND BOTANICAL GARDENS

Since its opening in 1893, Phipps Conservatory has been the nerve center of horticulture education in Southwestern Pennsylvania. Located just past the main entrance of Schenley Park in Oakland, the 13 rooms of the conservatory sit inside a Victorian-style glasshouse, where orchids, palm trees, ferns, a Japanese garden, a medicinal plant garden, and an assortment of floating water plants—to name just a sampling of the varieties on-site—await your discovery. Staying true to its fundamental mission as an education center, Phipps also hosts annual flower shows as well as occasional exhibits, lectures, and events.

Henry Phipps, a close friend of Andrew Carnegie's and, in his later years, a philanthropist, built the conservatory as a gift to the city of Pittsburgh. His explanation? He wanted to "erect something that will prove a source of instruction as well as pleasure to the people." Phipps even took pains to ensure that the conservatory would remain open on Sundays so that workers could stop by on what was their only day off.

From 2005 to 2006, the conservatory underwent a massive, $36 million renovation and expansion project resulting in an environmentally friendly welcome center and the Tropical Forest Conservatory, a 12,000-square-foot display room that features a different horticultural theme every two years.

MAP 2: 1 Schenley Park, 412/622-6914, www.phipps.conservatory.org; Sat.-Thurs. 9:30am-5pm, Fri. 9:30am-10pm; $15 adult, $11 child 2-18, $14 senior and student

RODEF SHALOM BIBLICAL BOTANICAL GARDEN

With a collection of more than 100 temperate and tropical plants, a small waterfall, a stream representing the River Jordan, and a desert scene depicting the biblical lands from Lake Galilee to the Dead Sea, the Biblical Botanical Garden at **Rodef Shalom Temple** is meant to symbolize universal love and the Bible. Many of the plants have biblical names (Moses in a Basket, Biblical Coat), and during each season, the garden focuses on a differing theme of Near Eastern horticulture. The experience of wandering the garden is meant to be something akin to a stroll through the Holy Land of ancient Israel, but even nonbelievers will enjoy relaxing among the beauty of nature; the temple is within walking distance of both

clockwise from top left: Phipps Conservatory in Schenley Park; the Cathedral of Learning on the University of Pittsburgh campus; the Carnegie Museum of Natural History

the Carnegie Mellon and Pitt campuses, and it sits across the street from the WQED studios (where, from the street, you can see a dinosaur sculpture dressed as Mister Rogers).

New special displays and educational programs are scheduled most seasons; call or visit the garden's website for updated information. Free public tours are given with a trained docent at 12:15pm on the first Wednesday of June, July, August, and September; tours can also be arranged for groups of eight or more, although it is highly recommended to make reservations two weeks in advance. Educational books and brochures about the art of horticulture are available for purchase on-site, and parking is free.

MAP 2: 4905 5th Ave., 412/621-6566, www.biblicalgardenpittsburgh.org; June 1-Sept. 15 Sun.-Thurs. 10am-2pm, Sat. noon-1pm, closed during winter; free

SCHENLEY PARK AND FLAGSTAFF HILL

A virtual oasis in the center of the city, the 456-acre Schenley Park sits on hundreds of acres of prime urban real estate in between Oakland's university district and Squirrel Hill. The park, which was donated to the city by Mary Schenley in 1889, features wooded trails that are particularly popular with after-work and weekend joggers. The park also boasts a soccer field, an ice skating rink, 13 tennis courts, a public swimming pool, and its very own lake. You'll also find **Phipps Conservatory and Botanical Gardens** and, across the street, another perennial favorite, **Flagstaff Hill.**

From the beginning of June through the end of August each year, free movies are shown on Flagstaff Hill, projected onto a jumbo outdoor screen. Show up on Wednesdays at sundown (usually around 9pm) with a blanket and picnic foods. No alcohol is allowed. On Sundays at sundown, family-friendly films are screened.

If your plans include exploring the park in depth, stop first at the informative Schenley Park Visitors Center, where a guide can suggest walking routes or jogging trails. Ask about free historical walks of Schenley Park, which are led on the first and third Sunday of every month at 1pm. The visitors center will also have scheduling information about the free kids' programs—storytelling, puppet shows—and the free National Geographic Film Festival, both of which take place throughout the summer.

Right next door is the **Schenley Park Cafe** (101 Panther Hollow Rd., 412/687-1800, www.pittsburghparks.org/schenleyparkcafe, Tues.-Sun. 10am-4pm with extended spring and summer hours), which offers free wireless Internet access and live folk and blues music on Sundays (July 2-Oct. 15 only, 12:30pm-3:30pm). The café offers trail maps of the park as well as coffee, light lunches, desserts, and a gift shop.

MAP 2: Schenley Park Café and Visitors Center, Panther Hollow Rd., 412/687-1800, www.pittsburghparks.org/schenley; daily 10am-4pm; free

SCHENLEY PLAZA

Modeled after Manhattan's Bryant Park and quickly on its way to becoming the Oakland area's most popular outdoor socializing spot, Schenley Plaza—which sits directly in between the main branch of the Carnegie Library and Pitt's Hillman Library—was a medium-sized parking lot less than a decade ago. Now a lush and inviting town square of sorts with a one-acre lawn, the plaza acts as a gateway to Schenley Park itself. Coincidentally, that was exactly the land's intended use when Mary Schenley donated the acreage to the city in 1890.

The plaza today is filled with movable chairs and café tables designed for socializing, high-quality food kiosks, free wireless Internet access, a large tented area to provide protection from the elements, 24-hour security, and an entertainment schedule that includes author appearances and live music year-round. Especially popular is **The Porch at Schenley** (221 Schenley Dr., 412/687-6724, www.theporchatschenley.com, Mon.-Fri. 11am-11pm, Sat. 10am-11pm, Sun. 10am-9pm), a full-service restaurant with a lovely outdoor patio that affords diners a wonderful view of the plaza.

One of the plaza's most exciting amenities is its Victorian-style **PNC Carousel** (Apr.-Oct. Mon.-Sun. noon-6pm, tickets $1.25). Featuring a colorful herd of animals that round the carousel to the accompaniment of old-fashioned pipe organ music, the ride is open to all ages and is wheelchair accessible.

MAP 2: 4100 Forbes Ave., www.pittsburghparks.org/schenleyplaza; free

SOLDIERS AND SAILORS MEMORIAL

One of America's largest museums dedicated to honoring and remembering its veterans, Soldiers and Sailors Memorial started out in the early 1900s with a much more local focus: It was originally intended only to recognize the sacrifice and patriotism of the Civil War veterans of Allegheny County. Today, however, the memorial represents all wars and all branches of service.

The building's massive Greco-Roman grand edifice—look for it on the corner of 5th and Bigelow across from Pitt's student union—was designed to resemble the mausoleum of Halicarnassus, one of the Seven Wonders of the Ancient World. The memorial's museum, however, will be of most interest to guests. Curios, uniforms, bric-a-brac, and other assorted gewgaws related to American-led battles—starting with the Civil War era and stretching all the way to Operation Iraqi Freedom—are displayed in glass cases. A special exhibition is dedicated to area women who've served in American wars.

MAP 2: 4141 5th Ave., 412/621-4253, www.soldiersandsailorshall.org; Mon.-Sat. 10am-4pm; $8 adult, $5 child and senior, free to veterans and current military

ST. PAUL CATHEDRAL

Known as the Mother Church of the Diocese of Pittsburgh, the Gothic-style St. Paul Cathedral in Oakland celebrated its 100th birthday in 2006. The 1,800-capacity church, with a 75-foot ceiling designed to resemble the hull of a ship, is undoubtedly one of Pittsburgh's most breathtaking. But the cathedral's true treasure is its massive organ, manufactured by the Rudolf von Beckerath Co. of Germany and generally considered to be one of the finest pipe organs in the world.

The building itself stands 247 feet tall, and a statue of St. Paul is mounted on the center pediment. Other statues depicting apostles and evangelists can be seen throughout the cathedral. Also impressive are the church's stained-glass windows, some of which represent Bible stories and the church's history in pictures. Take note of the large windows above the side doors, which document the life—and eventual martyrdom—of St. Paul himself.

To schedule a free tour of the cathedral, call the parish office at 412/621-4951 between 8am and 4pm (tour guides will only be granted to groups of five or more).

MAP 2: 108 N. Dithridge St., 412/621-4951, www.stpaulpgh.org; Masses Sun. 6:30am, 8am, 10am, noon, and 6pm as well as Mon.-Sat. 6:45am, 8:15am, and 12:05pm; call for tours; free

South Side

Map 3

GATEWAY CLIPPER FLEET

Located next to Station Square's Sheraton Hotel is a sloping dock that leads to the Gateway Clipper Fleet, a riverboat operation that since 1958 has been providing cruise tours both luxuriously elaborate and relatively simple along the city's three rivers.

As the most popular attraction in Pittsburgh, the Gateway Clipper Fleet claims to be the largest inland riverboat fleet in the country today. Yet the company began with just one solitary boat—a vessel purchased in Erie for $50. By 1959, the river tours on the 100-passenger capacity *Gateway Clipper* had proved so popular that two more 100-passenger vessels, the *Good Ship Lollipop* and the *Gateway Clipper II*, were added.

The fleet now contains six boats, all of them authentic reproductions of old working riverboats. Cruises happen throughout the year and in all sorts of weather. Passengers can experience a cruise tailored specifically for children, a formal evening cruise with dinner included, or dozens of other voyages. Visit the fleet online for more detailed information or to learn about chartering an entire ship. The sales office is open daily 9am-5pm.

MAP 3: Near Station Square, 412/355-7980, www.gatewayclipper.com; $20-65 adult, $10-28 child

SOUTH SIDE SLOPES

Just minutes away from the bustle and energy of East Carson Street, the South Side Slopes subneighborhood is Pittsburgh to the core. A winding maze of narrow traffic lanes and hillside steps weaves throughout this mostly blue-collar neighborhood, which was originally built for the immigrant workers who labored at the steel mills along the Monongahela River below.

The main attraction on the Slopes is the view itself; many roads rival even the view of Downtown seen from Mount Washington's Grandview Avenue, and beautiful views of Oakland and the South Side can also be had. To experience the various views for yourself, simply wander up 18th Street and poke around. The dozens of differing views will become clearly apparent as you stroll higher into the Upper Slopes, where you'll also see mixed-use development and upscale condos being built alongside the decrepit and decades-old row houses. Built mostly in the mid-1800s, the majority of houses in this particularly cramped region of Pittsburgh are only one room wide, two rooms deep, and up to three or four stories high. Should you find yourself truly turned around while exploring, simply head down any hill; nearly all roads lead back to East Carson Street. And as you climb up 18th Street, take note of the mural on the road's righthand-side retaining wall by local artist Rick Bach, who is also responsible for many of the metal sculptures and interiors found in the city's Mad Mex restaurants, as well as illustration work inside many of the older bars and restaurants of the South Side Flats.

St. Paul's Retreat Center (148 Monastery Ave., 412/381-7676, www.stpaulsretreatcenter-pittsburgh.org) is one of the more curious points of interest on the Slopes. The church was founded in the mid-1800s by four members of the Passionist Congregation who traveled to Pittsburgh from Italy. Today it acts as a spiritual facility open to anyone interested in deeply studying the Christian relationship with God. Call for scheduling information, as men's and women's retreats take place on differing weekends throughout the year.

St. Michael's Roman Catholic Church and Rectory (also known as St. Michael the Archangel Church, 21 Pius St., 412/431-5550, www.angelsarms.net), also located in the Slopes, is currently known as Angel's Arms Condominiums; it houses loft-style condos.

Another particularly popular event is the annual **Pittsburgh Step Trek,** a leisurely but organized walk through some of the most picturesque reaches of the South Side Slopes. The trek takes place every autumn; you can register online at www.southsideslopes.org. To take a self-guided tour, purchase a copy of Bob Regan's

The Steps of Pittsburgh (The Local History Co.), available from most local booksellers.

MAP 3: South of South Side Flats, www.southsideslopes.org

STATION SQUARE

Previously a cluster of railroad yards utilized by the Pittsburgh & Lake Erie Railroad Company, the 52-acre indoor shopping center and open-air entertainment complex known collectively as Station Square was converted into a center of commerce thanks to the midcentury decline in railway usage. The **Pittsburgh History and Landmarks Foundation** (100 W. Station Square Dr., Ste. 450, 412/471-5808, Mon.-Fri. 9am-5pm, www.phlf.org) spearheaded the renewal, which is likely the sole reason so many historical artifacts remain on-site. Of particular interest to those fascinated by Pittsburgh's industrial past is the massive, steel-purifying **Bessemer converter;** only two such converters exist in the United States. Look for Bessemer Court behind the Hard Rock Cafe. A fascinating selection of archival photographs can be viewed in the lobbies of the **Grand Concourse** restaurant and its adjacent **Gandy Dancer Saloon** (412/261-1717, www.muer.com/grand-concourse/index.asp). The main entrance of the restaurant is located on what was once the lower level of the P&LE Railroad Station, while the Gandy Dancer itself was formerly the P&LE's waiting room.

The complex's **Guest Services booth** is inside the Freight House Shops building and next to the **Station Square Express** (Fri.-Sat. noon-9pm, Sun. noon-5pm, ticket $1), a small train ride for kids. A wealth of brochures containing information about the Greater Pittsburgh area can be picked up for free at the booth.

Although still a relatively popular shopping and entertainment complex, Station Square has certainly seen happier days. Retail establishments and eateries in the main terminus have lately been closing with a depressing frequency, although across the Smithfield Street Bridge in the square's nightlife sphere, new businesses appear to open just as quickly as old ones fade away.

At **Bessemer Court,** you'll find the usual assortment of suburban chain restaurants (Houlihan's, Joe's Crab Shack). Those looking for an affordable and somewhat goofy way to explore Pittsburgh's waterways should stop by the **Just Ducky Tours booth** (125 W. Station Square Dr., 412/402-3825, Apr. 10-Oct., weekends only in Nov., $22 general, $15 child, www.justduckytours.com), also in Bessemer Court. The company's vintage World War II amphibious vehicles circle through the historical sights of Downtown before plunging into the water. Also headquartered at Station Square is the **Segway in Paradise** tour company (125 W. Station Square Dr., 412/337-3941, www.segwayinparadise.com, $59-97), which offers visitors

clockwise from top left: the Duquesne Incline; Gateway Clipper Fleet; Station Square

two- and four-hour tours of the city aboard their own Segway Personal Transporter.

MAP 3: Carson St. at the Smithfield Street Bridge, www.stationsquare.com

Mount Washington **Map 3**

★ THE DUQUESNE AND MONONGAHELA INCLINES

Definitely skip the taxi if you're planning an outing to Mount Washington; the most interesting way to arrive is certainly via one of the city's two remaining inclines—the hillside cable cars you may have seen inching up and down the mountain.

The **Monongahela Incline** is the easier of the two to reach on foot. The incline will scurry you up the hill and deposit you atop Grandview Avenue. Just a block away is Shiloh Street, home to a charming assortment of informal restaurants and cafés. From the corner of Grandview Avenue and Shiloh Street, make your way along the pedestrian path and look for the entrance to the **Duquesne Incline,** which would have been demolished in the mid-1960s if not for the efforts of the nonprofit Society for the Preservation of the Duquesne Incline; the society's volunteers have been operating the station since 1963.

Even if you don't plan to ride the Duquesne back down to Carson Street, don't miss the station itself, which is filled with historical newspaper accounts of Pittsburgh's incline system and archival photos and postcards of funiculars around the world. The view from the station's observation deck is absolutely jaw-dropping, and also worth a look is the Gear Room, where $0.50 gets you up close and personal with the machinery that makes the incline go round.

The inclines are certainly one of the city's most popular attractions for tourists, and for good reason. The two-minute, six-mile-per-hour ride, while a touch frightening for first-timers, is also exhilarating. As the cars slowly rise from their lower stations, Downtown Pittsburgh and the suburbs to the east and west appear. The Duquesne travels 400 feet up the hillside to reach an elevation of 800 feet, while the Monongahela travels 635 feet to reach a much lower 369-foot elevation. And given their ages (the Monongahela Incline has existed since 1870, although it was renovated in 1983 and 1994, while the Duquesne Incline was built in 1877), it's surprising to note just how smooth the experience is. Small children, however, often grow increasingly worried as the cars end their descent and gain traction toward the station houses; you might mention to any youngsters in your group that the car slows to a near dead stop about 10 feet from the bottom. It then easily inches its way home.

Keep in mind too that while the city refers to the inclines as "working museums," which is certainly an accurate descriptor, their primary function is that of public transport. You will almost always see more locals than tourists inside the cars, many of whom are Mount Washington residents who ride the inclines up and down the hillside each day (as this author did while briefly living on Mount Washington's Wyoming Street).

Bicycles may be taken on the Duquesne Incline only, although a double fare is required.

MAP 3: Duquesne Incline, 1197 W. Carson St. and 1220 Grandview Ave., 412/381-1665, www.duquesneincline.org, Mon.-Sat. 5:30am-12:45am, Sun. and holidays 7am-12:45am; Monongahela Incline, Carson St. at Smithfield Street Bridge, 412/442-2000, www.portauthority.org, Mon.-Sat. 5:30am-12:45am, Sun. and holidays 8:45am-midnight; $2.50 one way, $5 round-trip

Squirrel Hill and Point Breeze

Map 5

FRICK ART AND HISTORICAL CENTER

A complex of historical museums and buildings located on the eastern stretch of **Frick Park,** the Frick Art and Historical Center is bookended by its two most important structures. The **Frick Art Museum** displays a portion of the artworks collected by legendary Pittsburgh industrialist Henry Clay Frick, including paintings by Peter Paul Rubens (the majority of Frick's art investments can be found at the Frick Collection Museum in New York City). On the opposite end of the center is **Clayton;** it underwent a $6 million renovation in 1990 and can be explored on a guided tour.

Writing in *Architectural Digest,* the journalist Susan Mary enthused that Clayton is a triumph of restoration. Indeed, when the Fricks left for New York City in 1905, they had spent 22 years in Pittsburgh, and Clayton, of course, was a well-lived-in house. Much to the delight of modern-day visitors and historians, the Fricks failed to bring the majority of their belongings with them to New York; 93 percent of the house's artifacts are originals. Visitors can view children's toys in the nursery, bedroom furniture, and even the study.

Clayton was purchased for $25,000 in 1882, but at the time it boasted "only" 11 rooms. Less than a decade later, the architect Frederick J. Osterling was hired to spice up the building; he masterfully transformed it into the same 23-room mansion seen today.

Also on the grounds is the popular **Car and Carriage Museum,** where visitors can ogle 20 vintage automobiles, including Frick's

Pittsburgh's Disappearing Inclines

The Duquesne Incline makes its way down Mount Washington.

It was the late 1800s, and as the population of Pittsburgh's mill workers and coal miners quickly began to grow in number, the city also began to recognize a troubling site-specific problem. Because the land along the Monongahela River consisted mostly of mills and factories, the European migrants who worked there found it necessary to make their homes on the hills above. The precipitously steep hilltop neighborhoods—especially those above the South Side—were virtually inaccessible by either foot or horse. So in 1870, the two-car Monongahela Incline was constructed.

It rose from the base of the Smithfield Street Bridge and traveled up Mount Washington to what is now Grandview Avenue, operated by a relatively simple cable-pulley system: When one car traveled down, gravity pulled the other car up.

Eventually, more than 17 inclined planes—out-of-towners might refer to them as funiculars—were serving the city of Pittsburgh. But not only foot passengers utilized the hillside cable cars—light freight, horses, and wagons were also shuttled to and fro. Passenger fares ranged from one to five cents among the different inclines; heavy loads required extra payment.

The civil engineer responsible for the design and construction of the majority of the inclines in Pittsburgh was a Hungarian immigrant by the name of Samuel Diescher. After first settling in Cincinnati in 1866, where he built his first incline, Diescher eventually moved to Pittsburgh. He continued to build inclines elsewhere, however, including one in Johnstown, Pennsylvania, one in Wheeling, West Virginia, and two in South America.

Very few inclines exist today in the United States, although two shining examples remain in Pittsburgh: the Monongahela Incline and the Duquesne Incline. The Duquesne offers the superior view, although the Monongahela is much easier to access on foot; you'll find its entrance just across the street from Station Square on the South Side. Both inclines climb Mount Washington and dispatch passengers atop Grandview Avenue. One-way tickets are $2.50, and round-trips are $5.

1914 Rolls Royce Silver Ghost and Howard Heinz's 1898 Panhard, which some say was Pittsburgh's first car.

The Café at the Frick (412/371-0600, Tues.-Sun. 11am-5pm), on-site, is known as one of the city's top restaurants; it offers a daily tea service after 2:30pm.

MAP 5: 7227 Reynolds St., 412/371-0600, www.thefrickpittsburgh.org; Tues.-Sun. 10am-5pm; center, museums, and greenhouse free; Clayton guided tours $12 adult, $10 student and senior, $6 child; reservations recommended

FRICK PARK

Popular with bird-watchers and urban dog walkers alike, the 600-acre Frick Park is not only the city's largest park but also its most varied. Stretching in between the neighborhoods of Squirrel Hill and Point Breeze, the park is filled with playgrounds, various recreational facilities, dog runs, winding footpaths, red clay tennis counts, and even a bowling green.

Lesser known are the park's nearly two dozen phenomenal mountain-biking paths. With names like the Rollercoaster and the Worm Trail, it probably goes without saying that many of these routes are significantly challenging; even experienced cyclists are urged to stay away on rainy or poor-weather days.

MAP 5: Corner of Forbes Ave. and S. Braddock Ave., www.pittsburghparks.org/frick; daily 6am-11pm; free

JEWISH COMMUNITY CENTER AND THE AMERICAN JEWISH MUSEUM

Something of an all-inclusive recreational clubhouse where both Jews and non-Jews congregate, the Jewish Community Center features a state-of-the-art fitness center, a regular schedule of art classes, seminars, educational lectures, and theater performances, as well as the wonderfully contemporary American Jewish Museum, which is the only museum in the western half of the state dedicated to preserving the art, history, and culture of the Jewish diaspora.

The JCC, as it's often referred to locally, opened its doors way back in 1895 and was originally known as the Irene Kaufmann Settlement. The Kaufmann family and the National Council of Jewish Women were both responsible for the center, which was built in response to the rapidly growing number of Jewish immigrants settling in Pittsburgh. Today, people of all backgrounds are improving their bodies and their minds at the JCC. In fact, the center has proven so popular that a second facility now operates inside the **Henry Kaufmann Building** (345 Kane Blvd., Scott Township, 412/278-1975) in the South Hills.

MAP 5: 5738 Forbes Ave., 412/521-8010, www.jccpgh.org; Mon.-Thurs. 5:30Am-10Pm, Fri. 5:30Am-6Pm, Sat. 8Am-6Pm, Sun. 7:45Am-6Pm; Free

Moving the Lives of Kids Murals

Founded and largely organized by local artist Kyle Holbrook, the owner of Homewood's KH Design, the **MLK Community Mural Project** was quite likely the single largest demonstration of public art-making the city had ever seen when it first launched in the summer of 2007. Guided by professional Pittsburgh-area artists, more than 100 at-risk urban youths created a series of truly eye-catching murals throughout the city's East End, including locations in Wilkinsburg, Swissvale, East Liberty, and Edgewood. The project was expanded considerably during the following summer, and murals featuring everything from abstract art to historical figures to photorealistic depictions of actual neighborhood faces can be now be seen as far afield as Carnegie, McKeesport, Mt. Oliver, and Blawnox. The vast majority of the murals, however, can be found within the city limits.

Visit the MLK website (www.mlkmural.com) to view a complete map of mural sites and to learn about the occasional bus tours that visit the project's most important and impressive works of community art. Don't miss the 100-foot-long mural stretching along a portion of the Martin Luther King Jr. East Busway in East Liberty; it's at the corner of Ellsworth Avenue and Shady Avenue.

Bloomfield and Lawrenceville

Map 6

ALLEGHENY CEMETERY

More than 120,000 dead are currently at rest in the gorgeously landscaped Allegheny Cemetery, which covers some 300 acres smack-dab in the middle of Bloomfield and Lawrenceville. Composer Stephen Foster ("Oh! Susanna," "My Old Kentucky Home") is undoubtedly the cemetery's most recognizable name; a collection of difficult-to-follow signs point the way to his grave, which can be found in Section 21, Lot 30. (Stephen Foster's boyhood home is just a five-minute drive away at 3600 Penn Avenue, also in Lawrenceville, although it unfortunately is not open to the public. A historical marker can be seen on the house's front lawn.) Other Allegheny Cemetery notables include Don Brockett (Chef Brockett of *Mister Rogers' Neighborhood*), Thomas Mellon, and General Alexander Hays.

Chartered as a nonprofit organization in April 1844, Allegheny Cemetery is the country's sixth-oldest rural cemetery. And probably because it was modeled on the landscapes of fashionable English parks, the experience of strolling the grounds is rather pleasant and, during the sunlight hours, not the least bit creepy. Nonetheless, it's all too easy to get lost in the cemetery; even locals who jog or walk here sometimes find themselves turned around. The roads are winding and the grounds are quite hilly, so even though posted signs point the way to various plots and sections, things can get confusing. But not to worry: Both the Bloomfield and Lawrenceville ends of the cemetery have separate entry points, and groundskeepers patrol regularly in private cars.

MAP 6: 4734 Butler St., 412/682-1624, www.alleghenycemetery.com; Sept.-Apr. daily 7am-5pm, May daily 7am-8pm, June-Aug. daily 7am-7pm; free

ARSENAL PARK

Today it's a pleasant and sprawling green space filled with playgrounds, sporting facilities, and, of course, many of the young families who've been drawn to Lawrenceville because of its generally affordable real estate and convenient East End location. But Arsenal Park from 1814 until 1913 was known as the Allegheny Arsenal. Designed by Benjamin H. Latrobe, the arsenal functioned as a military barracks during the Civil War, the War of 1812, and the Mexican War. At one point during the Civil War, more than 1,100 civilian workers toiled here.

The arsenal was also a manufacturing site for weapons, and on September 17, 1862, somewhere between 70 and 100 men, women, and children perished when barrels of powder exploded. A bronze marker outside the park's restrooms now memorializes the victims of the blast, and next to the fence separating the park and the middle school sits an authentic IX Shell Gun Cannon that was constructed in 1865; a marker atop the cannon notes that it fired a total of 1,681 rounds. The arsenal's powder magazine now functions as a maintenance shed.

Popular with picnickers, area teenagers, and recreational sports leagues, Arsenal Park also offers tennis and basketball courts, two baseball fields, and plenty of space for a casual jog or walk.

MAP 6: Between 39th St., 40th St., Butler St., and Penn Ave., www.arsenalpark.org; daily dawn-dusk; free

THE CLEMENTE MUSEUM

Although tours of this truly passionate and loving monument to professional baseball legend Roberto Clemente, also known as "The Great One," can only be scheduled by making an advance reservation, the experience is nevertheless very much worth the trouble—especially for anyone with a serious interest in Major League Baseball or, for the matter, the immigrant experience in America.

Clemente was a Puerto Rican athlete who spent all 18 of his pro baseball seasons, from 1955 until his untimely death in 1972, with the Pittsburgh Pirates. Not only is he still considered one of the finest to ever play the game, he was also one of its most honorable and altruistic—the exact opposite of many modern-day pros, you might say—and he was well known for devoting much of his time off the field to serious humanitarian work.

At the two-story Clemente Museum, which is owned by professional advertising photographer Duane Rieder and located inside the historical Engine House 25, visitors will find literally thousands of pieces of Clemente memorabilia, including photographs and family snapshots, all manner of Clemente's former sporting gear, letters, telegraphs, and other personal curios, a large collection of bats, and even a set of actual seats from Oakland's Forbes Field.

MAP 6: 3339 Penn Ave., 412/621-1268, www.clementemuseum.com; tours given by appointment only, office open Mon.-Fri. 10am-5pm; $20 adult, $10 child

DOUGHBOY SQUARE

Doughboy Square, an arresting war monument celebrating area soldiers who gave their lives in World War I, is actually a triangle. At its base stands a statue of—what else?—a Doughboy. Most war historians agree that the nickname for World War I soldiers was derived from the white adobe soil that often coated them during training at a camp in Texas.

There's also a plaque at the statue's base listing the names of hundreds who perished not only in World War I, but also in World War II, the Korean War, and the Vietnam War. And just behind the statue sits the historical **Pennsylvania National Bank** building, a beautiful beaux arts structure that was built in 1902 and restored in the early 1990s.

A mixed-use development is being planned for the 3400 block of Butler Street, which sits adjacent to Doughboy Square. It will feature the **Doughboy Square Apartments** (www.doughboysquareapartments.com), home to 39 residential units and about 17,000 square feet of retail space on the street level.

MAP 6: East of 34th St., where Butler St. forks off from Penn Ave.

East Liberty and Garfield Map 6

THE CENTER FOR POSTNATURAL HISTORY

You say you want weird? Well, we've got your weird right here, smack dab in the heart of Garfield's Penn Avenue Arts Corridor, which is where you'll find the Center for PostNatural History—a truly odd and unexpected museum of bioengineered organisms. This is a collection, in other words, of plants, animals, insects, and other organisms that have been genetically modified or selectively bred. Yikes.

Founded in 2012 by artist Richard Pell, the center is "dedicated to the advancement of knowledge relating to the complex interplay between culture, nature, and biotechnology," according to its website. Through dioramas, photographs, taxidermy, and even living creatures, you'll encounter the "postnatural" world in exhibits on atomic age rodents and transgenic mosquitoes, for instance. You'll learn about the sort of engineered "frankenfood" produced by multinational chemical concerns. You'll visit Sea Monkeys and GloFish, and you'll be introduced to BioSteel goats. And hopefully, you'll be fascinated, disgusted, and terrified, all at once.

MAP 6: 4913 Penn Ave., Garfield, 412/223-7698, www.postnatural.org; Sun. noon-4pm, first Fri. of each month 5pm-8pm; free, but donations are accepted

PITTSBURGH ZOO AND PPG AQUARIUM

Much more than just a randomly selected menagerie, the 77-acre Pittsburgh Zoo and PPG Aquarium has been renovating and upgrading its facilities since 1980, when the once-staid exhibits first began their transformation into natural habitats. As a result, you won't see an abundance of depressing cages. Instead, winding pedestrian paths take visitors past the African Savanna and the Asian Forest, and even into a five-acre indoor rainforest housing 150 different plant species and more than 90 primates, including orangutans, cotton-top tamarins, and western lowland gorillas. Other naturalistic habitats include Cheetah Valley and a bear habitat, where Kodiak bears and black bears can be seen rummaging through rocky hills.

In fact, there are now literally thousands of animals representing hundreds of species. Don't miss the rare komodo dragon and the gila monster, found in the Reptile House. And if children are a part of your group, visit Kids Kingdom, an interactive facility with playground equipment that replicates animal motions, thereby teaching children to play just as a mole rat or a penguin might play.

Take care not to miss the PPG Aquarium, where polar bears, sea otters, and walruses frolic underwater. Keep in mind that balloons, pets, and tobacco products of any sort are banned from zoo premises.

MAP 6: 1 Wild Pl., Highland Park, 412/365-3640, www.pittsburghzoo.com; summer daily 9:30am-6pm, fall and spring daily 9am-5pm, winter daily 9am-4pm; $14 adult, $12 child 2-13, $13 senior

Greater Pittsburgh **Map 7**

ALLEGHENY OBSERVATORY

Although it was founded in 1859 for the purpose of educating the citizens of the City of Allegheny (which later became incorporated into the City of Pittsburgh), the Allegheny Observatory eventually

clockwise from top left: Frick Art and Historical Center; the Pittsburgh Zoo; cannon at Arsenal Park

Welcome to Braddock: the Urban Frontier

The small town of Braddock, Pennsylvania, sits about 10 miles southeast of Downtown Pittsburgh, and viewing it on a map likely won't prompt you to pay the borough a visit. In fact, assuming you pay attention to Pittsburgh-area news, you might assume it's a place to avoid: High-profile murders happen there occasionally, while Braddock politicians make headlines due to all-too-common corruption charges and illogical governing decisions. Perhaps the biggest recent news story to come out of Braddock was the 2010 closing of UPMC Braddock Hospital, which was located in the heart of town and which provided the place with much of its economic sustenance.

In total, since Pittsburgh's steel boom fully took hold in the early- to mid-20th century, Braddock has lost roughly 95 percent of its population. Approximately 2,000 people live there today, and both crime and decline have been at the center of Braddock's story for decades. However, for the first time since steel manufacturers lined the shores of Pittsburgh's three rivers, that story is beginning to change.

A new crop of do-it-yourselfers have turned Braddock's withered state into a type of industrial urban garden—a place where, as the borough's website (www.15104.cc) proudly proclaims, "reinvention is the only option." It's also a place where housing is so incredibly cheap that just about anyone can afford to live there, free to sow whatever seeds they so desire.

At the core of Braddock's DIY revolution is John Fetterman, a 6-foot 8-inch giant weighing in at nearly 400 pounds. Back in 2005, Fetterman utilized his master's degree from Harvard's Kennedy School of Government, along with his history of working in the region as a community organizer, to make a run as Braddock's mayor. He defeated the incumbent by one vote. Literally.

Since then, he's used his family's independent wealth, the connections he's made with congressional politicians, and his unprecedented knack for grabbing people's attention to promote both Braddock's weaknesses and its potential for post-industrial urban opportunity nationwide. To remind himself of what and who he governs, he has Braddock's zip code, 15104, tattooed on his left arm. The dates of all the murders that have occurred in Braddock on his watch are tattooed on his right arm.

As of this writing, Fetterman's goateed mug has been featured in the pages of *The Atlantic* and *Rolling Stone* magazines, and he's spoken at length on TV programs, including C-SPAN and *The Colbert Report*. Levi's clothing company recently donated more than $1 million to a number of Braddock-based charitable initiatives and has also partnered with the Independent Film Channel to produce a series of mini-documentary films about the "urban pioneers" who have come from far and wide to make Braddock their home and, in some cases, their place of business.

Much of Braddock is still in tatters, of course. Many houses and some entire residential blocks are completely vacant. Buildings crumble into unoccupied space and squatters use the remaining structures as garbage receptacles. Astute observers have said certain quadrants of Braddock look like something out of David Fincher's *Fight Club*.

But that's understandable. After all, a sizable corporate donation and a heap of media exposure can't undo years of neglect overnight. And yet concerned citizens have taken the initiative to establish such growing enterprises as **Braddock Farms** (www.growpittsburgh.org), for instance, which consists of 10 acres of organic vegetable gardens grown in vacant urban lots. Area kids tend to the Braddock Farms plots, harvesting and supplying herbs and vegetables to regional eateries.

Another such altruistic project in Braddock is **UnSmoke Systems** (www.unsmokeartspace.com), a creative space within a reclaimed Catholic school. Unsmoke Systems offers art for sale in the building's repurposed auditorium, and expansive studio space is available for a share of the building's utility bills.

A Braddock organization known as **Fossil Free Fuels** (www.fossil-freefuel.com) sells biodiesel gas that its employees have made out of fast food fryer oil. What's more, a growing number of artisans and craftsmen are now hawking their merchandise from once-forgotten Braddock storefronts. **New Guild Studio** (www.newguild-studio.com) offers "re-imagined liturgical art," according to its website, that blends "a respect for tradition with a healthy dose of modern techniques and materials." **Roadbourne Furniture,** meanwhile, makes and sells custom furniture using reclaimed materials. For more information about this unique small town and the many unusual opportunities available there, visit www.braddockredux.org.

In all, Braddock certainly isn't your typical tourist destination. But it's worth the visit if you're up for a history lesson that doesn't involve going to a museum, or a night out that doesn't involve bar-hopping.

There are in fact bars on the borough's main drag, but you might find yourself in an awkward scenario if you order any kind of beverage that requires fruity flavoring.

Your best bet—should you find yourself at the **Elks Lodge** (424 Library St., 412/271-1335) or just down the street at **Lucky Frank's Irish Pub** (312 Braddock Ave., 412/351-3878)—would be to order an Iron City beer and work your way into a conversation. The result might be a kind of tourism you've never quite experienced before.

And who knows? You may even run into a very large man with numbers tattooed on his forearms.

(Contributed by Matt Stroud, a Pittsburgh-based freelance journalist.)

Mayor John Fetterman

ran out of funds and was donated to the University of Pittsburgh, which today uses it as a research lab for its Department of Physics and Astronomy.

It's four miles north of Downtown in the 251-acre **Riverview Park** (www.pittsburghparks.org/riverview), and free public tours of the observatory are offered from April through October. Advance reservations are required. The highlight of the tour is a stop at the 13-inch Fitz-Clark refractor, through which visitors may view any number of celestial wonders, assuming the night sky is clear. Before gazing through the refractor, a short film is screened, and visitors are then taken on a walking tour of the building. Because of the private research going on at the observatory, visitors can only tour the facilities during the designated tour schedule. Once a year, however, an open house is held during which visitors are allowed to tour the observatory by following a designated path throughout the building; tour guides are not present. The event, which is also free and requires advance reservations, generally takes place toward the end of September.

The observatory also maintains a regular schedule of free astronomy lectures delivered by area scholars; regularly updated information is available at the observatory's website.

MAP 7: 159 Riverview Ave., Riverview Park, 412/321-2400, www.pitt.edu/~aobsvtry; tours Apr. 1-late Aug. Thurs. 8pm-10pm, Apr. 1-Nov. 1 Fri. 8pm-10pm; free

BAYERNHOF MUSIC MUSEUM

A gorgeous stone house overlooking the Highland Park lock and dam on the Allegheny River, Bayernhof was built by the late Charles B. Brown III, the founder and former CEO of Gas-Lite Manufacturing. Toward the end of Brown's life, he discovered the rather unique hobby of collecting rare automatic music machines. Before long, Brown got a bit carried away with his new obsession, and today, rare and antique machines can be found in every single one of Bayernhof's rooms. Thankfully, Brown had the foresight to add an amendment to his living will stating that upon his death, the instruments should be properly restored and the house should be opened to the public as a museum. Brown passed away in 1999, and now all visitors to Pittsburgh can enjoy the Bayernhof Music Museum.

The machines include a massive Seeburg Pipe Organ orchestra, a Wurlitzer "Style A" Automatic Harp, an Encore Automatic Banjo, a Wurlitzer 125 Military Band Organ, and a combination phonograph and music box known as a Reginaphone Music Box. It's also worth mentioning that completely aside from the music machines, Bayernhof itself is a wonderfully unique house, if a bit on the unconventional side. A hidden passageway takes visitors to a cave, for instance, that winds past small waterfalls and pools. And the entire south side of the house is glass-lined, affording beautiful views of Highland Park, Oakland, and Downtown.

MAP 7: 225 St. Charles Pl., O'Hara Township, 412/782-4231, www.bayernhofmuseum.com; two-hour tours given by appointment only at 10:30am or 2:30pm; $10

BEECHWOOD FARMS NATURE RESERVE

Considering it's the headquarters of the Audubon Society of Western Pennsylvania, it probably goes without saying that the Beechwood Farms Nature Reserve, which consists of five miles of walking trails and 134 acres of wilderness sanctuary, is a rather lovely and peaceful place. The trails are open to the public from dawn until dusk every day of the year.

The reserve is also home to the 125-seat **Evans Nature Center auditorium,** an **Audubon Nature Store,** a **bird feeder observation room,** and a **Natural History and Teacher Resource Library.**

Wildlife exists in abundance on the reserve; be prepared to spot deer, screech owls, and even red foxes. An artificially constructed pond built in 1981 is home to mallards and Canada geese. Visitors should also stop by the **Audubon Center for Native Plants,** a greenhouse and nursery complex whose mission is to educate gardeners and landscapers about the importance of working with native plants.

MAP 7: 614 Dorseyville Rd., Fox Chapel, 412/963-6100, www.aswp.org/locations/beechwood; Tues.-Sat. 9am-5pm, Sun. 1pm-5pm (Evans Nature Center); free

★ KENNYWOOD AMUSEMENT PARK

Since its founding in 1898, the long-surviving and much-loved Kennywood Amusement Park has become practically synonymous with the city of Pittsburgh itself. Over the past century, the park has survived fierce corporate battles, major changes in the industry, and even the Great Depression. But good old-fashioned fun trumps all, it seems, and today the park is still a hugely popular Pittsburgh-area attraction. New rides continue to be added each summer season, and in 1987, Kennywood was awarded National Historic Landmark status.

History aside, however, Kennywood is a can't-miss choice for Pittsburgh visitors both young and old. Roller coasters continue to be a favorite, especially the historical Thunderbolt and Jack Rabbit rides, as well as the terrifyingly fast Phantom's Revenge, which reaches speeds of 85 mph. The park also has its share of water rides and thrill rides, such as the catapulting SwingShot and the PittFall, a ride that simply drops its riders from a height of 251 feet to the ground below. But the fact that a decent number of classic rides are still in operation—like the paddleboats, the bumper cars, and the merry-go-round—probably lends the park its most authentic sense of classic greatness.

Live entertainment occasionally takes place at Kennywood, and operating hours and admission prices change according to season. Call or visit the park's website for the most up-to-date information. **MAP 7:** 4800 Kennywood Blvd., West Mifflin, 412/461-0500, www.kennywood.com; Memorial Day-Labor Day daily 10:30am-11pm; $39.99 adult, $26.99 child under 46 inches, $19.95 senior, Night Rider admission after 5pm $24.99

MONROEVILLE MALL

Cinephiles and horror fans in particular have for years been journeying to Pittsburgh with the intention of visiting just one solitary attraction: the Monroeville Mall. Built in 1969, the mall today consists of four anchor stores, more than 120 shops and restaurants, and 6,800 parking spots spread out over 1,128,747 square feet. But to splatter-film obsessives, it's more popularly known as the filming location of the original *Dawn of the Dead,* George Romero's hugely popular follow-up to his 1968 classic, *Night of the Living Dead.*

Dawn of the Dead is generally agreed upon as Romero's best film, and certainly one of the best zombie movies ever produced. Filming began in late 1977 and ended in February 1978. Romero's inspiration for the film happened during a visit to the mall in the early 1970s, when it was still one of the largest shopping centers of its type in the United States. He noticed the vacant faces and glazed-over eyes of the mall's shoppers, dutifully marching from store to store, and couldn't help comparing them to the living dead. A deal was struck with the mall's development company: Filming could take place between the hours of 10pm and 6am, when the mall was closed to the public.

Thousands of fans visit what is essentially a historical film set each year, and mall security has responded by tightening up considerably. Some visitors have even had their film or cameras confiscated after photographing memorable film locations, so consider yourself forewarned. Should you still care to brave the wilds of Monroeville Mall, however, do yourself a favor by first doing a quick Internet search; numerous fan sites list the exact locations of the film's most memorable scenes.

Horror fans might also consider making a pilgrimage to the borough of Evans City in Butler County; the opening graveyard scene in Romero's *Night of the Living Dead* was shot at the Evans City Cemetery. Much closer to the center of town is the East End neighborhood of Bloomfield, where legendary makeup artist and special effects man Tom Savini hangs his hat. Savini, who can often be seen around town, has worked on nearly every one of George Romero's films and today is a horror-film actor and director as well.

MAP 7: 200 Monroeville Mall Blvd. (Exit 57 on Business Rte. 22), Monroeville, 412/243-8511, www.monroevillemall.com; Mon.-Sat. 10am-9pm, Sun. noon-6pm

PENNSYLVANIA TROLLEY MUSEUM

Consisting of a historical trolley car house and a visitor education center, the Pennsylvania Trolley Museum is a documentation of the state's streetcars and of the era during which they were regularly traversing the Keystone State's urban areas.

The museum opened its doors in 1963, although the concept first dawned on the PTM founders in the early 1940s, when it seemed as if the cars—a truly quaint and important chapter of U.S. public transport history—were quickly disappearing from American cities. Today, a gift shop and a trolley car restoration site are a part of the facilities as well.

Admission includes a guided tour of the trolley car barn, which takes approximately 90 minutes to complete, as well as all the trolley rides you can handle along the museum's four-mile-long train track. Pictorial exhibits are always on display in the education center, and for an additional $2 charge ($1 children), visitors can tour the Trolley Display Building, a 28,000-square-foot site where 30 restored cars from the tri-state area are stored.

MAP 7: 1 Museum Rd., Washington, 724/228-9256, www.pa-trolley.org; summer Mon.-Fri. 10am-4pm, Sat.-Sun. 10am-5pm (call or visit website for off-season hours); $9 adult, $8 senior, $6 child 3-15

SEWICKLEY HEIGHTS HISTORY CENTER

Located on the former site of a working farm and surrounded by over 30 acres of gorgeous rolling pasturelands, the Sewickley Heights History Center is intended to be something of a reverential and historical monument to the upscale borough of Sewickley Heights. Ever since the Gilded Age of the early 1900s, in fact, when mill-owning industrialists relocated there from Pittsburgh in an effort to escape the city's omnipresent cloud of choking black smoke, Sewickley Heights has been well known as a haven for a small number of the city's wealthiest families.

The museum itself does a fine and respectable job of preserving the area's cultural and historical heritage, what with its decent collection of period photos, area artifacts, and antique carriages and automobiles. The museum also features a small theater where film footage of Sewickley's earliest days can be viewed. Educational lectures about what life was like in early-1900s Sewickley Heights are offered occasionally.

Perhaps the museum's most popular event is the annual Car, Carriage and Horse Show, a rather upscale nod to the many equestrian events that once took place here. It generally happens at the end of the summer, although a good number of other family-friendly and educational events are scheduled throughout the year; visit the museum's website for details.

MAP 7: 1901 Glen Mitchell Rd., Sewickley Heights, 412/741-4487, www.sewickleyheightshistory.org; Mon.-Fri. 3pm-5pm, Sat. noon-2pm; free

ST. ANTHONY'S CHAPEL

Although technically located in the northern neighborhood of Troy Hill, which isn't within walking distance of the North Side's more well-known attractions, the legendary St. Anthony's Chapel is nevertheless worth the trek. Tourists and other out-of-towners don't often come here to pray, but instead to examine the church's incredible collection of sacred Catholic relics. The collection is said to be the largest of its kind in the world outside of the collection found at the Vatican in Rome. St. Anthony's now owns approximately 4,200 pieces that are kept in 800 separate cases.

The chapel was founded in 1883 by a Belgian known as Father Mollinger; the current collection began when he rescued a number of reliquaries from Germany. Some he discovered in European pawnshops in the late 1800s, a time when many monasteries had splintered and the relics protected by those monasteries were stolen, lost, or otherwise misplaced.

The chapel itself is rather lovely, if not particularly large. Dark wood and stained-glass windows fill the interior, and the Stations of the Cross, beautifully carved out of wood, are remarkable.

As is the case with most collections of saints' relics, many of the pieces come complete with a touch of creepiness: You'll see saints' teeth, skulls, and bone fragments, for instance, although it's worth noting that gnarly body parts do not make up the bulk of the collection. There are also photographs, scraps of clothing, and other interesting bits.

Don't miss the small museum dedicated to Father Mollinger, which contains medicines and other items he used when curing the sick and dying. There's also a small gift shop.

MAP 7: 1700 Harpster St., Troy Hill, 412/323-9504, www.saintanthonyschapel.org; chapel open Sat.-Thurs. 1pm-4pm; tours conducted Sat. at 1pm, 2pm, and 3pm; audio tours available Sun.-Fri.; $3 donation

ST. NICHOLAS CROATIAN CATHOLIC CHURCH

A tiny parish whose now-shuttered sister church on the North Side was the first Catholic Croatian church in the United States, St. Nicholas Croatian Catholic Church has since been awarded status as both a National Landmark and a Pittsburgh Historical Landmark. Twenty murals by the Croatian artist Maxo Vanka are the church's claim to fame; many critics consider them to be his greatest masterpieces.

Painted in 1937 and 1941, and commissioned by the Reverend Albert Zagar, a fellow Croatian who at the time worked as the church's pastor, the murals depict mostly secular scenes of cultural and political significance: Croatian mothers grieving over their war-dead sons and images depicting the oppressed nations of Eastern Europe. According to Vanka, the majority of the images, of which only a few contain religious symbolism, were inspired by Hitler's Nazi occupation.

Oddly enough, St. Nicholas is equally famous for a rather unsettling reason: The church is widely believed to be haunted by the ghost of a former priest; church members and employees claim to have seen him tending the altar. When the North Side's St. Nicholas parish was closed and the congregation transferred to Millvale, many members refused to show up because of the rumored haunting. Even Vanka himself claimed to have spotted the priest while painting his famous murals.

MAP 7: 24 Maryland Ave., Millvale, 412/821-3438 or 724/845-2907, www.stnicholascroatian.com; call to arrange personal or group tours; free

TOUR-ED MINE AND MUSEUM

With a collection of more than 9,000 authentic mining artifacts dating as far back as the 1850s, the Tour-Ed Mine and Museum wonderfully documents the deep-mining and strip-mining histories of Southwestern Pennsylvania.

Schoolchildren especially enjoy the immersion experience of entering the Tour-Ed Mine, which was first mined for coal sometime around 1850 and eventually had its named changed to Avenue Mine. Since 1970, more than one million tours have been given at the site, each one led by experienced former miners. Tour groups will have a chance to examine mining tools and actual mining methods up close, and although the tour focuses partly on historical mining methods, modern advanced methods are also demonstrated and explained. Hydraulic machines are used to mine coal today, for instance, although in the mid-1800s it was largely dug by hand. Light jackets are recommended, as the mine's temperature remains steady at around 55°F year-round.

To ensure that every visitor has a chance to clearly view the demonstrations, tours never consist of more than 25 people. Visitors will also have a chance to view a working sawmill, as well as a reproduction of a 1900-era mine village, complete with a general store and a barbershop.

Just more than three miles away, you'll find the **Galleria at Pittsburgh Mills** (590 Pittsburgh Mills Circle, Tarentum, 724/904-9000, www.pittsburghmills.com, Mon.-Sat. 10am-9pm, Sun. 11am-6pm, www.pittsburghmills.com), an indoor and outdoor shopping center with a bowling alley, a movie theater, an IMAX 3-D theater, and numerous retailers.

MAP 7: 748 Bull Creek Rd., Tarentum, 724/244-4720, www.tour-edmine.com; Memorial Day-Labor Day daily 10am-4pm, last tour starts at 2:30pm; $10 adult, $9 child 12 and under

TRUNDLE MANOR

In a city like San Francisco or Portland, Oregon, Trundle Manor would almost certainly be a notoriously popular hot spot—the sort of bizarro, roadside Americana tourist trap locals would hustle their out-of-town visitors to with the fervor of a religious pilgrimage. But in Pittsburgh, you're unlikely to meet more than a handful of folks who've even heard of the place, and that's a true shame. Because while Trundle Manor isn't technically a museum—it's actually a private home, and tours need to be arranged in advance—it is nonetheless one of the oddest sites you're ever likely to experience in this corner of the Commonwealth.

Technically speaking, the manor is the private collection of two artists—Mr. Arm and Velda—who've filled their home with the sort of oddball curiosities one might have expected to see at an early-20th-century traveling carnival. You'll find taxidermied animals and other creepy dead creatures in glass cases, for instance. You'll see a groovy, *Juxtapoz* magazine-style art gallery, along with strange medical equipment, curious horror movie paraphernalia, and who knows what else. Trundle Manor's rather disturbing collection is always changing and growing, and in fact, visitors can even donate "dead things, medical devices, or booze" in lieu of actual money. Sounds like a real gas, eh daddy-o? (Just don't forget to bring along your sense of humor.)

MAP 7: 7724 Juniata St., Swissvale, 412/916-5544, www.trundlemanor.com; appointment only; call or text to schedule a visit during the weekend or evenings during the week; $20 minimum donation

Restaurants

Look for ★ to find recommended restaurants.

HIGHLIGHTS

★ **Best "New Pittsburgh" Restaurants:** Chef Kevin Sousa's **Salt of the Earth** kicked off Pittsburgh's current Contemporary American trend. Much newer is **Meat & Potatoes,** serving trendy interpretations of comfort food and Prohibition-era cocktails (page 138 and page 89).

★ **Most Authentic Pittsburgh Dining Experience:** Yes, Pittsburghers really do eat sandwiches with French fries inside. Join the locals at the original **Primanti Brothers** in the Strip District and try one for yourself. And while in Oakland, don't miss **The Original Hot Dog Shop,** a.k.a. "The O," a time-honored Pittsburgh junk food tradition (page 94 and page 104).

★ **Most Creative Interpretation of Mexican Street Food:** Culinary genius meets the simple Mexican street taco at **Yo Rita,** easily the city's most inventive finger-food outpost (page 115).

★ **Best Local Coffee Chain:** With 26 area locations, free Wi-Fi, and an eclectic atmosphere, **Crazy Mocha** has the locals flocking in droves (page 119).

★ **Best Place to Fuel Up After a Workout:** Shadyside's **Eden** abounds with tasty raw, vegan, and gluten-free treats, all of them practically guaranteed to restore your energy. If you need to fill up fast while still eating well, go for the brunch instead (page 120).

★ **Finest Grass-Fed Frankfurters:** You'll pay a pretty penny for the humanely raised sausages at Lawrenceville's gorgeous new **Franktuary** location. That's why the city's thriftiest gourmands stop by during the weekday happy hour, when dogs are half off (page 129).

★ **Best Brunch Spot:** Forget the greasy spoons and head instead to **Coca Café** for the goat-cheese-stuffed French toast, creative omelets, or eggs Bennie. Get there early or you'll be in for a long wait (page 130).

★ **Best New Meat Market:** Dig into the locally sourced beef at **Cure,** where you can be confident you're getting the most wholesome and ethically sourced flesh available, complete with an urban Mediterranean twist (page 131).

★ **Best Place to Share Small Bites and Gourmet Pizza:** What's the secret to the popping flavors of **Dinette?** Much of the bistro's produce is grown right overhead, on their very own rooftop garden (page 137).

★ **Best First Date Restaurant:** East Liberty's **Spoon** serves up artistic interpretations of fresh and local contemporary American entrées in a laid-back and intimate setting (page 138).

PRICE KEY

$ Entrées less than $10
$$ Entrées $10–20
$$$ Entrées more than $20

While hunting down especially refined dining options was once an uphill battle in Pittsburgh, the city has become something of a foodie's paradise in recent years. While farm-to-fork cuisine has been embraced here as it has in other metropolitan areas, local chefs nevertheless have a real knack for sneaking in just a hint of the Steel City's feel-good comfort food roots. Historically, this makes good sense: All of those mill and factory workers back during Pittsburgh's industry boom days certainly couldn't exist on (or afford) a diet of haute cuisine and foie gras. And so the most successful local chefs have a way of delicately reinventing the area's substantial classics with locally grown, in-season ingredients and a whole lot of friendly, hometown customer service.

Do remember, though, at your dive bars and cheap eats spots, that this is a town where both salads and sandwiches are frequently served with French fries on top, and where the double-carb nightmare known as a pierogi—a pasta dumpling filled with mashed potatoes and cheese—is considered something of a delicacy. And yes, Pittsburgh even has a food truck called Zum Zum that serves up "pierogi, *haluski,* and stuffed cabbage just like Grandma used to make."

Pittsburgh today is also rich in ethnic eateries, and not only of the Italian and eastern European varieties. Master sushi chefs now call Pittsburgh home, for instance, and throughout the East End, locals can gorge themselves on a daily basis at affordable Thai, Vietnamese, Indian, Ethiopian, and Filipino restaurants. While contemporary cuisine was relatively sparse within the city's limits just a few years ago, today it's easy to find in just about any neighborhood that's seen recent development. The very best bets for contemporary cuisine can be found in restaurants on the main drags of the Lawrenceville and East Liberty neighborhoods, though that certainly shouldn't deter you from venturing Downtown, or to neighborhoods like Point Breeze, Regent Square, and Squirrel Hill.

Perhaps the smartest manner in which to approach Pittsburgh's newfound culinary bonanza is to think of each neighborhood as a separate and unique dining experience: Bloomfield for Italian and comfort food restaurants, Oakland for ethnic and late-night bites, Mount Washington or Downtown for romantic fine dining. And on the South Side, you can always head to a bar after dinner if it's not quite time for the evening to end.

In other words, gastronomic delights can be found in even the furthest reaches of Pittsburgh, as long as you're willing to peek around the proverbial corner.

Downtown Map 1

Attempting to eat in Downtown on any sort of a strict budget is a difficult task. And should you find yourself working nine-to-five and searching out budget lunch options, things can get even stickier still. And yet there is good news: Many of the city's favorite food trucks have been making Downtown lunchtime appearances, and frankly, the overall trend is certainly still on the upswing. If you're truly in a bind, there's an abundance of fast-food joints, chain cafés, and sandwich shops in the area as well. You'll also find that many of the Cultural District's pricier places stay open late on weekends—and some weekdays—for the theater crowd, and many offer small plate selections after regular dining hours. Keep an eye out for prix fixe tasting menus at higher-end locales on the weekend—they're a great way to sample a whole lot of the menu while still being kind to your wallet.

AMERICAN

TAVERN 245 $$

Tavern 245 is yet another wonderful Downtown eatery that's opened in recent years; food is served all day, and the place stays open late. It's inside a 1950s-era building, and the vibe is good, kitschy fun; the atmosphere is casual but classy. The prices are just right for the quality and portion sizes. Tavern 245 offers up what might be the best salad in town, and their burgers combine just the right amount of crunch with slightly greasy juicy goodness.

MAP 1: 245 4th Ave., 412/281-4345, www.tavern245.com; Mon.-Fri. 11am-2am, Sat. 11am-3pm and 5pm-2am

ASIAN

HABITAT $$$

It's certainly a bit unusual for a hotel restaurant, of all things, to feature an oversized chef's table with a perfect view of a wide-open kitchen. But then again, Habitat, which is within the city's best-known new hotel, The Fairmont, is anything but average. The menu, featuring dishes from around the globe, might be thought of as the complement to the hotel's guests, who hail from around the globe themselves. And although many of the entrées with roots in Asian, Indian, and even European cooking are prepared in the kitchen's tandoor oven, or in a wok (pad thai, chicken *tikka masala,* Maine lobster curry), standard domestic fare (with an inevitable fusion twist) is also available. Try the Elysian Fields lamb loin or the half-pound Habitat burger for something special but simple.

MAP 1: 510 Market St., 412/773-8848, www.habitatrestaurant.com; Sun.-Thurs. 6:30am-2pm and 5:30pm-10pm, Fri.-Sat. 6:30am-2pm and 5:30pm-10:30pm

CONTEMPORARY AND NEW AMERICAN

BUTCHER AND THE RYE $$

If you needed any further proof that Pittsburgh's ever-expanding Downtown dining scene has finally come into its own, a night out at Butcher and the Rye should go a long way toward settling those doubts for good. Operated by the same team responsible for Downtown's runaway dining success, Meat & Potatoes, the two-story Butcher and the Rye features two dining rooms serving artisan-quality meat- and fish-based entrées with ingredients sourced from local farms. And while the big draw here is the 400-strong bourbon and rye menu (craft cocktails are also offered), the interior design and ambience is just as impressive. Think midcentury upper-crust hunting lodge, complete with antique wallpaper, taxidermied critters, and lamps made of faux antlers. For meat-lovers with a taste for the good life, this is an absolute can't-miss. Reservations recommended.

MAP 1: 212 6th St., 412/391-2752, www.butcherandtherye.com; Tues.-Thurs. 5pm-11pm, Fri.-Sat. 5pm-midnight

★ MEAT & POTATOES $$$

This hotshot gastropub in the Cultural District has been getting all-around rave reviews since first opening its doors in 2011, and for good reason: The menu centers around simple, fuss-free, and utterly delicious preparations of meat, potatoes, and veggies. The pot roast and hangar steak are standouts, and the $59 meat and potatoes for two (consisting of a 34-ounce rib eye, confit fries, housemade steak sauce, and marrow gratin) is a great way to splurge on a date. Portions are quite generous, and the Prohibition-era cocktails are already a citywide legend. Young creatives and professionals flock to this contemporary space after the business day ends.

Keep your eyes peeled for Pork & Beans, another anticipated project from Meat & Potatoes owner and head chef Richard DeShantz. It's rumored to be heading for either East Liberty or Lawrenceville, and comfort food and a beer garden will be on offer.

MAP 1: 649 Penn Ave., 412/325-7007, www.meatandpotatoespgh.com; dinner daily 5pm-11pm, until midnight on weekends, lunch Wed.-Fri. 11:30am-2pm, weekend brunch 10:30am-2pm

NINE ON NINE $$$

One of the more welcome additions to the Cultural District's contemporary dining scene, Nine on Nine is the sort of elegant establishment not often found in Midwestern or Rust Belt locales. Both the menu and the ambience are striking; grilled quail, wing of stingray, and Amish chicken are just a few of the unusual offerings, though the menu changes seasonally. They also offer a daily vegetarian entrée and are incredibly skillful at handling tricky dietary issues, such as gluten-free requests. The wine list is 29 names long, and the artfully prepared desserts are said to be just as majestic as the entrées. Happy hour is Monday-Saturday 5pm-7pm as well as Monday 9pm-11pm, and bar bites and drinks are available Monday, Friday, and Saturday 9pm-11pm.

MAP 1: 900 Penn Ave., 412/338-6463, www.nineonninepgh.com; lunch Mon.-Fri. 11am-2pm, dinner Mon.-Sat. 5pm-10pm

SIX PENN KITCHEN $$$

With its contemporary interpretations of classic American comfort food—gourmet burgers, buffalo chicken mac 'n' cheese, oven roasted pizzas—it's no surprise that Six Penn Kitchen is a constant favorite among Downtown theater-goers. The space is gorgeous with an upscale diner feel, and the food is simple but always fresh and expertly prepared. Six Penn is the kind of casual but delicious restaurant you find on every other block in a city like New York, and it's been a much-needed addition to the Downtown dining scene—especially since it's open all day, serves food late, and has a killer Sunday brunch (try the Boston cream beignets and the house-smoked bacon grits). If you work in Downtown or frequent the arts offerings in Pittsburgh, you'll probably wind up here quite often, and that's definitely not a bad thing.

MAP 1: 146 6th St., 412/566-7366, www.sixpennkitchen.com; Mon.-Thurs. 11am-11pm, Fri. 11am-midnight, Sat. 4:30pm-midnight, Sun. brunch 10:30am-2:30pm

LATIN AMERICAN

SEVICHE $$$

Seviche is one of the more adventurous restaurants to have popped up during the Cultural District's foodie renaissance. Quality seafood is offered in a variety of different preparations, and a seafood bar features seven different versions of the eponymous dish, in addition to a full menu of other Latin American goodies, such as empanadas, tostadas, and *croquetas* (fritters). Live Latin music and salsa dancing are also common events throughout the week, and the restaurant offers a 22 percent discount to Downtown residents each Tuesday (ID with 15222 zip code required).

MAP 1: 930 Penn Ave., 412/697-3120, www.seviche.com; Mon.-Thurs. 5pm-midnight, Fri.-Sat. until 1am

SEAFOOD

ORIGINAL FISH MARKET $$$

Tucked deep inside Downtown's Westin Hotel, the Original Fish Market serves what many claim to be the city's best sushi. (And for what it's worth, this author concurs.) A fantastic fresh seafood menu is also on offer—on it you'll find grouper, seared king salmon, ahi tuna, grilled swordfish, and the daily catch, among other house specialties—all of it flown in fresh twice daily. Better still is the fact that the Fish Market keeps such late hours; aside from a few greasy spoons on the South Side and the East End, this is one of Pittsburgh's better late-night dining options.

MAP 1: 1001 Liberty Ave., 412/227-3657, www.theoriginalfishmarketpgh.com; Mon.-Fri. 11am-1am, Sat.-Sun. 4pm-1am

ORIGINAL OYSTER HOUSE $

The men behind the counter at the Original Oyster House have been serving up giant fish sandwiches, breaded oysters, and cold mugs of beer for more than 140 years. This eatery in the heart of Market Square is the oldest bar and restaurant in the city; it's even been designated a historic landmark by the Pittsburgh History and Landmarks Foundation. The atmosphere—and the speedy service—remains much as it has been since the Oyster House's opening in 1870. Even Hollywood considers the restaurant particularly quaint: Scenes from 25 films, including *Striking Distance* and *Innocent Blood*, have been shot here.

MAP 1: 20 Market Sq., 412/566-7925, www.originaloysterhousepittsburgh.com; Mon.-Sat. 10am-10pm

PENN AVENUE FISH COMPANY $$

This relative newcomer to the Pittsburgh seafood and sushi scene has been pleasantly surprising guests in both its Downtown and Strip District (2208 Penn Ave., 412/434-7200) locations. Executive

clockwise from top left: Six Penn Kitchen; Meat & Potatoes; Nine On Nine

chef, catering genius, and fishmonger Henry Dewey set off with restaurant industry expert Angela Earley to give the Pittsburgh seafood scene a major facelift, and they've done just that. You simply cannot go wrong with the fish sandwiches—they are nothing like the sandwiches you might remember from church fish fries as a kid. If you're looking to buy some seriously fresh seafood to make sushi or other gourmet dishes at home, skip the trip to Wholey's, as the staff here is much friendlier; will give you expert tips on cut, preparation, and serving suggestions; and will remember your name when you inevitably return.

MAP 1: 308 Forbes Ave., 412/562-1710, www.pennavefishcompany.com; Mon.-Tues. 11am-4pm, Wed.-Fri. 11am-10pm, Sat. 6pm-10pm

Strip District

Map 1

Pittsburgh may not have a Chinatown, but it does have the Strip District—an international neighborhood brimming with everything from Asian grocery stores to Italian delis.

AMERICAN

DELUCA'S RESTAURANT $$

A truly rough-around-the-edges diner in the finest greasy spoon tradition, DeLuca's has held legendary status among Pittsburgh's breakfast aficionados for eons now; this is the place to bring an out-of-town visitor who wants to experience the *real* Steel City. The menu is exactly what you'd expect: massive plates full of eggs, bacon, and buttered toast. For something a bit different, try the fruit-filled pancakes; a regular order is so large you may not be able to finish it in one sitting. Or go for the breakfast burrito, but try not to snicker at the slices of processed American cheese melted on top. Remember: You've come for the *experience.*

MAP 1: 2015 Penn Ave., 412/566-2195; Mon.-Sat. 6am-3pm, Sun. 7am-3pm

PAMELA'S DINER $$

A much loved mini-chain, Pamela's Diner is your best bet for a quality, even-tempered breakfast experience; last night's date will feel just as comfortable munching on toast here as your visiting parents will. Truthfully though, the fare at any given Pamela's isn't much different than at your average greasy spoon—it's the crowd you'll run into that makes the difference: students, hipsters, and young parents, mostly. Most folks rave about the pancakes, though take care not to miss the omelets, which are some of the most satisfying in the city. There are five other locations throughout the city and suburbs: in Shadyside (5527 Walnut St., 412/683-1003), Squirrel Hill (5813 Forbes Ave., 412/422-9457), Oakland (3703 Forbes Ave.,

412/683-4066), Millvale (232 North Ave., 412/821-4655), and Mt. Lebanon (427 Washington Rd., 412/343-3344).

MAP 1: 60 21st St., 412/281-6366, www.pamelasdiner.com; Mon.-Sat. 7am-3pm, Sun. 8am-3pm

★ PRIMANTI BROTHERS $

Much more than just a restaurant, the original Primanti Brothers location in the Strip is a destination, a tourist attraction, and a staple of Pittsburgh's history. The rumors you've heard are true: A huge pile of French fries, and sometimes a fried egg, go *inside* the sandwich, which is already stacked sky-high with coleslaw and your choice of artery-clogging meat (roast beef and pastrami are favorites). Soups and salads can also be ordered, but most folks don't bother. Add a pop (soda) onto your order, and the combination will soak up even the worst of hangovers. There are city locations in Oakland (3803 Forbes Ave., 412/621-4444; Sun.-Wed. 10am-midnight, Thurs.-Sat. 10am-3am), South Side (1832 E. Carson St., 412/381-2583; Sun.-Thurs. 11am-2am, Fri.-Sat. 11am-3am), and Downtown (2 S. Market Sq., 412/261-1599; daily 10am-midnight), and more in the suburbs, so you've got few excuses to miss this venerable Pittsburgh institution. Check the website for a full list of locations. And yes, vegetarians can always order sandwiches without meat.

MAP 1: 46 18th St., 412/263-2142, www.primantibros.com; daily 24 hours

ASIAN

SUSHI KIM $$

Tucked away on a battered stretch of Penn Avenue between Downtown and the Strip, Sushi Kim is a local diamond in the rough: The decor exists somewhere between Asian pop culture and hipster kitsch, and the entrée list is split evenly between traditional Japanese and Korean dishes—about 40 in all. But most come for the sushi, which is some of the best in the Strip. Particularly amusing are the massive sushi boats, a sort of combo platter for the young-at-heart fresh-fish lover.

MAP 1: 1241 Penn Ave., 412/281-9956, www.sushikim.com; Mon. 5pm-9pm, Tues.-Thurs. 11:30am-2:30pm and 5pm-10pm, Fri.-Sat. 11:30am-10:30pm, Sun. noon-9pm

CAFÉS

LA PRIMA ESPRESSO COMPANY $

Some call La Prima the most authentic espresso shop in Pittsburgh, and if you show up during the morning rush, you'll see why. Clusters of middle-aged men gather around the front counter with espresso and Italian-language newspapers, and the baristas busily craft specialty drinks with speed and skill. (Look for the leaf or heart design that'll likely be etched atop your latte or cappuccino.) Even drip coffee is something special; there's almost always a Central American fair-trade or shade-grown selection on offer.

MAP 1: 205 21st St., 412/281-1922, www.laprima.com; Mon.-Sat. 6am-4pm, Sun. 8am-3pm

PRESTOGEORGE $

Part coffee and tea emporium, part specialty market, and part café, Prestogeorge has been a Strip District favorite for many years. It has loads of its own custom coffee blends roasted in small batches, along with make-your-own custom tea blends. Locals also love the handmade biscotti, and gift baskets make the perfect last-minute present for just about any occasion.

MAP 1: 1719 Penn Ave., 412/471-0133, www.prestogeorge.com; Mon.-Thurs. 8am-4pm, Fri. 8am-5pm, Sat. 7am-5pm

CARIBBEAN

KAYA $$

An island paradise in the heart of the Strip's warehouse district, Kaya represents the Caribbean arm of the local Big Burrito restaurant group. This is certainly Pittsburgh's premiere locale for Jamaican jerk chicken and Cuban sandwiches, and the menu changes daily, so dining often feels as much like a vicarious travel experience as it does a culinary adventure. The clientele leans toward the young, beautiful, and trust-funded, and the happy hour is a scene unto itself; saddle up for tropical island drinks or a martini.

MAP 1: 2000 Smallman St., 412/261-6565, www.bigburrito.com/kaya; Mon.-Wed. 11am-10pm, Thurs.-Sat. 11:30am-11pm, Sun. 11am-9pm

CONTEMPORARY AND NEW AMERICAN

BAR MARCO $$

Since opening in 2012 in the former location of Embury and the Firehouse Lounge, Bar Marco has quickly become one the city's top restaurants and nightspots, with rave reviews coming in across the country. Given the restaurant's reputation, food prices are surprisingly affordable, though you will want to order lots of "start" and "follow" plates (appetizers and entrées) to share. Begin with charcuterie, then order main dishes like mac 'n' cheese with rosemary and peppers or squash and sweet sausage. You'll also find a well-rounded wine list, though you should try at least one cocktail. Punch bowl social hours and the Sunday brunch are especially popular with local hipster types. The design is a bit sparse and can feel quite sterile during the daylight hours, but it turns into a much more welcoming space at night.

MAP 1: 2216 Penn Ave., 412/471-1900, www.barmarcopgh.com; Mon. 5pm-11pm, Tues. 5pm-midnight, Wed.-Sat. 5pm-2am, brunch Sat.-.Sun. 10am-3pm

Local Specialties

traditional Polish pierogi, ready to be cooked

Yes, there really is such a thing as Pittsburgh cuisine. The vast majority of it is not particularly good for you, but all of it is addictively delicious. For starters, there's the legendary **Primanti Brothers sandwich** (often pronounced with the "t" silent), which comes complete with French fries and coleslaw *inside*. Gnawing on a roast beef sandwich at the counter and washing it down with a pint of Iron City beer is a truly authentic Pittsburgh experience. According to Primanti's lore, the sandwich was created specifically for the hardworking men who once unloaded produce trucks in the Strip District in the middle of the night, so they could eat an entire meal with one hand while continuing to work with the other.

Of course, you can't mention a Primanti Brothers sandwich without locals instinctively imagining the Mancini's Bread it's served on. While Mancini's has expanded over the years to produce pepperoni rolls, cinnamon raisin bread, and even a few tasty artisanal loafs, it's their Italian loaf that even displaced locals recall so fondly. Frankly, the bread itself is an acquired taste—nothing fancy—but every true Pittsburgher has a Mancini's Bread story from their childhood. And yes, for those of you who've left the Steel City, Mancini's will gladly overnight-ship a box of four loaves for just $10.

Pierogi and **kielbasa** are regional

ELEVEN $$$

The aptly named Eleven (it's the 11th creation of the Big Burrito restaurant group) has lately become a particularly strong cornerstone of the fine contemporary dining scene in Pittsburgh. The philosophy is contemporary, too: As a serious adherent to the slow food movement, chef Greg Alauzen takes pains to include seasonal, regional ingredients in most dishes. You can expect all the usual suspects, of course: Elysian Fields lamb, pulled pork. But it's the gracefully prepared plates that truly make dining here a high-art experience. The wine list is nearly 150 names long.

MAP 1: 1150 Smallman St., 412/201-5656, www.bigburrito.com/eleven; Mon.-Thurs. 11:30am-10pm, Fri. 11:30am-11pm, Sat. 5pm-11pm, Sun. 11am-9pm

staples of Polish origin. A pierogi is a boiled potato and cheese dumpling deep-fried in butter, and a kielbasa (pronounced "keel-BAH-see" in Pittsburghese) is a smoked sausage, usually made of pork. The **Bloomfield Bridge Tavern** is the place to go to sample locally prepared Polish food at its finest—try the Polish Platter sampler dish.

Order a steak salad at just about any restaurant in Southwestern Pennsylvania, and you'll likely find a generous bed of fries scattered atop. This is a regional riddle that even local culinary experts don't understand, but how can you not love a city that loads its salads with red meat and fried carbs?

Speaking of beef, order your next T-bone or porterhouse steak **"Pittsburgh rare,"** and your meat will come charred on the outside and blood red on the inside. Allegedly, this trend reaches back to Pittsburgh's steel-making era, when steelworkers would bring raw steaks to work and then sear them on the nearest piece of burning hot metal just before lunchtime.

Try a **Devonshire sandwich** for lighter local lunch fare. The open-faced sandwich, made with either chicken or turkey, was invented here in 1936 by restaurateur Frank Blandi of early Le Mont fame. While the Devonshire boasts a heart-healthy white meat option, you probably won't be surprised to find that it's smothered in a creamy cheese sauce.

Most folks are aware that **Heinz Ketchup** has its roots in the Steel City. H. J. Heinz himself even taught Sunday School at the Grace Methodist Church in Sharpsburg. But few are aware that the **Clark Bar** and the **Klondike Bar** were born here, too. The Clark Bar was invented way back in 1886 on the city's North Side, where the Clark Building still stands. Today it houses the editorial team of the *Pittsburgh Tribune-Review.* The Klondike Bar was created by **Isaly's,** a company whose ice cream in particular remains legendary throughout the region.

To pass as a local, order another Isaly's creation—**chipped ham**—the next time you're at a Pittsburgh grocery store deli counter. Chipped ham is very thinly sliced; you can also order it "chipped chopped," meaning small clumps of the thinly sliced stuff. If you'd like to hunt down a taste of the original sensation, several independently owned markets just outside the city still carry Isaly's chipped ham and barbecue sauce; visit www.isalys.com for a list of local retailers.

Enjoy!

LATIN AMERICAN

GAUCHO PARRILLA ARGENTINA $$

Pittsburgh's newest and, well, only Argentinian wood-fired grill is simply a mouthwatering experience for local carnivores. The staff is highly knowledgeable and friendly, and that's a big plus, as you may need some assistance and recommendations during your first couple of visits. Though it's a BYOB, there's no corkage fee. The intimate space is warm and inviting, and it's a great choice for low-carb and gluten-free dieters. Don't get too full on appetizers, though, as the meats are the real menu highlights—most are served à la carte with a selection of condiments for just $3 each—sauces include *chimichurri, pimentón, ajo,* and the like.

MAP 1: 1607 Penn Ave., 412/709-6622, www.eatgaucho.com; Tues.-Sat. 11am-7pm

SNACKS AND DESSERTS

KLAVON'S ICE CREAM PARLOR $

You wouldn't necessarily know it from walking past the uninspiring facade, but this art deco drugstore and ice cream shop is the real deal. It opened way back in 1925, and all the trimmings are original, including the marble soda fountain and its attendant swivel stools, which are designed to look like soda bottle caps. Along with the regular assortment of sundaes and banana splits, Klavon's also stocks a wide array of old-school candy and even boasts a sandwich and soup menu for the sugar-phobic. Brooklynites, by the way, swear by the New York Egg Cream, so don't miss it.

MAP 1: 2801 Penn Ave., 412-434/0451, www.klavonsicecream.com; summer daily 11am-11pm, hours vary seasonally

PEACE, LOVE & LITTLE DONUTS $

It was only a matter of time before a family-friendly sweets shop like Peace, Love & Little Donuts opened up in the Strip, which transforms into one of city's busiest tourist attractions on the weekend. The bite-sized confections sold are offered with a staggering array of creative and candy-heavy toppings, most of them variations on the same sort of old-school donuts that Dunkin' Donuts specialized in long ago. A second location has since opened in Oakland (118 Meyran Ave., 412/379-3930, Mon.-Fri. 6am-6pm, Sat.-Sun. 11am-4pm), and the shop has branched out with franchise locations in Grove City, Cleveland, Nashville, and several Ohio locations. The maple bacon donut alone puts this little operation far ahead of any Krispy Kreme or Dunkin' pastry.

MAP 1: 2018 Smallman St., 412/489-7693, www.peaceloveandlittledonuts.com; Mon.-Fri. 6am-2pm, Sat. 8am-4pm, Sun. 9am-2pm

North Side

Map 1

While the North Side has seen a good deal of restaurant turnover in recent years, the majority of tourists who come to this part of town find themselves in the so-called North Shore area surrounding PNC Park. Chain restaurants and cafés serving bar food can be found there, and both PNC Park and Heinz Field have satellite locations of some of Pittsbugh's most popular eateries. Wander up to the commercial strip of East Ohio Street to find more restaurants, including "shot and a beer" bars and old taverns where patrons still toss their peanut shells on the floor. And when visiting the Andy Warhol Museum, don't hesitate to grab a bite in the downstairs

clockwise from top left: Peace, Love & Little Donuts; Eleven; The Original Fish Market

Markets and Grocery Stores

Pennsylvania Macaroni Company

Pittsburgh's most popular grocery store chain—by a long shot—is the locally headquartered Giant Eagle. More than 200 stores are located throughout Western Pennsylvania, West Virginia, Ohio, and Maryland, and just about every neighborhood in the city seems to have its own location. Some of the bigger locations even boast in-store cafés, video rental outlets, banks, and day-care centers. Other major area chains include **Shop 'n Save** (various locations, www.shopnsavefood.com, hours vary at each location) and **Foodland** (various locations, www.foodlandstores.com, hours vary at each location). Over the past few years, a number of Foodland stores have been bought out by **Shur Save** (various locations, www.shursavemarkets.com, hours vary at each location).

You'll find the city's solitary **Whole Foods Market** (5880 Centre Ave., 412/441-7960, www.wholefoodsmarket.com, daily 8am-10pm) in East Liberty, just east of the recently reconstructed Shadyside **Giant Eagle** (5550 Centre Ave., 412/681-1500, www.gianteagle.com, daily 6am-midnight), which for years now has been going head to head with Whole Foods in the battle for upscale customers. If eating healthy organic food is your thing but corporations aren't, head to the **East End Food Co-op** (7516 Meade St., 412/242-3598, www.eastendfoodcoop.com, daily 8am-9pm) in Point Breeze. The co-op has a wonderful in-store café, a fantastic organic produce selection, and probably the best bulk section in town.

The Strip District is home to unique grocery stores. Topping the list is the truly unique **Marty's Market** (2301 Smallman St., 412/586-7177, www.martysmarket.com, Mon.-Fri. 10am-8pm, Sat.-Sun. 9am-5pm, café and coffee bar open at 8am weekdays, 9am weekends), which is also home to a top-notch coffee bar and a café serving a popular weekend brunch. Marty's is something of a boutique grocer, with much of its fresh, high-quality food being sourced from area farmers. You'll find a made-to-order bakery here, a full-service butchery offering cheeses and ethically sourced meats, and much more.

Also in the Strip is **Wholey's Market** (1501 Penn Ave., 412/391-3737, www.wholey.com, Mon.-Thurs. 8am-5:30pm, Fri. 8am-6pm, Sat. 8am-5pm, Sun. 9am-4pm), a store so legendary in Pittsburgh that it often does double duty as a tourist attraction. Shoppers come here for the wide selection of fish and meats, while out-of-towners come to gawk at the plush farm animals in the dairy section that play musical instruments at the push of a button. Don't miss the sushi bar at the store's entrance.

Giving Wholey's a genuine run for its money in the fishmonger department is the relatively new **Penn Avenue Fish Company** (2208 Penn Ave., 412/434-7200, www.pennavefishcompany.com). If it swims, you'll find it here—everything from Arctic char and Chilean sea bass to soft-shell crabs and striped bass—and it'll most likely be the freshest-caught for many miles around.

Definitely check out the Strip's **Pennsylvania Macaroni Company** (2010 Penn Ave., 412/471-8330, www.pennmac.com, Mon.-Sat. 6:30am-4:30pm, Sun. 9am-2:30pm); call it "Penn Mac" if you want to sound like a local. You'll find an overwhelming selection of Italian pastas and sauces, and possibly the city's finest cheese counter.

The **Pittsburgh Public Market** (2401 Penn Ave., 412/281-4505, www.pittsburghpublicmarket.org, Wed.-Fri. 10am-4pm, Sat. 9am-5pm, Sun. 10am-4pm) has recently moved from its original Smallman Street location. With a diverse collection of dozens of separate vendors hawking everything from healthy take-away snacks, gifts, beauty products, accessories for pets, and of course, produce and grocery offerings galore, this is essentially Pittsburgh's answer to the historic Reading Terminal Market in Philadelphia.

Lotus Food Co. (1649 Penn Ave., 412/281-3050, daily 9am-6pm) is by far the most popular Asian grocery store in the Strip. It carries food items imported from North and South Asia, including durian fruit! For hard-to-find and specialty Japanese food stuffs, check out the small but packed **Tokyo Japanese Food Store** (5855 Ellsworth Ave., 412/661-3777, www.tokyostorepgh.com, Tues.-Sat. 10am-7pm, Sun. 10am-5pm) in Shadyside, which is fun to explore even when you're not planning to buy. You'll find everything from take-away sushi and bento boxes to Japanese bakery foods, Asian periodicals, Asian cookware and snacks, and imported Japanese cigarettes.

And if you're an especially frugal or health-conscious grocery shopper, you'll surely want to wield a cart throughout the aisles of **Trader Joe's** (6343 Penn Ave., East Liberty, 412/363-5748, www.traderjoes.com, daily 8am-9pm). The store sells organic, vegan, and whole foods at relatively low prices. A bit farther afield in the city's suburbs is **Back to Basics** (300 Mt. Lebanon Blvd., Mt. Lebanon, 412/343-8156, www.back2basicsinc.com, Mon. 10am-8pm, Tues.-Fri. 10am-6pm, Sat. 10am-5pm), a self-described "nutrition and dietary shop" known for its generous supply of vitamins and supplements. Slightly esoteric wellness services can also be had here, including naturopathy and iridology.

And finally, food shoppers on a budget will be pleased to learn that an outpost of the German-helmed **Aldi** (5631 Baum Blvd., www.aldi.us, Mon.-Sat. 9am-9pm, Sun. 9am-7pm) discount supermarket has opened in the city's East End, within easy walking distance of Whole Foods. A second Aldi location with the same store hours sits on the South Side (2628 E. Carson St.).

FUEL AND FUDDLE $

A popular college eatery centered around the dual themes of bar food and good beer, Fuel and Fuddle is the perfect place to eat when you can't quite decide what you're in the mood for. The menu consists of large plates of pub grub and finger foods such as chicken wings, Thai skewers, jack cheese quesadillas, and nacho plates. Beer specials change daily.

MAP 2: 212 Oakland Ave., 412/682-3473, www.fuelandfuddle.com; daily 11am-2am

HEMINGWAY'S $

Once a must-see stop on the city's bohemian café circuit, Hemingway's is now more of an epicenter for observing primal meathead behavior. The beer doth flow, and boy is it cheap. But get here before dark falls, and you might just find the English-pub atmosphere and its attendant pub-grub menu rather charming. What's more, Hemingway's commands an enviable location on the University of Pittsburgh campus, making it a perfect place to meet up for a burger or sandwich before a raging night out. Just make sure you go easy on the $1 Miller Lites, dawg.

MAP 2: 3911 Forbes Ave., 412/621-4100, www.hemingways-cafe.com; Mon.-Fri. 11am-2am, Sat. 6pm-2am

LEGUME $$

Although it first opened back in 2007 in the Regent Square neighborhood, the tables certainly turned on Legume's popularity when it relocated to North Oakland. Because the staff does the majority of its food processing in-house, including whole-animal butchery, vegetable canning, and grinding grain for pasta and polenta, the menu changes a bit each day; updated lunch and dinner menus can be viewed online. You're quite likely, though, to find an even mixture of creatively prepared pastas, meats, fish, and vegetables at this white-tablecloth restaurant, all of it gathered from small area farmers and food purveyors and artisans. Plates are always true works of art, and you'll never come across anything processed or otherwise prepared through industrial means.

MAP 2: 214 N. Craig St., 412/621-2700, www.legumebistro.com; Mon.-Fri. 11:30am-2pm and 5pm-9pm (till 10pm on Fri.), Sat. 5pm-10pm

★ THE ORIGINAL HOT DOG SHOP $

Much more than just a corner hot dog and pizza shop, "The O," as it's known locally, is nothing less than a Pittsburgh institution. Opened in 1960, it's probably safe to say that anyone who's ever spent time in the nearby Pitt dorms has a story to tell about the place. The all-natural dogs are world class, but most come for the ridiculously large baskets of cheese fries, or the cheap pizzas, or at least a six-pack. The O is always at its best after dark, when things are crowded and chaotic.

MAP 2: 3901 Forbes Ave., 412/621-7388, www.theoriginalhotdogshop.com; daily 10am-3:30am

UNION GRILL $$

If it's simple, hearty American fare you're after, you won't do much better in this stretch of town than the Union Grill. Burgers are the really big item, clocking in at around a half pound after cooking. Just about every entrée includes more food than the average person can consume in one sitting, from the sandwiches and veggie wraps to the chicken entrées and crab cakes. If you've managed to save room for dessert, make it a slice of the homemade pie, and when the weather's warm, request a sidewalk table for optimum Craig Street people-watching.

MAP 2: 413 S. Craig St., 412/681-8620; Mon.-Thurs. 11:30am-10pm, Fri.-Sat. 11:30am-11pm, Sun. noon-9pm

ASIAN

LULU'S NOODLES $

Living somewhere in between cafeteria-style casual dining and chic urban café, Lulu's Noodles is a favorite destination for budget-conscious Pitt and CMU undergrads looking for good value in a stylish setting. Portion sizes are generous, too: Order a noodle dish—the Singapore rice noodles are a good bet—and you'll have a tough time cleaning your plate. Noodle soups are also recommended, and if you're not terribly hungry, Lulu's is quite well known for its bubble tea.

MAP 2: 400 S. Craig St., 412/687-7777; daily 11am-10pm

OISHII BENTO $$

What a concept: A traditional Japanese *bento* restaurant right in the heart of the university district, featuring a mini-sushi counter, Japanese-style floor seating, and even a selection of Korean dishes. No wonder Oishii Bento—the name means "Yummy Lunchbox"—is such a raging success. Prices are reasonable, the menu is completely unique, and each order of food is its very own work of art. For a truly filling lunch, go with one of the meat or veggie rice bowls. For pure fun, though, simply pick and choose at random; aside from sleeping in and skipping class, Oishii Bento is certainly one of Oakland's most amusing midday distractions.

MAP 2: 119 Oakland Ave., 412/687-3335, www.oishiibento.com; Mon.-Fri. 10:30am-9pm, Sat. 11am-9pm

SPICE ISLAND TEA HOUSE $$

A pan-Asian legend that for eons now has been introducing Oakland's college community to Indonesian, Burmese, Thai, Cambodian, and Filipino food, Spice Island Tea House is one of the area's few can't-miss institutions. With the charming mismatched furniture and thatched-roof vibe, even a bad meal would still be fun—but nearly every Spice Island entrée is a crowd pleaser, especially the Indonesian and Thai rice dishes. (Some of the Burmese soups can be a bit scary.) Along with the restaurant's impressive selection of exotic loose-leaf teas, beer and wine are available.

MAP 2: 253 Atwood St., 412/687-8821, www.spiceislandteahouse.com; Mon.-Thurs. 11:30am-9pm, Fri.-Sat. 11:30am-10pm

SUSHI BOAT $$

Slightly cheaper than Oishii Bento (and with a bit more of a low-rent cafeteria vibe), Sushi Boat tends to fill up fast during peak lunch hours, especially as Pitt students arrive to grab a bite between classes. Both Chinese and Japanese dishes are served, although maki, nigiri, and sashimi sushi are the big draw; expect to pay around $1.50 per piece. For the biggest bang for your buck, go with the vegetarian rice bowl or the seafood fried rice platter. Sushi Boat can be very hit-or-miss in terms of quality, but then again, that can happen easily in Oakland, given the sheer volume of students and restaurants in the area.

MAP 2: 128 Oakland Ave., 412/681-1818; Mon.-Fri. 10:30am-9pm, Sat. 11am-9pm

CAFÉS

EAT UNIQUE $

Eat Unique is a great place to grab a healthy and filling bite when you're tired of all the chain franchises, pizza, and deep-fried delicacies Oakland has to offer. A modern and spotless cafeteria-style spot, Eat Unique also has a large selection of vegetarian options, from sandwiches and soups to grillers and wraps. Many ingredients are organic and locally sourced when in season, and everything is made fresh and in-house—even the desserts. And rest easy: You definitely won't find any fries on your salad here!

MAP 2: 305 S. Craig St., 412/683-9993, www.eatuniquecafe.com; daily 11am-8pm

INDIAN

INDIA GARDEN $$

Expect a somewhat chaotic atmosphere at India Garden, one of Oakland's most popular Indian joints (and most authentic, according to some). Every year, it seems, the food wins some sort of award from a Pittsburgh publication (including the *Pittsburgh City Paper*'s Best Indian award), and you'll certainly understand the hype after trying a savory curry, chicken tandoori, or *tikka masala.*

clockwise from top left: Lulu's Noodles; Eat Unique; Union Grill

Vegetarians also have cause to rejoice, as the meat-free dishes are absolutely celestial. (Try the eggplant.) Dinners are 50 percent off daily 4pm-6pm and 10pm-1am.

MAP 2: 328 Atwood St., 412/682-3000, www.indiagarden.net; Mon.-Fri. 11:30am-2:30pm and 5pm-11pm, Sat.-Sun. 12:30pm-11pm

ITALIAN

LUCCA $$$

If you're looking for an especially tranquil and laid-back Oakland dining experience, you're likely to fall in love with Lucca, one of the city's more luxurious Italian cuisine establishments. Young movers and shakers and swooning couples on dates flock here for the fettuccine, couscous, and caramelized onions, and also for the quaint decor and the staff's impeccable attention to detail. If money's not an issue and you've got a discriminating palate to impress, Lucca's your place.

MAP 2: 317 S. Craig St., 412/682-3310, www.luccaristorante.com; Mon.-Fri. 11:30am-2pm and 5pm-10pm, Sat. 5pm-11pm, Sun. 4:30pm-9pm

MEXICAN

MAD MEX $$

For lovers of quality Tex-Mex and massive food portions, it doesn't get much better than Mad Mex, a locally based restaurant-and-bar chain. The menu is an inventive collection of burritos, enchiladas, and quesadillas with a twist: portobello mushrooms inside, say, or tofu or chickpea chili. If it's the truly sublime you're after, go with the Dance Marathon Burrito (spinach, portobellos, and marinated chicken) or the Kristy's Big Sister's Red Velvet Burrito, complete with *pico de gallo* and zucchini inside. Graciously, food is half off every night 11pm-1am; expect long lines. Other locations are in Monroeville (4100 William Penn Hwy., 412/349-6767), Robinson (Robinson Township, 2 Robinson Plaza, Park Manor Dr., 412/494-5656), Cranberry (20510 Perry Hwy., 724/741-5656), the South Hills (2010 Greentree Rd., 412/279-0200), and the North Hills (7905 McKnight Rd., 412/366-5656).

MAP 2: 370 Atwood St., 412/681-5656, www.madmex.com; daily 11am-1am

MIDDLE EASTERN

ALI BABA $$

A longtime Craig Street favorite, Ali Baba is the Steel City's preeminent Middle Eastern deal. It's "the best Middle Eastern restaurant in Pittsburgh," according to *Pittsburgh* magazine—for 10 years running. And while prices may indeed be fit for a college-style budget, it's easy to pretend you're living large, what with the decidedly classy ambience. In other words, a student dive this most definitely is not, although Pitt and CMU types (and their parents and professors) are almost always in attendance. Food-wise, it's tough to go wrong, although the shish kebab dinner is particularly inviting, as is the *sheik el-mahshi* (roasted eggplant with seasoned lamb). The baklava is an especially agreeable dessert; be aware that the BYO policy extends to wine only.

MAP 2: 404 S. Craig St., 412/682-2829, www.alibabapittsburgh.com; Mon.-Fri. 11:30am-2:30pm and 4:30pm-9:45pm

SNACKS AND DESSERTS

CONFLICT KITCHEN $

Although it originally sat next door to the Waffle Shop, a now-shuttered breakfast café in East Liberty that also hosted a live talk show, the truly unusual and very important Conflict Kitchen has since been reinvented as a small food kiosk in Schenley Plaza. At this take-away booth, the cuisine served is entirely from countries with which the United States is currently in conflict. The featured country changes roughly every four months, and the cuisine is generally of the finger food and drinks variety. Multimedia events involving citizens of the featured countries are often scheduled.

MAP 2: 221 Schenley Dr., Schenley Plaza, 412/802-8417, www.conflictkitchen.org; daily 11am-6pm

DAVE & ANDY'S $

Without a doubt, this non-chain store is the finest purveyor of ice cream in Pittsburgh. The confections at Dave & Andy's are good for a reason: Ice cream is made the old-fashioned way, with wooden churns and rock salt. The result? Fresh, perfectly creamy ice cream offered in a regularly rotating selection of flavors. Ask for yours in a homemade waffle cone (also made fresh in-house), which includes a handful of M&Ms that plug up the hole at the bottom.

MAP 2: 207 Atwood St., 412/681-9906; Mon.-Fri. 11:30am-10pm, Sat.-Sun. noon-10pm

South Side

Map 3

The South Side is widely known as party central to most Pittsburghers, who fill the pubs and taverns on weekends. East Carson Street is where you'll find most of the action, including the majority of good places to eat. You'll find some ethnic options as well, including a wonderful French restaurant, a good number of Italian places, and two decent Japanese spots. Naturally, pizza shops abound.

AMERICAN

DOUBLE WIDE GRILL $$

Something of a themed restaurant that exists inside a heavily retrofitted old gas station, the Double Wide Grill does a beautiful job of paying homage to midcentury American car culture. Aside from an actual pickup truck suspended above the bar, a wonderful collection of auto-industry detritus hangs from nearly every surface. The menu features barbecue, pub-grub style food, and plenty of vegetarian and vegan options, with items such as the Hubcap Fries, Death Row Delmonico, and Build Your Own TV Dinner. The food, while certainly not Pittsburgh's finest, is generally of above-average quality.

MAP 3: 2339 E. Carson St., 412/390-1111, www.doublewidegrill.com; daily 11am-2am

FAT HEAD'S SALOON $$

Fat Head's is easily one of the South Side's best bar and grill joints, although it's more popularly known as a premiere East Carson locale in which to get good and tanked. Clearly, that has much to do with the three dozen or so imports and craft brews on tap, but pick up a menu between pints and you'll find that Fat Head's has much more than just alcohol on offer: in short, a pub-grub-on-steroids menu featuring mostly burgers, sandwiches, and the massive (and massively popular) "headwiches." Diners watching their waistlines, in other words, will want to proceed to Fat Head's with extreme prejudice.

MAP 3: 1805 E. Carson St., 412/431-7433, www.fatheads.com; Mon.-Thurs. 11am-midnight, Fri.-Sat. 11am-1am, Sun. 11am-11pm

GRAND CONCOURSE $$$

Located in the concourse of the old P&LE Railway station, and with seating for 500, the Grand Concourse is quite accurately known as one of Pittsburgh's most elegant and stately places in which to dine, complete with fully refurbished Edwardian-era architectural trimmings. It's also the largest restaurant in the city. The somewhat timid menu is largely seafood based; typical entrées include lobster ravioli, coconut shrimp, and Maryland crab cakes. For a slightly more informal experience, ask to be seated in the Gandy Dancer Bar, where oysters and clams can be ordered alongside old-style cocktails. Sunday brunch is quite an occasion, though more casual than evening dinner hours, and is popular during special occasions such as Mother's Day.

MAP 3: 100 W. Station Square Dr., 412/261-1717, www.muer.com; Mon.-Sat. 11am-10pm (Fri.-Sat. until 11pm), Sun. brunch 10am-3pm

THE ZENITH $$

A vegetarian café, an art gallery, and an antiques shop, all underneath the same roof? Believe it. The Zenith—formerly known as the Zenith Tea Room—is renowned locally for its $10 prix fixe Sunday brunch, where diners help themselves to an astounding spread of pastas, cakes, and breakfast-style entrées. But the weekly menu is equally interesting, consisting of creatively prepared casseroles, stews, and meat-free sandwiches. After your meal, stroll through Zenith's eclectic assortment of collectibles and vintage clothing. And definitely don't miss the restrooms, which are some of the most amusingly decorated in the city.

MAP 3: 86 S. 26th St., 412/481-4833, www.zenithpgh.com; Thurs.-Sat. 11:30am-8:30pm, Sun. brunch 11am-2:30pm

ASIAN

CAMBOD-ICAN KITCHEN $

Originally a legendary street food cart that fed the hungry bar-hopping masses of East Carson Street until the wee hours of most mornings, Cambod-ican Kitchen—now reinvented as a sit-down restaurant—has returned to Pittsburgh after a nearly three-year hiatus. Cambod-ican purists need not fret, however—the original "Cat on a Stick" (chicken shish kebab) is still for sale. So too is a wonderfully adventurous menu of fried noodles and wontons, curry rolls and fresh spring rolls, and a sampler platter big enough to share with one or two friends.

MAP 3: 1701 E. Carson St., 412/381-6199, www.cambodicankitchen.com; Tues.-Sat. 5pm-5am

NAKAMA JAPANESE STEAK HOUSE $$$

Depending on where you sit and what you order at the 200-seat, uber-trendy Nakama, a culinary experience here can become just about anything you'd like. Large groups and parties, for instance, flock to the smokeless hibachi tables for filet mignon and hibachi scallops, while late-night arrivals and the happy hour crowd gather around the massive island bar for carafes of sake and pints of Japanese beer. Arriving solo? Try sidling up to the sushi bar, which features a comprehensive menu of sashimi and veggie-based rolls alongside the usual standards.

MAP 3: 1611 E. Carson St., 412/381-6000, www.eatatnakama.com; Mon.-Sat. 11am-1am, Sun. 1pm-9pm

CAFÉS

BEEHIVE COFFEEHOUSE $

One of Pittsburgh's most iconoclastic locales in which to sip organic coffee while discussing Sartre and Nietzsche, the Beehive has been many different things to many different angst-ridden teens since its

clockwise from top left: Nakama Japanese Steak House; Grand Concourse; Cambod-ican Kitchen

opening in 1991. What it remains, however, is a pleasantly comfortable place to immerse one's self in the city's bohemian subculture. The Beehive's interior decor vibe is strictly thrift store—think mismatched furniture and kitschy wall murals. It also offers pinball, wireless access, used paperbacks in the vending machine, and the best-pierced baristas in Pittsburgh. In other words, the spirit of the South Side under one roof.

MAP 3: 1327 E. Carson St., 412/488-4483, www.beehivebuzz.com; Mon.-Thurs. 9am-1am, Fri.-Sun. 9am-2am

BIG DOG COFFEE $

Looking for a quiet South Side café that's a sort of locals-only spot, and a bit off the beaten East Carson Street path? You could certainly do worse than Big Dog Coffee, which is tightly tucked into a residential area but still within easy walking distance of the SouthSide Works shopping center. Owned by a Bulgarian violinist and his bassoonist wife, Big Dog sits in a restored, century-old former bakery, where it serves popular desserts and an unusual lunch menu that includes oatmeal, soups, sandwiches, cookies, and gelato. Coffee snobs take note: Big Dog serves Intelligentsia.

MAP 3: 2717 Sarah St., 412/586-7306, www.bigdogcoffee.net; Mon.-Fri. 6am-10pm, Sat.-Sun. 7:30am-10pm

CONTEMPORARY AND NEW AMERICAN

CAFE DU JOUR $$

With the ambience of an intimate European bistro, the flavor of Cafe du Jour has lately been tweaked by its two new owners—both of them young chefs who've introduced to the menu an impressive array of inventive Californian cuisine. This may not sound like much, but in a city where contemporary dining always seems to revolve around dishes from the old country, Cafe du Jour stands out in spades. And don't be afraid to let the servers guide your choices, as some are wont to do; after all, everything from the portobello soup to the cheese plates to the *cassoulet* (French stew) is simply stunning. If the weather's right, you'll want to make reservations for a patio seat. Credit cards are not accepted, so come prepared with cash.

MAP 3: 1107 E. Carson St., 412/488-9695; Tues.-Sat. 5pm-10pm

DISH $$$

Popularly known as one of Pittsburgh's best choices for a first date, Dish is actually a bar that just happens to serve some of the best-prepared small plates and soups on the South Side. Pasta, meat, and fresh fish dishes—as well as a long list of wonderfully sinful desserts—are also on offer. But for many, the real draw at Dish is its ambience: Lights are always turned down low, and the small tables and considerable lack of elbow room tend to make for a rather cozy dining or drinking experience. Fair warning: Reservations are recommended during the always-busy weekends. No credit cards are accepted.

MAP 3: 128 S. 17th St., 412/390-2012, www.dishosteria.com; Mon.-Sat. 5pm-2am

FRENCH

BRIDGE TEN BRASSERIE $$$

Pittsburgh doesn't have many truly authentic French restaurants, but Bridge Ten Brasserie is certainly one of them. As a professional travel writer, owner Dave DeSimone fell in love with French cuisine and the traditional, unpretentious restaurants it was served in. He filled a much-needed niche in the local restaurant scene by bringing a real French dining experience to the South Side. The décor is simple, and the food, of course is the real draw. The coq au vin and steak au poivre are menu standouts, but if you're with a group, do try to order as many dishes as you can, and then share. Save room for dessert, as there's usually a *tarte du jour.* Travelers will appreciate its proximity to the nearby Holiday Inn Express.

MAP 3: 20 S. 10th St., 412/586-5033, www.bridgeten.com; Mon.-Fri. 4:30pm-10pm, Sat. 11:30am-11pm, Sun. brunch 11am-2:30pm

GERMAN

HOFBRÄUHAUS PITTSBURGH $$

It's designed to resemble a centuries-old Munich beer hall of the very same name, and perhaps the most surprising thing about Hofbräuhaus is that, despite its location in the SouthSide Works shopping center, a sense of authenticity actually does shine through. There are long tables in the main hall where you can dine, European-style, with perfect strangers. Beer brewed on the premises adheres strictly to the Bavarian beer purity law. And there's also an abundance of live music, as well as an incredibly hearty (and seriously caloric) menu of bona fide Bavarian delicacies. A decidedly less adventurous selection of burgers, sandwiches, and salads is also available. And if you show up after dark, don't forget to visit the outdoor beer garden, with its fantastic view of the Monongahela River.

MAP 3: 2705 S. Water St., 412/224-2328, www.hofbrauhauspittsburgh.com; Mon.-Wed. 11am-midnight, Thurs. 11am-1am, Fri.-Sat. 11am-2am, Sun. noon-midnight

ITALIAN

PIZZA SOLA $

Formerly known as Pizza Vesuvio, Pizza Sola has managed to make a serious name for itself in Pittsburgh on the basis of one solitary gimmick that actually works: It approaches its pie-making as an actual craft. New York City-style thin-crust slices—the type you fold in half lengthwise and eat on the go—are what's on offer. Even better, the young employees behind the counter take their tradition seriously, tossing every pizza by hand with dough that's made fresh daily. The shop has recently added sandwiches, wings, salads, and desserts to its once-limited menu. Other locations are in Oakland (114 Atwood St., 412/681-7652) and East Liberty (6004 Penn Circle S., 412/363-7652).

MAP 3: 1417 E. Carson St., 412/481-3888, www.pizzasola.com; Mon.-Wed. 11:30am-midnight, Thurs.-Sat. 11:30am-3am, Sun. 12:30pm-midnight

MEXICAN

★ YO RITA $$

Operated by one of the city's most in-demand celebrity chefs, Kevin Sousa, Yo Rita almost instantly became a must-visit destination among local foodies when it opened in the former location of the Iguana Grill. The upscale menu offerings, which essentially consist of the most inventive and inspired collection of tacos this side of the Alleghenies, might best be thought of as Mexican-American fusion. Think root vegetable with quail egg, pork belly with sour cherries, or flank steak with red onion jam. High-end culinary experimentation is the order of the day, in other words. So if nachos or bean burritos are what you're after, keep looking.

MAP 3: 1120 E. Carson St., 412/904-3557, www.yoritasouthside.com; Mon.-Thurs. 4pm-10pm, Fri.-Sat. 4pm-11pm

SNACKS AND DESSERTS

THE MILK SHAKE FACTORY $

While this author admittedly has something of a mild ice cream addiction, just about everyone loves the old-fashioned, hand-spun milkshakes at this South Side gem. The Milk Shake Factory is something of a candy shop and ice cream shop all in one, so you might as well plan to indulge, picking up some chocolates from Edward Marc Chocolatier while you're there. Fifty-five smooth and creamy ice cream flavors await, along with the best chocolate confections in town.

MAP 3: 1705 E. Carson St., 412/488-1808, www.themilkshakefactory.com; Mon.-Sat. 10am-10pm, Sun. 11am-9pm

SPANISH

IBIZA TAPAS AND WINE BAR $$

Owned and operated by local restaurateur Antonio Pereira, who is also responsible for next-door's Spanish-themed restaurant Mallorca, Ibiza boasts 45 small plates—some hot and some cold—from both continental Europe and South America. Style and creativity are in full force, so be prepared to encounter an exceptional menu. Beef carpaccio, tuna tartare, and stuffed banana peppers with veal are just a few of the many offerings. Particularly obsessive foodies might consider requesting a table with a kitchen view, where the chefs toil on full display.

MAP 3: 2224 E. Carson St., 412/325-2227, www.ibizatapasrestaurant.com; Mon.-Thurs. 4pm-2am, Fri.-Sat. 4pm-1am

MALLORCA $$$

A traditional Spanish restaurant in the finest white-tablecloth style, Mallorca offers a premiere dining experience that is simply unequaled elsewhere in the city. Families and young couples on dates crowd the gated outdoor terrace or the often-packed dining room to gorge on Spanish- and Mediterranean-style seafood dishes or the exotic house specialties: roast suckling pig, say, or even goat. And just as they would in an actual Iberian eatery, diners often find themselves lingering to nosh, sample, and sip for hours. Not feeling particularly adventurous? Stick with the paella, for which Mallorca is justly famous.

MAP 3: 2228 E. Carson St., 412/488-1818, www.mallorcarestaurant.com; Mon.-Thurs. 11:30am-10:30pm, Fri.-Sat. 11:30am-11:30pm, Sun. noon-10pm

Mount Washington

Map 3

Although it once housed a station on the Underground Railroad and today houses families of turkey and deer, even to most locals Mount Washington is best known for only three things: the jaw-dropping view afforded from its Grandview Avenue, which stretches the length of its cliffside; the two inclines that traverse the side of the cliff to deliver you there; and Restaurant Row, the small collection of exceedingly romantic cafés and eateries where a plate of veal Lafayette and glass of pinot noir come complete with one of North America's most gorgeous urban views.

Technically, Restaurant Row is in the small neighborhood of Duquesne Heights, and if you reach Grandview Avenue by way of the Monongahela Incline, which sits directly across the street from Station Square, you'll have quite a hike if you intend to walk to a restaurant—it's approximately one mile. The Duquesne Incline, on the other hand, sits adjacent to the restaurants, but to reach it on foot from Station Square you'll need to walk past the Gateway Clipper Fleet, continue on through the parking lot, and then follow the footpath along the Monongahela River until you see the incline on your left. If you're not sure exactly where you're going, taking a taxi from your hotel would probably be your wisest choice.

It's important to note, however, that as Pittsburgh's fine-dining scene has slowly grown and improved over the years, the reputation of Mount Washington's eateries has declined. Which isn't to say that the food offered is necessarily poor, but rather, that it's significantly overpriced given its quality. In other words, if extraordinary food is what you're after, you can do much better elsewhere.

AMERICAN

GRANDVIEW SALOON & COAL HILL STEAKHOUSE $$

It's easy to understand why the Grandview Saloon's two dining levels—as well as its two outdoor patios—are consistently packed with tourists and locals: The view afforded from either deck is just as stunning and romantic as any other you'll find along Restaurant Row, and yet the prices are a bit lower because the atmosphere is more casual. The Grandview Saloon, in fact, is much more of a bistro than a fine-dining spot, a fact that the menu clearly reflects. Sandwiches, wraps, chicken salads, burgers, and hoagies are all available, although USDA prime steaks are as well. And if you're primarily interested in drinking, head to the restaurant's lower level, where you'll find a small horseshoe-shaped bar.

MAP 3: 1212 Grandview Ave., 412/431-1400, www.thegrandviewsaloon.com; daily 11:30am-10pm

LEMONT RESTAURANT $$$

The LeMont is a five-star locale offering traditional American cuisine, including seafood and old-school meat entrées. (The two house specialties, for instance, are steak Diane and chateaubriand.) And despite its hopelessly out-of-date decor, LeMont also continues to be something of a hit for wedding receptions and business meetings. Dessert selections are appropriately filling and rich. For men, a coat and tie are required. This is a reservation-only venue.

MAP 3: 1114 Grandview Ave., 412/431-3100, www.lemontpittsburgh.com; Mon.-Sat. 5pm-11pm, Sun. 10am-11pm

MONTEREY BAY FISH GROTTO $$$

Inside a high-rise building at the far western end of Grandview Avenue, the Monterey Bay Fish Grotto offers an award-winning selection of fresh fish, flown in daily and served in a visually striking glass-enclosed dining room. The setting is truly remarkable; every table has a phenomenal view of The Point. The steaks and seafood will definitely set you back, but this is one of the few Mount Washington restaurants that have kept up with quality and service. There's simply no debating the fact that your experience is certain to be unique and memorable. Various private banquet spaces can accommodate parties as small as 20 or as large as 100. And for a gathering that truly impresses, a private wine room with a 24-person capacity and a four-course prix fixe fish dinner can be reserved.

MAP 3: 1411 Grandview Ave., 412/481-4414, www.montereybayfishgrotto.com; lunch Mon.-Fri. 11am-3pm, dinner Mon.-Thurs. 5pm-10pm, Fri.-Sat. 5pm-11pm, Sun. 5pm-9pm

TIN ANGEL $$$

Tin Angel has long been a hit with tourists and locals, and it certainly didn't hurt business when President Bill Clinton and Prime Minister John Major dined here back in 1994. The American and Greek cuisine includes Black Forest filet mignon and stuffed grape leaves. You can expect the food quality and the Downtown city view to be on essentially the same level as at the row's other restaurants: Gazing out the window is almost guaranteed to be awe-inspiring, while your meal will likely be decent enough, but far too expensive.

MAP 3: 1200 Grandview Ave., 412/381-1919, www.tinangelpittsburgh.com; Tues.-Sat. 5:30pm-10pm

Shadyside

Map 4

The upscale shopping neighborhood of Shadyside has two main drags—Walnut Street and Ellsworth Avenue—and both are home to a wonderful mixture of pubs, cafés, high-end eateries, and ethnic restaurants. Strolling the length of either street doesn't take long, although I've saved you some of the trouble by listing some of the better options.

AMERICAN

HARRIS GRILL $$

Something of a contemporary American lounge with a sense of humor, Harris Grill manages to play different roles for different diners. The first floor has a standard pub feel, while the second floor (The Walnut Grill) is elegant, and even romantic, with dim lighting and a subtle Mediterranean theme. But take a look at the menu: Brittney Spears (chicken tenders), Jamaican Tacos Tonight (pulled jerk chicken tacos), Sammiches (Pittsburghese for sandwiches), and Scooter's Mom's Black Bottom (a giant chocolate cupcake stuffed with chocolate cream cheese icing and topped with a raspberry drizzle) are highlights. Harris Grill offers a great icebreaker atmosphere for first dates, but it's also fun with a big group of friends.

MAP 4: 5747 Ellsworth Ave., 412/362-5273, www.harrisgrill.com; Mon.-Sat. 11:30am-2pm, Sun. 10am-2pm

ASIAN

SOBA $$$

For exquisitely crafted pan-Asian cuisine and a moderately formal ambience, look no further. Soba consists of two full floors, with a dining room and a well-tended bar on each; half of Soba's patrons on any given night are there for the dry martinis and the schmoozing. Starry-eyed lovers and local pseudo-celebrities can be seen digging into vegetable samosas and lemongrass strip steak. A relatively recent facelift modernized and brightened the place up quite a bit. Wander up to the third floor and you'll find Umi, a fantastic Japanese restaurant also affiliated with the Big Burrito Group.

MAP 4: 5847 Ellsworth Ave., 412/362-5656, www.sobapa.com; Sun.-Thurs. 5pm-10pm, Fri.-Sat. 5pm-11pm

THAI PLACE CAFÉ $$

Lauded as one of the country's top Thai restaurants, Thai Place is conveniently situated in the heart of Shadyside's shopping district. That isn't to suggest that its ambience is anything special, which it most definitely is not. But for a flawless meal after a Saturday or Sunday of serious pavement pounding, it hits the spot perfectly. Pad thai, of course, is popular, but the more adventurous should consider the deep-fried squid, or even the boneless crispy duck. Thai curries are also especially mouthwatering. Other locations can be found in Wexford (12009 Perry Hwy., 724/935-8866) and Fox Chapel (1034 Freeport Rd., 412/784-8980).

MAP 4: 5528 Walnut St., 412/687-8586, www.thaiplacepgh.com; Mon.-Thurs. 11am-10pm, Fri.-Sat. 11am-11pm, Sun. noon-9:30pm

UMI $$$

On Soba's top floor but with its own separate entrance, Umi is probably Pittsburgh's most style-conscious Japanese eatery. The sushi and sashimi, prepared with high precision by a true *shokunin* (a master sushi chef), will set you back around $3 a piece. Not a terrible price to pay, considering that executive chef Mr. Shu is one of the city's top sushi celebrities. (Another is Chaya's Fumio Yasuzawa.) Fish-free dishes include teriyaki, miso soups, and even an octopus salad.

MAP 4: 5849 Ellsworth Ave., 412/362-6198, www.bigburrito.com/umi; Tues.-Thurs. 5pm-9:30pm, Fri.-Sat. 5pm-10:30pm

CAFÉS

★ CRAZY MOCHA $

Another branch of the ever-growing Crazy Mocha chain, now with more than two dozen separate locations, this café retains a slightly rarified air and something of a neighborhood feel as well, due to its choice location on Ellsworth Avenue. Menu items are just what you'd expect: A full range of coffee and espresso drinks, with sandwiches and cheesecakes behind the counter. But even regular ol' coffee drinkers get their orders delivered straight to the table—an interesting concept in the too-often discourteous world of independent cafés.

MAP 4: 5830 Ellsworth Ave., 412/441-9344, www.crazymocha.com; Mon.-Thurs. 7:30am-midnight, Fri. 7:30am-1am, Sat. 8am-1am, Sun. 9am-midnight

★ EDEN $

A tiny little restaurant and juice bar focusing on light and heart-healthy foods, Eden is one of the city's few eateries offering a predominantly raw-food menu. And while Eden resembles nothing so much as a pint-sized smoothie bar, you can expect to find all the healthy lifestyle standards, including sandwiches, wraps, garden salads, freshly squeezed juices, and, of course, smoothies. Many ingredients are locally sourced. Both vegetarian and non-veggie options are available, and brunch menu items such as waffles and breakfast burritos are served daily. Foodies won't appreciate the place much, but it's a great spot to grab a bite after your Pilates workout or spinning class.

MAP 4: 735 Copeland St., 412/802-7070, www.edenpitt.com; Mon. and Wed.-Fri. 5pm-10pm, Sat. 10am-2pm and 5pm-10pm, Sun. 10am-2pm

CONTEMPORARY AND NEW AMERICAN

CAFE ZINHO $$

The same crew responsible for the legendary but now shuttered Baum Vivant (as well as the Cultural District's recently closed Café Zao) operates this bistro-style eatery—an actual garage in a residential neighborhood that's been transformed into something of a culinary hipster's haven. The decor at Cafe Zinho is strictly thrift-store chic, complete with mismatched furniture and ironically bad art. But entrées and even desserts are strictly first-class, and artfully built: Think gourmet dishes complete with lamb, mussels, and even wild game. The veggie rice bowls and remarkably constructed salads regularly earn approving clucks from discriminating foodies as well.

MAP 4: 238 Spahr St., 412/363-1500; Mon.-Thurs. 5:30pm-10pm, Fri.-Sat. 5:30pm-11pm, Sun. 5:30pm-9pm

MEDITERRANEAN

CASBAH $$$

Offering certainly one of the city's most satisfying culinary adventures, Casbah is tough to miss: It's the tan stucco block built to resemble a Moroccan mosque. Expect a wide spread of Mediterranean and North African cuisine that's simply unmatched elsewhere in Pittsburgh, and be prepared to expand your version of the exotic while dining; a typical menu might offer Elysian Fields lamb with red wine jus, roasted duck broth soup, and Prince Edward Island mussels. The menu, which changes daily, is seasonally based and features fresh food from area farms. Wine lovers will find themselves pleased; the cellar is considered one of Shadyside's most selective.

MAP 4: 229 S. Highland Ave., 412/661-5656, www.bigburrito.com/casbah; Mon.-Sat. 11:30am-2:30pm and 5pm-10pm, Sun. 11am-2pm (brunch) and 5pm-9pm

PERUVIAN

LA FERIA $$$

As befits its fairly obscure culinary status (a Peruvian restaurant in *Pittsburgh?*), La Feria isn't the easiest eatery to find. First, walk into the lobby of Pamela's Diner, then head up the stairs. You'll find yourself in a Latin craft shop, but an interesting selection of Peruvian sandwiches, salads, and entrées can be ordered at the counter; a few tables are available for in-house dining. Specials change daily; regular standbys include empanadas (stuffed pastries), *pudin de pan* (traditional bread pudding dessert), and Peruvian coffee.

MAP 4: 5527 Walnut St., 2nd Fl., 412/682-4501, www.laferia.net; Mon.-Sat. 11am-10pm

SNACKS AND DESSERTS

OH YEAH! $

Oh Yeah! is a hardcore ice cream fiend's dream come true. Complete with an oversized ice cream scooper acting as a door handle, this creatively outfitted café serves up a wild menu of mix-ins and flavor combinations. Both vegan and sugar-free ice creams are available, as are more than 100 seriously unusual add-ins, including hemp protein and habanero pepper powder. The fact that the organic cream comes from Amish grass-fed cows takes some of the guilt out of this guilty pleasure. Libertarians will be pleased to learn that bitcoins are accepted as legal tender.

MAP 4: 232 S. Highland Ave., 412/200-5574, www.theohyeah.com; Mon.-Thurs. 7am-10pm, Fri. 7am-11pm, Sat. 8am-11pm, Sun. 8am-10pm

Squirrel Hill and Point Breeze

Map 5

One of the largest Jewish neighborhoods on the East Coast, Squirrel Hill is home to a number of kosher eateries. But walk the length of the neighborhood's perpendicular main drags, Murray and Forbes Avenues, and you'll discover just about everything else,

clockwise from top left: the ice cream scooper door handles at Oh Yeah!; Eden; Crazy Mocha in Shadyside

from a Korean bubble tea shop to one of the best bagel bakeries in Pittsburgh.

Point Breeze is largely a residential area where few restaurants are located. Self-caterers interested in healthy eating—but looking for a change of pace from Whole Foods—should check out the neighborhood's **East End Food Co-op** (7516 Meade St., 412/242-3598, www.eastendfoodcoop.com).

Located on the opposite side of Frick Park from Squirrel Hill, Regent Square's main drag exists along South Braddock Avenue, which can be covered from one end to the other on foot in about five minutes.

AMERICAN

D'S SIX-PAX AND DOGS $$

A perennial Regent Square favorite, D's Six-Pax and Dogs has possibly the biggest and most diverse selection of imported and microbrewed beer for sale in the city (more than 1,000 options). Particularly amusing is the walk-in cooler, where customers can browse the selection and pick their very own out-of-town six-pack. Hot dogs are exceedingly delicious as well—they aren't quite gourmet but they're close, and the list of free toppings is seemingly endless. It's a perfect choice when you're not up for greasy bar food but not hungry enough for a full meal. Veggie dogs are available.

MAP 5: 1118 S. Braddock Ave., 412/241-4666, www.ds6pax.com; Sun.-Wed. 11am-11pm, Thurs.-Sat. 11am-midnight

THE MAP ROOM $$

Operated by a British expat who has chosen to cover the walls of her cozy and smallish tavern with antique maps of the Old World, the Map Room is essentially an upscale pub where the bar food is decidedly more adventurous and of a slightly higher quality than you're likely to come across in most Pittsburgh pubs. Grilled chicken entrées, chowder soup, mussels, and bread pudding are the sorts of delights you'll find here. In other words, comfort food of a sort that perfectly accompanies a pint or two of Guinness, or maybe a cup of hot tea during yet another drizzly Steel City day.

MAP 5: 1126 S. Braddock Ave., 412/371-1955, www.beesharp.com/MAPROOM; daily 3pm-2am

SQUARE CAFÉ $

One of the neighborhood's most popular early-morning eateries, the Square Café acts as a fairly standard neighborhood diner during its daily breakfast and lunch service. Breakfast fare includes tofu scrambles, breakfast quesadillas, French toast with challah bread, and granola, while lunch service is standard American fare (meat and pasta dishes mostly) with a light fusion twist. Soups, salads, sandwiches, and wraps are also served, as is a fairly standard kids' menu featuring PB&J, macaroni and cheese, and chicken fingers.

MAP 5: 1137 S. Braddock Ave., 412/244-8002, www.square-cafe.com; Mon.-Sat. 7am-3pm, Sun. 8am-3pm

ASIAN

CHAYA JAPANESE CUISINE $$

As a general culinary rule of thumb, a Japanese restaurant filled with actual Japanese diners is usually a sign that you've found the real deal. Chaya, which boasts one of Pittsburgh's two best sushi chefs (Fumio Yasuzawa), operates under a similar assumption: Apparently, this is where the city's Japanese community congregates when they're feeling homesick. So what's all the fuss about? For starters, very few restaurants in town make their own wasabi in-house. And what's more, fresh fish for sushi and sashimi is flown in chilled—not frozen—from Japan or New York. The remainder of the menu features a baffling assortment of traditional seafood goodies that aren't easily found on American shores.

MAP 5: 2104 Murray Ave., 412/422-2082, www.chayausa.com; Mon.-Thurs. 5pm-9:30pm, Fri.-Sat. 5pm-9:45pm

CURRY ON MURRAY $$

Pittsburgh's East End is relatively rich in Thai dining options, but in Squirrel Hill, Curry on Murray is generally a can't-miss choice. As its name suggests, curries are the go-to menu item; but the various noodle dishes are also popular. Fair warning to those who aren't accustomed to authentic Thai food: This stuff is *spicy.* If you can't handle the heat, be sure to let your server know. It's not available year-round, but try to grab some of the shop's coconut ice cream if you've arrived during the summer months.

MAP 5: 2121 Murray Ave, 412/422-3120; Mon.-Wed. 4pm-9:30pm, Thurs. 11am-9pm, Fri. 11am-10pm, Sat. noon-10pm, Sun. noon-8:30pm

GREEN PEPPER $$

A self-described contemporary Korean lounge and bistro, Green Pepper is owned and operated by a husband-and-wife team who had no previous business experience to speak of. And yet due their obsession with fresh, locally-sourced ingredients and unfailingly polite customer service, this small eatery has caught on in a big way. If you've come for dinner, try the traditional Korean *bibimbap,* a massive bowl of rice topped with veggies, sliced meat, and a fried egg. And as it happens, Green Pepper is also home to Squirrel Hill's most amusing karaoke bar, where the singing and merrymaking continues long after the kitchen closes.

MAP 5: 2020 Murray Ave, 412/422-2277, www.greenpepperpgh.com; Mon. and Wed.-Sun. 11:30am-2pm and 5pm-10pm

CAFÉS

MAKE YOUR MARK ARTSPACE & COFFEEHOUSE $

Just as popular for its vegetarian-friendly light lunches (panini, quesadillas, and soups) as for its artistically prepared selection of fair trade and organic La Prima coffees, Make Your Mark has done just that in the formerly unremarkable Point Breeze business district, which is slowly becoming something of a dining and leisure destination. As the café's name suggests, patrons can leave their own mark on a wall covered in stainless steel sheets and magnets; other amenities include free Wi-Fi, a leafy backyard patio, and a truly tempting selection of cookies and desserts.

MAP 5: 6736 Reynolds St., 412/365-2117; Mon., Wed., and Thurs. 7am-7pm; Tues., Fri., and Sat. 7am-10pm

61C CAFÉ $

Looking for Squirrel Hill's hipster contingent? Chances are good that at least half of them are lounging at the 61C Café this very moment, hunched over laptops or people-watching on the outdoor patio. To reach the café from Oakland or Downtown, just hop on the 61C, its namesake bus. And once you're here, feel free to indulge your most obscure espresso drink desire; the majority of the 61C baristas are proud professionals. Pastries and teas are also on offer, and the wireless access is free to all.

A new location known as the **61B Café** (1108 S. Braddock Ave., 412/521-6161) recently opened in Regent Square; you can probably guess which public bus will take you there.

MAP 5: 1839 Murray Ave., 412/521-6161, www.61ccafe.com; Mon.-Thurs. 8am-11pm, Fri. 7am-midnight, Sat. 8am-midnight, Sun. 8am-11pm

CONTEMPORARY AND NEW AMERICAN

POINT BRUGGE CAFÉ $$

Located in the same spot as the city's historical Point Restaurant, Point Brugge Café was designed to feel and operate like a familiar neighborhood gathering spot. The atmosphere itself is a pleasant cross between traditional European sophistication and the laid-back vibe of the West Coast, while the dishes—Asian fusion and contemporary American, mostly—strike a balance between comfort food and modern decadence. As an added bonus, Belgian beers can often be found on tap. Reservations are recommended.

Also worth a visit is the café's sister restaurant in Highland Park, the appropriately named **Park Bruges** (5801 Bryant St., 412/661-3334, www.parkbruges.com), which offers an upscale twist on poutine and serves the city's best Liege waffles and eggs Benedict during brunch.

MAP 5: 401 Hastings St., 412/441-3334, www.pointbrugge.com; Tues.-Thurs. 11am-10pm, Fri.-Sat. 11am-11pm, Sun. 11am-9pm

ROOT 174 $$

One of beloved local chef Keith Fuller's newer culinary endeavors can be found right in the heart of Regent Square, and frankly, the location and neighborhood fit the cuisine quite perfectly. There are a lot of familiar dishes, like roast chicken, on the menu, but they all have unique and contemporary twists. This is one of the few edgier contemporary restaurants in town. Vegetarian options like vegan meatballs may even tempt a carnivore. The food is local and fresh, and the menu changes seasonally. If you have a chance, try Root's "Sunday Funday" on the third Sunday of each month; it's a five-course meal that Fuller puts together "off-the-cuff" for just $35, and it's served family-style, with the staff and customers eating together.

MAP 5: 1113 S. Braddock Ave., 412/243-4348, www.root174.com; Tues.-Thurs. 11am-10pm, Fri.-Sat. 11am-11pm, Sun. 11am-9pm

ITALIAN

MINEO'S $

Claiming to be any city's best pizza joint can be a controversial undertaking, but the family-owned Mineo's has the awards to prove it—dozens of them, from nearly every Pittsburgh publication—lining the walls of their no-frills cafeteria-style shop. It's tough to put a finger on exactly why the pies and slices are so delectable. It could be the generous piling on of cheese. Or maybe the always-fresh ingredients. Might be the sauces and toppings, both of which Mineo's steadfastly refuses to skimp on. And if you absolutely can't stop by during your time here, they'll happily overnight a pie anywhere in the United States.

MAP 5: 2128 Murray Ave., 412/521-9864, www.mineospizza.com; Sun.-Thurs. 11am-1am, Fri.-Sat. 11am-2am

MEDITERRANEAN

ALADDIN'S EATERY $$

Yet another ethnic restaurant in Squirrel Hill with a focus on healthy, natural foods, Aladdin's Eatery is now a chain with more than a dozen locations throughout Pennsylvania, Ohio, and Illinois. The vibe couldn't possibly be more independent and homegrown, however: The waitstaff is consistently friendly and helpful, the dining room is strictly smoke-free, and the owners even donate a bit of the profits to local charities. So, how about the food? Even better. The Middle Eastern and Mediterranean dishes can be made vegetarian or with meat; house specialties include a phenomenal hummus shawarma with pita and a *mujadara* plate (steamed lentils and rice with toasted onions).

MAP 5: 5878 Forbes Ave., 412/421-5100, www.aladdinseatery.com; Mon.-Thurs. 11am-10:30pm, Fri.-Sat. 11am-11:30pm, Sun. 11am-10pm

SNACKS AND DESSERTS

COOL ICE TAIPEI $$

If you're familiar with the explosively popular new culinary trend known as Taiwanese snow ice, you'll understand just how incredibly lucky Pittsburghers are to have Cool Ice Taipei at their disposal. *Xue hua bing,* as it's properly referred to, is a delightfully smooth and delicately ruffled dessert described as something of a cross between ice cream and the traditional shaved-ice snow cone known to every American child. It's not yet easy to find in the U.S., much less the Mid-Atlantic. The Taiwanese and Asian entrées and other items, including everything from Korean kimchi and fried squid balls to steamed pork dumplings and fresh fruit juices, are certainly passable, but the snow ice is the main attraction.

MAP 5: 5813 Forbes Ave, 412/521-8989, www.coolicetaipeipitt.com; Tues. 1pm-9pm, Wed.-Thurs. noon-9pm, Fri.-Sat. noon-10pm, Sun. noon-8:30pm

VANILLA PASTRY STUDIO $

Owned and operated by a former Pennsylvania Culinary Academy instructor of the Pastry Arts (seriously!), Vanilla Pastry Studio is something of a fantasy land for grown-ups with a serious sweet tooth. Offerings include everything from artistic wedding cakes to muffins, loaf breads, gourmet cookies, and cupcakes that more than a few locals claim are superior to those sold by the much-loved Dozen Bake Shop chain. This clean and modern shop also handles unique requests for weddings and special events; if there's an unusual sugary creation you'd like to commission, there's a good chance Vanilla Pastry can bring it to life.

MAP 5: 1130 S. Braddock Ave., 412/242-9820, www.vanillapastry.com; Tues.-Fri. 9am-6pm, Sat. 9am-4pm, Sun. 9am-3pm

WAFFALONIA $

With two locations in Pittsburgh (the other is a food kiosk in Oakland's Schenley Plaza), Waffalonia is a fun little eatery that'll satisfy even the sweetest sweet tooth. The made-from-scratch and freshly ironed authentic Belgian waffles can be topped with the ice creams, spreads, fruits, and other confections of your choosing. The strawberry, banana, and Nutella waffle is a healthier alternative, but if you want to get the full Waffalonia experience, you'll want to pick a flavor of Dave and Andy's ice cream. The menu, updated daily, is styled to look like an old-fashioned Eurorail departure board.

MAP 5: 1707 Murray Ave., 412/521-4902, www.waffalonia.com; Mon.-Thurs. 11am-10pm, Fri. 11am-11pm, Sat. 9am-11pm, Sun. 9am-10pm

Feasting at the Food Trucks

As any self-respecting foodie is certainly well aware, the food truck trend has seen a hugely popular revival in recent years throughout many major U.S. cities. Pittsburgh, as it happens, is no exception.

Dozens of entrepreneurial vendors have come and gone here over the past five years or so. And despite having to battle some of the most ridiculous rules and regulations (having to park in metered spots; only being able to buy permits in January; having to leave most locations after 30 minutes), many mobile food hawkers in Pittsburgh—just as in cities like Portland, San Francisco, Philadelphia, and New York—serve some of the most creatively unusual cuisine in the city. Fortunately, local vendors have banded together in an attempt to revise these small-town regulations; visit the website of the **Pittsburgh Mobile Food Coalition** (www.pghmobilefood.com) for the latest developments.

Bear in mind that quite unlike the dingy old food trucks of decade's past, many of today's mobile vendors are young, creative, and incredibly talented chefs, some of them serving up dishes superior to those you'll find in even the most popular East End bistros. Then again, some of the trucks are in fact mobile satellites of popular neighborhood eateries. And more than a few of the city's food truck pioneers have since gone on to open their own brick-and-mortar locations, thanks to the success of their savvy mobile enterprises.

Improved regulations or not, there's no arguing that the renewed food truck renaissance is here to stay. Most trucks update their menus and location schedules daily via Twitter and Facebook. And in Pittsburgh, you'll often see entire fleets parked near popular community events and festivals. Here's a brief list of some of the city's tastiest travelers.

- As the 2013 winner of the "Mobile Food" category in *Pittsburgh* magazine's annual Reader's Poll, **PGH Taco Truck** (www.pghtacotruck.com, @PghTacoTruck) easily serves up the freshest Mexican street food in town. They use local and organic ingredients and offer vegan and gluten-free options.
- **Oh My Grill** (www.ohmygrill.com, @OhMyGrill) offers (what else?) seriously toothsome grilled cheese sandwiches made with all-natural cheese. Don't miss out on the homemade dipping sauce.
- **Fukuda** (www.fukudapgh.com, @FukudaTruck) is already well-known for the signature sushi and experimental Japanese cuisine offered at its brick-and-mortar locale in Bloomfield. And now it's gone mobile. Yes, sushi from a truck. It's the first in the nation, and it's seriously good.
- The team from **Bella Christie and Lil Z's Sweet Boutique** in Aspinwall (www.asweetboutique.com, @bellachristiez) now transports the delectable cupcakes and mini-desserts on wheels, satisfying sweet teeth all over town in the process.
- The **Street Foods** venture (www.facebook.com/streetfoodspgh, @streetfoodspgh) was inspired by the worldwide travels of its owners, who now bring international street food of all sorts to the streets of Pittsburgh. Even better, the menu changes on a regular basis.
- **Zum Zum** (www.polishpierogi.com, @PGHPierogiTruck) delights locals and newcomers alike with twists on the traditional Pittsburgh favorites of pierogi, *haluski* (cabbage and noodles or dumplings), and stuffed cabbage.

Bloomfield and Lawrenceville

Map 6

Things have certainly changed in the neighborhood known as Pittsburgh's "Little Italy," which today is plentiful with ethnic eateries, including those of the Indian, Thai, and Polish variety. And yet Bloomfield today is still full of classic Italian restaurants, and every Pittsburgher seems to have his or her favorite.

Formerly something of a run-down industrial wasteland, Lawrenceville's revitalization efforts have continued apace over the past decade or so, and it's no surprise that so many talented restaurateurs have recently flocked to the area. You'll find a slew of great coffee shops, a good number of high-quality restaurants, and even a few ethnic eateries. You'll probably also see the occasional food truck parked along the main drag, especially during gallery exhibits and other community events.

AMERICAN

★ FRANKTUARY $

If you've only had the pleasure of visiting Franktuary's tiny Downtown location (325 Oliver Ave., Mon.-Fri. 11am-2pm), which sits on the ground floor of Trinity Episcopal Cathedral, you won't even recognize this much newer Lawrenceville outpost with plentiful seating in a wide-open space accented by the street facing open windows. The vibe is decidedly serious and upscale. Table service is offered, and there's even a beautiful bar serving microbrews, cider, and the ever-present craft cocktails. Of course, gourmet hot dogs are still the main feature, but these are no run-of-the-mill frankfurters, friends. Instead, you'll pay a premium for grass-fed and humanely raised meat and specialty sausages. Stop by Monday-Friday 4pm-6pm for happy hour and half-priced dogs. To spot the Franktuary food truck, follow the team on Twitter at @franktuary.

MAP 6: 3810 Butler St., 412/586-7224, www.franktuary.com; Mon.-Wed. 11am-midnight, Thurs.-Sat. 11am-2am, Sun. 11am-3pm

TESSARO'S $$

Red meat fanatics—burger lovers especially—should not miss out on a trip to one of the city's most mouthwatering eateries, Tessaro's, which looks and feels like a locals-only neighborhood eatery both inside and out and has been featured on many Food Network TV shows. Tessaro's regularly wins awards locally for serving the 'Burgh's best burgers, which weigh in as heavy as a half pound. The secret, some say, is the bits of steak and filet mixed with the meat. If the idea of a gourmet burger isn't grabbing you, try a char-grilled steak or chop instead. Potato salad connoisseurs will not want to pass up a side of this heavenly homemade comfort food, as Tessaro's serves what this author considers to be one of the very best in town. Try to grab a back booth near the kitchen window—watching the old-school chefs in action is half the fun.

MAP 6: 4601 Liberty Ave., 412/682-6809, www.tessaros.com; Mon.-Sat. 11am-11pm

ASIAN

THAI CUISINE $$

Of the two Thai restaurants to choose from in Bloomfield, Thai Cuisine is by far the more popular, and for good reason: The pad thai is some of the best in the city, the waitstaff are extremely good-natured and attentive, and the lunch menu is an absolute bargain. This is also a perfect choice for a first date, and with more than 100 items on the menu, even the most timid diners stand a decent chance of finding something to like. (More than two dozen meatless dishes are also offered.) Particularly popular is the *tom ka gai* (chicken coconut soup), which goes wonderfully with any entrée. Do save room for the black sticky rice with mango dessert if it's available.

MAP 6: 4627 Liberty Ave., 412/688-9661, www.thaicuisinerestaurant.net; Tues.-Fri. 11am-2:30pm and 5pm-10pm, Sat.-Sun. noon-10:30pm

TRAM'S KITCHEN $$

This is easily one of Pittsburgh's most popular Vietnamese restaurants, but even Tram's most loyal customers often feel compelled to describe the ambience with a qualifier, which I'll second: It's a hole in the wall. But sit down with a steaming bowl of *pho* (Vietnamese soup) and order a round of spring rolls, and you likely won't care; the food at Tram's is always fresh and bursting with flavor, especially the vermicelli topped with meat or vegetables. Tram's is also a great choice for vegetarian diners.

MAP 6: 4050 Penn Ave., 412/682-2688; Tues.-Sun. 10am-10pm, Sun. 11am-9pm

CAFÉS

★ COCA CAFÉ $$

Easily one of Pittsburgh's best coffeehouses in both food and drink quality as well as interior design, the arty Coca Café displays a regularly rotating selection of locally produced sculptures and multimedia work on the shelves and walls of its front room. In its back room, retro diner booths have been chopped up and refitted into attractive works of art, and even on roasting summer days the small back patio is shaded and pleasant. Grilled sandwiches and other finger foods are available, La Prima coffee is served, and Sunday brunch (smoked salmon omelets, vanilla-orange yogurt with granola) is of the particularly pleasing and high-end variety.

MAP 6: 3811 Butler St., 412/621-3171, www.coca-cafe.net; Tues.-Wed. 8am-3pm, Thurs.-Fri. 8am-5pm, Sat. 9am-5pm, Sun. 9am-2pm

ESPRESSO A MANO $

This Lawrenceville coffee shop is a hit with local creative types, and it can get especially packed in the summer months, which is also when the street-facing glass garage door is opened to the elements. The vibe is modern but warm, and the café is particularly popular for the artistic foam designs its baristas create when pouring lattes and cappuccinos. Craftsmanship, in other words, is a serious deal; coffee snobs won't go away disappointed.

MAP 6: 3623 Butler St., 412/918-1864, www.espressoamano.com; Mon.-Fri. 7am-9pm, Sat. 8am-9pm, Sun. 8am-6pm

CONTEMPORARY AND NEW AMERICAN

★ CURE $

The food at this hugely popular and genuinely sustainable restaurant, where diners eat family-style around simple wood tables, is local, fresh, and tinged with something of a Mediterranean twist. Head chef Justin Severino, a graduate of the Pennsylvania Culinary Institute, takes ethical farming practices quite seriously and is deeply involved with his suppliers. He's also a well-known supporter of ethical animal husbandry and slaughtering techniques. Serious carnivores, in other words, can indulge in the gorgeously prepared meats and fish without the guilt associated with supermarket or fast-food meat. As for the menu, it's tough to go wrong. Take full advantage of staff recommendations, as employees taste everything on offer and are well-versed on the ever-changing menu.

MAP 6: 5336 Butler St., 412/252-2595, www.curepittsburgh.com; Sun.-Mon. 5pm-9pm, Wed.-Thurs. 5pm-10pm, Fri.-Sat. 5pm-11pm

INDIAN

TASTE OF INDIA $

Don't be put off if you visit Taste of India around dinnertime and find the dining room nearly deserted—the crowd tends to thin after the midday all-you-can-eat buffet, a Pittsburgh trend that's repeated in nearly every area Indian restaurant. Nonetheless, the offerings at Taste of India unquestionably represent North Indian food at its finest, and the affordable portions are surprisingly generous to boot. It's tough to go wrong with any of the entrée

top: Franktuary; bottom: Cure

choices, but do consider ordering one of the fantastic *lassis* (a yogurt shake) with your meal.

MAP 6: 4320 Penn Ave., 412/681-7700, www.tasteofindiapittsburgh.com; Mon.-Thurs. 11:30am-2:30pm and 5pm-10pm, Fri.-Sat. 11:30am-2:30pm and 5pm-10:30pm, Sun. 5pm-10pm

ITALIAN

DEL'S BAR & RISTORANTE DELPIZZO $$

An always-packed and much-loved local standby, Del's is the place to go in Bloomfield if you want your Italian done *really* right. Hip and picturesque, however, it most certainly is not—the vibe is definitely much more along the lines of Grandma's kitchen than, say, chic eatery. That probably has much to do with the fact that Del's has long been a family-owned and -operated business; the main emphasis is clearly on classic Italian cooking, not to mention good value. Bring your visiting parents or out-of-town guests to Del's, and try something standard, like lasagna or a Parmesan dish.

MAP 6: 4428 Liberty Ave., 412/683-1448, www.delsrest.com; Mon.-Thurs. 11am-11pm, Fri.-Sat. 11:30am-midnight, Sun. 1pm-10pm

LATIN AMERICAN

TAMARI RESTAURANT AND LOUNGE $$$

Allen Chen, whose father owns some of Pittsburgh's most successful Chinese and Thai restaurants, shied away from the food service industry during his childhood. But he eventually took a strong interest in cooking and became a chef. He also discovered similarities in Asian and Latin food that he simply couldn't shake. He partnered with a friend to create the city's first Latin-Asian fusion bistro. The result is something like a tapas bar—where small dishes are served and generally shared among friends—that features not only Spanish dishes like seviche but also flavors from Mexico, China, Thailand, and Japan. The result is simply one of the best and most distinctive culinary options in Pittsburgh.

MAP 6: 3519 Butler St., 412/325-3435, www.tamaripgh.com; Mon.-Thurs. 11:30am-10pm, Fri. 11:30am-11pm, Sat. 4pm-11pm, Sun. 11am-9pm

POLISH

BLOOMFIELD BRIDGE TAVERN $

Although its days as one of the city's most progressive live-music venues are now little more than a memory, the BBT is still Pittsburgh's premiere locale for Polish food. To truly get into the spirit, order the massive Polish Platter, which includes *haluski* and *golumpski* (different varieties of cabbage) along with the requisite pierogi (fried dumplings) and kielbasa (sausage). Those expecting particularly attentive service or even a particularly ethnic experience might walk away disappointed, but come for the food and you'll leave with a very satisfied stomach every time. Showing up early is also a good idea, as the BBT's bar crowd generally convenes by early evening.

MAP 6: 4412 Liberty Ave., 412/682-8611, www.bloomfieldbridgetavern.com; Tues.-Sat. 5pm-2am

SNACKS AND DESSERTS

DOZEN BAKE SHOP $

It may have taken a while for the gourmet cupcake trend to fully infiltrate our fair city, but the hugely successful Dozen Bake Shop is nothing if not proof-positive that in Pittsburgh, at least, these meticulously designed treats are here to stay. Dozen's pricing is relatively affordable, and it's committed to using organic and locally sourced ingredients. Customers are encouraged to linger over a cup of Intelligentsia coffee while taking advantage of the free Wi-Fi and watching the magic happen in the wide-open kitchen.

MAP 6: 3511 Butler St., 412/621-4740, www.dozenbakeshop.com; Mon.-Thurs. 8am-6pm, Fri. 8am-9pm

LA GOURMANDINE $

Owned and operated by a French couple who previously lived and worked in Paris, this traditional French bakery quickly became a darling of the Pittsburgh foodie community when it opened in the summer of 2010. And while the hand-crafted pastries and other French sweets are certainly big draws, La Gourmandine is probably best known for its breads, baguettes, and baguette sandwiches. Combination specials for breakfast or lunch, usually involving some grouping of croissant, sandwich, and made-from-scratch quiche, are offered daily. And since the menu of freshly baked goods changes on a daily basis, you're quite likely to discover something new and unusual during each and every visit.

MAP 6: 4605 Butler St., 412/682-2210, www.lagourmandinebakery.com; Tues.-Fri. 7:30am-4:30pm, Sat.-Sun. 9am-2:30pm

East Liberty and Garfield **Map 6**

The culinary scenes in the up-and-coming and quickly gentrifying East Liberty and Garfield neighborhoods are arguably the city's most exciting—at least for the time being. Many of Pittsburgh's most progressive chefs have chosen to work in the area, where everything from traditional Ethiopian to Pan-Asian to comfort foods and independent coffee shops can be found. To explore the areas on foot, start just east of the Children's Hospital on Penn Avenue before continuing east into the heart of East Liberty, where the

Penn Circle area and North Highland Avenue both have quite a lot to offer.

AMERICAN

BRGR $$

As its cheeky moniker suggests, BRGR is a gourmet burger joint, complete with handmade milkshakes and the ambience of a fairly upscale restaurant. And while the dry-aged prime beef patties are excellent, so too are the burgers made with just about every ingredient one could imagine—salmon, turkey, roasted corn, black beans, shrimp, pork, and more. So yes, there are plenty of vegetarian options, and low-carb and gluten-free dieters can have their sandwiches created sans bun. BRGR, in fact, is very conscientious about dietary restrictions, despite the health impact those big beef patties might have on your arteries. There's a second location in Cranberry (20111 U.S. 19 and Freedom Rd., Cranberry Mall, 724/742-2333), and a roving food truck sits at the Grant Street and Forbes Avenue lot (Wed.-Fri. 11:30am-2:30pm).

MAP 6: 5997 Penn Circle S., 412/362-2333, www.brgrpgh.com; Mon.-Thurs. 11:30am-11pm, Fri.-Sat. 11:30am-midnight, Sun. 11:30am-9pm

STATION STREET $

You can satiate your hot dog craving at this hugely popular East End eatery known for its dogs and fries. Opened by local rock-star chef Kevin Sousa, this is also one of only two Pittsburgh restaurants currently serving poutine—a Quebecois delicacy of greasy French fried potato goodness topped with gravy and cheese curds. Yes, it sounds gross, but it's also mighty satisfying after a long night out at the bars. For those less adventurous eaters, the chili cheese and kimchi dogs are said to be sublime.

MAP 6: 6290 Broad St, 412/365-2121, www.stationstreetpgh.com; Mon.-Sat. 11am-9pm, Sun. noon-7pm

UNION PIG & CHICKEN $$

One of chef Kevin Sousa's more recent ventures is a barbecue joint styled with long wooden picnic tables and a classic red gingham check print throughout. And while the genuine St. Louis barbecue style is what's on offer, Union Pig whips up a mighty fine fried chicken as well. Order ribs by the rack or barbecue chicken in half or full sizes. Needless to say, this is a great place to go with family and friends—the highly regarded chefs take their craft seriously, and yet the atmosphere remains fun and decidedly lighthearted. Sides are conveniently served à la carte. If you'll be dining alone, the $10 barbecue sandwich combo with a side and drink is a true steal. The bar stays open until 2am Monday-Saturday.

MAP 6: 220 N. Highland Ave., 412/363-7675, www.unionpgh.com; Mon.-Thurs. 11am-10pm, Fri.-Sat. 11am-1am, Sun. 10am-9pm

ASIAN

PLUM PAN-ASIAN KITCHEN $$

Opened in the same space (and largely by the same team) as the sorely missed and seriously expensive gourmet Chinese restaurant known as Richard Chen, the more down-to-earth Plum seems offer simpler fare at much-easier-to-digest prices. Long-time Pittsburgh-area diners might like to think of Plum as something of an upscale Spice Island Tea House, which is a pan-Asian eatery in Oakland appealing to the university set. And yet the Thai, Indonesian, Vietnamese, Malaysian, and Chinese offerings at Plum manage to be appropriately sophisticated while still maintaining a semblance of affordability. The space itself is aesthetically gorgeous—not surprising, given the building's former tenant—and the newly installed sushi bar is said to be among Pittsburgh's very best.

MAP 6: 5996 Penn Circle S., 412/363-7586, www.plumpanasiankitchen.com; lunch Mon.-Fri. 11:30am-3pm and Sat. noon-3pm, dinner Mon.-Thurs. 5pm-10pm, Fri.-Sat. 5pm-11pm, Sun. 4:30pm-9pm

SMILING BANANA LEAF $

Pittsburgh isn't exactly lacking in Thai restaurants, but as for *quality* Thai restaurants—that's another story altogether. Which is exactly why this addition to Highland Park's growing culinary scene was greeted with so much anticipation. And aside from the restaurant's exceedingly small size and its understandably slow service during the busy dinner rush, there's not much to complain about. The curry and noodle dishes seem to be the biggest hits, although considering SBL's very reasonable rates (lunch entrées can be had for $7-8), a little experimentation may well be in order.

MAP 6: 5901 Bryant St., 412/362-3200, www.smilingbananaleaf.com; Mon.-Thurs. 11am-9pm, Fri.-Sat. 11am-10pm, Sun. noon-9pm

CAFÉS

ZEKE'S COFFEE $

As the neighborhood's very own small-batch coffee roaster, Zeke's is a genuine first for East Liberty. And yet while the roaster itself does offer free Wi-Fi, it's not necessarily the sort of place you'd feel comfortable spending the entire day. (There's just one table.) Instead, pick up a pound to brew at home and enjoy a to-go cup of Zeke's rocket-fueled drip coffee while you wait. Fair warning: You'll never be able to purchase grinds at the grocery store again.

MAP 6: 6012 Penn Ave., 412/670-6231, www.zekescoffeepgh.com; Mon.-Sat. 9am-6pm

CONTEMPORARY AND NEW AMERICAN

★ DINETTE $$

Yet another entrant into Pittsburgh's swiftly growing family of restaurants that proudly fly the locally-sourced-and-organic flag, Dinette is a brilliantly designed minimalist bistro offering gourmet flatbread pizzas along with what is easily one of the city's most sophisticated wine lists. And aside from its daily-changing menu, Dinette has quite a lot to brag about: *Pittsburgh* magazine named it one of the city's 25 best restaurants in 2010, while during the same year, owner and chef Sonja Finn ranked as a semifinalist for a prestigious James Beard Foundation award. For those with the money to spend, Dinette offers a culinary experience unique to just about any other you're likely to find within the city's limits.

MAP 6: 5996 Penn Circle S., 2nd level, 412/362-0202, www.dinette-pgh.com; Tues.-Thurs. 5pm-10pm, Fri.-Sat. 5pm-11pm

E2 $$

Located on a quiet but expanding block near the picturesque Highland Park Reservoir, E2 (pronounced "E-squared") is an absolute must for the high-end breakfast connoisseur. The menu provides some of the best—and most distinctive—brunch fair in the region. The menu changes from week to week, although standard fare runs the gamut from sugar-dusted beignets and perfectly poached eggs to some of the best donuts you've ever dreamed of. Late risers need not despair, though, as daily lunch and dinner menus of the rustic and locally sourced Mediterranean variety are now available. There's a corkage fee of $6 per bottle.

MAP 6: 5904 Bryant St., 412/441-1200, www.e2pgh.com; Tues.-Fri. 5pm-10pm, Sat. 9am-2pm and 6pm-10pm, Sun. 9am-2pm

THE LIVERMORE $$

Opened in 2013 in the former home of the Waffle Shop, and by the same team responsible for the overnight success known as Bar Marco, the Livermore has a seriously small space that befits its already-famous tapas and after-work snacks menu. Of course, whether the Livermore will eventually grow to join the East End's legions of New American hot spots still remains to be seen. For the time being, stop by for after-dinner drinks, most of which are of the pre-Prohibition and mid-20th-century American variety. Coolest detail: The bar was made from salvaged bowling alley wood.

MAP 6: 124 S. Highland Ave., 412/361-0600; Sun.-Tues. 11am-11pm, Wed.-Sat. 11am-1am

NOTION $$$

The East End certainly has been blessed with a culinary renaissance in recent years, and this relative newcomer, which opened in 2011, describes its cuisine as "an edible expression of creativity" and genuinely takes the game to a whole new level. The concept revolves around locally sourced, new American fare—the same as so many other area eateries—and yet Chef Dave Racicot significantly ups the ante with truly surprising prix fixe menu pairings and the most beautiful presentations you'll see outside of a glossy food magazine. Dress appropriately—this is most certainly a white tablecloth spot—and be prepared for a mighty large bill at the end of the night.

MAP 6: 128 S. Highland Ave., 412/361-1188, www.notionrestaurant.com; Tues.-Sat. 6pm-10pm

★ SALT OF THE EARTH $$$

Two years of planning culminated in the opening of Salt of the Earth in 2010, which at the time was easily the city's most anticipated restaurant in years. Much of that had to do with Salt's co-owner and chef, the venerable and avant-garde Kevin Sousa, who has lately become something of local—and even national—culinary legend. Sousa is a proponent of a culinary movement known as molecular gastronomy, in which the principles of science are brought into the kitchen. What's more, SOTE is the first restaurant at which Sousa has had the luxury of calling literally all the shots, and his genius truly shines through, with contemporary interpretations of everything from pork belly to lamb shoulder to a seriously forward-thinking cocktail menu. If you try one high-end eatery during your time in Pittsburgh, definitely make it this one.

MAP 6: 5523 Penn Ave., 412/414-9088, www.saltpgh.com; Mon.-Sat. 5pm-1am

★ SPOON $$$

Fawning food critics nationwide can't seem to say enough about Spoon, one of the East End's favorite avant-garde eateries, where seasonal and locally sourced ingredients are combined with unparalleled creativity. The brilliant menu is the result of executive chef Brian Pekarcik's intimate knowledge of food and its many possibilities: how to match seemingly dissimilar foods, for instance. Consider a dish known as Ahi Tuna Two Ways, which pairs a sushi crab roll with a noodle salad.

MAP 6: 134 S. Highland Ave., 412/362-6001, www.spoonpgh.com; Mon.-Thurs. 5pm-10pm, Fri.-Sat. 5pm-11pm, Sun. 5pm-9pm

clockwise from top left: People's Indian Restaurant; Plum Pan-Asian Kitchen; Dinette

ETHIOPIAN

TANA ETHIOPIAN CUISINE $$

For those inexperienced with the cuisine, Ethiopian dishes are generally eaten with the hands, while using a soft yet sturdy type of flatbread called *injera* in place or a fork or spoon. To get a feel for the flavors, order a combination platter, which allows diners to sample up to five different meat and vegetable dishes. And yet just about anything found on the menu is likely to please the adventurous foodie; after battling it out for years with Abay, another nearby Ethiopian spot, Tana is now the city's solitary Ethiopian restaurant.

MAP 6: 5929 Baum Blvd., 412/665-2770, www.tanaethiopiancuisine.com; Mon.-Thurs. 5pm-10pm, Fri.-Sat. 11:30am-2:30pm and 5pm-11pm, Sun. 5pm-10pm

FRENCH

PARIS 66 BISTRO $$

As a self-described purveyor of "everyday French cuisine," this crepe hub prides itself on being the exact opposite of the stereotypical French restaurant in America: It's both affordable and non-exclusionary. At the same time, it manages to retain an entirely authentic vibe, thanks no doubt to the owner and head chef, both of whom were trained as master crepe makers in France. Designed to look, smell, and feel like a Parisian sidewalk café, Paris 66 also serves up French pizza, Parisian pastries, and made-daily French desserts. Brunch is served on Sunday.

MAP 6: 6018 Penn Circle S., 412/404-8166, www.paris66bistro.com; Mon.-Thurs. 11am-10pm, Fri.-Sat. 11am-11pm, Sun. 10am-3pm

INDIAN

PEOPLE'S INDIAN RESTAURANT $

Its exterior may not be the most welcoming, but show up for the weekday all-you-can-eat lunch buffet and you'll immediately understand why Garfield's best-kept culinary secret probably won't be a secret for long. Featuring spicy cuisine from the northern Indian state of Punjab, People's Indian Restaurant has a menu extensive enough for vegetarians and meat-eaters alike. Smoky tandoor dishes are especially smart picks, as is the chewy and puffy Punjabi naan (Indian bread). Ten dollars will buy you the buffet plus tip with a bit left over. Evening entrées (chicken *korma, vindaloo*) are equally affordable.

MAP 6: 5147 Penn Ave., 412/661-3160; Mon.-Sat. 11:30am-10pm

ITALIAN

SPAK BROTHERS PIZZA $

Owned and operated by ambitious siblings who grew up in the city's suburbs, this Garfield-area pizzeria serves truly delectable versions of typical pizza shop fare. The Spaks, however, have also carved out a unique niche as purveyors of vegetarian and vegan offerings not available anywhere else in the region, the vast majority of which are so surprisingly flavorful that even meat-loving omnivores have become regular customers. Meat-free wings, tacos, cheese steaks, and even meatless sausage and pepperoni are all available. And what's more, the shop largely sources local and sustainable ingredients.

MAP 6: 5107 Penn Ave., 412/362-7725, www.spakbrothers.com; Mon.-Thurs. 11am-10pm, Fri. 11am-11pm, Sat. noon-11pm, Sun. 3pm-10pm

Nightlife

It can be easy enough at times to holler and moan about Pittsburgh's distinctive lack of serious nightlife options, but remember: This is a small town, and although the city's nightlife scene almost certainly has a little something to offer almost everyone, chances are good that you may have to dig deep to truly find what you're looking for.

For instance, where bigger urban areas may have dozens of gay clubs, or 10 different jazz bars, Pittsburgh may be home to only five or six. Maybe fewer. Maybe more. The major difference, however, lies in the sense of community that's ever-present in the neighborhood bars and in the tiny East End art galleries that transform into cutting-edge live music venues on weekend nights.

To a large degree, nightlife in Pittsburgh is synonymous with two separate South Side destinations: There's the main drag of East Carson Street, which has been described as the longest uninterrupted stretch of bars in the country. There's also the shopping and tourist-friendly destination known as Station Square, which is home to a complex of hard-partying dance clubs. If you're looking for a scene that's slightly grittier and significantly more authentic, check out the hipster bars dotting the East End neighborhoods of Lawrenceville, Bloomfield, and East Liberty; a good number of them also double as art galleries and intimate concert venues.

Making nice with the locals and the regulars, though, is probably the best way to learn about Pittsburgh's entertaining and often hidden nightlife secrets. For instance, while local pubs generally close

Look for ★ to find recommended nightlife.

HIGHLIGHTS

★ **Most Creative Cocktails:** With its pre-Prohibition vibe, its highly skilled mixologists dressed in period costume, and its complicated menu of old-school cocktails, **Acacia** is the city's premier 1920s pseudo-speakeasy (page 149).

★ **Best Dance Club:** The dance clubs at Station Square seem to open and close with alarming frequency, but the current top dog is certainly **Whim,** with its high-end laser-light system and always creative theme nights (page 154).

★ **Best Live-Music Venue:** Easily the most intimate live-music experience in the city, **Club Café** is the place to catch up-and-coming singer-songwriters just before they break into the mainstream. Jazz, blues, and folk legends perform here regularly as well (page 154).

★ **Best Lounge:** There's nothing else in the city quite like uber-stylish **Skybar,** home to Pittsburgh's solitary rooftop pool and lounge. Kick back by the outdoor fire pit or even in your own private cabana (page 156).

★ **Best Mixed Gay-and-Straight Bar:** Shadyside's upscale **Spin Bartini & Ultra Lounge** is just as popular with heteros as it is with the East End's growing gay community, making it the perfect place for a little late-night cruising (page 157).

★ **Best Neighborhood Bar: Squirrel Hill Café,** known to locals as "The Cage," has been around forever, yet welcomes all comers with open arms. This is the bar where everybody knows your name (page 158).

★ **Best Themed Brewpub:** Located in a disused Catholic church where genuine pews are used for seating and beer tanks sit atop the altar, **Church Brew Works** has been Pittsburgh's favorite holy house of sin for some two decades now (page 159).

★ **Best Dive Bar:** Hipsters and locals alike adore its cheap swill with equal fervor. It's **Gooski's,** Pittsburgh's most authentic house of late-night debauchery (page 159).

★ **Best Bar for a First Date:** Chatting over tacos and Coronas at the effortlessly hip **Round Corner Cantina** may be the perfect way to vet that potential significant other you've been eyeing (page 162).

for the night at 2am, there are after-hours bars and unusually creative nightlife events that even many Pittsburgh natives don't know about. So belly up to the bar, get to know your neighbor, and start exploring the Steel City like the locals do: with an always open-minded attitude, and with good friends in tow.

Downtown

Map 1

LIVE MUSIC

ANDY'S WINE BAR

A sort of accompanying nightspot to the Fairmont's in-house restaurant, Habitat, Andy's Wine Bar is a light lunch spot, a live jazz club, and a contemporary wine bar all in one. Inspired by the city's two most notable Andys—Warhol and Carnegie—Andy's Wine Bar is also home to a fantastic collection of artifacts that were discovered underground during the building's site excavation. The live jazz shows (always free) are a history lesson unto themselves, regularly featuring some of the city's finest musical talent. Performances take place 6pm-9pm Tuesdays and Wednesdays, 7:30pm-10:30pm Thursdays, and 8pm-midnight Fridays and Saturdays. See the website for lineup details.

MAP 1: 510 Market St. (Fairmont Pittsburgh lobby), 412/773-8884, www.andyswinebar.com; Sun.-Thurs. 2pm-midnight, Fri.-Sat. 2pm-1am; no cover

LITTLE E'S

Considering that the opening of Little E's put an end to a lengthy stretch during which Pittsburgh essentially had no full-time jazz clubs, it's little surprise that the live music performances have been so overwhelmingly successful. Warm, relaxing, and truly intimate, Little E's feels something like an undiscovered secret or a hidden downtown bar, complete with exposed brick walls, a decent cocktail list, and a menu featuring soups, salads, sandwiches, and Cajun-influenced entrées. Blues musicians perform regularly as well. See the website for specific performance dates and times.

MAP 1: 949 Liberty Ave., 2nd Fl., 412/392-2217, www.littleesjazz.com; Wed.-Sun. 5:30pm-12:30am, $10 for patrons not buying food and drinks

Strip District

GAY AND LESBIAN

LUCKY'S TAVERN

If the now-defunct Pegasus location on Liberty Avenue was long known as the most crucial nexus of Steel City gay culture—and it was—then you might think of Lucky's (official name: Real Luck Café) as that long-gone club's slightly lesser-known older cousin. Lucky's has been around *forever,* and you've probably driven past it without even knowing: It's tucked back behind the green wooden shamrock sign where Penn Avenue meets the 16th Street Bridge. Aside from the super-friendly crowd, the nude male dancers are probably the biggest draw, although the pet-friendly deck doesn't hurt either. Lucky's is fairly popular with lesbians as well.

MAP 1: 1519 Penn Ave., 412/471-7832, www.realluckcafe.com; daily 4pm-2am; no cover

LIVE MUSIC

ALTAR BAR

Although it had a fairly impressive run as a nightclub where cocktail waitresses often dressed up in Catholic schoolgirl uniforms, the Strip District's Altar Bar, which is inside one of the city's many churches-turned-businesses, is now a live music venue featuring pop and rock bands. And while the experience of catching a show here isn't entirely unlike the experience you might have at Mr. Small's, the city's other concert venue located inside a disused church, bands performing at Altar Bar tend to be of the slightly less impressive variety: tribute acts and cover bands, for instance, make frequent appearances, as do horrorcore hip-hop acts and washed-up death metal bands.

MAP 1: 1620 Penn Ave., 412/206-9719, www.altarbar.com; Mon., Wed., and Fri. noon-6pm and during events; $5-15

CLUB ZOO

After a long and successful run as Metropol, an industrial music dance club that doubled as one of the most popular live music venues in the city, this converted warehouse in the Strip has been reborn as Club Zoo. Technically, Club Zoo is an under-21 spot where high schoolers can congregate in an alcohol-free environment. But much as at Metropol, live music is also a big seller; marquee-level alternative and hip-hop acts can easily draw thousands of fans. With its post-apocalyptic warehouse vibe, Club Zoo is a particularly amenable place to catch guitar-heavy rock or electronic acts.

Holy Houses of Sin

Consider for a moment one of Pittsburgh's oddest development trends: Over the past couple of decades, plucky entrepreneurs here have been transforming old and abandoned churches into bars, cafés, nightclubs, and restaurants. Is it a testament to the industrious nature of the Steel City, or just plain ol' blasphemy? You be the judge.

A restaurant and brewpub that serves some of the tastiest gourmet pizzas in town, **Church Brew Works** (3525 Liberty Ave., Lawrenceville, 412/688-8200) opened about 20 years ago in the shuttered St. John the Baptist chapel. Sure to be especially offensive to the ultra-devout are the brewpub's steel and copper tanks, which occupy the place of honor upon the altar.

Located in the industrial burgh of Millvale, St. Ann's became the site of Pittsburgh's most radical church transformation when a recording studio by the name of **Mr. Smalls** (400 Lincoln Ave., Millvale, 412/821-4447) moved in. Small's has since grown to become one of the city's most popular concert halls, and it now serves up an almost nightly mix of punk, reggae, heavy metal, and hip-hop.

One of Pittsburgh's most sinful transformations has taken place in (where else?) the Strip District, where **Altar Bar** (1620 Penn Ave., 412/206-9719, www.altarbar.com) can now be found in what was once known only as St. Elizabeth Church. Previously a naughty nightclub featuring cocktail waitresses in Catholic schoolgirl uniforms, Altar Bar is now a live music venue, where pop and rock acts perform regularly.

There's also **The Union Project** (801 N. Negley Ave., Highland Park, 412/363-4550, www.unionproject.org), a multipurpose space inside the former Union Baptist Church. Quite unlike the aforementioned locales, the Union Project is the sort of place where good deeds are done on a regular basis: Visual artists create here, community organizers organize here, and inner-city youth gain valuable life skills and work experience here. To make a financial donation to the Union Project, call or visit the organization's website.

One of the city's newest chapel transformations has taken place out in Carnegie, where a former Italian Catholic Church, Holy Souls, is now a fast-food-style Indian restaurant known as **Café Delhi** (205 Mary St., 412/278-5058). The place even has a BYOB policy.

And if you're planning on patronizing some of these businesses but still haven't settled on accommodations, consider bunking down for a night at **The Priory** (614 Pressley St., 412/231-3338 or 866/377-4679, www.thepriory.com), a charming and recently upgraded bed-and-breakfast on the North Side that was once a Benedictine monastery. It's within easy walking distance of Downtown, breakfast is served inside the old refectory, and wireless Internet access is available in all rooms and throughout the premises.

And bunking down permanently in a former church is a realistic option here as well. The architecturally unique condos and lofts of the **Angel's Arms Condominiums** (1 Pius St., 412/363-4000, www.angelsarms.net), located in the South Side Slopes, were built upon the structure of the former St. Michael the Archangel church. Prices currently start at around $300,000.

MAP 1: 1630 Smallman St., 412/201-1100, www.clubzoo.net; Fri.-Sat. 7:30pm-1am; $10 Fri., $12 Sat.; live music tickets start at $20

Oakland

Map 2

BARS

PETER'S PUB

Only at Peter's Pub can one experience all the raucousness and debauchery of a Pitt frat party without actually having been invited. University athletes and the type of undergrads who obsessively follow the NCAA playoffs are whom you can expect here; also count on ridiculously affordable daily beer specials, some as cheap as $1. On the second floor is a separate bar, as well as a dance floor that quickly grows sweaty and crowded on weekend nights. Draft beers are strictly of the pale yellow variety, and yes, they're actually served in red plastic cups, keg-style.

MAP 2: 116 Oakland Ave., 412/681-7465, www.mypeterspub.com; Mon.-Sat. 11am-2am, Sun. noon-2am; $1-5 Thurs.-Sat. after 9pm on deejay or live music nights

LOUNGES

AVA

Following a very long and successful run in East Liberty, AVA only recently moved into its new North Oakland digs, where craft cocktails are served alongside classic-cool deejay parties. AVA during the day is nothing if not a laid-back and fashionable lounge at which to enjoy a beer or a specialty martini alongside jazz, hip-hop, or world music. And for the time being, it appears as if the club's networking events for creative professionals and its cutting-edge dance nights will be marching on at the new location.

MAP 2: 304 N. Craig St., 412/363-8277, http://avapgh.wordpress.com; Mon.-Fri. 8am-2pm and 6pm-2am, Sat. 6pm-2am, Sun. 10am-2pm; no cover, $5-10 events

KBOX KARAOKE HOUSE

Featuring authentic Asian-style private karaoke rooms, KBOX is definitely a first for the Steel City, where karaoke usually happens in Iron City-soaked dive bars in front of crowds of drunken revelers. In the East, however, karaoke is a social and much more serious pastime that's often shared only with friends—thus, the private room. KBOX, which is open to all ages, is popular with Asian students from nearby CMU, American college kids, and even young professionals and families. Roughly 100,000 songs are on tap, including about 13,000 in English. Each room is kitted out with a 50-inch flat-screen TV, a video-on-demand system, and a pro-quality Shure microphone. Snacks and Asian entrées are available. KBOX does not serve alcohol, but for a 20 percent service fee you can BYOB.

MAP 2: 214 S. Craig St., 412/621-2860, www.kbktv.com; Wed.-Thurs. and Sun. 2pm-midnight, Fri.-Sat. 2pm-2am; $59/room or $12/person Fri.-Sat. 7pm-2am; $44.25/room or $9/person Wed.-Thurs. 7pm-midnight, Fri.-Sat. 2pm-7pm, Sun. 2pm-midnight; $29.50/room or $6/person Wed.-Thurs. 2pm-7pm

MINT HOOKAH BAR & LOUNGE

A number of hookah bars serving the city's college community have popped up in Oakland over the years, but Mint, the current front-runner (and the longest-lasting), seems to be the place that's finally done it right. Weekdays here are quiet and relaxed, and thanks to the free Wi-Fi, many students bring laptops and work while trip-hop and other chill music plays. Weekends, however, bring full-on deejay ragers, transforming Mint into more of a club atmosphere. Movies screen on Wednesdays, and belly dancers entertain the crowd on Saturday nights. The ol' hubble bubble will set you back anywhere from $10 to $18.

MAP 2: 416 Semple St., 412/681-4040, www.mintpgh.com; Sun.-Wed. 5pm-1am, Thurs. 5pm-2am, Fri.-Sat. 5pm-4am; no cover

South Side

Map 3

BARS

★ ACACIA

Although the formerly Strip District-based Embury cocktail bar briefly occupied this space, some say the Prohibition-themed Acacia offers an even more authentic experience. Many of the mixologists behind the bar at Acacia are attired in period-appropriate costume, right down to the suit vest and the waxed handlebar mustache. And although you'll pay a princely sum for the artistically crafted cocktails, many of which call for incredibly complicated preparations, it's more than worth it just to soak in the detail-rich speakeasy atmosphere. Interestingly, bourbon seems to be something of a house specialty.

MAP 3: 2108 E. Carson St., 412/488-1800, www.acaciacocktails.com; Mon.-Sat. 5pm-2am; no cover

BAR 11

With an atmosphere that much more closely resembles a house party than an actual bar, it's perhaps surprising that the unmarked Bar 11 has stayed such a well-kept secret for so long. No need to mince words, however: Bar 11 is a tried-and-true dive; the even-tempered waitstaff and the creative party-favor shtick keep things exciting. The room is perpetually lit by black lights and covered in aluminum foil, and patrons are encouraged to draw on each other with highlighter pens.

MAP 3: 1101 Bradish St., 412/381-0899; Tues.-Sat. 8pm-2am; no cover

DEE'S CAFÉ

Less of a dive bar than a home away from home for some of the South Side's most ambitious imbibers, Dee's is dirty, dank, and perpetually clouded in smoke; it's one of the few bars in the city exempt from the smoking ban. Best of all, it's cheap and probably the most fun you'll have in any of Pittsburgh's shot-and-a-beer bars, especially if you hang around long enough to get to know the locals. What does the crowd look like? Picture a Nine Inch Nails concert, circa 1994: combat boots, trench coats, Manic Panic hair, etc. The crowd at the upstairs bar, where pint glasses are strictly verboten, is a touch older and more upscale. Action around the billiards tables on both levels is always in full effect.

MAP 3: 1314 E. Carson St., 412/431-1314, www.deescafe.com; Mon.-Sat. 11am-2am, Sun. noon-2am; no cover

JACK'S BAR

Take our word for it: No one goes to Jack's, which probably has greater name recognition than any other watering hole along the South Side strip, for its beverage selection. Nor do they go for the atmosphere, the ambience, or the music. That's because Jack's is the city's meat market *par excellence,* plain and simple. Being that this is Pittsburgh, that generally means an overabundance of thick-necked men in white ball caps and coeds with teased hair and high heels. It also means an almost nightly procession of fistfights, so do hang on tight to your Iron City should you find yourself packed into a far corner. In true Steel City style, Jack's never closes its doors, except when forced by Pennsylvania law.

MAP 3: 1121 E. Carson St., 412/431-3644, www.jacksbarpittsburgh.com; daily 7am-2am; no cover

LAVA LOUNGE

One of the many South Side spots operated by the owners of the Beehive Coffeehouse, Lava Lounge looks a lot like it sounds. Picture a tavern where, say, the Flintstones might pass an evening, and you'll start to get the idea: Tables, booths, and high-backed chairs are all designed to resemble a liquid molten lava flow. Even the interior design is creatively cave-like. Do be aware that draft beer isn't available; wine, pricey imports, and cocktails of the Trader Vic's variety are what you'll be drinking. Unknown rock bands play in the back room periodically. Deejays spin '80s and '90s records most evenings, although other curious events, like spelling bees and heavy metal nights, are also popular.

MAP 3: 2204 E. Carson St., 412/431-5282, www.lavaloungepgh.com; Mon. and Sat. 5pm-2am, Tues.-Fri. 4pm-2am, Sun. 8pm-2am; Sun.-Thurs. no cover, Fri. and Sat. $3

LOCAL BAR + KITCHEN

Something of a downscale lounge with a good kitchen and a rustic pub atmosphere, Local is known for having the neighborhood's largest heated and enclosed rooftop deck. Margaritas, martinis, and other cocktails are popular, but if you're looking for a quality selection of craft beer on tap, go elsewhere. The kitchen does a good job with standard American pub grub, including pizza, wings, soups, and sandwiches.

MAP 3: 1515 E. Carson St., 412/431-1125, www.localpgh.com; daily 11am-2am; no cover

OVER THE BAR BICYCLE CAFÉ

Although Pittsburgh has steadily grown into something of a seriously enthusiastic bicycling city, the arrival of this bike-themed bar and café felt, to some degree, like a genuine confirmation that the cycling scene in Bridge City had become an important and lucrative big business. At OTB, you'll find bicycling tchotchkes and memorabilia hanging from—and nailed onto—nearly every available surface. Cyclists eat and drink here regularly, and even the delightfully toothsome pub-grub menu pays homage to the sport. Group rides are occasionally scheduled, and the microbrew list is comparable to those at most other East Carson Street watering holes. Naturally, arriving on two wheels is strongly encouraged. OTB has a second location at the **North Park Boathouse** (10301 Pearce Mill Rd., Allison Park, 724/940-5000, daily 11am-midnight).

MAP 3: 2518 E. Carson St., 412/381-3698, www.otbbicyclecafe.com; Mon.-Fri. 11am-11pm, Sat. noon-11pm, Sun. noon-10pm; no cover

PIPER'S PUB

A drinking and dining mecca for the city's British expat community, Piper's Pub has all the charm of an authentic English pub. At the bar, selections on draft include Strongbow, Old Speckled Hen, Smithwick's, and Boddingtons; the single-malt scotch menu is dozens of names long, and bottled beers are available from all across the British Isles and beyond. A large dining room fills the majority of the bar, which is perfectly fitting, considering how tasty the pub grub is; try the Ploughman's platter (a cheese plate with apple slices and gherkins) or the Guinness stew. Traditional Irish bands perform most weekend nights, and live footie matches are even beamed in via satellite. Weekend brunch is served Saturday and Sunday 8:30am-3pm.

MAP 3: 1828 E. Carson St., 412/381-3977, www.piperspub.com; Mon.-Fri. 11am-midnight, Sat.-Sun. 8:30am-midnight; $1-5 Thurs.-Sat. after 9pm on deejay or live music nights

ROWDY BUCK

Run by the same creative entrepreneurs responsible for the Double Wide Grill and the Lava Lounge, among others, Rowdy Buck has a wonderful faux-western theme, complete with lumberjack-style bartenders wearing flannel, a log cabin-like interior, and gourmet hot dogs on the menu. Aside from the obvious trend factor, it's not quite clear why pre-Prohibition cocktails are served, although there certainly are enough specialty drinks, craft beers, and bourbons at the Buck to keep anyone busy. Naturally, fake antlers abound, and some of the seats are made to look like tree stumps. It's all a bit cutesy, but it works. Pub-grub entrées with kitschy Wild West names are available, and yes, the rumors are true: You actually can cook your own s'mores.

MAP 3: 1323 E. Carson St., 412/431-2825, www.rowdybuck.com; Mon.-Sun. 4pm-2am; no cover

THE SMILING MOOSE

The Moose is something of an unofficial headquarters for the city's tattooed contingent, goth girls, old-school punk rockers, aging skinheads, and Vespa-driving mods. Perhaps not surprisingly, fistfights aren't uncommon. Obscure speed metal and punk bands play free shows in the back of the bar most weekends; if the noise gets to be a bit too much, simply slip up to the tiny second-floor bar, where conversation and a game of billiards can be more easily accomplished.

MAP 3: 1306 E. Carson St., 412/431-4668, www.smiling-moose.com; Tues.-Sat. 11am-2am, Sun.-Mon. 2pm-2am; $5-10 Sat.

SMOKIN' JOE'S

The success of Smokin' Joe's, which from the outside appears to be simply yet another in an endless procession of bars, is based on a relatively simple philosophy: Stock a larger variety of beer than the guy next door. *Way* larger. We're talking hundreds and hundreds, some on draft, some in the massive cooler just inside the front door. In a nutshell, that's why serious drinkers come to Joe's. The interior is rather cramped and plain, and although budget wing nights are a draw for some, the pub grub really isn't much to write home about (try Fat Head's next door if you're really hungry). Insider's tip: Don't pass up Joe's just because the bar is packed to overflowing; there's often ample seating on the second-floor balcony.

clockwise from top left: Spin Bartini; Mario's East Side Saloon; Brillobox

MAP 3: 2001 E. Carson St., 412/431-6757, www.smokinjoessaloon.com; Mon.-Thurs. noon-2am, Fri.-Sat. 10am-2am, Sun. 11am-2am; no cover

TIKI LOUNGE

It ain't Trader Vic's, but it comes mighty close. Tiki Lounge is the city's solitary Polynesian-themed bar, a fact that's made all too clear even to the casual passerby—just keep your eyes peeled for the massive Tiki god in the front window. (You'll have to pass through his massive mouth before gaining entry to the lounge.) Inside, it's something of a South Pacific paradise, with wooden masks, bamboo stalks, and Hawaiian island paraphernalia lining the walls, including an indoor waterfall. The cocktail menu is equally exotic: Choose from such wonders as a Headhunter, a Fu Manchu, and a Coconut Kiss. Deejays light up the relatively small dance floor with pop and house music on weekends.

MAP 3: 2003 E. Carson St., 412/381-8454, www.tikilounge.biz; Mon.-Sat. 4pm-2am, Sun. 8pm-2am; no cover downstairs, $5-10 upstairs

DANCE CLUBS

★ WHIM

Perhaps the city's swankiest and most architecturally impressive dance club, Whim more or less manages to eschew the cheeseball aesthetic of the standard Station Square meat market. The vibe is somewhat European, what with the club's minimalist, brushed-metal furniture and the dance floor's multihued laser lights. Outside the VIP areas, the seating offers a great view of the often-packed dance floor. And naturally, special event nights ('80s, hip-hop, Top 40) with discounted drink specials abound; check the website for details.

MAP 3: 1 E. Carson St., 412/281-9888, www.whimpitt.com; Thurs.-Sat. 9pm-2am; $5-10, $20 and up special events and parties

LIVE MUSIC

★ CLUB CAFÉ

No other live music experience in Pittsburgh comes anywhere near to that at Club Café, which likes to call itself the city's premiere "wired" nightclub. (Many shows are filmed live; an *Austin City Limits*-style TV program and a DVD series have already been produced.) The room is so small, and the seating so close to the stage, it's practically possible to reach out and touch the performers mid-song. Music is generally of the singer-songwriter variety; past artists include Damien Rice, Jill Sobule, and Citizen Cope. Blues and indie-pop bands also show up with some regularity; the crowd generally consists of well-behaved young professionals. Hours are subject to change based on the performance schedule (see the website for details).

MAP 3: 56 S. 12th St., 412/431-4950, www.clubcafelive.com; bar daily until 2am; first show daily 7pm, door opens at 6pm; second show daily 9pm, door opens at 8pm; $5-25

REX THEATRE

Formerly a movie theater with a fantastic art deco facade, the Rex has since transformed itself into a midsize concert venue without actually, well, transforming much. The reclining theater seats were never removed, for instance, so even during big-name punk shows, the energy level can feel rather lackluster. The popcorn and candy counter in the front lobby remains as well; it's now a bar. The occasional alternative burlesque performance or independent film screening also takes place. Better still, the theater's original art deco signage can still be seen. See the website for show times and dates.

MAP 3: 1602 E. Carson St., 412/381-6811, www.rextheatre.com; $10-30 performances

LOUNGES

DIESEL

Located in the same space that once housed the legendary Nick's Fat City, Diesel is a sort of a glossy, two-venues-in-one nightlife establishment. Comprising two levels and featuring dance floors and multiple bars, the weekend experience comes complete with big-name deejays, high-tech lighting, and overpriced VIP bottle service. There's even an all-white, mezzanine-level VIP lounge. *Très chic!* Head-bangers should take note, however, that rock, pop, and metal shows are also a big draw at Diesel, although discerning live music fans do frequently complain about the club's sound quality. Diesel can also be rented for private events.

MAP 3: 1601 E. Carson St., 412/431-8800, www.dieselclublounge.com/pittsburgh; Thurs.-Sat. 9pm-2am and during live events; $5-25

S BAR

Something of a cross between a martini bar, a meat market, and a chilled-out lounge where Pittsburgh's beautiful people come to play, S Bar manages to remain upscale and decidedly hip at the very same time. Deejay nights are a big draw—Mega Man, Sean Perry, and Jazzy Jeff have all previously graced the decks. And although the atmosphere at S Bar is certainly more slick and glossy than at your average East Carson Street watering hole, the dance floor is fairly democratic—you'll generally find a decent mix of college kids, B-boys, hipster types, and young professionals mixing it up.

MAP 3: 1713 E. Carson St., 412/481-7227, www.sbarpgh.com; Mon.-Sun. 6pm-2am; no cover

★ SKYBAR

Home to Pittsburgh's only rooftop pool and lounge, the open-year-round Skybar would almost certainly seem more at home in Miami's South Beach than it does on the gritty East Carson strip. Still, the city skyline somehow looks lovelier way up here in the air, where evening tables and even cabanas can be reserved. Outdoor fire pits and a retractable roof complete the atmosphere. Unfortunately, memberships are required; you'll find an application online.

MAP 3: 1601 E. Carson St., 412/651-4713, www.skybarpgh.com; Thurs. and Sat. 7pm-2am, Fri. 4pm-2am; no cover before 11pm, $7 after 11pm

VILLA SOUTHSIDE

A clean and minimalist bar and nightclub that also offers a fairly extensive tapas and appetizer menu, the two-story Villa Southside is owned and operated by the same family who ran Bruschetta's, the Italian eatery that formerly occupied this very space. Villa, however, is certainly a departure, considering that the dance floor, the modernist stone deejay booth, and the high-end lounge furniture topped with candles are the major draws. There's also a large outdoor patio, which is perfect on warm nights, and a plethora of plasma TVs screening—you guessed it—pro sports.

MAP 3: 1831 E. Carson St., 412/431-3535, www.villasouthside.com; Wed.-Fri. 5pm-2am, Sat. 7pm-2am; no cover

Mount Washington

Map 3

BARS

REDBEARD'S

Just steps from the lobby of the Monongahela Incline and the overlook decks of Grandview Avenue, Redbeard's is probably the only Mount Washington bar that doesn't come complete with an intimidating, locals-only feel. Of course, the majority of the folks who line the bar and fill the back booths *are* locals, but Duquesne University students in particular flock here for the many discount beer and wings nights. Redbeard's can accommodate quite a crowd on warm summer evenings, which is also when the umbrella-covered patio seating fills up especially fast. A second location in Downtown, **Redbeard's on Sixth** (144 6th St., 412/261-2324, daily 11am-2am), fills up with sports fans after work and during Steelers and Penguins games.

MAP 3: 201 Shiloh St., 412/431-3730, www.redbeardspgh.com; daily 11am-2am; no cover

Shadyside

Map 4

BARS

MARIO'S EAST SIDE SALOON

This location was for many moons home to the now-defunct Doc's Place, which always felt something like a pre-game frat party, but with manners. Mario's East Side Saloon is operated by the same team responsible for Mario's South Side Saloon, although, thankfully, the old Doc's Place vibe still seems more or less in place. The upper-level outdoor patio (where smoking is allowed) is just as fun, and the burgers are just as burnt as they ever were. Not a bad choice if you're up for a low-key night with a relatively young crowd.

MAP 4: 5442 Walnut St., 412/681-3713, www.mariospgh.com/eastside; Mon.-Thurs. 4pm-2am, Fri.-Sat. 11am-2am; no cover

GAY AND LESBIAN

★ SPIN BARTINI & ULTRA LOUNGE

Located in the former home of the Cuban-themed Club Havana, this stylish and fashion-forward lounge doesn't specifically market itself as a gay club. Still, Shadyside's GLBT crowd does seem to have claimed Spin as yet another boast-worthy attraction in what is quickly becoming known as a gay neighborhood. As for the interiors and the experience itself, both are very much what you'd expect from a club referring to itself as an ultra lounge: The liberal and open-minded patrons are generally stylish and upscale, as is the club itself. Dressing to impress is strongly encouraged. Live jazz shows and cabarets are occasionally staged, while Spin is strictly a dance club scene on Fridays and Saturdays.

MAP 4: 5744 Ellsworth Ave., 412/362-7746, www.spinbartini.com; daily 4pm-2am; no cover Mon.-Fri., $5 and up Sat., Sun., and special events

LOUNGES

ALTO LOUNGE

Alto is a relatively sophisticated lounge that is literally awash in a collection of calming blue lights. Its success has much to do with the fact that there's nothing else quite like it in the immediate vicinity. And although it largely caters to Shadyside's grad student and young professional population, this is also the perfect choice for a first date—the minimalist decor seems a bit futuristic and a touch romantic, at all once. The cocktail menu is decidedly high-end. You'll also find bottle service, an impressive wine list, and a modest offering of appetizers.

MAP 4: 728 Copeland St., 412/682-1074, www.altolounge.com; Wed.-Sun. 5pm-2am; no cover

Squirrel Hill and Point Breeze

Map 5

BARS

SILKY'S SPORTS BAR & GRILL

If Squirrel Hill's hipster havens or its ethnic cafés aren't exactly your idea of a good time, consider Silky's, a welcoming sports bar with a friendly, nonexclusionary vibe. During particularly important sporting contests—or any time the Steelers are playing—Silky's can get a bit overrun with rowdy and often overzealous fans. But any other day of the week, it's a perfectly anonymous place to unwind with an Iron City beer, a burger, and a side of fries. And although it appears small from the outside, Silky's two floors and upper balcony are actually quite roomy, making it a smart choice for large groups.

MAP 5: 1731 Murray Ave., 412/421-9222; daily 3pm-2am; no cover

★ SQUIRREL HILL CAFÉ

Don't bother calling it the Squirrel Hill Café, as it's fairly unlikely that anyone will know what you're talking about. Known locally as "The Cage," this is a relatively unimposing room filled only with cafeteria-style booths, two TV sets tuned to sports or news, and a small balcony that opens only on busy nights. But don't be fooled: The Cage has long been one of the city's most popular scenester bars, largely because of Squirrel Hill's popularity with musicians and artists. But even though rents have risen here, the vibe at The Cage remains. Grad students from CMU and Pitt have long populated the bar's booths; show up during the afternoon to spot English teachers grading term papers while sipping pints of Guinness or Penn Pilsner.

MAP 5: 5802 Forbes Ave., 412/521-3327; Mon.-Tues. 4pm-2am, Wed.-Sat. 11am-2am, Sun. 6pm-2am; no cover

Bloomfield and Lawrenceville

Map 6

BARS

BELVEDERE'S ULTRA-DIVE

Essentially a dive bar of the decidedly hip variety, Belvedere's also frequently doubles as a live music venue, hosting classic punk bands and newer hip-hop and indie acts. The city's all-female roller derby league often holds its after-parties here following bouts. And while themed parties take place regularly, including a popular '80s night and karaoke and bingo nights, the real draw at Belvedere's is the truly unique energy and ambience of the place: gritty, honest, dirty, and downright fun.

MAP 6: 4016 Butler St., 412/687-2555, www.belvederesultradive.com; daily 11am-2am; $2-5

BLOOMFIELD BRIDGE TAVERN

Although popularly known as Pittsburgh's best choice for authentic Polish dining, the BBT, as it's known locally, is also a popular neighborhood bar and live-music destination. There isn't anything too terribly exciting on tap, although the bar's parking lot and its front porch always fill with bike messengers and activist types during the weekly Thursday Dollar Night, when import and craft-brewed bottles past their expiration date are hawked for a buck each. Drum and bass events are staged weekly, as are acoustic open-mic nights. Live rock bands, either touring or local, usually play on Friday and Saturday nights.

MAP 6: 4412 Liberty Ave., 412/682-8611, www.bloomfieldbridgetavern.com; Tues.-Sat. 5pm-2am; no cover

★ CHURCH BREW WORKS

Located in a lovingly restored Catholic church where actual pews are used for seating and massive beer tanks sit atop the altar, this Lawrenceville brewpub and restaurant offers one of Pittsburgh's most unusual drinking and dining experiences. The award-winning beers brewed here include a light and a dark lager, an English pale ale, a stout, and a specialty brew that changes on a monthly basis. And yet Church Brew Works is probably just as well known for its gourmet pub grub menu, featuring high-end interpretations of pasta, seafood, salads, sandwiches, and the ever-popular brick-oven pizza. The church itself, by the way—formerly known as St. John the Baptist—is fairly stunning; its collection of stained glass windows alone is worth the trip.

MAP 6: 3525 Liberty Ave., 412/688-8200, www.churchbrew.com; Mon.-Thurs. 11:30am-midnight, Fri.-Sat. 11:30am-1am, Sun. noon-9pm; no cover

★ GOOSKI'S

Call it a dive, call it a hipster hangout, or call it Pittsburgh's most legendary neighborhood watering hole—just make sure that before leaving town you spend at least one weekend night at Gooski's, preferably with a pitcher of cheap beer in front of you. It's long been known as one of the hardscrabble Steel City's most representative hangouts, but the true beauty of Gooski's lies in its diametrically

Pittsburgh's Brewing Craft Beer Scene

Pittsburgh's craft beer scene, which was nearly non-existent a decade ago, has exploded. Some might say this makes perfect sense; there's an old joke in Pittsburgh that the city is roughly 10 years behind the rest of the country when it comes to trends of any sort. Still, for a town of just 300,000 souls, the options for ale affectionados have reached surprising proportions. And it doesn't appear as if anyone's complaining.

The **Pittsburgh Craft Beer Week** website (www.pittsburghcraftbeerweek.com) is rich with information about local brewers and area beer news. Inaugurated by the nonprofit **Pittsburgh Craft Beer Alliance** in 2012, PCBW stages annual springtime events.

Robert Musson's *Brewing in Greater Pittsburgh* (Arcadia Publishing, 2012) explores the region's wide-ranging beer history, which dates back to 1765. *Craft Pittsburgh* (www.craftpittsburgh.com) is a quarterly magazine covering craft beer news and events throughout the area.

The North Side's **Penn Brewery** (800 Vinial St., 412/237-9402, www.pennbrew.com; Mon.-Sat. 11am-midnight) is Pittsburgh's oldest and largest microbrewing mainstay. Authentic German beers have been produced here since 1986, and the on-site German-flavored restaurant has long been a local favorite. Order a pint and a kielbasa Reuben in the outdoor *Biergarten,* where Bavarian-style *oompah* musicians wail away on accordions.

You simply can't experience the craft beer scene in Pittsburgh without bellying up to the bar at the legendary **Church Brew Works** (3525 Liberty Ave., 412/688-8200, www.churchbrew.com, Mon.-Thurs. 11:30am-11pm, Fri.-

opposed clientele: Saddle up to the bar, and you'll soon find yourself in conversation with an unemployed steel worker, or maybe a tough-talking motorcycle maven. Area hipsters—many who aren't from the area at all, but who've driven for miles just to make the scene—fill the bar's booths and the billiards room. On Saturday nights, local garage rock bands perform.

MAP 6: 3117 Brereton St., 412/681-1658; daily 11am-2am; $4-7 live music shows

INDUSTRY PUBLIC HOUSE

Offering an even mixture of American comfort food, artisanal cocktails, and craft beer, the Industry Public House hits a perfect ambience between pre-Prohibition trendiness and gritty, industrial modernity. It's sometimes referred to as a gastropub, and it's certainly true that the carb-heavy menu is nearly as impressive as the ridiculously long list of microbrews on tap. The wine and whiskey are also top-notch, and the creatively named cocktails are generous on the pour.

MAP 6: 4305 Butler St., 412/683-1100, www.industrypgh.com; daily 11am-2am; no cover

Sat. 11:30-midnight, Sun. noon-9pm), an award-winning, full-service brewpub located inside a restored, early 20th-century Catholic church. Don't miss it.

The search for odd and obscure beers is sometimes half the fun, but if you'd prefer to have someone else do the heavy lifting (not to mention the driving), **PA Brew Tours** (www.pabrewtours.com) shuttles enthusiasts to breweries and brewpubs throughout the state. Choose from half a dozen pre-planned tours, many of them based in and around the Pittsburgh area, or take a one-of-a-kind tour customized that meets your needs and interests. Pricing starts at $39 per person.

One of the city's more unusual craft beer events is **TAPPED,** a regular series of pop-up beer gardens that appear in various up-and-coming hotspots around town. To find out if an event is being planned during your visit, check out www.facebook.com/tappedpgh, or visit the website of **Epic Development** (http://epicdevelopmentspgh.blogspot.com), the forward-thinking economic development firm behind the events.

The city's longest-running mini-beer festival is the always-popular **Steel City Big Pour** (www.constructionjunction.org/pages/bigpour), which is best described as a beer week-style party that takes in just one day. The Big Pour happens in early September inside Construction Junction, a used building materials retailer, which lends the event something of an authentic and hard-edged ambiance. All manner of area craft beers can be sampled, and a local brewery usually creates a beer that can only be tasted at the Big Pour.

NEW AMSTERDAM

It's certainly no coincidence that one of Pittsburgh's favorite bastions of hipster cool, the bar and café known as New Amsterdam, is smack-dab in the heart of Lawrenceville's main drag, which is quickly transforming into one of Pittsburgh's most exciting destination neighborhoods for the creative set. As for the bar itself, which is a squat brick square of a building with a garage door entrance opening onto the sidewalk, it's quite unlike anything else in the area. The exterior is plastered with a gorgeous skull-motif mural by the local artist Matt Spahr, and the food and drinks—wings, mac and cheese, fish tacos—pay appropriate homage to the neighborhood's blue-collar traditions. Whether you're looking to refuel or simply do a bit of people-watching, this new Lawrenceville tradition is a solid choice.

MAP 6: 4421 Butler St., 412/904-2915, www.newamsterdam412.com; Mon.-Fri. 4pm-2am, Sat.-Sun. noon-2am; $5-10 for special events

REMEDY

Formerly home to the Floridian-themed Ray's Marlin Beach Bar & Grill, where seafood was served and dance parties took place on the top floor, Remedy has thankfully managed to retain much of what made Ray's such a well-loved spot. At its core, Remedy is still a quirky neighborhood hot spot with obscure microbrews on tap and old-school hip-hop on the jukebox. The bar's best feature, though, may be its large and unusual layout; with three floors and an outdoor deck, Remedy can sometimes feel like a few different bars packed into one building. Art shows are a regular feature, as are the deejay-hosted weekend dance parties. The menu is filled with both vegetarian and comfort food options.

MAP 6: 5121 Butler St., 412/781-6771, www.remedypgh.com; Mon. and Sat. 4pm-2am, Tues.-Fri. 3pm-2am, Sun. 12:30pm-2am; no cover

★ ROUND CORNER CANTINA

Easily of one the Lower Lawrenceville area's hottest and most-talked-about drinking and dining destinations, Round Corner Cantina is a gorgeously decorated Mexican-style bar and eatery catering to the same sort of young and artsy crowds that frequent Brillobox and the nearby New Amsterdam. Formerly a neighborhood dive, the cantina has been thoroughly refurbished with retro hand-painted signage and rickety wooden seating. The menu features a surprisingly authentic selection of Mexican street food and imported Mexican beer, and the outdoor patio is one of the neighborhood's most pleasant surprises.

MAP 6: 3720 Butler St., 412/904-2279, www.roundcornercantina.com; Mon.-Wed. 5pm-midnight, Thurs.-Fri. 5pm-2am, Sat. 2pm-2am, Sun. noon-midnight; no cover

THUNDERBIRD CAFÉ

If you're looking for an authentic dive bar in the East End—in other words, one that hasn't long ago been gentrified by college students—the Thunderbird Café might just be your place. And what's more, although the Thunderbird was previously known as little more than a cheap spot to get good and sloshed, it's now known as a cheap spot to get good and sloshed while taking in live music, often of the indie-rock or alt-country variety. It's also not a bad place to wind down after knocking down the bowling pins at Arsenal Lanes, which is just down the street on the corner of Butler and 44th Streets.

MAP 6: 4023 Butler St., 412/682-0177, www.thunderbirdcafe.net; Mon.-Thurs. and Sun. 11am-midnight, Fri.-Sat. 11am-1am; $3-15 during live music shows

GAY AND LESBIAN

BLUE MOON

A seriously low-key neighborhood pub—basically a dive bar for Lawrenceville's GLBT crowd—the Blue Moon is not exactly the city's classiest queer joint. But if it's a truly judgment-free zone you're looking for, look no further. Because while a night out here can be equal parts rude and rambunctious, it can also be a wildly good time, assuming you're willing to let loose and let go of your inhibitions. (Trannies and drag queens, for instance, are especially fond of the Blue Moon.) The frequently scheduled events (drag and fashion shows, for instance) are just as fun, and equally goofy. And don't miss the back-room bar, with its vintage bar and back patio.

MAP 6: 5115 Butler St., 412/781-1119; Mon. 4pm-1am, Tues.-Sat. 5pm-2am, Sun. 5pm-1am; no cover

CATTIVO

A surprisingly massive gay bar and dance club tucked away in a somewhat sketchy area of Lawrenceville, Cattivo is especially popular with Pittsburgh's lesbian crowd. But make no mistake: Cattivo isn't a high-end lounge, and the interiors are certainly nothing to shout about. The crowd, however, is said to be exceptionally friendly and accepting; Steelers games are shown on a big screen; and a pub-grub-style kitchen serving pizza, hoagies, and wings stays open until 1am. Every Friday and Saturday night, deejays get the crowd moving in Cattivo Sotto, the bar's lower-level dance floor.

MAP 6: 146 44th St., 412/687-2157, www.cattivo.biz; Tues.-Sat. 4pm-2am; $5-10 after 9pm

LIVE MUSIC

BRILLOBOX

One of Pittsburgh's top see-and-be-seen spots for the bedhead crowd, Brillobox is run by a husband-and-wife team who relocated here after establishing themselves in New York City's contemporary art world. (The name is a nod to the eponymous Warhol work.) The ground floor is strictly a drinking establishment where Cat Power and M.I.A. records serenade the city's hipster glitterati; the owners' tastefully displayed paintings and sculptures decorate the walls and shelves. Live music takes place on the second floor, which conveniently has its own bar tucked into the back corner. Local pop and indie-rock bands perform about as often as do national touring acts. Other popular happenings include deejay nights, like the now-legendary Pandemic events, and the occasional multimedia art show or literary event.

MAP 6: 4104 Penn Ave., 412/621-4900, www.brillobox.net; Mon.-Sat. 5pm-2am; no cover downstairs, $6-15 upstairs

MR. SMALL'S THEATRE

Cleverly located inside the nave of the former St. Ann's Catholic church in Millvale, Mr. Small's is a midsize venue with near-perfect acoustics. Performers run the gamut, although hip-hop, indie rock, and metal acts make up the vast majority of the club's schedule. What's more, a professional-grade recording studio is on-site, and the company also maintains its own low-key record label. For aspiring rock stars, Small's offers occasional workshops and music camps. See the website for show times and dates, as well as recording studio availability.

MAP 6: 400 Lincoln Ave., 412/821-4447, www.mrsmalls.com; $10-50 performances, VIP balcony seating available at additional cost

31ST STREET PUB

Owned and operated by a heavily tattooed Harley-Davidson enthusiast, the 31st Street Pub is the Steel City's official headquarters for gritty garage rock, punk, and all other subgenres generally associated with black leather and power chords. The crowd tends to be equally underworldly; depending on which band is on the bill you might spot aging junkie punks, skinheads, heavy metal fans, or smartly coifed hipsters. If you're looking to get soused, you've come to the right place. Domestic beer, served in red plastic cups, is exceedingly cheap, and Jägermeister is available on tap.

MAP 6: 3101 Penn Ave., 412/391-8334, www.31stpub.com; pub hours Wed. 3pm-9pm, Thurs.-Fri. 3pm-2am, Sat. 9pm-2am; Thurs.-Sat. shows start at 10pm, most shows start at 9pm; $10 in advance, $12 at the door

East Liberty and Garfield **Map 6**

BARS

HARVARD & HIGHLAND

One of the more recent additions to what is quickly becoming a nationally recognized food-and-drink empire, Harvard & Highland is helmed by the heavily tattooed Kevin Sousa, a uniquely creative master chef who takes pride in constructing edible works of art for the regular Joe. Harvard & Highland, however, which rests above Sousa's Union Pig & Chicken, is purely a cocktail bar. But even if the retro Prohibition whimsy found at Acacia, for instance, happens to rub you the wrong way, you'll still want to give H&H a fair shake. Molecular mixology is the term given to the manner in which drinks are created, and aside from the bar's breezy New England ambience, you might find other surprises: Guest mixologists from out of town sometimes work the bar. And the menu will only improve with time.

MAP 6: 220 N. Highland Ave., 412/363-7675, www.sousapgh.com/harvard-highland; Mon.-Thurs. 5pm-1am, Fri.-Sat. 5pm-2am, Sun. 5pm-11pm; no cover

KELLY'S BAR

Once a no-name neighborhood dirt-bag bar, the lovingly refurbished Kelly's is practically synonymous with East End style and sophistication, but in a slightly retro and ironic sense. With its art deco design, Wurlitzer jukebox, and Tiki-themed back deck, it's no surprise that Kelly's has played such an important role in the recent revitalization of East Liberty. The bad news is the too-cool-for-school waitstaff, some of who are infamous for their inattentiveness. You'll soon forget about all that, however, after getting your hands on one of the bar's expertly mixed cocktails or a jerk-chicken burger from the surprisingly competent kitchen.

MAP 6: 6012 Penn Circle S., 412/363-6012; Mon.-Thurs. 5pm-midnight, Fri.-Sat. 5pm-2am; no cover

SHARP EDGE BEER EMPORIUM

Respected by beer snobs locally, and even countrywide, the Sharp Edge is perhaps best known for its extensive selection of obscure Belgian drafts. With more than 300 internationally crafted beers available, there's something for everyone, no matter which European or developing nation you'd like to explore in pint or bottle form. Few of the imported selections come cheap, of course; try the mystery brew if you're drinking on a budget. Burgers, sandwiches, pizzas, and other assorted American finger foods are also a big draw. If you'd prefer your dinner party quiet, grab a table in the back room. A Downtown location, **Bistro 922 Penn** (922 Penn Ave., 412/338-2437), is surprisingly roomy and offers 36 taps and nifty beer gift baskets. Other outposts include one in Sewickley called **Bistro Sewickley** (510 Beaver St., 412/749-0305); another in suburban Peters Township known as the **Brasserie** (102 Gallery Dr., 742/942-2437); and the **Creekhouse** (288 W. Steuben St., 412/922-8118), located in the West End neighborhood of Crafton.

MAP 6: 302 S. St. Clair St., 412/661-3537, www.sharpedgebeer.com; Mon.-Thurs. 11am-midnight, Fri.-Sat. 11am-1am, Sun. 11am-9pm; no cover

LIVE MUSIC

GARFIELD ARTWORKS

Although technically a visual arts gallery, Garfield Artworks is also one of the most prolific live-music venues in town, booking an almost nightly schedule of underground rock bands, avant-jazz artists, goth and industrial outfits, and the occasional electroclash spectacle. This is thanks in no small part to the locally notorious Manny Theiner, a longtime music promoter who has been bringing indie bands to Pittsburgh for over two decades. The digs aren't much to look at—GarfArt is nothing more than a big open box, sometimes with a plastic tub of free beer stashed in a far corner. No

clockwise from top left: Redbeard's; Church Brew Works; Sharp Edge Beer Emporium

matter, though—the disaffected and mostly teenaged concertgoers tend to provide more than enough visual stimulation. See the website for concert dates and times.

MAP 6: 4931 Penn Ave., 412/361-2262, www.garfieldartworks.com; $10 cover, show prices vary

MODERNFORMATIONS GALLERY

Much like its down-the-street neighbor Garfield Artworks, ModernFormations is also first and foremost an art venue, yet it hosts a wonderfully cutting-edge calendar of indie- and art-rock groups. When particularly popular acts pass through, MoFo can find itself packed from wall to wall, so take care to arrive early when the next up-and-coming band stops by. See the website for details on performances and other events. Insider's tip: If you're feeling hunger pains between bands, grab an order of fresh spring rolls from Pho Minh, the Vietnamese place next door.

MAP 6: 4919 Penn Ave., 412/362-0274, www.modernformations.com; gallery Thurs. 7pm-9pm, Sat. 1pm-4pm; $5-15 live music

Greater Pittsburgh

Map 7

LIVE MUSIC

CARNEGIE LIBRARY MUSIC HALL

Although the Music Hall at the Carnegie Library's Homestead branch has been hosting musicians and performers of all stripes for decades now, it was only recently transformed into the sort of midsized concert venue that hosts national rock, pop, and indie bands. Touring jam bands and reunited classic acts are also a big draw; comedy shows and the occasional play are sometimes booked as well. And while local fans have been known to kvetch about the venue's uncomfortable seating and its strict no-alcohol policy, the good news is that shows are all-ages. Designed in the tradition of the grand American music hall, this is an ideal antidote to the significantly grungier rock venues in the city. Doors open a half hour before scheduled performances.

MAP 7: 510 E. 10th Ave., Munhall, 412/368-5225, www.librarymusichall.com; phone ticketing Mon.-Fri. noon-5pm; $20 and up

MOONDOG'S

Moondog's isn't particularly easy to get to without your own method of transportation—it sits way north of the city in a blue-collar burgh along the Allegheny River—but if authentic local and national blues music is your bag, it's absolutely worth the trip. When live music isn't happening, Moondog's acts as a cozy neighborhood pub. But on most weekends, local blues acts and singer-songwriters like Norm Nardini take the stage. Sometimes true blues legends show up; over the past decade and a half, Moondog's has hosted the likes of Keb' Mo', Koko Taylor, and Junior Wells. See the website for show times and dates.

MAP 7: 378 Freeport Rd., Blawnox, 412/828-2040, www.moondogs.us; Wed. 3pm-6pm, Thurs. 3pm-midnight, Fri. 3pm-2am, Sat. 7pm-2am, closed Sun.-Tues. unless there is a scheduled show; $15 and up performances

Arts and Culture

Look for ★ to find recommended arts venues.

HIGHLIGHTS

★ **Best Contemporary Art Gallery:** With frequent freebie shows displaying everything from printed letterpress art to kitschy installations, and even live music and odd performance art, **SPACE** is consistently on the creative cutting edge (page 174).

★ **Best Oddly Hilarious Comedy Club:** With its clubhouse atmosphere, quirky stand-up shows, and unusually excellent roster of workshops for aspiring comedians, the nonprofit **Arcade Comedy Theater** offers a far-from-average performing arts experience (page 174).

★ **Best Place to Get Your Rock On:** The North Shore's **Stage AE** has that amphitheater sound, but it's small enough to host edgy pop and indie rock acts that haven't quite hit the mainstream (page 179).

★ **Best Theater:** Popularly known as Pittsburgh's most forward-thinking theater, the adventurous **City Theatre** stages new works, spoken word, and the occasional world premiere (page 181).

★ **Best Art-House Cinema:** Take a journey back to the Golden Age of cinema at **Oaks Theater,** a restored art deco theater built in 1941 (page 189).

Here's an idea for a potentially explosive experiment: Once you arrive in Pittsburgh, ask a local musician, and then a visual artist, a journalist, a photographer, a dancer, and an actor what each one has to say about the state of the arts here. If history is anything to go by, you'll want to duck soon to avoid the flying hyperbole.

Which isn't to say that the members of Pittsburgh's creative class have particularly bad attitudes, or that they don't approve of the music and art being created here. On the contrary, the general consensus among the town's right-brained types seems to be that when it comes to competing in the arts on an international scale, our community simply isn't living up to its potential. And because Pittsburgh is a sizable city that feels so much like a small town, and because the living is so cheap and easy in Southwestern Pennsylvania, potential is probably the one word you'll keep humming to yourself if you spend enough time here.

Naturally though, more than a few creative types have taken full advantage of the town's growing opportunities. In years past, for instance, the East End neighborhoods of Garfield and East Liberty have seen the once-bedraggled Penn Avenue corridor transformed into a collection of contemporary galleries. And recently, scores of locally grown conferences and lecture series have continued to draw impressively large crowds.

Of course, as is to be expected in any midsize urban area with limited resources, Pittsburgh artists tend to pick up and leave with

Free Parking Sundays

Those on a tight budget should consider planning Downtown cultural excursions on a Sunday, as all street parking is free and most garages offer all-day parking for just $5. Many Downtown galleries and shops are open until 5 or 6pm on Sundays (finally!), and matinee performances at favorite Cultural District venues are often a steal, especially when compared to the price of evening performances. What's more, a good number of Downtown restaurants offer affordable brunch and prix fixe (tasting) menus on the weekend as well. So on Sundays, find a great spot, leave your car put, and take advantage of the Free Fare Zone offered by Port Authority's light rail system, known locally as the T. It includes all four Downtown stops and both North Shore stops, which offer easy access to PNC Park, Heinz Field, Rivers Casino, and the rest of the North Shore's attractions.

alarming frequency; the city's economic and cultural gatekeepers have long been scratching their heads and hoping for a solution to the apparent brain-drain. Grassroots arts organizations and community groups like the Sprout Fund have been doing their part, spending copious amounts of time and money in an attempt to make Pittsburgh a more attractive and a more exciting place to live and play.

So what exactly does the future of creative expression look like in the Steel City? Certainly, some things are expected to improve: The August Wilson Center for African American Culture finally opened to the public after years of planning and fund-raising, for instance. Pittsburgh is also now home to ToonSeum, one of only three cartoon art museums in the country. And the Lawrenceville neighborhood is becoming nationally known for its DIY arts and crafts scene. In the meantime, the city's creative population—potentially explosive as it may well be—will no doubt continue to soldier on.

Downtown

Map 1

CINEMA

HARRIS THEATER

As a member of the Pittsburgh Filmmakers family of art house cinemas, Harris Theater is one of the most progressive places in town to watch movies. And aside from a few adult bookstore video booths and special screenings at Cultural District galleries, it's the only theater in the Downtown area. Independent and foreign films are what you'll find here, although since many movies screen only for a limited time, move quickly if something grabs your interest.

If you're in town specifically for the annual Three Rivers Film Festival, you'll be spending a lot of time at the Harris, which will quite likely be the closest theater to your Downtown hotel.

MAP 1: 809 Liberty Ave., 412/682-4111, http://pfm.pittsburgharts.org; general admission $8; event ticket prices vary

CONCERT VENUES

A. J. PALUMBO CENTER

Although technically the home of the Duquesne University Dukes and Lady Dukes basketball teams, the A. J. Palumbo Center frequently transforms into a pop and rock concert hall after dark. Only the biggest artists at the top of their game perform here; years past have seen Public Enemy, Jane's Addiction, Green Day, and Counting Crows take the stage. Other entertainment and sporting events happen occasionally, such as wrestling and boxing. Insider's tip: To avoid being crushed on the floor during a rock show, arrive early and grab a seat in the general admission bleachers nearest the stage.

MAP 1: 600 Forbes Ave., 412/396-5140, www.duq.edu/about/campus/aj-palumbo-center

CONSOL ENERGY CENTER

It's true that plenty of Pittsburghers still mourn the loss of our city's architecturally stunning Civic Arena, the former home of the Stanley Cup-winning Pittsburgh Penguins. However, it turns out that the replacement—almost directly across the street—isn't half bad. The LEED Gold-certified CONSOL Energy Center is packed with amenities: a brewpub, a 12,000-square-foot Penguins team store, a dozen escalators, a fine dining restaurant, and (according to the center's website) the widest seats of any NHL stadium, at 24 inches. Big-name pop acts and rock bands perform regularly as well, as will the Pittsburgh Power, the city's new Arena Football League pro team.

MAP 1: 1001 5th Ave., 412/642-1800, www.consolenergycenter.com

GALLERIES

FUTURE TENANT

The Pittsburgh Cultural Trust hosts this project of Carnegie Mellon University, an ever-changing art space where exhibitions might take the form of amateur installations, literary events, video art presentations, or pretty much anything else the creative mind can conceive. Given the truly experimental nature of Future Tenant, shows can understandably be somewhat hit or miss. And although use of the space isn't technically limited to artists from the CMU community, the works of the school's students and faculty are certainly represented with frequency. MFA exhibitions take place at the end of each school semester.

MAP 1: 819 Penn Ave., www.futuretenant.org; gallery hours vary; free

★ SPACE

SPACE is undoubtedly one of city's most contemporary-minded arts emporiums, despite its veteran status in the gallery scene. And with deejays, live music, and hordes of the city's prettiest young things showing up *en masse* for nearly every event, openings tend to more closely resemble house parties than the stale wine-and-cheese happenings found at your average gallery. Special attention is paid to local artists whose work may be otherwise ignored or overlooked, especially those photographers, visual artists, or installation builders who consistently push the envelope. Guest curators organize large and very popular group shows often.

MAP 1: 812 Liberty Ave., 412/325-7723, www.spacepittsburgh.org; Wed.-Thurs. and Sun. 11am-6pm, Fri.-Sat. 11am-10pm; free

WOOD STREET GALLERIES

Certainly one of Pittsburgh's most ambitious contemporary galleries, Wood Street, which is publicly funded by the Pittsburgh Cultural Trust, is so named because of its location above the Downtown Wood Street T station. Exhibitions are decidedly hit or miss but are almost always worth at least a cursory look. Multidisciplinary artists from Pittsburgh and, indeed, around the world, have shown here; the curators seem to have especially weak spots for industrial-themed installation art and wildly contemporary video art. Conceptual photography projects show up occasionally, and the space also houses the trust's shared office space program, which provides resources, supports, and tools to smaller local arts organizations.

MAP 1: 601 Wood St., 412/471-5605, www.woodstreetgalleries.org; Wed.-Thurs. 11am-6pm, Fri.-Sat. 11am-8pm, Sun. 11am-5pm; free

PERFORMING ARTS

★ ARCADE COMEDY THEATER

Downtown Pittsburgh's destination for comedy, Arcade Comedy Theater is a nonprofit 75-seat space that hosts all manner of comedy, from stand-up to improvisational acts and everything in between. The atmosphere is as fun as the performances, complete with a pinball machine in the lobby. Ticket prices are affordable. Arcade Comedy Theater also offers a slew of courses and workshops for aspiring comics and for children just beginning to explore the craft.

MAP 1: 811 Liberty Ave., 412/339-0608, www.arcadecomedytheater.com; $5-20

clockwise from top left: Benedum Center for the Performing Arts; Arcade Comedy Theater; Heinz Hall

BENEDUM CENTER FOR THE PERFORMING ARTS

Formerly known as the Stanley Theater, the Benedum Center is another of Pittsburgh's Downtown Cultural District cornerstones. The Pittsburgh Opera, the Civic Light Opera, and the Pittsburgh Ballet Theater all use the building as a home base, so patrons are often seasonal subscribers. This is also where mainstream Broadway fare (*Cats, Phantom of the Opera*) can be found. And as for the venue's simply stunning $43 million restoration? Let's just say that it's no wonder the Benedum is now on the National Register of Historic Places.

MAP 1: 719 Liberty Ave., 412/456-6666, www.trustarts.org/venues/benedum.aspx; $31-149

BYHAM THEATER

At just over 200 years old, the Byham Theater (originally known as the Gayety Theater, and then as the Fulton) remains one of the most important cornerstones of the city's Cultural District theater scene. And although the Gayety was largely a vaudeville house and the Fulton a movie theater, today the main stage presents a mixture of dance, ballet, theater, and even live music. The fully restored, 1,500-seat interior is nothing but classic American music hall; apparently no detail was spared. Imagine a luxurious lobby, a full balcony, and friendly ushers who escort latecomers to their seats with a flashlight. The Byham is a true American classic.

MAP 1: 101 6th St., 412/456-1350, www.trustarts.org/venues/byham.aspx; $19-55

CABARET AT THEATER SQUARE

The Civic Light Opera most certainly has a long and storied history in Pittsburgh. It premiered back in 1946 with a production on the Pitt campus before moving into the Civic Arena, and then Heinz Hall, before finally settling in at the Benedum Center. The 265-seat Cabaret at Theater Square, however, is less than 10 years old, and it's there that the CLO's cheery and accessible brand of musical theater is performed year-round. And although the majority of the Cabaret's guests enjoy musical revues and family-friendly shows like *Nunsense* from within the comfort of a traditional theater seating, the dinner-and-a-show option is available as well. Late-night cabaret entertainment also takes place at the adjacent **Backstage Bar** (655 Penn Ave., 412/325-6769, www.trustarts.org/visit/facilities/backstage), which features outdoor dining and always-free entertainment.

MAP 1: 665 Penn Ave., 412/325-6766, www.clocabaret.com; $40-65

Bob Marley in the Steel City

Quite inadvertently, the city of Pittsburgh became a very important historical footnote in the history of Rastafari and reggae music on September 23, 1980. That was the day the great Jamaican singer/songwriter Bob Marley played his very last concert, at Downtown's Stanley Theater. Today, the Stanley is known as the **Benedum Center for the Performing Arts.** Should you wish to pay tribute to the man otherwise known as the third world's first pop superstar, you can do so by visiting the Benedum at 719 Liberty Avenue in the Cultural District. Soon after Marley's final public performance, the artist died of cancer in a Miami hospital at the age of 36.

HEINZ HALL

Anyone interested in taking in a performance by the Pittsburgh Symphony Orchestra will need to settle in at Heinz Hall, which is the ensemble's Downtown home base. And although not currently at the very top of its game—as it was during conductor Lorin Maazel's tenure—the PSO has consistently been recognized by experts around the world as one of the country's greatest orchestras. The hall itself is a splendidly restored former hotel and boasts such features as an adjustable orchestra pit and an outdoor garden plaza with a waterfall. Guided tours are available to groups of eight or more.

MAP 1: 600 Penn Ave., 412/392-4900, www.pittsburghsymphony.org, $35-175

PITTSBURGH PUBLIC THEATER (AT THE O'REILLY THEATER)

Unbeknownst to even most locals, the O'Reilly Theater was designed by superstar architect Michael Graves, a name you might recognize if you've lately perused the kitchenware aisle at Target (Graves is also a product designer). The 650-seat theater opened in late 1999, and it was built specifically with acoustic excellence in mind. It's also the only theater space Downtown featuring a "thrust" stage, meaning that the audience surrounds the stage floor on three sides in a U shape. Performances are suitably eccentric while still maintaining mainstream appeal; successful Off-Broadway and comedy shows seem to do well.

MAP 1: 621 Penn Ave., 412/316-1600, www.ppt.org; $28-55

Strip District

Map 1

GALLERIES

SOCIETY FOR CONTEMPORARY CRAFT

Located in an industrial warehouse space, the Society for Contemporary Craft has been presenting exhibitions both duly conservative and wildly eccentric for more than 30 years. The permanent collection includes blown glass by Dale Chihuly and rare chairs by the likes Frank Gehry and Mr. Imagination; clay, metal, and fiber crafts are also on display. Temporary exhibitions might feature anything from decoupage collages by inner-city high school kids to outsider art from the Deep South and even utilitarian Native American crafts. The gallery's relatively small gift shop, known simply as **The Store,** generally carries handmade purses, scarves, and stationery, as well as decorative items made of glass and wood. You'll also find a small selection of home furnishings, such as lamps, tables, and chairs. Jewelry, toys, and other small gift items are popular and generally well stocked.

Should you find yourself at the Steel Plaza T station Downtown, be sure to check out the society's satellite gallery, inside the One Mellon Bank Center building. The satellite gallery is open daily until midnight. Exhibits at both galleries are free.

MAP 1: 2100 Smallman St., 412/261-7003, www.contemporarycraft.org; Mon.-Sat. 10am-5pm; free

North Side

Map 1

CINEMA

CARNEGIE SCIENCE CENTER RANGOS OMNIMAX THEATER

Leave it to the smart folks at the Carnegie Science Center to improve ever so slightly on the already fascinating IMAX theater experience, a high-quality, large-screen film format where the picture is usually three stories high, or roughly 50 feet. The Carnegie's screen, however, is four stories high. It's also concave, so that the on-screen action takes place not just in front of you, but also on both sides. Thankfully, the seats recline, so there's no need to worry about painful neck strain. Laser shows are especially popular and are set to popular music, and the midnight Pink Floyd laser show has been flocked to by students, local music lovers, and old hippies for years. Discounted tickets are available for seniors and children and when purchased with a general admission ticket to the Science Center.

MAP 1: 1 Allegheny Ave., 412/237-3400, www.carnegiesciencecenter.org; $8 adult, $13 double feature or laser show

CONCERT VENUES

★ STAGE AE

Near the site of the old Three Rivers Stadium, this North Shore concert hall is the newest addition to Pittsburgh's live music scene, hosting cutting-edge rock and pop acts that have yet to develop household-name status. It was designed to look, sound, and feel like the popular LC Pavilion in Columbus, Ohio. And that's a good thing, since Pittsburgh has long been lacking a venue that's larger than a club but smaller than an amphitheater.

MAP 1: 400 North Shore Dr., 412/229-5483, www.promowestlive.com/pittsburgh

PERFORMING ARTS

NEW HAZLETT THEATER

Located smack-dab in the middle of the Central North Side, the nonprofit New Hazlett is something of an anything-goes, all-purpose arts facility. Plays are staged on a regular basis, but so too are live music and spoken word performances, as well as various literary and artistic community gatherings. Performing arts organizations of all sorts pop up regularly at the New Hazlett, although new work by both the contemporary Dance Alloy troupe and the decidedly quirky Barebones productions theater company can be seen with some regularity.

MAP 1: Allegheny Square E., 412/320-4610, www.newhazletttheater.org

Oakland

Map 2

CINEMA

MELWOOD SCREENING ROOM

On the second floor of Pittsburgh Filmmakers (a film, video, and photography production center and training facility in North Oakland), Melwood Screening Room is the city's premiere locale for ultra-unusual indie films. When Matthew Barney's Cremaster Cycle came to town, for instance, the Melwood was the no-brainer choice to host. Student films play in this 130-seat venue as well, as does the local phenomenon known as Film Kitchen, a monthly independent film and video series featuring a selection of mostly locally made shorts.

MAP 2: 477 Melwood Ave., 412/681-5449, http://pfm.pittsburgharts.org; general admission $8; Film Kitchen $5; event ticket prices vary

CONCERT VENUES

CARNEGIE MUSIC HALL

Tucked into the same building as the Carnegie Museums of Art and Natural History, the beautifully restored and antique Carnegie Music Hall is a 1,928-seat venue often described as "acoustically perfect." That's good news for the patrons of the Pittsburgh Chamber Music Society, a group that performs regularly; folk concerts organized by Calliope, a local folk music society, take place as well. And the Carnegie Lecture Series brings to the music hall an always-impressive rotation of literary celebs.

MAP 2: 4400 Forbes Ave., 412/323-1919, www.pittsburghchambermusic.org

PETERSEN EVENTS CENTER

Constructed by the University of Pittsburgh in 2002 as a home for the Pitt Panthers basketball team, the main stadium at Petersen Events Center can seat roughly 10,000 fans, and that's not including club and luxury seats. Sports and fitness isn't the only game, however; top-selling pop and hip-hop acts like Counting Crows and Outkast perform frequently. In fact, Downtown's Mellon Arena is the only large-capacity venue in town with more seating. Alcohol isn't available at this venue.

MAP 2: 3719 Terrace St., 412/323-1919, http://web-smg.athletics.pitt.edu

GALLERIES

MILLER GALLERY AT CARNEGIE MELLON UNIVERSITY

Founded in 2000 by Regina Gouger Miller, an artist and alumna of CMU's School of Art, the 9,000-square-foot, three-story Miller Gallery is one of the city's most surprising and accessible venues of contemporary art, where exhibitions are always free to the public. As a division of the school's College of Fine Arts, it's also a place where members from the greater Pittsburgh community—including those who don't normally travel in artistic circles—are encouraged to widen their interpretation and understanding of contemporary art. Arts-related lectures and special events are occasionally scheduled.

MAP 2: Purnell Center for the Arts, 5000 Forbes Ave., 412/268-3618, http://millergallery.cfa.cmu.edu; Tues.-Sun. noon-6pm

PERFORMING ARTS

CHARITY RANDALL THEATRE

One of the three performance spaces used by the University of Pittsburgh's Theatre Department (the other two are the Henry Heymann Theatre, just downstairs, and the Cathedral of

Learning's Studio Theatre), the Charity Randall Theatre is an intimate, 478-seat auditorium. This is where the vast majority of student-run performances take place; Shakespeare is particularly popular, and years past have seen a similar glut of student-friendly fare (George Bernard Shaw, Andrew Lloyd Webber). Artists-in-residence working at Pitt can often be seen performing alongside the student actors.

MAP 2: Forbes Ave. at Bigelow Blvd., 412/624-7529, www.play.pitt.edu; $12-25

PITTSBURGH PLAYHOUSE

Situated in a somewhat obscure stretch of South Oakland (if you can find Magee-Women's Hospital, you're close), the Pittsburgh Playhouse is home to a professional company known as The Rep, as well as three student companies based at the nearby Point Park University: a children's theater company, a dance company, and a standard theater company. In other words, there's a *lot* going on at the playhouse during any given month—indeed, there are 235 performances annually—so there's a good chance that no matter your specific arts preference, you'll be able to find something that grabs your attention.

MAP 2: 22 Craft Ave., 412/621-4445, www.pittsburghplayhouse.com; $9-20

South Side

Map 3

GALLERIES

SILVER EYE CENTER FOR PHOTOGRAPHY

Aside from the occasional student shows that take place at Pittsburgh Filmmakers' Melwood Photography Gallery, the Silver Eye Center is the city's solitary locale dedicated exclusively to the photographic arts. The gallery has two small but inviting rooms that showcase Pittsburgh-based artists and artists from around the world. Independent films are occasionally screened at Silver Eye, and lectures, panel discussions, portfolio critiques, and workshops are also held.

MAP 3: 1015 E. Carson St., 412/431-1810, www.silvereye.org; Tues.-Sat. noon-6pm; donations accepted

PERFORMING ARTS

★ CITY THEATRE

Known as one of the city's most well-respected companies, City Theatre is tucked away in a cozy, red-brick building just a block from the corner of East Carson and 13th Streets. The 270-seat main studio has something of an industrial warehouse feel, a vibe that works especially well when the performance is particularly edgy.

top: Future Tenant; **bottom:** Irma Freeman Center for Imagination

Artistic director Tracy Brigden has been leading the company since 2001 and has since produced monologues, world premieres, and even an oddly avant-garde live music experience with Pittsburgh's own Squonk Opera.

MAP 3: 1300 Bingham St., 412/431-2489, www.citytheatrecompany.org; $35-65

Shadyside

Map 4

GALLERIES

MENDELSON GALLERY

The Mendelson Gallery is particularly interesting and worth a visit not only for its extensive collection of impressive modern selections (works by Keith Haring, Robert Mapplethorpe, and Thad Mosley have been featured in the past) but also because this East End gallery doubles as the home of its owner, Steve Mendelson, and was once a bordello confiscated by the IRS. Mendelson has recently opened a sister gallery in Paris's fashionable Sixth Arrondissement.

MAP 4: 5874 Ellsworth Ave., 412/361-8664, www.mendelsongallery.net; Wed.-Sat. noon-5pm; free

PITTSBURGH CENTER FOR THE ARTS

A self-described "nonprofit community arts campus," the Pittsburgh Center for the Arts is a unique resource center for visual artists. Artists-in-training can sign up for one of the center's ever-popular studio classes, while working professionals can apply to the residency program that takes place at various sites throughout the city. The work displayed in the gallery is produced largely by Southwestern Pennsylvanians with various skill levels. You'll find works by well-established artists displayed alongside pieces by newcomers.

MAP 4: 6300 5th Ave., 412/361-0873, www.pittsburgharts.org; Tues.-Wed. and Fri.-Sat. 10am-5pm, Thurs. 10am-7pm, Sun. noon-5pm; gallery admission $5 adults, $4 seniors, $3 students, children 12 and under free

Squirrel Hill and Point Breeze

Map 5

CINEMA

MANOR THEATER

Since the closure of Forward Avenue's Squirrel Hill Theatre, the four-screen Manor Theater is now the neighborhood's solitary cinema house. Still, it continues to screen a decent number of so-called big-budget indie films—movies that have a somewhat limited release, in other words, but that generally aren't too terribly left of center. Family fare and children's pictures also screen regularly, which makes good sense given the abundance of youngsters in this family-friendly neighborhood.

MAP 5: 1729 Murray Ave., 412/422-7729, www.manorpgh.com; $9.25 adult, $6.50 matinee before 6pm, $6.50 senior and child

REGENT SQUARE THEATER

A 300-seat, single-screen art-house cinema, Regent Square Theater is on the opposite side of Frick Park from Squirrel Hill. Regent Square, like Oakland's Melwood Screening Room and Downtown's Harris Theater, is a member of the Pittsburgh Filmmakers family; that means that eclectic films both domestic and foreign are the order of the day.

MAP 5: 1035 S. Braddock Ave., Pittsburgh, 412/681-5449, http://pfm.pittsburgharts.org; general admission $9; event ticket prices vary

PERFORMING ARTS

THE SPACE UPSTAIRS

Just above Construction Junction, this huge experimental and informal performance venue has been home to many outstanding drama and dance performances, contemporary installations, and multimedia works, many of which offer little to no separation between performer and audience. With its raw, hardwood-floored warehouse atmosphere, the venue makes for a unique and intimate experience quite unlike any other in the city. Contemporary dance company The Pillow Project is an artist in residence.

MAP 5: 214 N. Lexington St., 412/225-9269, www.thespaceupstairs.org

Shaking Up the Boards

Looking for theater that's a touch more progressive than the standard Cultural District fare? Consider tracking down a performance by one of the following contemporary companies.

Already legendary in Pittsburgh for its *Midnight Radio* series—which is something of an ultramodern version of Garrison Keillor's *A Prairie Home Companion*—**Bricolage** (www.webbricolage.org) is one of the hottest theater companies in Pittsburgh today. It produces a wide range of original work and adaptations, as well as truly unique interactive experiences.

Also pushing the live entertainment envelope is **The Microscopic Opera Company** (www.microscopicopera.org), which offers short and ultramodern chamber operas in seriously intimate spaces. Microscopic's recent fourth season will undoubtedly be remembered for its truly mesmerizing *Night of the Living Dead* interpretation.

On the contemporary dance front, **The Pillow Project** (www.pillowproject.org) is worth paying attention to. Something of a cross between a multimedia dance company and an experimental performance art collective, this group has already created a fascinating body of free-form dance work, including flash mob-like public performances.

Bodiography Contemporary Ballet (www.bodiographycbc.com) is another Pittsburgh dance win, bringing a much-needed dose of new life and modernity to classical ballet. The company produces a range of genre-blending, inspirational works that seamlessly meld contemporary music and visual design with the technical rigors of ballet.

And finally, while the much-loved **Quantum Theatre** (www.quantumtheatre.com) may have begun the trend of producing theatrical works at decidedly non-theatrical locations around town, the idea seems to have spread like wildfire over the past few years. It's become quite common in Pittsburgh for small companies and spontaneous collectives to produce immersive, small-budget works in unexpected locations—everything from wide-open public areas to abandoned warehouses, and even cramped private apartments. Keep an eye out in local cafés and galleries for flyers announcing these on-the-fly "shoestring theater" works.

Bloomfield and Lawrenceville

Map 6

GALLERIES

BOX HEART

Much like the emerging artists who live in the neighborhood, Box Heart gallery is a grassroots sort of place where handmade jewelry, handmade soaps, and other crafts can be found among paintings and other items of visual art by local up-and-comers. The gallery annually hosts the much-loved Art Inter/National Exhibition, inspired by the renowned Carnegie International, which has attracted artists from as far away as Iran, Chile, and China, to explore how space and environment influence the creative process.

MAP 6: 4523 Liberty Ave., 412/687-8858, www.boxheart.org; Sun. 1pm-5pm, Tues. 11am-6pm, Wed.-Sat. 10am-6pm; free

FE GALLERY

This all-volunteer-based (and volunteer-run) gallery and interdisciplinary nonprofits arts venue proves that sometimes you can get what you don't pay for. Located in a gorgeous Lawrenceville setting, Fe has shown a vast array of work by both local and international artists in genres ranging from painting and photography to contemporary installation and film. It also provides outreach programs and workshops to underserved communities and groups throughout the region. The gallery and space are able to exist through a combination of space rental fees for private events and the charitable support of local businesses, many of which are also located in Lawrenceville.

MAP 6: 4102 Butler St., 412/254-4038, www.fegallery.org; Tues.-Fri. noon-3pm, Sat. noon-4pm; free

PAINT MONKEY

While not necessarily a gallery per se, Lawrenceville's Paint Monkey is the city's only BYOB paint-and-sip make-it-yourself studio. Class themes vary from the cheeky (paint your pet nights) to the more eccentric (Day of the Dead sugar skulls), although works by classic painters are covered as well. All classes are aimed at beginners, though more advanced creative types will especially appreciate the fun, laid-back studio environment. Paint Monkey provides cups, corkscrews, napkins, and a tub of ice for keeping drinks chilled. You bring the booze and snacks. See the website for a complete calendar and to make reservations.

MAP 6: 100 43rd St., Studio 212, 412/770-4923, www.beapaintmonkey.com; hours and class prices vary

East Liberty and Garfield **Map 6**

GALLERIES

THE IRMA FREEMAN CENTER FOR IMAGINATION

Essentially a cross between a community outreach center, an arts school, and a gallery, the seriously ambitious mission of Garfield's Irma Freeman Center for Imagination involves "enrich[ing] and diversify[ing] the local community by building positive experiences in a multicultural, progressive setting." Quite a mouthful, to be sure. But the center's cofounder, Sheila Ali, has already developed a

Art All Night

Without a doubt, one of the most popular and beloved local arts and crafts events is Lawrenceville's **Art All Night,** a 22-hour overnight creative extravaganza that takes place during the last full weekend each April in varying locations throughout the neighborhood. Art All Night is a non-juried art show featuring the works of hundreds of established and aspiring artists in the Pittsburgh area.

The festivities begin on Saturday afternoon as artists drop off their work and volunteers quickly curate, hang, and place all the pieces. At 4pm the doors are opened, the music begins, and activities for families and children kick off—there's always a designated space with kid-friendly art, though the rest of the show is uncensored.

There are also many participatory art events—like Cardboard City, where visitors can help build a crowd-sourced city with a mix of cardboard, adhesive, paints, and markers, and the Ironed City Plastic Art Project, during which participants help iron ordinary plastic grocery bags into designs that will later be used in public art projects.

Starting at around 9pm, the mood is decidedly more adult and rowdy, but by the following Sunday morning it's quite chill, with much smaller crowds still enjoying the artwork.

Since the show is not juried and all are invited to participate, some work is obviously more interesting and desirable than others. Notably, the furnishings and sculpture seem to keep getting better each year, and many well-established artists of all mediums now support the Art All Night party.

Participation and attendance are both free. Visit www.artallnight.com for the most up-to-date details on the event and its artists.

fairly extensive schedule of classes, including yoga, mosaic-making, and green technology workshops designed to be taken by parents and their children. The center's summer camp has become quite well respected for the more mature and expressive approach it takes in working with child artists. The center also showcases visual arts exhibits, including a rotating selection of paintings by the late Irma Freeman herself—an incredibly prolific Pittsburgh artist who also happened to be Ali's grandmother. See the website for dates, times, and prices for workshops, classes, and other special events.

MAP 6: 5006 Penn Ave., 412/924-0634, www.irmafreeman.org; gallery Sat. 2pm-5pm and by appointment; free

MOST WANTED FINE ART

Owned and operated by the artist Jason Sauer, a transplant from Texas, whose work generally consists of large-scale installations and even demolition derby cars, Most Wanted is yet another Garfield-based contemporary art gallery featuring occasional live performances by punk, indie, and wildly experimental bands. Community outreach events happen on an occasional basis, as do events featuring poets and other performing artists. The gallery is also home to the Art Car project and the Stuff n Such Society. Openings are held during monthly first Friday Unblurred gallery

Gallery Crawls

The neighborhood-wide art gallery crawls that occur in Pittsburgh on a regular basis make for loads of good fun, even if contemporary art isn't necessarily your thing.

The Pittsburgh Cultural Trust sponsors the **Gallery Crawl in the Cultural District,** a free quarterly event that tends to take on something of a party atmosphere as the night wears on. As many as two dozen Downtown galleries, museums, and other venues are generally involved, and aside from simply showcasing new visual art, live music, dance, theater, film, and even architecture are also occasionally featured. Visit www.trustarts.org for specific dates and times, as well as a complete schedule of events and exhibits, all of which are free.

In a coordinated effort with the Cultural Trust's Gallery Crawl, the Pittsburgh Downtown Partnership hosts its quarterly **Night Market** at the same time. The Night Market brings dozens of vendors to the streets offering everything from crafty wares to tasty treats. Visit www.downtownpittsburgh.com for a list of dates and vendors, and for information on other special events, such as crafting workshops and art demonstrations.

The significantly edgier **Unblurred** gallery crawl happens on the first Friday of each month. The vast majority of its exhibitions and performances take place inside the galleries and cafés of the Penn Avenue Arts Corridor in Garfield and East Liberty. And as with the Cultural District's crawl, live performances are a big part of the Unblurred experience; expect to witness anything from spoken word to live music, and from modern dance to glass blowing. Visit www.friendshippgh.org/paai/unblurred for monthly schedules.

crawls. See the website for information on the gallery's music and performance schedule. New exhibits open the first Friday of each month; the performance and special event schedules vary. Other visits are by appointment only.

MAP 6: 5015 Penn Ave., 412/328-4737, www.most-wantedfineart.com; free

PITTSBURGH GLASS CENTER

Not content to exist simply as a static gallery, the nonprofit and architecturally stunning Pittsburgh Glass Center is also an education hub. Aspiring glass blowers can attend classes, including flameworking, casting, and hot glass workshops. Show up during an evening exhibition and you'll find staff members and student glass blowers alike demonstrating their skills and often selling their wares; glass jewelry is an especially popular item. Or simply peruse the current exhibition at the Hodge Gallery—stunning creative glass art and mixed-media shows happen regularly. The gallery is open late during first Friday gallery crawls. See the website for current dates, times, and prices for classes and workshops.

MAP 6: 5472 Penn Ave., 412/365-2145, www.pittsburghglasscenter.org; Mon.-Thurs. 10am-7pm, Fri.-Sun. 10am-4pm; $5 suggested donation

PERFORMING ARTS

KELLY STRAYHORN THEATER

Located in the heart of East Liberty's quickly gentrifying business district, the historic Kelly Strayhorn doesn't support a home theater company, but rather opens its doors to a widely diverse range of events and performances. Its name comes from two former East Liberty locals who made it big: stage man Gene Kelly and jazz great Billy Strayhorn. Typical events at this intimate 350-seat theater include modern dance performances, ethnic festival celebrations, plays from local and touring companies, and films that explore the African American experience.

MAP 6: 5941 Penn Ave., 412/363-3000, www.kelly-strayhorn.org

Greater Pittsburgh

Map 7

CINEMA

★ OAKS THEATER

It's no wonder the Oaks Theater was named Best Independent Movie Theater by the readers of *Pittsburgh City Paper;* as a 70-year-old institution, it's one of the very few movie houses in town that genuinely evokes the Golden Age of cinema. Even better, seating is most definitely not limited—430 film fanatics can gather together at the Oaks, which, yes, is still a one-screen operation. And while independent and foreign films are shown throughout the week, a regular series of midnight cult classics (films by David Lynch, George Romero, and the like) takes place as well. A popular event known as Cine Brunch, during which a light brunch is served prior to the screening of a film classic, happens at 10am, usually on the second Saturday of each month.

MAP 7: 310 Allegheny River Blvd., Oakmont, 412/828-6311, www.theoakstheater.com; $8 adult, $6 matinee before 6pm, $6 senior and child; $10-15 for special screenings and series; $5 for all Tues. screenings

CONCERT VENUES

FIRST NIAGARA PAVILION

As Western Pennsylvania's largest concert venue, First Niagara Pavilion is essentially Pittsburgh's version of Denver's Red Rocks Amphitheater, or the Gorge Amphitheater in the Pacific Northwest. Formerly known as the Post-Gazette Pavilion, and before that the Coca-Cola Star Lake Amphitheater, this is where the touring summer festivals stop on their way through the tri-state area; Lilith Fair, Phish, and the Grateful Dead have all taken the stage in years past. Tickets can be purchased for the seating area near the stage, which is in fact covered by a pavilion. Most show-goers prefer the cheaper general admission tickets, however, with which you'll stake out a spot on the grass. Keep in mind that the Pavilion is roughly a 45-minute drive from Downtown Pittsburgh.

MAP 7: 665 Rte. 18, Burgettstown, 724/947-7400, www.firstniagarapavilion.net

PEPSI-COLA ROADHOUSE

Imagine going to a dinner theater way out in the sticks, but instead of a murder-mystery taking place on stage, you're being entertained by a country-and-western act from a bygone era. That's the scene at the Pepsi-Cola Roadhouse, where hundreds of show-goers squeeze in around tables to nosh on barbecue ribs and nod their heads to Kenny Rogers or Dwight Yoakam. Video projection screens and a state-of-the-art sound system fill the roadhouse, so even if you don't happen to be right up against the stage, it's practically guaranteed to be an unequivocally intimate experience.

MAP 7: 565 Rte. 18, Burgettstown, 724/947-1900, www.pepsiroadhouse.com

GALLERIES

JAMES GALLERY

One of the city's most respected houses of contemporary, modern, and older works, James Gallery exhibits work not only by Pittsburgh's top artists, but also by national and international artists of note. Work displayed represents all manner of media, including sculpture, photography, and fiber arts, and many of the artists represented by the gallery are available for site-specific commissions. The gallery is also known for its framing work through its joint venture, Frame Foundry, as well as for its commissioning of works for both corporate and public sector projects.

MAP 7: 413 S. Main St., Pittsburgh, 412/922-9800, www.jamesgallery.net; Mon.-Sat. 9am-5pm; free

MANCHESTER CRAFTSMEN'S GUILD

Something of a cross between an educational music and arts facility, a gallery, and a concert space with an on-site recording studio, Manchester Craftsmen's Guild is one of the local scene's most intriguing and culturally philanthropic arts institutions. It's in out-of-the-way Manchester, not far from some of the city's roughest North Side neighborhoods, and it's appropriate that the guild also offers arts and photography classes to disadvantaged high schoolers. Grown-ups can take courses as well, although many folks who flock here do so for the notable jazz concert series. Anyone is free to wander into the main lobby, however, which doubles as the guild's ever-changing, multimedia art gallery. The class and workshop schedule is available online.

MAP 7: 1815 Metropolitan St., Manchester, 412/322-1773, www.manchesterguild.org; hours vary; jazz performance tickets $25-100; free gallery admission

UNSMOKE SYSTEMS

A multipurpose art gallery and events venue housed in a former Catholic school, UnSmoke Systems is one of the many "urban reuse" projects that have helped to transform the dilapidated town of Braddock into a nationally known community of cutting-edge creative types. Currently, UnSmoke hosts artists-in-residence who work in the building's converted studio spaces. But as with the town of Braddock itself, its doors are open to just about anyone in need of space for a creative project or event.

MAP 7: 1137 Braddock Ave., Braddock, www.unsmokeartspace.com; hours vary; free

PERFORMING ARTS

HILLMAN CENTER FOR PERFORMING ARTS

On the Shady Side Academy campus, this multi-stage performing arts venue has brought in an impressive array of theater, dance, and musical performances, as well as cultural and academic speakers. Both Attack Theatre and the Pittsburgh Ballet Theatre have held performances here, while the 2013 season attracted the likes of Cirque Zuma (something of an African Cirque de Soleil) and Berkeley professor Michael Pollan. The Hillman Center for Performing Arts is anything but your average high school auditorium. The gorgeous Richard E. Rauh proscenium theater (complete with full orchestra lift) accommodates 641 people, while the much more intimate Peter J. Kountz black box theater seats 120. Most performances are held on Saturdays at 7:30pm.

MAP 7: 423 Fox Chapel Rd., Fox Chapel, 412/621-4445, www.shadysideacademy.org; $15-25

Sports and Activities

Due to the ongoing success of its professional sports teams—the Steelers, the Pirates, and the Penguins—Pittsburgh has been known as "The City of Champions" (or "Champyinz" in some circles) since the 1970s. It's only fitting, then, that the city and its outlying areas provide ample opportunities for training, competition, and playing hard.

The city's most popular leafy escapes, Schenley Park and Frick Park, provide recreation and respite. Entering their gates feels like entering an entirely different world, right in the center of town. Joggers and walkers can enjoy miles of trails inside Schenley Park, and the mountain-biking paths that run through Frick Park are said to be some of the best in the country. And unlike in some bigger towns, locals are generally amenable to welcoming out-of-towners into Ultimate Frisbee or pickup basketball games.

Naturally, Pittsburgh's three rivers (Allegheny, Monongahela, Ohio) offer ample opportunities for water activities, such as boating, canoeing, rowing, and yachting, all of which take place throughout the warmer months. The city also provides a plethora of tennis courts and swimming pools. During winter, venture deep into Schenley Park and you'll find families ice skating in an ever-popular rink, and skiing and snowboarding excursions aren't more than an hour away in the Laurel Highlands. No matter what the season, you won't need to dig deep during your time in Pittsburgh to discover just about any sort of outdoor fun.

Look for ★ to find recommended recreation.

HIGHLIGHTS

★ **Best Way to Explore the Allegheny River:** Cruising the length of the Allegheny River with **Kayak Pittsburgh** is a wonderfully relaxing way to experience the Steel City (page 200).

★ **Best Public Swimming Pool:** Built by the wealthy industrialist Henry W. Oliver, the South Side's **Oliver Bath House** is a gorgeous spot for an afternoon dip. The indoor pool is heated, and it even boasts a splendid cathedral ceiling (page 210).

★ **Best Yoga Studio for Beginners:** Friendly, welcoming, and never stuck-up: That's the in-house attitude at **Amazing Yoga,** making it the smart choice for nervous yoga newbies (page 215).

★ **Best City Park for Serious Mountain Bikers:** The challenging trails that crisscross **Frick Park** are some of the most pulse-pounding in the entire state (page 216).

★ **Best Place for a Bromance:** Forget the man cave and take your best buds out for an action-packed day at **Steeltown Paintball Park** (page 220).

★ **Sickest No-Charge Skatepark:** With endless concrete bowls and a wealth of street skating accoutrements, it's no wonder **3 B's Action Park** is considered one of the Greater Pittsburgh area's best spots to push wood (page 223).

Downtown

HIKING AND BIKING TRAILS

ELIZA FURNACE TRAIL

Also known as the **Jail Trail** because of the route it takes behind the Downtown Allegheny County Jail, the Eliza Furnace Trail is a 3.5-mile-long bike path that is technically an extension of the Three Rivers Heritage Trail. Much of the route runs right alongside a major expressway, and it would be misleading to pretend that more than a small stretch or two of the Eliza Furnace is a peaceful pathway. Its beauty, however, lies in its location; the trail starts smack-dab in the center of Downtown, and it has a convenient exit point in North Oakland, right in between the Pitt and CMU campuses. This is an obvious boon to any of the thousands of East Enders who work Downtown, as any other route into the city is fraught with unruly traffic and undue stress.

To enter the trail from Downtown, travel south on Grant Street, away from the Strip District and toward the Monongahela River. The trail literally abuts the river, so keep going and you'll eventually run into it.

MAP 1: Trailhead starts in Downtown and ends in Oakland, north of Schenley Park, www.city.pittsburgh.pa.us/trails

ICE SKATING

THE RINK AT PPG PLACE

The Rink at PPG Place is Downtown Pittsburgh's version of the winter skating experience at Manhattan's Rockefeller Center (although PPG is actually 2,000 square feet larger). Located directly south of Market Square in the shadow of Philip Johnson's dramatic PPG Place building, the rink opens for business every year on Light Up Night in November and closes in early March. The experience of circling the rink's lighted Christmas tree, especially after dark, is absolutely unforgettable. Lunchtime monthly passes have become increasingly popular among the downtown professional set.

MAP 1: PPG Place, 412/394-3641, www.ppgplace.com/rink; winter Mon.-Thurs. 11am-10pm, Fri.-Sat. 11am-midnight, Sun. noon-8pm; $8 adult, $7 child and senior; skate rental $3

SPECTATOR SPORTS

Basketball

DUQUESNE DUKES

College basketball fans who can't score tickets to a Panthers match might instead check out the Duquesne Dukes, a much-lauded Atlantic 10 Conference crew that calls Duquesne University home.

Pittsburgh on Two Wheels

biking on Three Rivers Heritage Trail

In 1990, Pittsburgh's cycling community received a mighty blow when *Bicycling* magazine named it one of the 10 worst biking cities in the United States. Since then, the city has seen quite a turnaround, though it is admittedly still not a complete biker's paradise. Pittsburgh motorists, for instance, still show little respect for roadside cyclists. **Bike Pittsburgh** (www.bikepgh.org), a local grassroots bicycle advocacy group that curates untold numbers of bike-related events in the city and holds considerable sway with the powers-that-be in Harrisburg, has been instrumental in fostering the city's cycling community, improving biker safety, and seeing that bike lanes and other resources became an integral part of all city planning. In the last five years or so, an astounding number of bike lanes have been added to local neighborhoods and previously inaccessible or dangerous areas.

In 2008, Bike Pittsburgh launched the **Car Free Fridays** initiative, which has since become quite popular with local residents. The organization provides Car Free Friday action kits to assist residents in challenging their neighbors and coworkers to leave their cars at home. It also promotes local events that offer ample bike parking and other bike-friendly amenities, organizes local bike pools, and provides commuter bike maps.

If you'll be in town in August, Bike Pittsburgh's annual **BikeFest** is not to be missed. Bike Fest usually runs for about two weeks and features loads of different cycling themed events, rides, and parties. The annual **Pedal Pittsburgh** ride (www.pedalpgh.org) also takes place in August and makes for a great alternative way to tour the city and meet like-minded locals.

Bike shops have lately been opening at a surprisingly rapid clip, while **Free Ride** (214 N. Lexington Ave., inside Construction Junction, www.freeridepgh.org), a DIY-style society that recycles and reuses old bikes, continues to supply Pittsburghers of all income levels with affordable wheels. There are even two new bicycle magazines being published in Pittsburgh: *Urban Velo* (www.urbanvelo.org) and *Bicycle Times* (www.bicycletimesmag.com).

Visit Bike Pittsburgh's website for a complete list of two-wheeled events and resources. The site also provides a wealth of printable maps, which can come in quite handy due to Pittsburgh's unique geographical layout and terrain.

According to *U.S. News & World Report*, the Dukes have nearly as much prowess in the classroom as they do on the court: The magazine recently ranked the school's athletic program 15th in terms of graduation rates.

MAP 1: 1302 Forbes Ave., A.J. Palumbo Center, 412/232-3853 (tickets), www.goduquesne.com; $10 pp, group and student discounts available

Football

PITTSBURGH POWER

Co-owned by the legendary Steelers Hall of Fame receiver Lynn Swann, the Pittsburgh Power is a team new to the Arena Football League—it was added in 2011 during a four-team league expansion. Currently being coached by Derek Stingley, the team plays home games at the CONSOL Energy Center, where tickets can often be had for as little as two for $99. Incidentally, the team holds open tryouts every fall at the Southpointe Fieldhouse (www.southpointefieldhouse.com) in Canonsburg; anyone with the requisite courage is welcome to give it a go. And as for the team's color scheme? You guessed it: black and gold.

MAP 1: 1001 5th Ave., CONSOL Energy Center, 888/769-2011, www.consolenergycenter.com, www.pittsburghpowerfootball.com; $15-180; season tickets available

Hockey

PITTSBURGH PENGUINS

Less popular than the Steelers but followed with much more seriousness and intensity than the Pirates, the Penguins arrived in Pittsburgh in 1967 when the NHL expanded by adding six clubs. And although the team's first two decades were fairly unremarkable, the tables began to turn significantly when the legendary Mario Lemieux was added to the roster in the mid-1980s. Indeed, in 1992 the Penguins took home the Stanley Cup for the second time in a row.

Today, "Super Mario" Lemieux is the Penguins' owner, and following a fairly bitter dispute concerning the club's future, the Pens have since relocated to the brand-new CONSOL Energy Center.

For information about purchasing individual game tickets or season tickets, visit the team website or the CONSOL Energy Center box office. Tickets are also available for sale by season ticket holders at www.ticketmaster.com/ticketexchange.

MAP 1: 1001 5th Ave., CONSOL Energy Center, 412/642-1800, www.consolenergycenter.com, http://penguins.nhl.com; $45-215

North Side

Map 1

GUIDED AND WALKING TOURS

PNC PARK TOURS

You don't necessarily need to be a Pirates fan to enjoy a tour of the ball club's newest North Side stadium. In fact, given that PNC Park is considered by many baseball insiders to be one of the country's finest parks, this is an experience that even a non-sports fan might find worthwhile.

Naturally, tour participants will have a chance to view sections of the park not open to fans during game time. Some of the experiences include a trip down to the field itself and an up-close-and-personal view of the batting cages and even the press box, which is generally considered the best seat in the house.

MAP 1: 115 Federal St., 412/325-4700, http://pirates.mlb.com; tours Mar.-Sept. Mon.-Fri. and one Sat. per month at 10am, noon, and 2pm; $7 pp

HIKING AND BIKING TRAILS

THREE RIVERS HERITAGE TRAIL

Stretching for nearly 40 miles along both sides of the Allegheny, Monongahela, and Ohio Rivers, the well-maintained Three Rivers Heritage Trail begins as a concrete path on the North Shore, where it runs right alongside the Allegheny River. The trail is an absolute treat for urban cyclists, joggers, and walkers. The length of the trail running through the North Shore is also where you'll find the **Vietnam Veterans Monument,** the **Korean Veterans Memorial,** and the gigantic, striking, and somewhat controversial (because of its lumpy appearance) **Mister Rogers statue.**

The Vietnam memorial, which features life-size statues of soldiers returning home from war to greet their families, stands mere feet from the Allegheny shoreline and almost exactly between Heinz Field and PNC Park. It's capped by an egg-shaped canopy meant to symbolize a hibiscus flower, which represents rebirth and regeneration and is native to tropical regions throughout the world, including Southeast Asia. The Korean War memorial is a bit farther east; it represents the 2,401 Pennsylvanians who died during the war. (California is the only state in the country that suffered more losses.) The memorial features a number of tall but thin blocks, fanned into a semicircle design. During certain times of the day, columns of sunlight, which the memorial's designer hoped would represent aspects of both shared and individual experiences, stream through the blocks. There are also commemorative plaques on the site documenting the war's chronology and a memorial wall engraved with names of the fallen soldiers. You'll find the

Biking The Great Allegheny Passage

If you live in Pittsburgh, driving to Washington, D.C., is a bore. The turnpike Is long and lugubrious, and the dwarfish hills roll on forever. At five hours, the drive is *just* too long, and once you hit the beltway traffic, Pittsburghers regret ever leaving home.

But thanks to the **Great Allegheny Passage** (www.gaptrail.org), biking to the nation's capital is an overland adventure. Cyclists can now pedal from southern Pittsburgh to Cumberland, Maryland, and from there take the **C&O Canal Towpath** (www.bikewashington.org/canal) straight into Washington. Based on a retired railroad line, the Great Allegheny Passage (GAP) winds along the **Youghiogheny River,** bisects **Ohiopyle State Park,** passes over the **Laurel Highlands,** and slices through quirky Pennsylvania towns. The trail has recently been connected to the **Montour Trail** (www.montourtrail.org), which will ultimately extend 46 miles from Moon Township to Clairton.

Now complete, the passage is among the longest, most scenic rails-to-trails projects in North America. And with the right preparation, almost anybody can ride it.

The path is mostly even gravel, and although cyclists have to pump the entire way (there's not much coasting), the level ground makes for easy progress. Travelers will relish the views of hills and water, and every few hours a freight train huffs its way across the river, its whistle echoing down the valley. You'll cross truss bridges and pass hidden factories, and—most titillating of all—you'll pass through **Big Savage Tunnel,** a 3,295-foot-long tunnel that cuts clean through **Big Savage Mountain,** Don't worry, though—the inside is lighted.

Most bikers only ride parts of the trail—from Pittsburgh to Ohiopyle, where they meet friends for white-water rafting ventures, or from Pittsburgh to Cumberland, thus completing the 150-mile tour. The full mega-transect to D.C. takes about a week; more and more riders complete the C&O section each year. Sensible people will prefer the late spring or early fall, as the region gets hot and humid in summer. Keep in mind that lodging is often seasonal, and the towns are pretty spread out (if you're leaving West Newton, for instance, Connellsville lies a full 26 miles down the way).

Cyclists can ride the Great Allegheny Passage on their own, or they can call a touring companies. **Bike the Gap** (www.bike-the-gap.com, 412/303-0566) is one of the better touring outfits. In addition to its two-day and five-day package tours, Bike the Gap also provides custom tours, and it handles all trip planning logistics, from reserving hotels to arranging transportation for your luggage. Package tours range $100-200; custom tours are priced upon request.

Whatever your level, the trip doesn't require a lot of cross-country training, only a good road bike, ample supplies, and some maintenance skills. Whether you try an afternoon excursion or a seven-day odyssey, the Great Allegheny Passage will almost certainly take *you* for a ride.

(Contributed by Robert Isenberg, a writer and stage performer based in Pittsburgh. His book about traveling in post-war Yugoslavia, The Archipelago, *is available from Autumn House Press.)*

Mister Rogers statue atop the Manchester Bridge Pier, which sits just outside the south entrance to Heinz Field.

Continue east along the path, with the river on your right, and soon the walkway will turn to dirt. Eventually the massive Heinz factory will appear on your left; much of it was recently converted into loft apartments.

The dirt trail turns to rock and begins to peter out around the 40th Street Bridge, at which point you'll have to turn around and head back to the city. Another option would be to explore the 13-acre **Millvale Riverfront Park,** which sits underneath the bridge. The park is home to a gazebo, a covered picnic pavilion, and the training facility of the Three Rivers Rowing Association.

To discover the route's other stretches, take note of the map-covered plaques that line the trail. An interactive online map and downloadable PDF maps of the Three Rivers Heritage Trail can be found online at www.friendsoftheriverfront.org.

MAP 1: Heinz Field to the 40th Street Bridge, alongside the Allegheny River, www.friendsoftheriverfront.org

ROWING AND KAYAKING

★ KAYAK PITTSBURGH

Kayak Pittsburgh offers what may very well be the most enjoyable and affordable way to explore Pittsburgh's waterways. The company rents flat-water kayaks that even the completely inexperienced can easily navigate. Canoes, hydrobikes, and stand-up paddle boards are also available. To reach the rental shack, cross the 6th Street Bridge (also known as the Roberto Clemente Bridge) from Downtown and head toward the North Side; the shack sits underneath the staircase, adjacent to PNC Park. Kayak Pittsburgh also does business at the North Park Boathouse, where rowboats, bicycles, pedal boats, and canoes can also be rented.

MAP 1: Under the north side of the 6th Street Bridge, 412/969-9090, www.kayakpittsburgh.org; Mon.-Fri. 11am-dusk, Sat.-Sun. 10am-dusk; rental rates $8-22 per hour

SPECTATOR SPORTS

Baseball

PITTSBURGH PIRATES

There certainly aren't many Major League Baseball teams in existence today with records as disappointingly poor as that of the Pittsburgh Pirates. Following a 2009 defeat by the Chicago Cubs, for instance, the Pirates earned the unfortunate distinction of having the longest consecutive run of losing seasons not just in baseball but in any North American professional sport. Ouch.

Still, diehard fans continue to follow the team on television and, to a slightly lesser degree, at the ballpark. With the team's 2013 winning season, however, game day attendance has certainly improved, and PNC Park is truly delightful.

What's more, Buccos game tickets are affordable and exceedingly easy to come by, even on game day. Seats can be found for as low as $17 at www.stubhub.com, while general admission bleacher tickets (purchased at the PNC Park box office) go for just $9 in advance. Due to new dynamic ticket prices, general admission tickets are generally more expensive on game day.

MAP 1: PNC Park box office, corner of Federal and General Robinson Sts., 800/289-2827 (tickets), http://pirates.mlb.com; $9 general admission (bleacher seats)

Football

PITT PANTHERS

The University of Pittsburgh's Pitt Panthers football squad has a particularly impressive history, with possibly an even more impressive list of famous alumni. Dan Marino, Tony Dorsett, Mike Ditka, Pop Warner, and scores of NFL players have all spent time as Panthers. Perhaps fittingly, the team now plays its home games at Heinz Field, which is also the home base of the Pittsburgh Steelers. The Panthers' most intense rivalry is with the West Virginia University Mountaineers; the two teams meet every Thanksgiving for a game known as the Backyard Brawl. The Brawl is an experience not to be missed, although tickets are hard to come by. Pitt and the Penn State Nittany Lions also maintain a healthy rivalry.

To purchase game tickets, visit the team's website or www.peterseneventscenter.com. You can also purchase tickets at the Petersen Events Center Ticket Office (corner of Desoto and Terrace Streets in Oakland). The office is open Monday-Friday 8:30am-5pm.

MAP 1: 100 Art Rooney Ave., Heinz Field, 412/648-7488 or 800/643-7488 (tickets), www.pittsburghpanthers.com; $50 general admission, $25 student with University of Pittsburgh Student ID; $85-285 sideline, end zone, box, and club seats

PITTSBURGH STEELERS

As the fifth-oldest team in the NFL, and the franchise with perhaps the most widespread fan base of any professional football club, it's no exaggeration whatsoever to think of the Pittsburgh Steelers as a way of life—or even a religion—for many locals. Indeed, Steelermania and Pittsburgh culture can easily be thought of as one and the same. And although the Steelers in 2008-2009 managed to claim an unprecedented sixth Super Bowl victory—the first and only team in the history of the NFL to do so—it's probably fair to say that the so-called "Super Steelers" of the 1970s still stand out in most fans' minds as the crew to permanently define the organization.

Steelers tickets are notoriously hard to come by. Season ticket holders get nearly all of the seats, and most holders have had their seats for generations, since the days of Three Rivers Stadium. In fact, a good way to know you're finally a local is when you have a friend who offers or tells you he has a way to get tickets (or you finally work your way to season tickets after years and years on the waiting list). Your best bet is the scalpers who troll outside all home games, but be forewarned that scalping is technically illegal; purchase tickets (none of which are guaranteed to be authentic) at your own risk. Fans can also try calling the Steelers ticket office at 412/323-1200.

MAP 1: 100 Art Rooney Ave., Heinz Field, 412/323-1200, www.steelers.com; $100-900

Oakland

Map 2

ICE SKATING

SCHENLEY PARK SKATING RINK

The Schenley Park Skating Rink, located near the park's tennis courts and baseball fields, is open from November through March. Inline skaters and roller hockey players often fill the rink during the summer months. And since students from nearby Pitt and CMU flock here on weekend nights, the rink can be a decent place to take a first date—or to find a first date. Should your coupling turn into something more serious, consider returning on February 14 for the annual Valentine's on Ice event.

MAP 2: 1 Overlook Dr., 412/422-6523, www.pittsburghpa.gov/citiparks/schenley-skating-rink; call for hours; $4 adult, $3 senior and child (17 and under); skate rental $2.50

PARKS

SCHENLEY PARK

Donated to the city by Mary Schenley in the late 1800s and designed by William Falconer, Schenley Park is home to 456 green acres of inner-city paradise. From the Carnegie Library in Oakland, simply stroll over the Panther Hollow Bridge and toward the expanse of hills and trees; you'll likely forget you're smack-dab in the center of a city in no time.

Recreation opportunities are many and varied on the fields and greens of Schenley, which is one of the largest city-operated parks in the eastern region of the country. Along with its 13 tennis courts, swimming pool, soccer field, running track, ice skating rink, and

Catching Steelermania

a Steelers fan's "terrible van"

No matter how long or short your visit to Pittsburgh, and no matter the time of year or the purpose of your stay, and regardless of your interest in professional sports, you're nearly guaranteed at some point to find yourself in the midst of a conversation about the Pittsburgh Steelers, our town's six-time Super Bowl-winning NFL superstars. It's been said, in fact, that Pittsburgh's popular culture and Steelers culture are essentially one and the same. And if you're lucky, you may even run into a local fan afflicted with a full-fledged case of Steelermania.

In the summer of 2010, the Carnegie Mellon art professor Jon Rubin beautifully documented Steelermania by curating "Whatever It Takes" at the school's Miller Gallery; it was an awe-inspiring exhibition of Steelers fan collections both passionate and bizarre. It introduced the city to a wide variety of Steelers superfans, including Ron Vergerio, better known as "Steeler Ron" (www.steelerron.com), who has spent the past decade covering nearly every inch of his body with Steelers-themed tattoos.

Local artists and crafty fans around the country get in on Steelermania. In local gift shops and on websites like eBay and Etsy, I've seen Steelers-themed nail decal art, headbands and hats, dog sweaters and caps, wall art, scrapbooking supplies, home decor, a dizzying amount of jewelry, plush toys, holiday ornaments, carved pumpkins, stained glass work, stationery, purses and totes, door wreaths, wooden clocks, leg warmers, high heels, pillows, and even racy lingerie.

Perhaps not surprisingly, Steelers fans also host a seemingly endless number of blogs and podcasts about the team. **Steeler Addicts** (www.steeleraddicts.com) and **Steeler Nation** (www.steelernation.com) host popular bulletin board-style forums about the team. **Steel City Blitz** (www.steelcityblitz.com) and **Steelers Depot** (www.steelers-depot.com) host equally admired podcasts.

To experience a taste of Steelermania without even leaving your own hometown, pay a visit to one of the hundreds of Steelers bars around the country; these are pubs where displaced Pittsburghers and other fans gather during game days to cheer on the black and gold. A directory of national and even international Steelers bars can be found online at www.steelersbars.com.

hiking trails, there's an 18-hole golf course and a relaxing, somewhat secluded lake. And if you're interested in schmoozing with the college crowd, head to Schenley Park's Flagstaff Hill (it's across the road from Phipps Conservatory), where CMU students play, sunbathe, and flirt whenever the weather's warm.

MAP 2: Boundary St. at Schenley Dr., 412/682-7575, www.pittsburghparks.org

SPECTATOR SPORTS

Basketball

PITT PANTHERS

Probably the most popular b-ball squad in the city, the University of Pittsburgh's Pitt Panthers are a Big East crew frequently ranked near the top of the league. Home games are played at the recently built Petersen Events Center (www.peterseneventscenter.com)—it's generally favored by sports journalists as one of the county's finest college basketball arenas. Also of interest at Petersen is the **McCall Panthers Hall of Champions.** Located in the center's lobby, it displays decades worth of Pitt athletics achievements. The hall is open Monday-Friday 9am-5pm, as well as during all men's basketball games. Tours of the Petersen Events Center are available Monday-Friday 9am-4pm and must be scheduled less than one month in advance.

MAP 2: 3719 Terrace St., Petersen Events Center, 412/648-8076, www.pittsburghpanthers.com; $60-140

SWIMMING POOLS

SCHENLEY PARK POOL

As one of the most popular public swimming spots in the city, the Schenley pool on scorching summer days can feel just as crowded as a Florida beach during spring break. Undoubtedly, that has much to do with its convenient location near Central and South Oakland, neighborhoods with a lot of concrete, a lot of young people, and very few private swimming pools.

The facility itself is fair, but not outstanding. There isn't much shade to speak of, although the pool is appropriately large. Young children (as well as the young at heart) will appreciate that Schenley Park's ubiquitous ice cream truck passes by dozens of times a day.

MAP 2: 1 Overlook Dr., Schenley Park, 412/422-4266; mid-June to early Sept. Mon.-Fri. 1pm-7:45pm and Sat.-Sun. and holidays 1pm-5:45pm; daily admission $4 adult 16 and older, $3 child 3-15

TENNIS

SCHENLEY PARK TENNIS COURTS

It's easy to understand why the courts in Oakland's Schenley Park are so popular with Pittsburgh's racket enthusiasts. For starters, the park features an impressive 13 courts that sport hard, Plexipave surfaces. And with so many courts to choose from, players are almost certain to find at least a few spaces open on any given day of the week, even though the area quite often hums with activity. The area is well lit, and all courts are in wonderful condition—which is saying something, given that the city-sponsored facilities are free and open to the public. Do be aware that the courts, which sit next to Schenley Park's soccer and softball fields, are often in use Saturday mornings and weekday evenings by city-sponsored tennis clinics or tournaments.

MAP 2: Overlook Dr., Schenley Park, 412/244-4188, www.pittsburghparks.org

South Side

Map 3

GUIDED AND WALKING TOURS

GREEN GEARS PEDI CABS

Truth be told, the Green Gears Pedi Cabs company wasn't started with the intention of offering city tours, but rather as a way to shuttle foot-weary tourists and drunk sports fans from stadium to bar or restaurant, say. And yes, these really are genuine pedicabs: They're entirely human-powered, often driven by former bicycle messengers. Thanks to the company's overwhelming popularity among locals and out-of-towners alike, the cabs can now be rented for bar crawls, wedding parties, or just about any other event you can imagine. Green Gears does offer pre-planned city tours, although they tend to be open to new and unusual suggestions.

MAP 3: 1720 Wrights Way, 412/343-7334, www.greengearspedicabs.com; fares vary by driver but average $60/hour or $1/city block

JUST DUCKY TOURS

Nearly every decent-sized American town with river real estate now has an amphibious vehicle city tour. Pittsburgh's version, headquartered at Station Square, is Just Ducky Tours. The tour, which passes through Downtown, parts of the North Shore, and the Monongahela and Ohio Rivers, takes place in a vintage World War II amphibious vehicle, able to traverse both land and sea. Tours are roughly an hour long; expect to be pelted with miscellaneous Pittsburgh trivia and bad jokes. Just Ducky operates April through October and on weekends only in November.

MAP 3: 125 W. Station Square Dr., 412/402-3825, www.justduckytours.com; adults $22, child 3-12 $15, child 3 and under $5

clockwise from top left: Pittsburgh Vintage Grand Prix; a Segway tour; Just Ducky Tours

PITTSBURGH HISTORY AND LANDMARKS FOUNDATION TOURS

The Pittsburgh History and Landmarks Foundation is a nonprofit preservation group whose members work to save the city's most important structures from demolition or misuse. In an effort to educate the public about certain buildings and parts of the city they may have otherwise passed by without so much as a single thought, the group has organized wonderfully educational guided walking tours.

The tours are a smart place to start for anyone interested in learning about the historical relevance of the city, packed as they are with intriguing well-researched trivia. Most tours are roughly an hour long, and although donations are encouraged, all tours are free. Some of the more popular excursions include an architectural tour of the South Side, a look at the Old Allegheny County Jail, and a stroll through Downtown's historical Fifth and Forbes Corridor.

MAP 3: 100 W. Station Square Dr., Ste. 450, 412/471-5808, www.phlf.org; check website for schedule; free

THE PITTSBURGH TOUR COMPANY DOUBLE DECKER TOURS

As the city's solitary hop-on, hop-off bus tour, the Pittsburgh Tour Company offers one of the most convenient and thrilling ways to explore the city. Tours take place aboard a genuine mid-20th-century double-decker bus from London. The bus travels from the SouthSide Works plaza to Station Square before heading to the Rivers Casino on the North Shore, the Heinz History Center and Wholey's Fish Market in the Strip District, and then to Downtown before returning again to the SouthSide Works.

MAP 3: 445 S. 27th St., SouthSide Works, 412/381-8687, www.pghtours.com; all-day passes $25 adult, $15 child

SEGWAY IN PARADISE

It's a fairly safe bet to assume that the majority of the people reading this book don't own a Segway and have never ridden one but have always wanted to give it a try. If that's you, and if you're in Pittsburgh, you're in luck. A local sightseeing organization now offers two-hour tours aboard the battery-powered, self-propelled scooters. Appropriately enough, Segway in Paradise pioneers begin their exploration at the Carnegie Science Center on the North Side before heading over the Allegheny River to Point State Park, through Downtown, and then over the Monongahela River to Station Square before looping back.

MAP 3: 125 W. Station Square Dr., 724/625-3521, www.segwayinparadise.com; $59-97

Pittsburgh's Quirkiest Tours

a Pittsburgh Tour Company double-decker bus

As Pittsburgh's popularity as a tourism destination continues to slowly grow, so too does its selection of sightseeing tours. Over the last few years, a good number of exceptionally quirky and unique Pittsburgh tours have entered the marketplace, and while some proved unpopular with visitors and ultimately disappeared, others have gone on to become local mainstays. The following is a selection of can't-miss tours for anyone genuinely interested in digging deep into the city's history and culture.

'BURGH BITS AND BITES FOOD TOUR

During these unique culinary walking tours of various Pittsburgh neighborhoods, tour-goers wander through the Strip District, Lawrenceville, Bloomfield, Brookline, Dormont, and several other local neighborhoods, sampling regional foods and learning about local culinary history along the way. Tours are generally two hours long and cost $37 per person (www.burghfoodtour.com, 800/979-3370).

GREEN GEARS PEDICABS

The drivers of Green Gears (so named because of the cabs' non-polluting eco-friendliness), Pittsburgh's only bicycle-powered pedicab service, pedal along the streets of the South Side, the North Shore, Downtown, Lawrenceville, and the Strip District. The charge is roughly $1 per block; the pedicabs can also be rented for special events and have become quite popular for use during promotional events (www.greengearspedicabs.com, 412/343-7334).

HAUNTED PITTSBURGH GHOST TOURS

As the self-described "archivists of Pittsburgh's nightmares," the guides of Haunted Pittsburgh host walking tours and pub crawls in Oakland, the

SPECTATOR SPORTS

Football

PITTSBURGH PASSION

Formed in 2002, the Pittsburgh Passion is a professional, all-women's contact football team and a member of the National Women's Football Association (NWFA). Oddly, the majority of the players had very little football experience before joining the Passion.

South Side, and Mount Washington on Saturday nights from May through Halloween. Haunted incline tours are especially popular during October, and the Haunted Oakland tour is great a great way for new students to get to know the area, its history, and its many legends and haunts. Virtual tours are also available. Tours are $15-18 per person (www.hauntedpittsburghtours.com, 412/302-5223).

MIKE'S CARRIAGE SERVICE

Featuring romantic horse-drawn carriage tours throughout Downtown and Station Square, Mike's refers to itself as "Pittsburgh's premier source for horse-drawn entertainment." Station Square rides are $20-50, and tours of Downtown are $135 (www.caustelotfarms.com, 412/913-0664).

RIVERQUEST

Formerly known as Pittsburgh Voyager, the RiverQuest organization offers a wide range of river-based educational programs for both children and adults. Tours take place aboard the *Explorer,* an eco-friendly triple-decker boat; passengers use the city's rivers as something of a living classroom, where they learn about science, sustainability, and more. Visit the website for more information, as tour times and program schedules vary widely. For public sails, tickets are $5.95 for children ages 3-12, $9.95 for adults and children over 12. Adventure voyages, scouting programs, field trips, summer camps, and other special events are also held throughout the year (www.riverquest.org, 412/231-2712).

PITTSBURGH PARTY PEDALER

It's unlikely that you've ever seen or experienced anything quite like the Pittsburgh Party Pedaler, which is basically a miniature pub on wheels, complete with 12 seats, a bench on the back end, and a keg on the front. Seriously. This Dutch-built contraption requires every seated "partier" to pedal—you'll be riding at no more than five mph—and most routes traverse the tourist-friendly areas of the North Shore, where the city's pro sports stadiums are located. Riders supply their own food and beverages (www.pittsburghpartypedaler.com; $325-385).

THE PITTSBURGH TOUR COMPANY

If hop-on/hop-off double-decker city bus tours are your thing, the Pittsburgh Tour Company covers all the local basics (and you can't miss their bright red double-decker coaches). The tour has stops in more than 20 Pittsburgh neighborhoods and attractions. Buses leave year-round from the SouthSide Works. Private tours and a land and water tour (offered in conjunction with the Gateway Clipper Fleet) are also available. All-day tour passes are $25 per adult, $15 for children ages 10 and under (www.pghtours.com, 412/381-8687).

Some had barely played the game at all, and instead came from softball, volleyball, soccer, basketball, lacrosse, or hockey backgrounds. But make no mistake, team members have matured into some tough ladies—they've since won a National Championship and four Divisional Championships, and are now the most recognized team in the league, even picking up some TV deals along the way. The Passion plays home games from late April through mid-June at Station Square's new Highmark Stadium.

MAP 3: 510 W. Station Square Dr., Highmark Stadium, 412/224-4900, www.pittsburghpassion.com; $15

Rugby and Wrestling

RUGGERS PUB

Although the combative sport of rugby is still a relative novelty in North America, its popularity in Pittsburgh seems to be growing. The **Pittsburgh Rugby Club,** for instance, claims more than 300 members of all ages and both sexes and is also a do-good nonprofit organization that occasionally helps out with various community service projects. To get a feel for the size and intensity of Pittsburgh's rugby scene yourself, show up at Ruggers Pub, which also serves as the Pittsburgh Rugby Club's local headquarters. The players congregate and refuel here after local matches. The experience of seeing a team fill the pub after a win can be quite eye-opening, especially for Americans who know little about the, uh, ruggedness of the sport. Naturally, matches are shown on the telly, but if you'd rather hit the field yourself, contact the area club at www.pghrugby.com. For information about joining the **South Pittsburgh Hooligans Men's Rugby Club,** call 412/734-8998 or visit www.southpittrugby.com. And if you'd simply like to see the teams rumble, head over to www.pghrugby.com and view the upcoming schedules; most matches take place in Boyce Park.

MAP 3: 40 S. 22nd St., 412/381-1330, www.ruggerspub.com; daily 11am-2am; free

Soccer

PITTSBURGH RIVERHOUNDS

Founded in 1999, the Riverhounds are not only Pittsburgh's first professional soccer club, but also the only pro soccer team in the immediate tri-state area. Currently coached by Peters Township native Justin Evans, the Riverhounds play in the National Division of the USL Pro Division, and home games are played at Station Square's 3,500-seat Highmark Stadium. And because this is Pittsburgh, after all, the team even has its own group of hardcore supporters, who call themselves the Steel Army; the Army meets often at Piper's Pub on the South Side.

MAP 3: 510 W. Station Square Dr., Highmark Stadium, 412/224-4900, www.riverhounds.com, www.highmarkstadium.com; season tickets $150-240, check website for individual ticket prices

SWIMMING POOLS

★ OLIVER BATH HOUSE

Possibly the most interesting of all the public pools is also the only one located indoors, and it's open year-round. The Oliver Bath House was built by Oliver Iron and Steel in 1910. The corporation's owner, a successful industrialist by the name of Henry W. Oliver, had it constructed specifically for his employees who had nowhere else to bathe. Five years later, Oliver presented the structure as a gift to the city. With its cathedral ceiling and blue-tiled, well-heated pool (the water is usually around 80°F), the bathhouse is the absolute picture of peace and serenity (especially during adult swim). It's especially popular with area seniors.

MAP 3: 38 S. 10th St., 412/488-8380, http://pittsburghpa.gov/citiparks/oliver-bath-house; Mon.-Fri. 9am-9pm, Sat.-Sun. noon-9pm; daily admission $4 adult 16 and older, $3 child 3-15

ORMSBY POOL

If there were a competition for the most conspicuous and oddly located public pool, Ormsby would win it, hands down. Yet on the flip side, you won't have any trouble finding the place: Simply drive or walk across the Birmingham Bridge toward the South Side, and once you reach East Carson Street, there it is, right on the corner of one of the city's busiest intersections. This isn't necessarily a bad thing, although if you don't like the idea of the world at large being able to see you in your bathing suit, you'd probably be better off swimming elsewhere. Then again, its convenience is exactly what makes Ormsby such a popular place: Where else can you perform a cannonball splash one minute and then be gulping down a cold pint of Iron City Light the next? And aside from the many pubs on the Carson Street Strip, the pool also sits right next door to a public library, is just down the street from the SouthSide Works shopping center, and is an easy walk to dozens of popular neighborhood cafés and boutiques.

MAP 3: 79 S. 22nd St., 412/488-8377; mid-June to early Sept. Mon.-Fri. 1pm-7:45pm, Sat.-Sun. and holidays 1pm-5:45pm; daily admission $4 adult 16 and older, $3 child 3-15

YOGA, MEDITATION, AND MARTIAL ARTS

BREATHE YOGA STUDIO

In a 1,400-square-foot studio in the heart of the South Side Flats, Breathe Yoga offers beginning and intermediate Hatha classes, including Iyengar classes, and a Yoga Basics class, which focuses on simple breathing and posture techniques. That doesn't begin to describe the school's full schedule, however. Breathe also squeezes in the occasional Middle Eastern dance class, as well as capoeira and modern dance instruction. There's also a full schedule of workshops focused on specific aspects of yoga and spirituality.

MAP 3: 1113 E. Carson St., 3rd Fl., 412/481-9642, www.pittsburghyoga.com; drop-in yoga classes $15

Fitness For the Anti-Jock

In a town where the act of consuming a 16-ounce can of Iron City Beer is spoken of as a metaphor for exercise (locals like to talk of "pumping a pint of Iron"), it's only fitting that sundry sports and recreational activities abound for the beer-bellied, the uncoordinated, the unathletic, and the otherwise altogether out-of-shape. Which isn't to say that Pittsburgh's myriad offbeat outdoor pursuits aren't physically demanding. Consider the local chapter of the Hash House Harriers, for instance: a motley crew of men and women who jog for miles upon miles throughout the city's back streets, stopping only occasionally to raise their spirits, you might say, at a neighborhood tavern.

But whatever your current level of physical vigor, you're almost certain to find some sport or activity of interest in Pittsburgh. In other words, welcome to the City of Champions, where even a 255-pound running back named after a mass-transit vehicle (the Pittsburgh Steelers' Jerome Bettis, a.k.a. "The Bus") can become an honest-to-goodness American hero.

HASH HOUSE HARRIERS

A self-described "drinking club with a running problem," the Hash House Harriers were formed in the 1930s by a group of British soldiers stationed in Malaysia. Looking for a creative way to combine exercise with social activity, they modified the English game of hares and hounds into something of a drinking contest. Today, Hash House Harriers clubs, known as kennels, exist in just about every major city on Earth—Pittsburgh included. To put it simply, a hash is a combination of a long-distance jog, a scavenger hunt, and a keg party. Membership is just $15 per year. Anyone is welcome to join in; for more information email firstcontact@pgh-h3.com, or go online at www.pgh-h3.com.

LAWN BOWLING

Lawn bowling, an ancient Roman game that was first introduced to America by the British, is perfect for players young and old, regardless of physical fitness. Unlike the variety of bowling that takes place along a wood-paneled lane, in lawn bowling part of the strategy involves knocking an opponent's ball out of play. The city's two bowling greens are in Point Breeze's Frick Park—not far from the Henry Clay Frick estate—and are the only such courts in the region. Open bowling takes place on Thursday evenings and many Saturday afternoons, provided there is no league or tournament match scheduled. First-time guests receive free admission, after which there is a $10 charge per bowler. Free lessons are also available. For more information, call 412/782-0848 or visit the **Frick Park Lawn Bowling Club** website at www.lawnbowlingpittsburgh.org.

PINBALL WIZARDS

If you know much at all about pinball, you'll no doubt be impressed to learn that Pittsburgh is home to the World Pinball Championships, an annual series organized by PAPA (www.papa.org), the Professional Amateur Pinball Association. The championship games take place in suburban Scott Township. Do be aware, however, that the majority of the flipper fanatics here will be adults, not children. More than $33,000 in prize money changes hands during the tournament; the winner takes home $7,500. Pittsburgh is also home to the Pittsburgh Pinball open and hosts the largest league in the country. Pinball has become so popular in the region, in fact, that there is now a large pinball museum and showroom just north of the city: **Pinball Perfection** (231 Perry Hwy., Westview, 412/931-4425; hours vary; www.pinballperfection.com). For more information about the local pinball scene, the Pittsburgh league, and area pinball events and challenges, visit www.coinball.com.

ROCK & BOWL

Looking for an unusual way to spend an evening that involves ugly shoes, loud music, and cheap beer in plastic cups? You might try paying a visit to **Arsenal Lanes** (212 44th St., 412/683-5992, www.arsenalbowl.com) in Lawrenceville. The lanes are especially known for their Wednesday night event, Rock & Bowl, where hipster types bowl to the accompaniment of a local rock band. The night will set you back $8, which includes all the frames you can squeeze in between 9pm and the stroke of midnight. And there's no need to feel self-conscious about your nonexistent bowling skills; while some of Pittsburgh's best bowlers frequently congregate at Arsenal Lanes, they tend to steer clear of these events.

ULTIMATE FRISBEE

A noncontact team sport that combines elements of soccer, basketball, and American football, Ultimate Frisbee was created in 1960 by college students who originally tossed around pie dishes. Today the sport is played internationally, and more than 50 countries hold tournaments. Contrary to popular belief, however, UF players must be in top physical shape to perform well. The local organization known as **Pittsburgh Ultimate** (www.pittsburgh-ultimate.org) is home to seasonal leagues, college teams, a women's league, and a junior league. Pickup games are usually held once a week, and locations, dates, and times vary by season. Pickup games, however, are often held at the West Penn Recreation Center in the Polish Hill neighborhood. Visit the organization's website for a current pickup schedule or to contact league representatives if you're interesting in pursuing the sport in a more serious fashion.

VINTAGE CARS, BUGGIES, AND ROBOT RACES

Oakland's Schenley Park is the site of two of the city's most revered and unique races, the Pittsburgh Vintage Grand Prix and Carnegie Mellon University's buggy races. For over 30 years now, the annual **Pittsburgh Vintage Grand Prix** (www.pvgp.org) has been drawing vintage racers and auto enthusiasts to town and has since grown to include races throughout the month of July and vintage car shows throughout the year.

If cars aren't your thing, CMU's buggy races (www.cmubuggy.org), held during the university's legendary **Spring Carnival,** are sure to bring a smile to your face. Students and even alumni groups create small, aerodynamic buggies throughout the year that are then raced with nothing more mechanical than gravity and a little human push. Tech types will also want to head onto CMU's campus itself during Spring Carnival, when the school's legendary robot races (known as Mobots) take place. **Mobot races** (www.cs.cmu.edu/mobot) are open to students, alumni, and members of the local community, and CMU's School of Computer Science even sells a beginner's kit with everything aspiring engineers need to get started.

WAVE POOLS

Pittsburghers are rather fond of the city's three **wave pools,** all of which are wheelchair accessible and open every day from June through September (with some exceptions). Adult admission is $4; kids 6-12 and adults over 60 pay $3; kids 5 and under pay $1. The pool in **Boyce Park** (675 Frankstown Rd., 724/325-4677) is the most conveniently located if you're staying in the city; there's a snack bar and plenty of sunbathing space on the premises. **Settler's Cabin Park** in Oakdale (1225 Greer Rd., 412/787-2667) boasts trails, log cabins, a diving pool, and a wave pool. **South Park** (Buffalo Dr., 412/831-0810) also has a wave pool, as well as 9- and 18-hole golf courses, an ice skating rink, 33 lighted tennis courts, and a model airplane field.

Shadyside

GYMS AND HEALTH CLUBS

FITNESS FACTORY

There's much to recommend about Shadyside's Fitness Factory, which sits right on the border of Shadyside and the recently gentrified corner of East Liberty. For starters, the membership rates are seriously competitive at just $49 per month or $299 per year (and they haven't gone up for a very long time). In fact, with the exception of Edgewood's new Planet Fitness location, you're not likely to find a better deal anywhere in town.

The equipment is relatively run-of-the-mill, although much of it has been recently updated, including the addition of a climbing wall, but there seems to be more than enough of almost everything, and lines rarely form around even the most popular pieces of equipment. And while you won't find a pool or sauna, there is a tanning bed as well as a steady stream of eardrum-shattering house music blasting from the sound system. The clientele is generally friendly, accommodating, and college-aged.

MAP 4: 212 S. Highland Ave., 412/362-6306, www.fitnessfactorypgh.com; daily 24 hours; $10/day

X SHADYSIDE

Although X Shadyside claims to be the city's only 24-hour health and fitness club, it's actually not—the gym closes at 6pm on Saturday and Sunday nights. Still, it is one of only a handful of gyms in the city where you can get round-the-clock workout access, and the facilities, by the way, are top-notch. Free weights are plentiful and seemingly brand new, but the machines, which work the body's muscles with an almost uncanny precision, are even better. X Shadyside has no swimming pool or steam room, but it does boast its own room of cardio equipment and a spacious studio where yoga and aerobics classes take place (all classes are included in the price of a gym membership, which is roughly $70 a month).The average exercisers tend to be the same sorts of people you'd see shopping along Shadyside's streets: gorgeously styled young women and men.

MAP 4: 5608 Walnut St., 412/363-9999, www.xshadyside.com; daily 24 hours; $20/day

PARKS

MELLON PARK

Unlike the majority of Pittsburgh's other public parks, Mellon Park is relatively tiny. If you've ever visited the Pittsburgh Center for the Arts, you've also been in Mellon Park—it's the green space that surrounds the center. The area directly behind the center is a gorgeously restful and hilly expanse—it's also one of the city's quaintest locales for an afternoon or evening picnic. On the opposite side of bustling 5th Avenue you'll find Mellon Park's Tennis Bubble, a court with a bubble-like covering that protects players from the biting cold throughout the winter and early spring.

MAP 4: Corner of 5th Ave. and Shady Ave., 412/682-7575, www.pittsburghparks.org

TENNIS

MELLON PARK TENNIS CENTER

Ever driven past a structure on 5th Avenue near Penn Avenue that resembles a giant inflatable dome and wondered what went on there? Now you know: It's nothing less than an indoor, year-round tennis court. Known locally as the Tennis Bubble, the dome itself measures an impressive 118 feet wide by 265 feet long. Most enthusiasts will be pleased to learn that the playing surface is a Premiere Court (a slightly cushioned hard court), and that when the dome is removed during the summer months, use of the courts is free to the public. (Inexplicably, the bubble isn't removed every summer.) Players should call ahead to reserve one of the bubble's five courts. The bubble, which maintains a pleasant temperature of 65°F, is open every day of the week.

MAP 4: 6425 5th Ave. at Beechwood Blvd., 412/665-4017 or 412/475-0689; daily 7am-11pm; court rental $20-30 per hour

YOGA, MEDITATION, AND MARTIAL ARTS

★ AMAZING YOGA

One of the city's most popular and progressive yoga studios, Amazing Yoga now has three locations, including the Shadyside studio and one each in Wexford (2606 Brandt School Rd., 724/935-2240) and on the South Side (1506 E. Carson St., 412/681-1092). Taking an introductory class at Amazing Yoga is the perfect choice for anyone who still considers the practice a bit mystical or odd, largely because the reigning philosophy is one of acceptance, community, and all-inclusiveness. Snotty attitudes are a big no-no, in other words, which may explain why Amazing has won the *Pittsburgh City Paper*'s "Best Yoga Studio" and "Best Yoga Teachers" awards for the past six years in a row. Baptiste power yoga is the predominant style practiced at Amazing. A 30-day unlimited pass, good at any Amazing location, is $125. The studio offers online classes as well.

MAP 4: 730 Copeland St., 412/681-1092, www.amazingyoga.net; drop-in classes $15

Squirrel Hill and Point Breeze

Map 5

ADVENTURE SPORTS

THE CLIMBING WALL

An intense full-body workout, a sometimes terrifying experience, a serious mental test, and an absolute blast: That pretty much sums up the sport of indoor rock climbing, which can be practiced safely and affordably at The Climbing Wall at The Factory in Point Breeze. Beyond the basic introductory class, private advanced lessons and kids' lessons are also available. Can't make it to Point Breeze? Make the scene instead at the SouthSide Works' **REI** (412 S. 27th St., 412/488-9410, www.rei.com), where shoppers who are REI members can ramble up an indoor wall before picking up a new pair of discounted Merrells.

MAP 5: 7501 Penn Ave., 412/247-7334, www.theclimbingwall.net; $30 introductory class (includes equipment rental); $12 all-day passes; monthly memberships $65

PARKS

★ FRICK PARK

The largest of the city's parks, Frick Park practically begs walkers, joggers, and bikers to get lost among its many trails and forested areas. But strolling the valleys and hills is hardly the only recreational option. Frick also has playgrounds that are perfect for families with small children, as well as a wide-open field where dogs are allowed to run leash-free. You'll also find red clay tennis courts and a lawn bowling green (the only public court in Pennsylvania), where competitive seniors can be found whiling away the afternoon.

MAP 5: Corner of Forbes Ave. and S. Braddock Ave., 412/682-7575, www.pittsburghparks.org

Bloomfield and Lawrenceville

Map 6

BOWLING

ARSENAL LANES

With much more to offer than your standard neighborhood bowling alley, it's no surprise that Lawrenceville's Arsenal Lanes has become such a popular hang-out spot for the East End's artiest inhabitants. The Wednesday night Rock & Bowl event—where live rock acts perform directly on the lanes—draws an especially large crowd, although so too do the many other special nights, including Friday's ever-popular karaoke night. Probably the alley's best feature, however, is its Upstairs Saloon, which overlooks the smaller and somewhat hidden Hollywood Bowl room, an intimate bowling space filled with bright-shining lights.

MAP 6: 212 44th St., 412/683-5992, www.arsenalbowl.com

ROWING AND KAYAKING

THREE RIVERS ROWING ASSOCIATION

Pittsburgh's Three Rivers Rowing Association is a nonprofessional group that organizes rowing and kayaking activities and events on the Allegheny River. Anyone is welcome to join in or become a member, regardless of age or experience. The TRRA has two facilities, one on Washington's Landing under the 31st Street Bridge and another in the Millvale Waterfront Park, underneath the 40th Street Bridge. But exploring the association's website before stopping by would be prudent; there you'll find detailed information about kayak tours, rowing classes and events, listings for sweep and sculling classes, information about joining a dragon boat team, and quite a bit more. Call for information about purchasing an annual membership, which provides access to all TRRA facilities and equipment. Activities generally take place between April and November.

MAP 6: 412/231-8772, www.threeriversrowing.org; annual membership dues $395 adult, $735 families, $220 student; membership rates include full facility usage, kayak, scull, sweep, and dragon boat usage, and program discounts

SKATEBOARDING

WEST PENN SKATE PARK (POLISH HILL BOWL)

The Polish Hill Bowl, as it's known to locals, is the easiest to reach if you don't have a car. It's also not far from Gooski's—convenient should you care to do a bit of pre- or post-session drinking. The 77A and 77B buses pass by the park, as does just about every other

Three Rivers Park

Thanks in large part to the tireless work of a group of Pittsburgh civic and business leaders who in 1999 created an organization known as the Riverlife (www.riverlifepgh.org), Pittsburgh is finally in the midst of creating what will surely be known as one of the country's most gorgeous and inspiring riverfront parks. Currently being referred to as **Three Rivers Park,** and at roughly 80 percent completion at the time of writing, the project is brilliantly utilizing the city's huge amount of urban waterfront property, which includes both banks of the Ohio, Allegheny, and Monongahela Rivers. Once it's finished, the city will be home to an interconnected riverfront park system some 13 miles long.

The gorgeous South Shore Riverfront Park, a new Convention Center plaza, the Monongahela Wharf landing, a pedestrian walkway on the Hot Metal Bridge, and a massive restoration of Point State Park and its legendary fountain have all been completed, while other projects—including a green boulevard along the Allegheny Riverfront, the Mon Wharf switchback ramp, and a connector between Point Start Park and the Mon Wharf—are underway. And while the entirety of Riverlife's construction plans aren't scheduled to be complete until 2020, it will no doubt be a genuine thrill to watch as Pittsburghers slowly develop more intimate and meaningful connections with their native waterways—a goal that has unfortunately not been realistic for city dwellers here, until now. Visit www.riverlifepgh.org for updates and access information.

54C, but be sure to ask the driver if his or her route passes through Polish Hill. True to its name, the park doesn't offer much more than a bowl, albeit a relatively nice one. Some street skating facilities are also on-site.

MAP 6: 450 30th St., 412/622-7353; daily dawn-dusk

SPECTATOR SPORTS

Rugby and Wrestling

KEYSTONE STATE WRESTLING

Wrestling fans have a new Pittsburgh home at "the Moose" in Lawrenceville, which is the city's exclusive location of Keystone State Wrestling matches. And Pittsburgh, as it happens, has its own fair share of larger-than-life wrestling personalities—"Iceman" Tony Johnson, Lord Zoltan, Bobby Badfingers, and "Dr. Devastation" Lou Martin come to mind. As is the case on the professional wrestling circuit, you'll see tag team matches and ridiculous beefs between competitors at Keystone State events. Some ladies also get in on the action. It's all in good fun, but those easily offended might want to check out some of the club's photo galleries online, to see what they're in for before match day.

MAP 6: 120 51st St., Lawrenceville Moose (Moose Lodge 581), 412/681-5958, www.kswa.net; $10

East Liberty and Garfield Map 6

PARKS

HIGHLAND PARK

Located in an East End neighborhood of the same name, Highland Park sits on an overlook atop the Allegheny River, close to the Pittsburgh Zoo. Because of its enviable vista, the park is especially popular with joggers but also with walkers who enjoy circling the 0.75-mile path around the reservoir, a historical city site officially known as Reservoir No. 1. The sand volleyball courts are a popular destination in the summer, as is the swimming pool, which is the only long-course pool in Pittsburgh.

MAP 6: Highland Ave., 412/682-7575, www.pittsburghparks.org

Greater Pittsburgh Map 7

ADVENTURE SPORTS

GO APE ZIPLINE PARK

Pittsburgh's one-and-only treetop adventure is just a few miles north of town in North Park. The Go Ape course rests atop the park's 63-acre lake, and even if you're not up for the zipline fun, the scenic views themselves are simply breathtaking. The course is made up of dozens of rope ladders, dizzying crossings, two Tarzan swings, and five ziplines. The course is leveled in five sections, with each going higher and higher. Don't worry if you're a bit faint of heart, though, as there are bypass routes throughout the course for those who might chicken out. The adventure takes between two and three hours to complete, though I recommend making a day of it and enjoying the park's other amenities as well. Operating hours vary; check website for details.

MAP 7: North Park, 303 Pearce Mill Rd., Allison Park, 412/935-1766, www.goape.com; Mar.-May weekends and select weekdays, daily Jun.-Aug., Sept.-late Nov. weekends and select weekdays, closed Dec. 31-Mar. 1; online reservations recommended; adult $55, child 10-17 $35

PITTSBURGH INTERNATIONAL RACE COMPLEX

Formerly known as Beaverun Motosports Complex, the Pittsburgh International Race Complex is the region's world-class racing, training, and testing facility. The race course itself features 12 turns and a 1,700-foot straight-away, and the complex offers kart racing on the 0.8-mile Wilson circuit. There's also a vehicle dynamics training area and multiple spectator events. Karts are $20 per

10-minute session or $50 for three 10-minute sessions. Pitt Race Driving Academy for teens is $249 per four-hour session and $400 for an intensive all-day session.

MAP 7: 201 Penndale Rd., Wampum, 724/535-1000, www.pittrace.com; daily noon-8pm; additional times based on events and rentals

★ STEELTOWN PAINTBALL PARK

Lovers of war games and grown-ups who are still kids at heart with surely get a thrill at Steeltown Paintball Park. Get ready to strategize, duck for cover, and surprise your enemies (or best friends) on the fun but challenging field. Taking a paintball hit does sting, and you should plan to wear gear that covers you completely. For those with younger children, Steeltown offers "Splatmaster" paintball, which uses a lower velocity spring-loaded gun and smaller paint cartridges. The park is often rented out for birthday, corporate, and other private parties, so do check online before your visit. Equipment rental pricing includes everything you need, from your gun to a full-face mask, though you can bring your own equipment if you prefer. Due to liability issues, however, paintballs must be purchased on-site. A $150 annual pass includes free open play sessions and equipment rentals.

MAP 7: 500 Huntington Ave., Emsworth, 412/443-9287, www.steeltownpaintballpark.com; daily 10am-6pm; $15 during open play times; $10 equipment rental

GUIDED AND WALKING TOURS

RIVERS OF STEEL HERITAGE TOURS

Comprising 3,000 square miles throughout seven counties of Southwestern Pennsylvania, the Rivers of Steel Heritage Area was created by U.S. Congress in 1996. The purpose was to honor the culture and the American way of life that existed hand-in-hand with the industry of Big Steel—an industry that no longer exists in this part of the county.

In Pittsburgh's Homestead neighborhood, however, it's now possible to tour the areas where steel production took place. Tours and their themes occasionally change, so it's best to call or check the organization's website before planning a trip. Past tours, however, have explored the infamous site of the Homestead Steel Strike of 1892 and the remains of the Carrie Furnace. Visitors can also take narrated, self-guided tours of the immediate area by renting audio devices with headphones.

MAP 7: 338 E. 9th Ave., Homestead, 412/464-4020, www.riversofsteel.com; about $20

Steel City Strolls

Much like San Francisco, a town to which Pittsburgh is occasionally compared, Pittsburgh has many neighborhoods that are hilly, rough-hewn, and generally best explored on foot or atop a bicycle. The guided walking tours organized by the **Pittsburgh History and Landmarks Foundation** are a good place to start—they're packed with intriguing historical and architectural trivia, and most are only an hour long.

Once you get your footing, try striking out on your own. The Greater Pittsburgh area is filled with rarely visited but historically curious pockets; to enjoy the city's more obscure reaches, head to the Pennsylvania section of the Carnegie Library or any local bookstore and look for locally published guides and maps, many of which aren't widely distributed outside the area. *Seeing Pittsburgh,* by Barringer Fifield (University of Pittsburgh Press), includes both walking and driving architectural tours; *60 Hikes Within 60 Miles: Pittsburgh,* by Donna Ruff (Menasha Ridge Press), offers diverse hiking suggestions in the city and beyond; *The Steps of Pittsburgh,* by Bob Regan (Local History Co.), is a fascinating guide to the city's 712 sets of outdoor steps; and *The Bridges of Pittsburgh,* also by Bob Regan (Local History Co.), is considered the definitive guide to the city's hundreds of cross-river spans. And when you're ready to get out of town, pick up *Quick Escapes Pittsburgh,* by Michelle Pilecki (Globe Pequot), which offers a rundown of 25 mini-vacations in mostly tranquil settings.

GYMS AND HEALTH CLUBS

WRIGHT'S GYM

As the only certified Krav Maga training facility in the Pittsburgh area, Wright's Gym is serious about self defense. The gym also offers courses in Brazilian jiu-jitsu, Muay Thai kickboxing, and even wrestling, in addition to having all of the amenities you'd expect in a fitness facility, from cardio and weight equipment to heavy bags and locker rooms. Wright's is a few minutes' drive outside of town, but it has a surprisingly loyal following and is especially popular with women. Prices are based on courses and vary. Beginning through advanced levels are taught.

MAP 7: 20 Foster Ave., Crafton-Ingram Shopping Center, Crafton/Ingram, 412/921-1530, www.wrightsgym.com; daily 24 hours; prices vary

ICE SKATING

AIRPORT ICE ARENA

A good place to learn ice skating basics is the Airport Ice Arena, where future hockey players and figure skaters also train. Public events are scheduled when the place isn't being used by professional sports organizations. Located in Moon Township not far from the Pittsburgh International Airport, Airport Ice Arena offers a professional-level rink, and a number of different courses and programs for young ice skaters, figure skaters, and hockey players in training. The seven-week Learn to Skate program ($120, includes rental skates), for instance, is geared toward pre-teens, as is the eight-week Learn to Play Hockey course ($149), which is only offered occasionally. Check the website for upcoming clinic dates and registration info.

MAP 7: 330 Hookstown Grade Rd., Parkway West, Moon Township, 412/264-2222, www.airporticearena.com

ICE CASTLE ARENA

The indoor Ice Castle Arena in Castle Shannon is open year-round; public skating takes places on two NHL regulation-size rinks. Beginning adult skaters and children can take lessons at the Ice Castle, which is also a perfect location to host a child's birthday party.

MAP 7: 990 Castle Shannon Blvd., Castle Shannon, 412/561-9090, www.icecastlearena.com; call for hours; $7 general admission, $3 skate rental, child 5 and under free

SKATEBOARDING

AE RIDE SKATEPARK

Located behind the Cranberry Municipal Center and constructed over the course of just one day (with help from the Pittsburgh-based American Eagle Outfitters corporation), AE Ride is a free park featuring ramps, rails, stairs, platforms, and benches—a street skater's dream come to life. There are also quarter-pipes, launch ramps, and small half-pipe ramps.

MAP 7: 2525 Rochester Rd., Cranberry, 724/776-4806, www.cranberrytownship.org; daily dawn-dusk, weather permitting; free

IMPERIAL SKATEPARK

Generally agreed upon as the best and most challenging skate park in the Greater Pittsburgh area, Imperial Skatepark is nothing less than a concrete dream. You'll find a beautifully constructed concrete snake run, a kidney-shaped pool, and small ramps scattered throughout. There's also a standard street area with rails, as well as a half-pipe. The park is well lit and open late, and BMX riders are welcome.

MAP 7: 810 Rte. 30, Findlay Township's Clinton Community Park, www.findlay.pa.us; spring/summer daily 8am-11pm, winter daily 8am-9pm, weather permitting; free

MCKINLEY SKATEPARK

Located in Beltzhoover's McKinley Park, this skate park is often empty during the day. Offering a four-foot metal half-pipe and a decent collection of street obstacles, the park can be accessed by taking the Liberty Tunnel out of the city and then turning left onto Route 51 South. From there, hang another left onto Bausman Street; you'll soon see the park on your left. Thrift store connoisseurs should take care not to miss the nearby **Red White & Blue Thrift Store** (935 Ohio River Blvd., 412/766-6098).

MAP 7: Bausman St., Beltzhoover; daily dawn-dusk; free

PENN HILLS EXTREME SPORTS PARK

Located in Duff Park and not far from the Penn Hills Shopping Center on Rodi Road, the Penn Hills Extreme Sports Park is free to the public and open to skateboarders, in-line skaters and BMX riders. And because area teens actually contributed ideas when it came time to design the park's layout, the end result was fairly impressive; obstacles include a mini-ramp, a quarter-pipe, a pyramid, stairs, ledges, and a number of movable boxes.

MAP 7: 102 Duff Rd., Penn Hills, 412/795-3500, www.pennhills.org; daily dawn-dusk; free

SHERADEN SKATE PARK

A decent enough park unfortunately constructed with prefabricated parts, the West End's Sheraden Park features quarter-pipes, a so-called fun box with a ledge, and a number of rails for sliding and grinding.

MAP 7: Tuxedo St., Sheraden, 412/255-2539; daily dawn-dusk; free

★ 3 B'S ACTION PARK

This is one of the city's newer public skate parks, generally considered by locals to be one of the very best. The medium- and large-sized concrete bowls and the street skating areas are conveniently located near the Boyce Park wave pool. Aside from the park's wealth of rolling concrete real estate, skaters also appreciate the fact that Boyce is free to all comers. Not quite so popular with the locals, though, is the over-enthusiastic pad and helmet rule; you'll need to be covered in something approaching plastic armor if you hope to spend any serious time here.

MAP 7: 675 Old Frankstown Rd., Monroeville, Boyce Park, www.alleghenycounty.us/parks/bpfac.aspx; daily dawn-dusk; free

SKIING, SNOWBOARDING, AND SNOWMOBILING

The ski and snowboarding season in Western Pennsylvania generally runs from mid-December through mid-March, weather conditions permitting. But even when the powder isn't falling, it's usually still possible to hit the slopes, as the area's better resorts cover their mountains in artificial snow when Mother Nature fails to provide.

Snowmobile hobbyists might want to visit the website of the **Pennsylvania State Snowmobile Association** (www.pasnow.org,

888/411-7772), which works to maintain trails and a high level of snowmobiling safety throughout the state.

For more information about ski areas and resorts statewide, consult the Pennsylvania Ski Area Association at www.skipa.com.

BOYCE PARK

The ski slopes at Boyce Park won't be of much interest to the advanced skier, but they're ideal for beginners and the generally timid. And because Boyce Park is in nearby Monroeville, this is the perfect choice for a day trip or a quick ski after work. Snowboarders have access to two quarter-pipes and one of the longest half-pipes in Pennsylvania. Adult slope fees are a reasonable $10 a day during the week and $14 on weekends.

MAP 7: 675 Old Frankstown Rd., Monroeville, 724/733-4665 or 724/733-4656, www.alleghenycounty.us/parks/bpfac.aspx

HIDDEN VALLEY FOUR SEASONS RESORT

Hidden Valley Four Seasons Resort is in the picturesque Laurel Highlands, about 60 miles east of the city. Although it started life more than 50 years ago as a family-run bed-and-breakfast, it now offers a year-round schedule of activities, including downhill and cross-country skiing, hiking, biking, and golfing. The ever-popular Seven Springs Resort is nearby, as is the white-water rafting destination of Ohiopyle. Hidden Valley has 28 different trails and slopes. Adult season passes are $499.

MAP 7: 1 Craighead Dr., Hidden Valley, 814/443-8000 or 866/443-7544 (snow reports), www.hiddenvalleyresort.com; daily 9am-9pm; adult lift tickets $30-54 weekends, $25-30 weekdays

NEMACOLIN WOODLANDS RESORT

This is a truly luxurious vacation spot offering all manner of recreation possibilities, including adventure sports (off-road driving, fly-fishing), culinary classes, and the occasional wine tasting. Skiers and snowboarders can take advantage of 10 separate slopes and a half-pipe atop the 2,030-foot Mystic Mountain. Snow tubing is also big. Nemacolin is in Fayette County, about 60 miles southeast of the city. Adult season passes are $129. A 30-minute dog sledding ride will set you back $125, or $150 for two riders.

MAP 7: 1001 LaFayette Dr., Farmington, 724/329-8555 or 866/344-6957, www.nemacolin.com; adult day pass $38, cross-country skiing or snowshoeing $20

SEVEN SPRINGS MOUNTAIN RESORT

The peak at Seven Springs Mountain Resort has an elevation of nearly 3,000 feet with a vertical drop of 750 feet; it boasts 14 slopes and 17 trails. Its longest trail is 1.25 miles long. No wonder Seven Springs is one of the area's most popular ski resorts. (*Ski Magazine* rated it the number-one resort in the mid-Atlantic.) The expert-level snowboard park is 400 feet wide and 500 feet long.

MAP 7: 777 Waterwheel Dr., Champion, 800/523-7777 or 800/452-2223 (snow report), www.7springs.com; daily lift tickets $38-68

SPECTATOR SPORTS

Horse Racing

LADBROKE AT THE MEADOWS

About a half-hour drive south of Pittsburgh is Ladbroke at the Meadows, a harness facility with a year-round racing schedule; its website proclaims it as "Greater Pittsburgh's best-kept secret." That may be something of a stretch, but because of its somewhat secluded location near the town of Canonsburg, it is true that the Meadows doesn't see the sort of traffic it probably deserves. Admission and parking are both free at the Meadows, which offers both casual and fine-dining options. Check out the facility online for live racing schedules and wagering information, or call any one of the Meadows's off-track betting locations if you'd rather not visit the track: New Castle (2004 W. State St., 724/654-2221), Harmarville (1 Anchor Dr., 412/828-0610), Coraopolis (7700 University Blvd., 412/262-3100), or West Mifflin (7025 Clairton Rd., 412/650-9000).

MAP 7: 210 Racetrack Rd., Washington, 724/225-9300, www.themeadowsracing.com; free

Rugby and Wrestling

PITTSBURGH HARLEQUINS RUGBY FOOTBALL CLUB

Especially serious are the players of the Pittsburgh Harlequins Rugby Football Club. The club was founded in 1973 and today is a member of the USA Rugby Football Union, the Mid-Atlantic Rugby Football Union, and the Potomac Rugby Union. The team plays on a green known as Founders Field, which is about 16 miles from Downtown Pittsburgh in Indianola. Visit the team's website for an updated game schedule.

MAP 7: Eisele Rd. at Cove Run Rd., Founders Field, Indianola, www.pittsburghharlequins.org; free

TENNIS

WASHINGTON'S LANDING TENNIS COURTS

A 42-acre island formerly known as Herr's Island, about two miles east of Downtown on the Allegheny River, the formerly blighted area referred to as Washington's Landing is today a collection of expensive townhomes, a marina, a rowing center, and one of the most gorgeously situated public tennis courts in all of Pittsburgh. With an unbelievably beautiful riverside setting, it almost wouldn't matter if the courts were uneven and cracked. And while three of the five courts are in fact in poor condition, two are perfectly usable.

That less-than-perfect situation doesn't often create a problem, because due to its somewhat obscure location, the courts usually see very little action, even on perfect weather days.

The playing surface is hard, and there are no lighting or restroom facilities. To find the courts, drive north along the 31st Street Bridge (from the Strip District toward Route 28), then take a left onto the downward-sloping ramp that sits mere feet from the end of the bridge. Take a left at the bottom of the ramp and follow that road until it dead-ends into the tennis courts' parking lot.

MAP 7: Washington's Landing, 200 Waterfront Dr., Pittsburgh, 412/255-2539; free

WATER PARKS

SANDCASTLE

Sandcastle is one of the Pittsburgh area's premiere amusement parks, second in popularity only to Kennywood. The park is in Homestead next to the Waterfront shopping complex and boasts 14 water slides, a wave pool, hot tubs, and a children's area. Special events include "Dive in Movies," during which family-friendly films are projected above a pool, and the "Waves Under 18 Party," a dance party that, yes, takes place in a wave pool. After dark, the over-21s head to Sandbar, an on-site outdoor nightclub. Hours vary throughout the season and for special events and festivals. Visit the website prior to scheduling your trip.

MAP 7: 1000 Sandcastle Dr., Homestead, 412/462-6666, www.sandcastlewaterpark.com; daily $31.99 adult, season pass $54.99

YOGA, MEDITATION, AND MARTIAL ARTS

STILL MOUNTAIN TAI CHI AND CHI KUNG

Because Pittsburgh doesn't have much of an immigrant Chinese community to speak of, you won't find the martial art of tai chi practiced in public parks here as it is in, say, San Francisco's Washington Square. But the ancient form of Chinese exercise is taught at kung fu and martial arts studios around town, including Still Mountain Tai Chi and Chi Kung.

The practice at Still Mountain leans toward Chinese Buddhism and involves a combination of martial arts, spiritual development, and health. A wide variety of classes and workshops take place at the Still Mountain studio, including classes that involve weapons, self-defense, and meditation workshops. Tuition per month for group classes is $100; private sessions are $60 per hour or $30 per half hour; a one-hour taped session with instruction and critique is $75; and private group sessions are $60 for the first person and $15 for each additional person.

MAP 7: Mount Lebanon, 412/480-9177, www.stillmountaintaichi.com

Various Locations

FISHING

FISH PITTSBURGH

The city and surrounding regions are home to popular angling clubs, and the community has grown so large local fishers have pulled together the blog and member forum site Fish Pittsburgh. There's a tab on the site with a thorough list of local fishing groups, including contact information for each. Anglers of all skill levels use the blog and forum to share the scoop on their favorite fishing holes.

www.fishpittsburgh.com

KEYSTONE BASS BUDDY CIRCUIT

The largest fishing tournament club in the state of Pennsylvania, the Keystone Bass Buddy Circuit is something of a cross between a social club and a competitive team. Members gather often to practice their respective angling techniques in Western Pennsylvania's rivers. For more information about the group or to download a membership application, visit the not-for-profit organization's website.

www.kbass.com

GUIDED AND WALKING TOURS

PITTSBURGH NEIGHBORHOOD TOURS

Partly conceived and created by the city's own tourism bureau, the wonderfully educational Pittsburgh Neighborhood Tours were designed for anyone, tourists and longtime locals alike, who would like to explore the city's unique and culture-rich areas. On the Neighborhood Tours website, you'll find reams of insider information about neighborhoods like Bloomfield, Mount Washington, the Strip District, and the South Side. Detailed self-guided tour suggestions are available for each of the featured neighborhoods.

412/481-0561, ext. 17, www.pittsburghneighborhoodtours.com, free

Shops

While Pittsburgh hasn't really been thought of as a premiere shopping destination since its midcentury heyday as a booming steel town, an eclectic and thriving new boutique scene has created quite a buzz over the last several years, thanks in large part to highly visible and much adored local designers and retailers, as well as the continued revitalization of the East Liberty and Lawrenceville neighborhoods.

Yet as Pittsburgh rapidly sheds its outdated Rust Belt image, local artists and entrepreneurs still embrace an unsurpassed work ethic and fierce loyalty to their customers and supporters. Beloved local shops and hipster boutiques alike pride themselves on quality, value, and friendly home-town service. Moving beyond your run-of-the-mill seasonal sales and trunk shows, many Pittsburgh shop owners have broken the mold of traditional retail success by doing the unexpected. Some, like Pageboy Salon & Boutique in Lawrenceville, for instance, are providing full-service style. Others, like Broke Little Rich Girl, a fashion-forward shop disguised as a food truck, are even putting their boutiques on wheels. And others still, including a quirky gift shop known as Wildcard, are engaging with customers through regular events and DIY classes.

Inside the city itself, especially in the shopping havens of Shadyside, Oakland, Squirrel Hill, and, most recently, Lawrenceville and East Liberty, you'll find a plethora of establishments to please even the pickiest of shoppers. And because Pittsburgh is still home to a significantly large senior citizen population, its antiques shops,

Look for ★ to find recommended shops.

HIGHLIGHTS

★ **Best Place to Grab a Gift for Your Girlfriend:** Ladies love the dizzying array of scarves, jewelry, bags, accessories, and other assorted bling at **Lucy's Handmade Clothing** (page 235).

★ **Best Place to Stock Your New Dream House:** The high-quality and sustainable furniture lines at **Hacienda** are amazing, especially when paired with the shop's unique decor and handmade artwork (page 235).

★ **Easiest Way to Keep Your Mountain Bike in Tip-Top Shape:** Pay a visit to the friendly folks at **Thick Bikes,** a fantastic neighborhood spot for bike repairs, used and new cycles, and all manner of biking paraphernalia (page 241).

★ **Best Place to Find Vintage Clothes You Can Actually Wear:** East Carson Street's **Highway Robbery** carefully selects only those vintage pieces that can be seamlessly integrated into modern wardrobes (page 241).

★ **Best Place to Pamper Your Pooch While Meeting Other Local Animal Lovers:** Shadyside's **Petagogy** has an impressive selection of premium, grain-free, and biologically appropriate foods for both dogs and cats, including many hard-to-find brands (page 249).

★ **Best Place to Overhaul Your Wardrobe:** It's tough to go wrong at **Mid-Atlantic Mercantile,** a boutique specializing in high-quality, sustainable, and ethically sourced clothing made in small batch runs for both men and women (page 257).

★ **Best Place to Find a Little Bit of Everything:** Since it offers everything from handmade T-shirts and housewares to uber-creative gift cards and jewelry, you just can't beat **Wildcard,** ground zero for the city's crafting scene (page 258).

★ **Best Places to Beautify:** When it comes time to rejuvenate your skin, consider the all-natural and age-defying methods offered at **Bloom Organic Skincare Parlor.** Anyone needing a color change or correction, meanwhile, will want to consult with **Dye by Daquila** (page 259 and page 263).

★ **Best Place to Outfit Your New Apartment:** Stock up on nifty boxes, tins, baskets, and other affordable housewares at **Urban Cottage** (page 259).

★ **Best Spot to Cop That New Mixtape:** In addition to having the latest in urban menswear fashion, **Time Bomb** promotes both local and nationally known hip-hop artists and deejays. Pick up a $5 mixtape, and you might just discover the world's next Mac Miller (page 263).

thrift stores, and vintage and consignment stores tend to offer incredible selections at very reasonable prices.

What's more, Pittsburgh has become quite a haven for the arts and crafts scene, thanks in large part to the city's affordable housing and studio costs and its history of manufacturing. Shoppers can expect to find one-of-a-kind, handcrafted goods by local designers and artisans in boutiques throughout the city. Be sure to inquire about open studio hours and clean-out sales for a chance to see these talented Pittsburghers at work, and to pick up unique finds at a fraction of their regular retail prices. Keep an eye out for popular events like the annual Handmade Arcade, a local arts and crafts fair that has become so highly anticipated and well attended that it is now held at the David L. Lawrence Convention Center, in order to accommodate the 8,000-plus shoppers that flock there in a single day.

Keep in mind that many independently owned boutiques and shops may change their hours seasonally or to accommodate special festivals and neighborhood events. Call or check online before your shopping journeys commence to get the most up-to-date hours of operation. Many shops also offer special promotions and coupons online, which can be a great way to save a few bucks while still supporting local retailers.

Downtown

Map 1

ARTS AND CRAFTS

BOUTIQUE 208

Although it started out as a modest pop-up shop, Boutique 208 has already become something of a local DIY crafting institution, offering only items that have been handmade by local artists and designers. Shoppers will find made-by-hand art and accessories, from purses, picture frames, tote bags, and T-shirts to jewelry, stationery, and home furnishing items, in this modestly sized and well-edited shop. Special events and how-to classes are occasionally scheduled.

MAP 1: 208 6th St., 412/566-3600, www.boutique208.blogspot.com; Wed.-Fri. 11am-2pm and 4pm-8pm, Sat. 11am-8pm, Sun. 11am-5pm

BOOKS AND MUSIC

AMAZING BOOKS

Although it has gone through quite a few recent mutations, this is essentially the same shop that was previously located on the Penn Avenue Arts Corridor, where it was known as Awesome Books. Today, Amazing Books is the Downtown area's only used bookstore, and alongside the standards—literary fiction,

Shops on the Move

Broke Little Rich Girl

With the Pittsburgh creative scene flourishing, many area artists, designers, and even entire retail establishments have taken their goods mobile. As a result, the city is now graced with an ever-growing number of arts, crafts, and makers markets, as well as pop-up shops and even complete mobile boutiques based on the successful food truck phenomenon.

ARTS AND CRAFTS MARKETS

Founded in 2004, **Handmade Arcade** (www.handmadearcade.com) has since become one of the most beloved arts and crafts events in the city. The one-day DIY bonanza is usually held in early December (perfect for holiday shoppers) and now takes place at Downtown's David L. Lawrence Convention Center, the better to accommodate the hundreds of vendors and the thousands of shoppers who flock there each year. The event also boasts an impressive number of hand-on demonstrations. Many Handmade Arcade vendors also sell their wares at other arts and crafts events throughout the year, and Handmade Arcade does support and even sponsor similar efforts throughout the year.

The popular nomadic market known as the **I Made It! Market** (www.imadeitmarket.com) began as an effort to assist local crafters and artists in bringing their wares to the public. It's since grown into a hugely popular destination event that takes place several times a year at popular Pittsburgh destinations. Previous markets have been held in shopping districts such as Bakery Square and SouthSide Works, and the collective often partners with local businesses and festivals as well. The team hosts workshops and other hands-on crafting events throughout the year. A complete event schedule is maintained on the website, and new events are added regularly.

POP-UP SHOPS AND EVENTS

Pop-up shops, boutiques, and even experiential environments have become quite the rage in Pittsburgh in recent years. In 2012, the Downtown Pittsburgh Partnership even launched several pop-up initiatives, including **Project Pop-Up: Downtown** (www.downtownpittsburgh.com), which was aimed at refilling vacant commercial real estate spaces. The initiative was so successful, in fact, that three of the pop-up shops have since moved in long-term: **Boutique 208** (208 6th St., 412/566-3600, www.boutique208.blogspot.com), **Dream Ice Cream** (359 Liberty Ave., 412/540-5393, www.dreamicecream.com), and Amazing Books (929 Liberty Ave., 412/471-1899, www.amazingbookspgh.com).

Sponsored by the nonprofit organization Leadership Pittsburgh Inc., the **Pop Up Pittsburgh!** project (www.popuppittsburgh.com) has been successful in revitalizing previously blighted neighborhoods by developing temporary and low-cost shops, events, and experiences. The project has created pop-up events including movie screenings, so-called community vows (where residents have taken public renewal vows to assist each other in developing their neighborhoods), block parties, and even festivals. All upcoming events are listed online.

The pop-up concept has proven so successful in the area that **CityLAB** (www.citylabpgh.org) has designed a series of pop-up projects they plan to take on the road. Their goal is to share the unique Pittsburgh experience with residents of other cities in an attempt to influence them to relocate to the 'Burgh. CityLab has also seen success in creating the **Garfield Night Market** (N. Pacific Ave. btwn. Penn Ave. and Dearborn St., 412/434-7080, www.garfieldnightmarket.org), an endeavor that features popular food trucks along with independent vendors who sell everything from small-batch roasted coffee to handmade messenger bags, jewelry, and housewares.

MOBILE BOUTIQUES

Not to be outdone by the local food truck scene, Pittsburgh fashion has also found itself some wheels and hit the road, bringing affordable boutique offerings to neighborhoods throughout the region. The most successful and beloved of mobile fashion mavens thus far has been **Broke Little Rich Girl** (www.brokelittlerichgirl.com, @BLRGInc). BLRG owner Samantha Lugo has single-handedly rewritten the formula for boutique success in Pittsburgh by fitting out a big blue step van, stocking it full of unique and one-of-a-kind fashion finds, and rolling through the city each day to settle in different neighborhoods. The mobile boutique is loved by local fashionistas, and best of all, Broke Little Rich Girl prides itself on helping women look great without breaking the bank.

Meanwhile, **Roadie Fashion Truck** (@Roadiefshntruck) has been generating rave reviews and plenty of press for owner/stylist Cailey Breneman, who hawks vintage and antique fashion finds on the road. Roadie's pickup truck and Jeep Liberty can be found at any number of festivals, markets, and other neighborhood events throughout the year, and her eye for vintage fashion finds has not gone unnoticed. Breneman uses Facebook and Twitter exclusively to announce all her upcoming appearances.

counter-cultural authors, psychology, and philosophy, to name just a few—the store also has a decent-sized selection of works by local authors and poets, and an impressive collection of first editions. Most standard titles sell for about half the original cover price. If you're short on funds, bear in mind that the owners are always in the market for high-quality used books; check the website to see what they're currently buying.

MAP 1: 929 Liberty Ave., 412/471-1899, www.amazingbookspgh.com; Sun. noon-4pm, Mon.-Wed. 11am-6pm, Thurs. 11am-8pm, Fri. 11:30am-sunset

SHOPPING DISTRICTS AND CENTERS

THE SHOPS OF ONE OXFORD CENTRE

The go-to shopping location for Pittsburgh's wealthiest citizens, the Shops of One Oxford Centre—located inside a glass atrium within an impressive 45-foot glass tower—are nearly all breathtaking, either for their beauty or their staggering price tags. Surprisingly enough, most all the shop owners and staffers are quite helpful and friendly, and willing to assist with both corporate sales needs as well as budget-minded customers. Some of the retailers include Emphatics, Kountz & Rider, and St. Moritz Chocolatier. The exclusive Rivers Club has a home in the building; there's also a small newsstand, a high-end hair salon, and a modest food court.

MAP 1: Corner of 4th Ave. and Grant St., 412/391-5300, www.shopoxford.com; Mon.-Sat. 10am-5pm

Strip District **Map 1**

ARTS AND CRAFTS

LOOM EXQUISITE TEXTILES

It's no wonder sewing and fabric fiends rave about Loom—it has the most impressive selection of cloth in the city. This awesome little boutique is jam-packed with high-quality and hard-to-find fabrics, tassels, trims, patterns, buttons, buckles, bling, how-to books, and even vintage couture clothing and jewelry. It also stocks rugs, fine textiles, and various home decor items. Sewing classes and private instruction are also available, as are interior consultations, custom upholstery, and window treatments. If you're wondering where a local designer found the fabric for that pillow or tote you just bought, chances are you can find it yourself at Loom. Crafters and quilters will love the selection of designer print fabrics.

MAP 1: 2124 Penn Ave., 412/586-4346, www.loomshowroom.com; Mon.-Sat. 10am-4pm, also by appointment

CLOTHING AND ACCESSORIES

★ LUCY'S HANDMADE CLOTHING

Lucy's is an unexpected little gem right in the heart of Pittsburgh's Strip District—a corner of the city that's much better known for its gourmet food offerings. Once you work your way past the fun finds that are usually displayed out on the sidewalk, you'll find the main floor packed with pashmina scarves, jewelry, handbags, and other unique accessories, while the second floor contains an impressive array of beautiful, handmade clothing—all at surprisingly affordable prices. The owner and store's namesake, Lucy, is incredibly warm, friendly, and helpful, and her boutique is the perfect place to find that statement piece, beautiful scarf, or other one-of-a-kind find to set you apart from the crowd. Locals also love Lucy's for its unique sweaters and other knitwear.

MAP 1: 2021 Penn Ave., 412/885-0327, www.lucyshandmadeclothing.com/onsale.shtml; daily 9am-5pm

HOME DECOR AND FURNISHINGS

★ HACIENDA

Across the street from the Cork Factory Lofts in the Strip District, Hacienda offers the very best high-quality, eco-friendly, and sustainable furniture in the area. Carrying sought-after lines like Terra Sur, Urban Woods, and Environment Furniture, Hacienda's furnishings are perfect for creating a contemporary dream home with a perfectly warm and rustic feel. The shop also offers rare, unique, and one-of-a-kind decor and home accents, as well as curated works by featured artists that pair perfectly with the furniture pieces on offer. Custom work and in-home design consultations are also available. And remember: While the prices may seem high, the items you're splurging on at Hacienda will almost certainly become lifetime investments.

MAP 1: 2350 Railroad St., Cork Factory, 412/904-4477, www.haciendafurniturepittsburgh.com; Tues.-Wed. and Fri.-Sat. 11am-5pm, Thurs. 11am-6pm

HOT HAUTE HOT

Specializing in eclectic and truly one-of-a-kind furniture pieces, the artists at Hot Haute Hot select used, vintage, or antique furniture items and customize each with a unique touch of creativity and top-notch craftsmanship. In other words, this is the perfect showroom for anyone on the hunt for a singular gem. The shop also creates custom items on commission for interested shoppers and for commercial spaces. To put it plainly, Hot Haute Hot is the polar opposite of your run-of-the-mill, standard contemporary furniture shop.

MAP 1: 2124 Penn Ave., 412/338-2323, www.hothautehot.net; Mon.-Fri. 10am-5pm, Sat. 9am-5pm, Sun. 11am-3pm

SHOPPING DISTRICTS AND CENTERS

STRIP DISTRICT

Although the Strip District is often referred to as Pittsburgh's only 24-hour neighborhood, the hardiest shoppers will want to arrive during the daylight hours on Friday, Saturday, or Sunday, when the widest variety of curbside vendors and street performers set up shop along Penn Avenue. And while you'll certainly find specialty boutiques—antiques stores and home decor shops, for instance—it's worth keeping in mind that the Strip is very tourist-friendly, and as such it's home to dozens of little stores hawking touristy trinkets of questionable quality. You'll find knockoff Steelers T-shirts and Pittsburgh-themed memorabilia of all sorts, including postcards, ball caps, and books. The Strip is also something of a public market, and with a bit of poking around it's possible to procure everything from gourmet coffee and cheeses to imported Italian meats and high-end kitchen gadgets. The best fun, however, can usually be had by simply wandering the streets and exploring at length. And don't forget to check out Smallman Street, which runs parallel to Penn Avenue and is home to a few unusual shopping surprises of its own.

MAP 1: Penn Ave. and Smallman St. btwn. 16th and 24th Sts., www.neighborsinthestrip.com

Oakland

Map 2

ARTS AND CRAFTS

IRISH DESIGN CENTER

The real gems at the Irish Design Center, an Irish import shop offering all the standard tchotchkes (rings, books, etc.), are the authentic sweaters and other cozy knits and linens. All are hand-knit, and all are absolutely the real deal (not mass-produced, in other words). What's more, the knits—blankets, throws, pullovers, and shawls—are all uniquely styled. The shop also offers Celtic travel services and distinctive themed tours of Ireland. But if you can't quite afford a world-class tour of the Emerald Isle, not to worry: Simply pick up a bottle of Inis perfume, which has been described by more than one devotee as "Ireland in a Bottle."

MAP 2: 303 S. Craig St., 412/682-6125, www.irishdesigncenter.com; Mon.-Fri. 10am-5:30pm, Sat. 10am-5pm; open late during holiday shopping season

BOOKS AND MUSIC

CALIBAN BOOKSHOP

Specializing in rare first editions, leather-bound books, and fine arts and philosophy tomes, Caliban Bookshop carries the sort of printed curiosities you simply aren't going to stumble across at the neighborhood Barnes & Noble. Treasures seem to show up almost daily, and if you're looking to sell something rare and counterculture-esque, Caliban may be looking to buy. They even make house calls and provide appraisal services to individuals and institutions. Just about every last item from the *McSweeney's* catalog is stocked, and a tiny music store, Desolation Row, can be found in the back corner. Caliban also operates The Warehouse (412/242-9040), a Wilkinsburg storage facility that's home to nearly 150,000 books; visits are by appointment only.

MAP 2: 410 S. Craig St., 412/681-9111, www.calibanbooks.com;
Mon.-Sat. 11am-5:30pm, Sun. 1pm-5:30pm, open most Thursdays till 8pm

PHANTOM OF THE ATTIC COMICS

With a new and much roomier location right above **Top Notch Art Center** (412/355-0444, www.tnartsupply.com) on Oakland's South Craig Street (look for the giant pencil), Phantom of the Attic has long been a Pittsburgh comic book institution. Regulars tend to show up in droves every Wednesday, when upwards of 100 new issues are added to the shelves. The inventory, in other words, is serious. And because Phantom's well-lit space is so sprawling and large, you're nearly guaranteed to find what you need. Meanwhile, the shop's previous location—directly across the street—is now home to **Phantom Games** (406 S. Craig St., 412/682-6290), a favorite hangout for the Dungeons & Dragons set. Although not affiliated with the Oakland location, two other Phantom of the Attic comic stores are in Greentree (2351 Noblestown Rd., 412/921-6229, www.phantomoftheattic.com) and Monroeville (3766 William Penn Hwy. 2, 412/856-4403, www.phantom-attic.com).

MAP 2: 411 S. Craig St., 412/621-1210; Mon.-Sat. 10am-7pm, Sun. 10am-5pm

UNIVERSITY OF PITTSBURGH BOOK CENTER

Not content to exist solely as a locale for new Pitt students to purchase textbooks and school supplies, the massive Pitt Book Center has such a well-stocked selection of fiction and nonfiction titles, as well as gifts and accessories, that students will barely need to stop by a Barnes & Noble during their four years here. Nonstudents, of course, are always welcome at the Book Center, which boasts a particularly well-stocked regional section and mountains of clothing and gift items emblazoned with the Pitt logo. Be prepared to leave all your belongings in a locker at the store's entrance before browsing.

MAP 2: 4000 5th Ave., 412/648-1455, www.pittuniversitystore.com;
Mon., Tues., and Thurs. 8:30am-6pm, Wed. 8:30am-8:30pm, Fri. 8:30am-5pm, Sat. 10am-5pm, Sun. noon-4pm

GIFTS AND SPECIALTY SHOPS

SNOW LION IMPORTS

Snow Lion Imports is Pittsburgh's first and only location for Tibetan and Himalayan arts, artifacts, religious items, and handicrafts, the vast majority of which were acquired by the owners during trips to Nepal, India, and Tibet. The shop's South Craig Street location carries items such as silver and turquoise jewelry, books and CDs, statues, Tibetan singing bowls, prayer flags, bags, clothing, prayer wheels, and a truly impressive collection of Tibetan carpets. Located in the shop's far corner is **Sherpa Gear** (www.sherpaadventuregear.com), a separate store offering a wide variety of trekking and adventure travel clothing; Sherpa Gear sends a portion of its proceeds to underprivileged Nepalese kids.

MAP 2: 201 S. Craig St., 412/687-5680, www.snowlionimports.com; Mon.-Fri. 11am-5:30pm, Sat. 11am-4pm

SKATEBOARDING AND BICYCLE SHOPS

IRON CITY BIKES

Located in the heart of South Oakland, the somewhat rough-around-the-edges Iron City Bikes carries a wide variety of high-quality bicycles, accessories, apparel, and merchandise from manufacturers including Norco, Surly, Velocity, ToPeak, and Haro. Iron City also provides bicycle maintenance services, and it boasts an amazing collection of used bikes starting at just $20 each. Be forewarned that while staffers are extremely knowledgeable, they can seem a bit intimidating to cycling newbies.

MAP 2: 331 S. Bouquet St., 412/681-1310, www.ironcitybikes.com; Mon.-Fri. 11am-7pm, Sat. 11am-5pm, Sun. noon-4pm

South Side **Map 3**

ARTS AND CRAFTS

FIREBORN STUDIOS

Every piece of functional pottery sold in this South Side studio and shop is created on the premises by Fireborn's founders, the master potters Dan Vito and Donna Hetrick. They also stock experimental works, one-of-a-kind objects, and discontinued items, often at deeply discounted prices. Heavily inspired by the 19th-century Arts and Crafts movement, the gallery is as warm, accessible, and inviting as the work found inside it, and Fireborn's "fat" mugs are the best thing to happen to coffee since the home grinder. Fireborn also provides classes for aspiring potters of all skill levels, and their kiln openings offer a rare chance to observe freshly glazed pots and other creations as they transform into beautiful works of art.

MAP 3: 2338 Sarah St., 412/488-6835, www.fireborn.com; Tues.-Thurs. noon-6pm, Fri.-Sat. noon-4pm

CLOTHING AND ACCESSORIES

FIGLEAF

A great alternative to the more expensive shops just down the road, this bright and trendy little South Side boutique has become a favorite for younger area shoppers. It's known for its eye-catching window displays and color-coded organization, and the clothing styles are akin to what one might expect to find at a Forever 21 or H&M, but without all the dizzying clutter and jam-packed racks. Even older and pickier shoppers are known to stop in to indulge in Figleaf's amazing accessory and costume jewelry selection. Figleaf has lately become so popular, in fact, that a few additional boutiques have opened recently in the nearby states of Ohio and Kentucky.

MAP 3: 1406 E. Carson St., 412/431-7700, www.figleafshop.com; Mon. and Wed.-Sat. 11am-7pm, Tues. 1pm-6pm

JUPE BOUTIQUE

Co-owned by fashion professionals Cara Moody and Amanda Hall, Jupe was opened with the aim of bringing fresh, contemporary fashion to area customers at price points they could actually afford. And though Jupe does stock a few higher-end lines, which goes a long way toward helping to diversify the store's inventory, most pieces are from designers like Free People, Mink Pink, and Soda Blue. Appropriately enough, Jupe (French for "skirt") took home several "best of" awards from local publications during its first few years of business. Jewelry, shoes, and accessories can also be picked up, and Jupe's new sister shop in Lawrenceville, **Panello** (3703 Butler St., 412/621-2640), offers the same amazing selection at great prices.

MAP 3: 2306 E. Carson St., 412/432-7933, www.jupeboutique.com; Mon.-Sat. 11am-7pm

GIFTS AND SPECIALTY SHOPS

CULTURE SHOP

A wonderfully unique import shop offering clothing, accessories, and gifts from (mostly) India and the Far East, the Culture Shop feels something like a cross between a Haight-Ashbury head shop and a magic store straight out of a Harry Potter novel. Bohemian accoutrements abound: incense, peasant dresses, silver rings, and statues bearing the likeness of Ganesha. But many come specifically for the striking jewelry, as should you, assuming you're looking for something expressly unique without the requisite high price tag. Strapped for cash or feeling nostalgic for your college days? There's always Nag Champa!

MAP 3: 1602 E. Carson St., 412/481-8284; Mon.-Wed. noon-9pm, Thurs.-Fri. noon-10pm, Sat. 11am-10pm, Sun. noon-5pm

HOME DECOR AND FURNISHINGS

PERLORA

Offering trendy contemporary furniture, Perlora is located in a retrofitted building that is now a loft-style showroom. Perlora also staffs a few interior designers who can help with projects of all sizes, which makes sense given the ultra-modern and traditional designs for sale, not to mention the ergonomic chairs and mattresses available. And while it's true that Perlora's furniture can be pricey, the originals are quite striking and not easily available elsewhere in the city. Also worth a visit is **Perlora Leather** (2837 Smallman St., 412/434-7425), a Strip District showroom featuring, of course, contemporary leather furniture.

MAP 3: 2220 E. Carson St., 412/431-2220 or 800/611-8590, www.perlora.com; Mon.-Sat. 10am-6pm, Sun. noon-5pm

PET SUPPLIES AND GROOMING

A DIAMOND IN THE RUFF

Known as much for its grooming services as for its signature alternatives to harsh pet shampoos and alcohol-containing conditioners, this popular South Side pet spa and boutique truly is a diamond in the rough. You'll be thrilled at your pooch's fresh new scent, and Diamond in the Ruff also stocks a full line of shampoos and conditioners specially engineered to bring out the best qualities of different fur types and colors. Therapeutic scrubs, mud masks, and facial scrubs for Spot are also available. Spa packages include a moisturizing paw treatment and complimentary teeth brushing. Be aware that the last bath is given two hours before closing time, and appointments are strongly recommended.

MAP 3: 155 S. 18th St., 412/381-2200, www.diamondinruff.com; Mon. and Wed. 8am-5:30pm, Thurs. noon-8pm, Fri. 8am-6pm, Sat. 8am-4pm, Tues. by appt. only; grooming $35-65 dogs, $35-45 cats

SHOPPING DISTRICTS AND CENTERS

SOUTHSIDE WORKS

An outdoor shopping center complete with exclusive boutiques, big-box chain stores, cafés and restaurants, a movie theater, and even high-end apartment buildings, SouthSide Works has earned a reputation as one of the city's most successful retail projects. Clothiers include Urban Outfitters, BCBG Max Azria, Puma, Forever 21, H&M, and American Eagle Outfitters. You'll also find Sur la Table, Golden Triangle Bike Rental, Double Decker Tours, two full-service banks (Citizens and PNC), and a slew of restaurants like the Cheesecake Factory, Hofbräuhaus Pittsburgh, and

Claddagh Irish Pub. Parking is surprisingly affordable, and a recently built Hyatt House hotel is on-site. Don't miss the human-size chess board, directly behind REI.

Grab a bike for the day so you can work your way through the entire South Side Flats neighborhood. Farther west on South Street, you'll find eclectic boutiques, independently owned bars and restaurants, music venues, theaters, coffee shops, and more. If you don't wear out your legs or wallet, you'll ultimately find yourself at Station Square, where you can grab a ride up the incline to Mount Washington to enjoy great views of the city. For more information, visit the **Guest Services kiosk** in the main piazza right outside of the Cheesecake Factory.

MAP 3: Corner of 27th St. and E. Carson St., 412/481-8800 or 877/977-8800, www.southsideworks.com

SKATEBOARDING AND BICYCLE SHOPS

ONE UP SKATE

Something of a cross between an upscale boutique and an old-school skate shop, One Up quickly became a South Side institution after opening its doors in 2003. The store boasts an impressive collection of skate shoes and apparel, with labels like Vans, Adidas, and Dickies all well represented. Check out the dizzying array of beautifully shiny skate decks—neatly stacked floor to ceiling on brackets. The quite knowledgeable and surprisingly friendly staff offer private skate lessons by appointment at Mr. Smalls Funhouse in Millvale.

MAP 3: 1409 E. Carson St., 412/432-7007, www.oneuppgh.com; Mon.-Tues. and Thurs. noon-7pm, Wed. and Fri.-Sat. noon-8pm, Sun. noon-5pm

★ THICK BIKES

Originally located in Brooklyn, Thick Bikes is a full-service repair shop that has been fabricating chromoly bicycle frames and other custom parts since 1996. And while the small showroom is packed tight with some of the best bikes and cycling products on the market, including a wide selection of used cycles and messenger gear, Thick Bikes is probably best known among locals for its honesty and its concern for safety. For those ready to make a serious investment, the shop also deals in made-to-order bicycles—some so stylish they'll even have drivers drooling.

MAP 3: 62 S. 15th St., 412/390-3590, www.thickbikes.com; Mon.-Sat. 10am-6pm

VINTAGE AND ANTIQUES

★ HIGHWAY ROBBERY

To describe Highway Robbery owner Kate Colussy as a vintage clothing savant would probably be an understatement; she has an eye for what she calls "vintage casual" style, and it's one you don't

clockwise from top left: Hip'tique; Mid-Atlantic Mercantile; Petagogy

often find outside of the most pricey and pretentious big city retro boutiques. Highway Robbery has a carefully curated selection of clothing that represents roughly the last six or seven decades of fashion, with each and every piece being hand-selected to blend effortlessly into modern wardrobes—reasonable price tags and all. Colussy is obsessed with customer service, and the store has a wonderfully bright and airy ambience.

MAP 3: 1411 E. Carson St., 412/251-0818, www.highwayrobberyvintage.com; Mon.-Sat. noon-8pm, Sun. noon-5pm

Shadyside

Map 4

ARTS AND CRAFTS

PITTSBURGH CENTER FOR THE ARTS

In addition to the gallery, which displays a rotating schedule of visual art and installations by both emerging and established artists, PCA maintains a wonderful gift shop with a large variety of pieces, all of them created by locals. The shop's collection has grown to include work by more than 200 artists from throughout Western Pennsylvania, and in just about every medium imaginable, from fiber, ceramic, and glass work to jewelry, photography, and paper arts. Especially popular is the annual yART sale, which runs from Black Friday through the first week of January; it features uniquely gorgeous work at bargain basement prices.

MAP 4: 6300 5th Ave., 412/361-0873, www.pittsburgharts.org; Tues.-Wed. and Fri.-Sat. 10am-5pm, Thurs. 10am-7pm, Sun. noon-5pm

CLOTHING AND ACCESSORIES

DIANA MISETIC

Designer and former Bosnian refugee Diana Misetic has been a local fashion institution since she opened her first boutique, Little Black Dress, years ago. Having moved on from her LBD days, Misetic now releases two ready-to-wear collections each year, in addition to providing custom designs for the likes of Princess Mary of Denmark and Bridget Regan of the rock band Flogging Molly, and collaborating on a custom gown with pop-art icon Burton Morris. Naturally, Misetic's custom designs don't come cheap: expect to pay anywhere from $300 to thousands for a dress. Pieces from Misetic's off-the-rack collections have fairly average designer price tags. A stop by this showroom and working studio is a must for any style maven.

MAP 4: 809 Ivy St., 412/363-6442, www.dianamisetic.com; by appointment

E.B. PEPPER

This shop is an absolute must for women who consider themselves among the city's most stylish; the lower level at E.B. Pepper consists mainly of career and formal attire, while the top floor is not to be missed for its endlessly chic casual wear. You'll find suiting by the ever popular Milly, casual clothing by Nikka, as well as all the standards in premium denim, such as Citizens of Humanity and Paper Denim & Cloth. The store is perhaps best known, however, for its mascot: Ms. Pepper's pet pug, Chloe, who practically lives at the store.

MAP 4: 5411 Walnut St., 412/683-3815, http://ebpepper.blogspot.com; Mon. 9am-5pm, Tues. and Thurs.-Sat. 9:30am-5:30pm, Wed. 9:30am-8pm, Sun. noon-5pm

HIP'TIQUE

Hip'tique has been one of the Shadyside neighborhood's best kept secrets since its opening in 2005. Co-owned by two best friends, this personality-rich boutique offers clothing, accessories, and decor by youthful and up-and-coming designers such as Tracy Reese, Central Park West, Plenty, Akiko, and others. Full of character, a little bit funky, and with relatively affordable prices, Hip'tique is a perfectly eclectic mix of high-end fashions and laid-back attitudes. Definitely make an appointment for personal styling (i.e., private shopping) if you have the time and need to break out of a fashion rut.

MAP 4: 808 Ivy St., 412/361-5817, www.hiptiquepa.com; Tues.-Sat. 10:30am-6pm, Sun. noon-4pm

MAXALTO

Simply visiting MaxAlto, a super funky and fun little boutique where customers sit on plush velvet couches while deciding what to purchase, is an experience in and of itself. The shop carries lines by Betsey Johnson, Anna Sui, LAMB, Lilith, and others of similar ilk. The decor is unique and spunky: antique hatboxes used as shoe displays, fitting rooms with long velvet curtains. The owner is particularly nice, and wonderful sale items can always be found in the back of the shop.

MAP 4: 5426 Walnut St., 412/683-0508, www.maxaltofashion.com; Mon.-Tues. and Thurs.-Sat. 10am-5pm, Wed. 10am-7pm

MODA

Carrying designer collections and "it" labels from Alexander Wang and Michael Bastian to Joe's Jeans, Woolrich, Theory, and Rogan, Moda is one of the Pittsburgh area's most fashion-forward clothing stores for men, complete with a decent shoe collection and a

Wearing Pittsbugh Pride

While the fashion world at-large may be known as superficial and fickle, Pittsburgh's latest bout of economic growth seems to have instilled a genuine sense of civic pride among the city's twenty- and thirty-something sets. As a result, a surprisingly large number of them have been proclaiming their rekindled Steel City love by launching independent, DIY-style T-shirt companies to much success and fanfare.

The often-ironic Pittsburgh tee has lately become such a local staple that designers now have their own annual T-shirt art show, known as **PGHTEE** (http://pghtee.com). Recent shows have included loads of shirts on display and available for sale, screen printing workshops with area artists, and even craft beer tastings.

To pick up some wearable Pittsburgh pride of your own, start by visiting **Neighbor Teaze** (www.neighborteaze.com) online, where vintage-style shirts touting various Pittsburgh neighborhoods are on offer. **ChampYinz** (www.champyinz.com) is another local favorite, with many of its designs referencing area sports culture.

Other area T-shirt purveyors of note include the decidedly punk-influenced **Commonwealth Press** (1931 East Carson St., 412/431-4207, www.cwpress.org); **Tee Rex Syndicate** and the **Cotton Factory** (5440 Penn Ave., 412/362-0748, www.teerex.com, www.cottonfactory.com), a custom design and novelty screen print shop known for its presence at nearly every arts and crafts event in town; and **Fresh Factory** (www.myfreshfactory.com), a t-shirt company that offers the softest and best fitting tees (along with handmade jewelry and other items) emblazoned with inside-y local jokes.

Those who are already know and love the Burgh will also adore **Clockwise Tees** (400 North Lexington St., 800/260-6022, www.clockwisetees.com), a local screen print shop that makes the branded gear for many local retailers and boutiques; **Believe Merch** (www.believemerch.com), a sports-related t-shirt line that swept the city back in 2007 with its "Believe" tee, when the Steelers got their first new coach in over a decade; and the **Pittsburgh Startup Tshirt Project** (www.pghstartuptshirts.com), a collective from the folks behind Rust Built (www.rustbuilt.org); it's dedicated to promoting and supporting the local entreprenuerial scene by offering tees emblazoned with the logos of new startups in town

T-shirts and other graphic items from all of these efforts are available at independent gift shops and fashion boutiques around the city, and are also stocked at the **Heinz History Center's** gift shop (1212 Smallman St., 412/454-6000, wwww.heinzhistorycenter.org). Many print shops also have open studio hours and tours; check online for hours and availability.

(Contributed by Carrie Ann, a designer and lifestylist based in Pittsburgh and Philadelphia.)

somewhat snooty staff. While the store does carry a small but fantastic selection of suiting, its primary focus is more casual, ready-to-wear merchandise, like designer denim, casual button-downs, graphic tees, and trendy accessories and watches.

MAP 4: 5401 Walnut St., 2nd Fl., 412/681-8640, www.modapittsburgh.com; Mon.-Fri. 11am-7pm, Sat. 10am-6pm, Sun. noon-5pm

PURSUITS

A bit more bohemian and New Age-y than your average women's clothing store in Shadyside, Pursuits is a wonderfully eclectic boutique that carries way too many brands to mention. Don't expect big-name designer gear, but rather relaxed fashions, dresses, and more affordable indie labels. If you're going for a more effortless, bohemian-chic vibe, you'll find everything you need (and then some) at Pursuits, without breaking the bank. Candles and other accessories are also available.

MAP 4: 740 Filbert St., 412/688-8822, www.pursuitspittsburgh.com; Mon.-Sat. 10:30am-5:30pm, Sun. noon-4pm

GIFTS AND SPECIALTY SHOPS

KARDS UNLIMITED

Hardly your average card store, this Shadyside favorite is more of a well-edited novelty shop that also carries an impressive stock of books, comics, graphic novels, posters, candles, T-shirts, wrapping papers, and unusual jewelry items, such as jewel-encrusted cigarette cases and lighters. Anyone looking for witty gifts from Knock Knock, stylish Blue Q products (for home and body), or yummy-smelling Yankee candles would do well to take a look, as Kards Unlimited's selection is the largest in town.

MAP 4: 5522 Walnut St., 412/622-0500, http://kardsunlimited.com; Mon.-Sat. 9:30am-9pm, Sun. noon-5pm

KAWAII GIFTS

Shadyside's fantastic Kawaii Gifts (the store's name is Japanese for "cute") stocks the region's largest (and arguably only) selection of Japanese imports, including collectible vinyl toys, plushies, housewares, stationery, miniatures, and more. Stuffed floor to ceiling with toys and baubles in every color of the rainbow, Kawaii is a must-visit for fans of brands like San-X, Iwako, Momiji, and Ugly Dolls. But despite Kawaii's eye-catching inventory, the store can be easy to miss, as it's tucked away at the bottom of a small staircase off Walnut Street.

MAP 4: 5413-B Walnut St., 412/687-2480, www.shopkawaii.com; Mon.-Sat. 11am-7pm, Sun. 11am-5pm

SCRIBE

Self-described as Pittsburgh's premiere paper boutique, Scribe is the perhaps the city's finest destination for all things communication related. It offers the most distinctive letterpress, stationery, and print design work from the likes of Gilah, Rifle Paper Company, Ink + Wit, Retro 1951, and others. Scribe's calligraphy and gift-wrapping services are extraordinary, and the boutique stocks a lovingly curated collection of journals, notebooks, greeting cards, and fine wrapping papers and ribbons. Unlike similar neighborhood stationery shops, Scribe's customer service is welcoming and unpretentious. Appointments are preferred for custom orders.

MAP 4: 731 1/2 Filbert St., 412/682-1644, www.scribepgh.com; Tues. noon-6pm, Wed. 11am-7pm, Thurs.-Sat. 11am-6pm, Sun. 11am-3pm

TOADFLAX

This gorgeous floral shop and gift boutique offers a true feast for the senses, thanks in large part to the bouquets of the fine freshly cut flowers—displayed in large modern vases—dotting the otherwise minimalist decor. Whether you're selecting a single lily or rose stem, or asking the shop to arrange a bouquet for that special someone, Toadflax does an exquisite job. Arrangements come complete with unobtrusive greens, premium paper, and satin ribbon. The shop also stocks gift items at all price points, including fine candies and chocolates, richly scented premium soy-based candles, coffee-table books, skin and body-care products, crystal goods, and modern ceramic and blown-glass vases.

MAP 4: 500 Walnut St., 412/621-2500, www.toadflax.com; Mon.-Fri. 10am-5:30pm, Sat. 10am-5pm

HEALTH AND BEAUTY

DEAN OF SHADYSIDE

With a location in the Hillman Cancer Center (5115 Centre Ave., 412/647-2811) in addition to its large Shadyside salon, it's no wonder Dean of Shadyside is such a well-loved Pittsburgh salon. Though not generally thought of as one of the trendier salons in town, Dean of Shadyside was nevertheless one of first in the area to offer Great Lengths hair extensions. Today, Dean's is the only area salon specializing in hair for cancer patients, including extensions and thickening treatments; wig specialists are also on staff. All hair loss services are provided in a suite apart from the main salon for maximum privacy. Manis, pedis, waxing, and all other traditional salon services are available.

MAP 4: 5404 Centre Ave., 412/621-7900, www.deanofshadyside.com; Mon. noon-8pm, Tues. 9am-6pm, Wed.-Thurs. 10am-8pm, Fri. 9am-5pm, Sat. 8am-4pm; haircuts $25-75

HOME DECOR AND FURNISHINGS

WEISS HOUSE

Carrying high-end furniture lines like B&B Italia, Cassini, and Ligne Roset, Weiss House employs a highly educated crew of interior designers who specialize in custom work, contemporary kitchen design, and residential renovations. The store has a large selection of carpeting, as well as exotic wood flooring materials. Recently added items include Asian antiques—all of them hand-selected and one of a kind. Weiss House also has home decor items and gifts, such as coffee-table books and candles. And don't sweat it if you're not a design expert—the staff is super friendly and laid-back, and they even have complimentary candy bars for guests (just don't touch anything while you're eating them).

MAP 4: 324 S. Highland Ave., 412/441-8888, www.weisshouse.com; Mon.-Fri. 10am-6pm, Sat. 10am-5pm

KIDS' STORES

THE PICKET FENCE

Budding fashionistas will be right at home in this charming Shadyside children's boutique. The Picket Fence carries lines like Room Seven and Appaman in addition to clothing for both new moms and babies, specialty toys, household decor, candles, and gifts. Fashion-forward moms flock to the store often to get their hands on up-and-coming labels that aren't readily available in other area shops, or even online.

MAP 4: 5425 Walnut St., 412/246-0350, www.picketfenceshadyside.com; Mon.-Tues. 10am-5pm, Wed.-Sat. 10am-6pm, Sun. 11am-4pm

PITTSBURGH TOY LENDING LIBRARY

As the name implies, the Pittsburgh Toy Lending Library isn't a standard retail outlet, but rather a volunteer-run cooperative based in Shadyside. And although the library does feature an indoor play space for kids aged six and under, the real jewel is the truly rich collection of more than 300 children's toys that can be temporarily rented and brought home, just like a library book. You do have to be a member to rent toys, but anyone can sign up for a membership. Check the website for an application, or fill one out at the library. First visits to the library are free; after that, membership levels range $30-250 per year. Parents willing to volunteer receive the lowest rates. The kids' play space is open to both members and nonmembers for private party rentals.

MAP 4: 5401 Centre Ave., 412/682-4430, www.pghtoys.org; Mon., Wed., and Sat. 9:30am-1pm, Tues. and Thurs. 9:30am-5:30pm, Fri. 9:30am-2:30pm

S.W. RANDALL TOYS & GIFTS

With the ambience of an old-fashioned toy store and a huge collection of dolls, unique toys, and gifts that you simply won't find at a department or discount store, S.W. Randall has been one of Shadyside's most treasured gems for years. Just off of Walnut Street, this truly magical shop is a rare treat for children and grown-ups alike. Staffers are wonderfully talented at recommending uncommon, age-appropriate gifts, and can place special orders for most items, including collectible dolls. Fans of Yo-Yos will be delighted to learn new skills and tricks at the shop's Sunday Yo-Yo club,

Squirrel Hill and Point Breeze

Map 5

ARTS AND CRAFTS

KNIT ONE

Simply put, Knit One is every knitter's paradise. A large and well-lit store decorated with woven area rugs, Knit One also offers the largest amount and widest variety of both yarns and knitting classes in the city. Classes run the gamut from the relatively simplistic (Introduction to Lace Knitting) to the advanced (Modular Knitting; Intarsia Method). Even the inventory itself is artistic, displayed as it is in modular shelving that is cleverly attached to the shop's walls. Knit One's owner offers private lessons to help even the most impatient and distracted of aspiring crafters complete their own yarn-spun creations.

MAP 5: 2721 Murray Ave., 412/421-6666, www.knitone.biz; Mon. noon-5pm, Tues. and Thurs. 10am-8pm, Wed., Fri., and Sat. 10am-5pm, Sun. noon-4pm

BOOKS AND MUSIC

JERRY'S RECORDS

Vinyl enthusiasts have been known to travel from as far away as Japan to dig through the crates holding more than one million records at this Squirrel Hill institution, named by no less an authority than *Rolling Stone* magazine as one of the best record shops in the country. The size of the selection simply boggles the mind; there seem to be sections devoted to just about every genre of music on earth, including some you probably never knew existed. Turntables and accessories are also sold, and prices on all but the rarest of finds are surprisingly affordable. Jerry's son operates a mini-shop inside the store known as **Whistlin' Willie's 78s** (412/478-4023, www.whistlinwillies.com); it's an exclusive purveyor of reasonably priced 78 rpm records.

MAP 5: 2136 Murray Ave., 412/421-4533, www.jerrysrecords.com; Mon.-Sat. 10am-6pm, Sun. noon-5pm

CLOTHING AND ACCESSORIES

CHARLES SPIEGEL FOR MEN/THE GARAGE

Certainly one of the best spots in Pittsburgh for unique and high-quality designer clothing, this location is technically two stores in one. Charles Spiegel for Men claims a wide swath of the space, and on these racks you'll find a great mix of suiting, including pieces by Eton of Sweden, Etro, and Coppley Custom Clothing. The Garage offers much more casual and trendy gear, perfect whether you're at the club or a local café. And aside from the atmosphere being especially warm and friendly, it's also the best place in town to take your boyfriend if he needs to kick it up a notch in the style department.

MAP 5: 5841 Forbes Ave., 412/421-9311, www.charlesspiegel.com; Mon., Wed., Fri., and Sat. 10am-6pm, Tues. and Thurs. 10am-9pm, Sun. noon-5pm

SHOES

LITTLE'S SHOES

While Pittsburgh today has more to offer the modern, stylish man than ever before, there was a time when Little's was one of the city's only independently owned shops offering a large collection of well-chosen, casual men's shoes. The shop is quite large and seemingly always overstaffed, and on the many racks and shelves you'll find everything from sneakers to formal styles. Brands include reliable, standard fare like Kenneth Cole, Clarks, Birkenstock, Diesel, Cole Haan, Puma, and Steve Madden. In the women's section, which is significantly larger than the men's section and offers much trendier choices, you'll also find handbags and accessories. Try to avoid showing up on busy Saturdays.

MAP 5: 5850 Forbes Ave., 412/521-3848 or 800/646-7463, www.littlesshoes.com; Mon.-Sat. 9:30am-9pm, Sun. noon-5pm

SKATEBOARDING AND BICYCLE SHOPS

BIKETEK

In the heart of Squirrel Hill and just steps from **Pro Bikes** (5876 Forbes Ave., 412/586-5497, www.probikesllc.com), another bike shop of very similar ilk, Biketek is perhaps the city's most mainstream and suburban-esque cycling shop. With a vibe and an interior design not unlike that of an REI store, Biketek offers a very wide range of very expensive rides, along with a professionally trained staff to sell them to you. Bike repair and bike-fitting services are also available, along with cycling apparel and accessories.

MAP 5: 5842 Forbes Ave., 412/521-6448, www.biketek.com; Mon.-Thurs. 11am-8pm, Fri.-Sat. 11am-5pm, Sun. noon-4pm

FREE RIDE

Staffed by the sort of cycling enthusiasts you'd expect to find leading a Critical Mass rally, Free Ride is a recycle-a-bike shop where old and discarded rides are given a new lease on life. The program works like this: Bikes are donated to Free Ride in a generally sorry state of disrepair. Volunteers spend hours in the shop bringing the bikes up to code. The resulting mountain bikes, road bikes, and BMX bikes are then sold at affordable rates.

The deal is even better if you already own a beat-up ride: The mechanics at Free Ride will help out with repairs at no charge, and will even educate riders about bike maintenance along the way. But here's the rub: Anyone who receives free assistance is asked to give back by volunteering a bit of his or her time at the shop. Marxism on two wheels and a saddle seat, you might say.

MAP 5: 214 N. Lexington St., inside Construction Junction, 412/254-3774; www.freeridepgh.org; shop Sat. 1pm-5pm, check website or call ahead for volunteer and drop-in class hours

VINTAGE AND ANTIQUES

AMBIANCE BOUTIQUE

Subsidiaries of Bethlehem Haven, a nonprofit organization established to provide assistance to homeless women in the Pittsburgh area, both of the city's Ambiance Boutiques are lovely little thrift shops stocked full of both new and consigned designer labels, accessories, and home furnishings. It's not uncommon to come across pieces by Thakoon, Theory, Zac Posen, Jean Paul Gaultier, and similar designers for a fraction of their retail prices. Conveniently located in Squirrel Hill and Oakmont (Allegheny River Blvd., 412/828-1946), the shops even carry formal evening wear and usually a large collection of shoes, all at very reasonable prices. Ambience also opens its space for private after-hours shopping parties (perfect for birthday girls of all ages) and has recently started listing its most desirable items for sale online.

MAP 5: 1722 Murray Ave., 412/421-2100, www.ambianceboutique.org; Mon., Wed., and Fri.-Sat. 11am-6pm, Tues. and Thurs. 11am-8pm, Sun. noon-5pm

CONSTRUCTION JUNCTION

Though not technically a vintage or antiques shop per se, Construction Junction is actually Pittsburgh's used building-materials supply warehouse, and an excellent place to find anything and everything for that home-improvement project you're working on—everything, that is, from decorative doors and windows to old toilets, filing cabinets, and plywood. And because the shop was started with the intention of keeping construction supplies out of landfills, everything is available for literally a fraction of the price you'd pay at a big-box building supply store. Perhaps not surprisingly, Construction Junction is a favorite among Pittsburgh's DIY community.

MAP 5: 214 N. Lexington St., 412/243-5025, www.constructionjunction.org; Mon.-Fri. 9am-6pm, Sat. 9am-5pm, Sun. 10am-5pm

DESIGNER DAYS BOUTIQUE

An upscale consignment shop where only the most exclusive designer labels (Prada, Gucci, Chanel) are sold at often shockingly low prices, Designer Days is operated by the National Council of Jewish Women, which works to improve the lives of women and children in the Pittsburgh area. Everything from casual and career clothing to eveningwear is carried, as well as designer accessories, handbags, and women's shoes. Private shopping parties for your club or organization can also be hosted here; visit the shop's website for details. Consignment sales are accepted Tuesday through Friday 11am-4pm, although advance appointments are required.

MAP 5: 5873 Forbes Ave., 412/441-0330, www.designerdaysboutique.com; Mon., Wed., and Fri.-Sat. 10am-6pm, Tues. and Thurs. 10am-8pm, Sun. noon-4pm.

Bloomfield and Lawrenceville

Map 6

ARTS AND CRAFTS

GALLERY ON 43RD STREET

Lifelong weaver Mary Coleman's shop is just off of the hustle and bustle of Lawrenceville's Butler Street. It features one-of-a-kind arts and crafts from throughout Western Pennsylvania. Coleman's impressive rugs, runners, and placemats can be seen throughout the gallery shop, and while you won't find the latest cutting-edge or controversial exhibit, you can always expect to find beautifully crafted and tasteful work in more traditional mediums, such as ceramics, pottery, and porcelain. In other words, Gallery on 43rd Street is the perfect place to find a gift for the parents or a lovely tea kettle and mug for Grandma.

MAP 6: 187 43rd St., 412/683-6488, www.galleryon43rdstreet.com; Tues.-Sat. 11am-6pm

BOOKS AND MUSIC

THE BIG IDEA INFOSHOP

A volunteer-run bookshop specializing in leftist politics, queer issues, and other radical and alternative cultures, the Big Idea originally existed only as a small corner of a small room in the original Mr. Roboto Project in Wilkinsburg. Along with the standard collection of neo-anarchist lit, the shop also stocks a good selection of zines and other independent publications. Volunteers are always needed, and the store hosts numerous discussion groups. A small café sells coffee, tea, and vegan snacks.

MAP 6: 4812 Liberty Ave., 412/687-4323, www.thebigideapgh.org; Wed.-Fri. 11am-9pm, Sat.-Sun. 11am-7pm

COPACETIC COMICS

Much more than just a run-of-the-mill comic book shop, Copacetic is also home to one of the city's better collections of independent and self-published comics, books, and zines. It also stocks a huge library of classic lit (everything from Homer to Whitman), classic and obscure DVDs, and jazz and indie CDs. Regardless of its eclectic and well-edited inventory, though, the truth is that many of Copacetic's best customers stop by just for a chance to shoot the bull with owner Bill Boichel—a veritable encyclopedia of American pop culture and perhaps Pittsburgh's chattiest boutique owner. Copacetic is in a Polish Hill building that also houses **Mind Cure Records** (412/621-1715, www.mindcurerecords.com), an indie shop specializing in vinyl, and **Lili Coffee Shop** (412/682-3600), a friendly neighborhood joint with great treats.

MAP 6: 3138 Dobson St., 3rd Fl., 412/251-5451, www.copaceticcomics.com; Tues.-Thurs. 11am-5pm, Fri.-Sat. 11am-7pm, Sun. noon-4pm

EAST END BOOK EXCHANGE

Not unlike Downtown's Boutique 208, the East End Book Exchange started out as a pop-up shop. It's since grown into a fully respectable general interest store on Bloomfield's main drag, where it sells a great selection of mostly used titles—everything from fiction and history to travel and cooking—with some rare volumes thrown in for good measure. A small section features work by local authors and poets. Vintage armchairs are scattered throughout the store, and local visual artists often display their work on the shop's walls. The EEBX buys books, but don't expect to unload your old romance novels; the shop is clearly curated by someone who knows their stuff.

MAP 6: 4754 Liberty Ave., 412/224-2847, www.eastendbookexchange.com; Tues.-Sat. 11am-7pm, Sun. 10am-4pm

MIND CURE RECORDS

Owned and operated by a one-time employee of the legendary Jim's Records (now Sound Cat Records), Mind Cure is an all-vinyl record shop specializing in punk rock and its many brethren: metal, indie-rock, post-punk, and much more. Of course, you're just as likely to find obscure jazz and blues records, and there's always something unusual in the bargain bins. Mind Cure even releases its own records by local acts, and often re-releases old Pittsburgh punk classics on vinyl. Located in the same Polish Hill building are **Copacetic Comics** (412/251-5451, www.copaceticcomics.com) and **Lili Coffee Shop** (412/682-3600).

MAP 6: 3138 Dobson St., 412/621-1715, www.mindcurerecords.com; Mon.-Sat. noon-8pm, Sun. noon-5pm

THE MUSE STAND BOOKSTORE & MORE

In the heart of the Bloomfield business district, the Muse Stand is a small and fairly sparse bookshop offering an even mixture of new and used books, new magazines, and bookstore-style gifts and accessories. While the nearby East End Book Exchange is the spot to hit if you're looking for something esoteric or intellectual, the Muse Stand is a better choice for your more mainstream fare and for bestselling titles of the Stephen King and Harry Potter variety.

MAP 6: 4524 Liberty Ave., 412/904-4004, www.themusestand.com; Tues.-Sat. 10am-6pm, Sun. 10am-3pm

RATHER RIPPED RECORDS

Although it first opened its doors more than 40 years ago in Berkeley, California, the decidedly quirky and vinyl-friendly Rather Ripped now calls the Lawrenceville neighborhood home. And as is seemingly the case with every great record store, the very generalist inventory seems to change with the wind: Everything from folk, jazz, and blues to post-punk, world music, and comedy records can be spotted during an average digging session. Rather Ripped also stocks a good bit of music and movie memorabilia, including T-shirts, and there's always a good selection of one-dollar vinyl and two-dollar CDs.

MAP 6: 4314 Butler St., 412/253-3445, www.ratherripped.com; Thurs.-Sat. and Mon. 11am-7pm, Sun. 11am-5pm

720 RECORDS

Previously based in East Liberty, the new 720 Records shop in Lawrenceville offers a stunning selection of vinyl records, cassettes, and CDs ranging from soul and jazz to funk and old-school hip-hop. It's also home to a coffee shop that sells sandwiches and light bites, and a modest but well-curated selection of urban wear. Historically speaking, 720 Records has been Pittsburgh's go-to shop for crate diggers and professional DJs, which means you're not likely to find a better selection of battle records, rare groove albums, or house breaks on vinyl anywhere else in the city.

MAP 6: 4405 Butler St., 412/904-4592, www.720records.com; Tues.-Sat. noon-7pm, Sun. noon-5pm

SOUND CAT RECORDS

This long-running Pittsburgh institution, originally known as Jim's Records, and then Paul's CDs, gained not only a new name but also a new owner when it became Sound Cat Records in mid-2012. Now operated by longtime Paul's CDs employee (and local indie-rock hero) Karl Hendricks, Sound Cat is essentially the same store it always was, and that's a very good thing. Something of a local headquarters for aficionados of eclectic sounds, Sound Cat's Bloomfield location is a tiny little box of a store, and yet its supremely well-edited collection is consistently top-notch. You'll find the best of the best in terms of traditional blues and jazz, world music, hip-hop, and indie-rock. DVDs and a small magazine section are also popular, as is the used CD bin in the front of the store. The aloof staffers are nevertheless exceedingly knowledgeable and can special-order just about anything.

MAP 6: 4526 Liberty Ave., 412/621-3256, www.soundcatrecords.com; Mon.-Thurs. 11am-7pm, Fri. 11am-8pm, Sat. 10am-7pm, Sun. noon-5pm

UNIFAUN RECORDS

Yet another recent entry into the retro retail explosion in Pittsburgh, Unifaun is a mostly vinyl shop specializing in the sort of inventory that drives record store geeks out of their basements: psych, soul, prog-rock, classic Americana, and old-school jazz, for starters. Unifaun also offers a modest selection of used CDs and has plans to start selling new vinyl in the near future. Even if you're not planning on buying, this tiny store is still worth a look, if only to check out the impressive collection of 1960s and '70s promo music posters on display.

MAP 6: 5417 Butler St., 412/781-2027; Wed.-Sat. noon-7pm, Sun. noon-5pm

CLOTHING AND ACCESSORIES

★ MID-ATLANTIC MERCANTILE

This shop stocks sustainable and ethically created styles for both men and women and is hands-down the best source for raw Japanese denim in Pittsburgh. All the labels carried—Rogue Territory, Tellason, and Naked & Famous, to name just a few—are manufactured in small batches with the utmost attention paid to durability and detail. Owner Emily Slagel is nearly always on-site to offer a wealth of information about the shop's goods, and the spacious and naturally lit fitting rooms ensure you won't wind up with buyer's remorse. If you have a chance to visit one of Lawrenceville's "Shop Late Nights"—the second Thursday of each month—you'll find free snacks, drinks, discounts, and other goodies.

MAP 6: 4415 Butler St., 412/904-4530, www.midatlanticmercantile.com; Tues.-Sat. 11am-7pm, Sun. noon-4pm

SOMETHING BORROWED

Something Borrowed is a godsend for the cash-strapped bride-to-be or homecoming queen; this boutique provides a carefully curated selection of fine gowns and other couture wear available for both rental and purchase. The shop is minimal and the service excellent. Something Borrowed is also great for visitors coming into town for a special event, say, who don't want to fuss with packing and formal wear. Coordinated accessories and jewelry are also available, and dress reservations can be made in advance by phone or on the boutique's website.

MAP 6: 4707 Liberty Ave., 412/682-1083, www.somethingborrowedboutique.net; Tues.-Wed. and Fri. 11am-5pm, Thurs. 3pm-8pm, Sat. 11am-3pm

GIFTS AND SPECIALTY SHOPS

DIVERTIDO

Those looking for fresh and inspired gift ideas would do well to stop by Lawrenceville's Divertido. This hip little shop offers a selection of handmade totes and purses, beautiful silk scarves, affordable jewelry, fun greeting cards, retro-style dinnerware and home decor, and lots of nontraditional gifts for babies and kids (including casual garb, unusual toys, and some really cool children's books). Helpful but not overly pushy staffers make selecting gifts for even your pickiest friends and loved ones a breeze, but consider yourself warned: All but the most disciplined of shoppers will likely leave with more than a few gifts for themselves, too.

MAP 6: 3609 Butler St., 412/687-3701, www.divertidoshop.com; Mon.-Wed. and Fri.-Sat. 11am-6pm, Thurs. 11am-8pm

HOUSE OF THE DEAD

Where on earth but Pittsburgh—the longtime home of George Romero and Tom Savini, and the filming location of 1968's *Night of the Living Dead* and its sequel, *Dawn of the Dead*—could a boutique devoted entirely to zombies possibly exist? At HOTD, you'll find oddball apparel, DVDs, tons of zombie movie memorabilia and collectible items, books, artwork, comics, games, jewelry, and who knows what else? HOTD also organizes zombie-related events around town and is even affiliated with Pittsburgh Adrenaline's **House of the Zed** (www.pittsburghadrenaline.com, 412/667-8362), a real-life military-style adventure experience in which a team of participants attempts to defend a real house against "zombies."

MAP 6: 4110 Butler St., 412/687-0510, www.houseofthedeadpgh.com; Tues.-Sat. 11am-7pm, Sun. 11am-5pm

★ WILDCARD

Described by one Yelp.com reviewer as "one of the coolest shops selling handmade goods I've ever been to," this Lawrenceville darling easily lives up to its online reputation. With the store's eye-popping colors and impressive inventory, which includes greeting cards, stationery, wallets, jewelry, T-shirts, and tons more (much of it made by Pittsburgh crafters), Wildcard is part gift shop and part art gallery, all wrapped up in one handsomely designed little package. In addition to showcasing new exhibits from local artists and crafters each month, Wildcard is also home to the Pittsburgh Craft Collective, which boasts an array of arts-and-crafts classes on everything from yarn spinning to polymer clay jewelry making. The store also hosts craft nights and other unusual DIY-themed events for area creatives.

MAP 6: 4029 Butler St., 412/224-2651, www.wildcardpgh.com; Mon.-Wed. and Fri.-Sat. 11am-7pm, Thurs. 11am-8pm, Sun. 11am-5pm

HEALTH AND BEAUTY

★ BLOOM ORGANIC SKINCARE PARLOR

Erinn Thompson's serene skin-care studio has quickly built a fiercely loyal customer base, and for good reason: Aside from being an expert esthetician and arguably the best waxer in town, Thompson only uses all-natural, organically sourced products in a gorgeous Victorian parlor. What's more, she consistently protects her customers' privacy and peace of mind—you won't bump into your neighbor in the waiting room—and all treatments are custom-ized. Bloom also offers a complete menu of waxing and tinting services in addition to high-quality eyelash extensions, and men will especially enjoy Thompson's facials and back treatments.

MAP 6: 5220 Butler St., 412/849-1891; www.bloomskincare.net; by appointment only; basic services $50-150

PAGEBOY SALON & BOUTIQUE

More of an all-around style headquarters than simply a salon and boutique, Pageboy exudes an aesthetic that celebrates individuality, resourcefulness, and beauty. Indeed, the collective Pageboy experience includes a full-service salon, personal styling and shopping, midcentury modern furnishings, and both men's and women's apparel and accessories from a range of local and national indie designers. With its exposed brick and duct work and its crafty displays, this Lawrenceville gem is truly a one-stop shop for both your personal and lifestyle needs.

MAP 6: 3613 Butler St., 412/224-2294, www.pageboypgh.com; Sun. 10am-5pm, Mon. 11am-6pm, Wed.-Fri. 11am-8pm, Sat. 10am-6pm; basic services $25-150

HOME DECOR AND FURNISHINGS

ASIAN INFLUENCES

Each and every item in this Butler Street homage to the Far East has been personally selected by shop owner and interior designer Susan Fischer. Many of her antique and one-of-a-kind pieces were acquired during years of shopping and auction-going, both in the United States and abroad. This is an ideal boutique to visit, then, if you're looking for something a bit exotic with which to beautify your home or office. Unique lamps and lighting fixtures are sold at Asian Influences, which is also something of a paradise for those who love containers like baskets, boxes, and tins.

MAP 6: 3513 Butler St., 412/621-3530, www.asianinfluences.com; Wed.-Sat. 11am-6pm

★ URBAN COTTAGE

Although its inventory is somewhat similar to that of Lawrenceville's Wildcard, Urban Cottage sets itself apart from most other home decor and gift shops with its significantly more polished and professional approach; think rustic-modern meets midcentury kitsch. Or imagine the accessories floor at your local Anthropologie, for instance, and then throw in a bit more eclectic charm and personality—that's Urban Cottage. Along with its amazing selection of unique wares for the home, other unusual odds and ends can be spotted, including jewelry and even vintage finds. If you've just moved to town, this is the perfect place to pick up an affordable stash of decorative baskets, crates, and boxes for keeping your new digs organized. The shop itself is cute as can be, and the owner is often on hand to answer questions and share decorating ideas.

MAP 6: 4602 Penn Ave., 412/683-1950, www.urbancottagedecor.com; Tues.-Fri. 11am-6:30pm, Sat. 11am-4pm

KIDS' STORES

YOBRO

Self-described as a company offering "apparel for little dudes," Yobro is one of the city's kiddie-fashion newcomers; it has also single-handedly filled a long neglected gap in the boys' fashion scene. Yobro's line of tees, hoodies, thermals, and other boy basics are stylish, super soft, and durable, and their namesake logo gear is beyond cute. Most of Yobro's T-shirts, in fact, are so well-designed that dads would probably wear them too, if they came in large enough sizes. And even better, the brand operates with the secondary mission of bringing attention to children's charity organizations, donating 10 percent of its sales to different charitable efforts. Hours change seasonally; visit the website for up-to-date details.

MAP 6: 3818 Butler St., 412/407-7689, www.yobroapparel.com; daily 11am-5pm

SHOES

BEST-MADE SHOES

Aside from brands like Dansko and Alegria, you won't find the most fashion-forward shoes at Bloomfield's Best-Made. You will find the city's best selection of comfort footwear, custom shoes, and orthotics, all being sold by board-certified pedorthists and master shoemakers. If you have any foot, leg, or back pain, and have trouble finding shoes that fit properly, rest assured that a trip to Best-Made will have you feeling a heck of a lot better in very little time. In addition to offering custom shoes and custom molded orthotic inserts, the family-owned Best-Made also provides the largest selection of Birkenstock shoes and orthotics in the area, stocks extra large and wide width sizes, and accepts Medicare and most major insurance plans for diabetic and other medically necessary footwear. And if you're having trouble

clockwise from top left: walkway to Eastside; Highway Robbery; Time Bomb

getting around, they even make house calls for consultations and fittings.

MAP 6: 5143 Liberty Ave., 412/621-9363, www.bestmadeshoes.com; Tues.-Sat. 10am-4pm

PAVEMENT

It was a desperately needed and instantly adored addition to the city's shoe scene when it opened back in 2006, and even today Pavement boasts a carefully and creatively curated assortment of designer shoes, as well as a complementary selection of clothing and hand-made accessories, jewelry, and gifts from designers and labels such as Ella Moss, Free People, Irregular Choice, Prairie Underground, and Alternative Apparel. Thanks to its urban rustic-chic vibe (think gallery-white walls and track lighting juxtaposed against antler sculptures and vintage decor), you'll never want to leave. Perhaps not surprisingly, the owners and staff are exceedingly knowledgeable and stylish, and as an added bonus, Pavement only stocks merchandise from eco-conscious vendors. Originally a Butler Street retail pioneer, Pavement has since grown into a full-fledged Lawrenceville classic.

MAP 6: 3629 Butler St., 412/621-6400, www.pavementpittsburgh.com; Mon.-Wed. and Fri.-Sat. 11am-6pm, Thurs. 11am-7pm, Sun. 11am-3pm

SHOPPING DISTRICTS AND CENTERS

16:62 DESIGN ZONE

Officially starting in Pittsburgh's Strip District before reaching the Lawrenceville neighborhood, the 16:62 Design Zone is essentially Pittsburgh's arts, crafts, and interior design district. As such, it's overflowing with galleries, boutiques, and open studios. And as Lawrenceville has found itself home to some of the best independently owned and operated shops in the city (Wildcard, Pavement, Pageboy, Bloom Organic Skincare, and Who New? all come to mind), shopping in the 16:62 Design Zone has become a great way to support local artists. Numerous events are organized throughout the year, including the annual **Joy of Cookies Cookie Tour** (www.lvpgh.com/cookietour) and the hugely popular **Art All Night** party (www.artallnight.com), where guests enjoy a full 24 hours of art and music. Most area studios offer open houses, and tours are held throughout the year. Exhibit openings are generally timed with first Friday gallery crawls, during which local galleries and shops stay open late and offer complimentary snacks and drinks along with a bevy of special events and programming. For more information about the area, visit www.lvpgh.com.

MAP 6: Btwn. Penn Ave. and Butler St. from 16th to 62nd Sts., www.1662designzone.com

VINTAGE AND ANTIQUES

WHO NEW?

Easily the best place in Pittsburgh at which to track down mid-century decor, Who New? is owned and operated by two men who might best be described as 20th-century design encyclopedias. The shop carries a wide-ranging selection of retro home furnishings, the vast majority from the 1950s through the '70s, including an incredible selection of vintage barware and kitchen items. The owners are more than willing to bargain, and if you're looking for something specific they don't have, they'll even help you hunt it down. Danish modern fans will not be able to leave without a new furniture purchase or two. A few new novelties (baby onesies, greeting cards, and toys) are also available.

MAP 6: 5156 Butler St., 412/781-0588; Wed.-Sat. noon-6pm, also by appointment

East Liberty and Garfield Map 6

CLOTHING AND ACCESSORIES

★ TIME BOMB

Time Bomb is Pittsburgh's premier destination for cutting-edge urban fashion. The store's continued success is owed largely to boisterous owner Brian Brick's presence and uncanny ability to stock the newest designers and lines before they achieve mainstream success. Time Bomb is a local hub for mixtapes and is the exclusive Pittsburgh distributer of lines like Evisu and Crooks & Castles. It's known for hosting an impressive array of hip-hop artists, deejays, and other trendsetters of the urban culture scene. And don't be offended if Brick tells you to "get your life right"—it's become something of his signature phrase and Time Bomb's unofficial store motto.

MAP 6: 200 S. Highland Ave., 412/661-2233, www.timebombshop.com; Mon.-Sat. noon-8pm

HEALTH AND BEAUTY

★ DYE BY DAQUILA

Daquila's precision cut and expert hair coloring services are among the best you'll find in Pittsburgh, especially if you're looking for a modern, fashion-forward, or avant-garde style. Staffers at this effortlessly hip yet personable salon are all Parisian trained, and it shows, especially with their Ballyage and corrective coloring technique. Daquila offers a wide variety of cut, color, highlight, treatment, and styling options to suit almost every need or occasion. And the salon is also popular with the gents, due to its complimentary bang and nape touch-ups (for existing customers), not to mention its reasonable rates—men's cuts start at just $25. As customers frequently complained of parking issues at the salon's previous Penn Circle South location, Daquila recently moved to a more intimate setting in Pittsburgh's Morningside neighborhood. Check online for current discounts; promotional savings of 15 to 25 percent for students and new customers are often available.

MAP 6: 1710 Jancey St., 412/361-0900, www.daquilahair.com; Tues. 10am-8pm, Wed. 10am-7pm, Thurs. noon-8pm, Fri.-Sat. 10am-4pm; basic women's services $25-180, basic men's services $10-50.

MCN SALON

Since relocating to East Liberty's increasingly fashionable Eastside retail development (www.shopeastside.net), MCN Salon has improved considerably on its classic urban-chic vibe—think rich, cherry-wood floors, fresh flowers, and a killer view. Specializing in color but also offering haircuts, textures, waxing, manicures, pedicures, and more, MCN consistently gets rave reviews from loyal customers. And definitely don't forget to say hello to Josie, the owner's English bulldog and the unofficial salon mascot.

MAP 6: 5932 Penn Circle S., 412/441-5151, www.mcnsalon.com; Tues.-Wed. 9am-8pm, Thurs. 10am-8pm, Fri. 9am-6pm, Sat. 8am-5pm

HOME DECOR AND FURNISHINGS

THE SHOP IN EAST LIBERTY

For those who appreciate a healthy dose of high style in their home furnishings but still want to support local craftspeople, the Shop in East Liberty couldn't be a better compromise. You'll find a wide-ranging collection of relatively affordable handcrafted jewelry, design-friendly home goods, and very reasonably priced paintings and prints. Check the "New Arrivals" section of the website if you're looking for something particularly unusual. Speaking of which, the kitchen and tabletop accessories sold are some of the most distinctive I've seen anywhere.

MAP 6: 214 N. Highland Ave., 412/450-0258, www.theshopinel.com; Tues.-Thurs. 11am-6pm, Fri.-Sat. 11am-7pm

PET SUPPLIES AND GROOMING

THE DOG STOP

Offering a wonderful service for busy dog owners who don't like the idea of leaving their pets at home alone, the Dog Stop takes pains to make sure your favorite hound stays happy, healthy, and socialized—with people as well as other dogs—throughout the day. The Dog Stop also offers full-service boarding 365 days a year. And along with the on-site Doggie Retail Store, there are separate play spaces for dogs of all sizes, and even a "lounge" for low-energy pups. A second location in the South Hills (2858 Banksville Rd.,

412/364-7867) features 10,000 square feet of climate-controlled play space, and a third Dog Stop was scheduled to open in the Strip District in late 2013. Boarding is $28-34 per night; day care is $24 per full day for the first dog, $15 for each additional dog; grooming costs $28-55; and self-wash service is $10 for dogs under 25 pounds, $15 dogs 25 pounds and up. Discount packages are available for all services.

MAP 6: 1140 Washington Blvd., 412/361-0911, www.thedogstop.net; day care Mon.-Fri. 6:30am-7pm, Sat.-Sun. 10am-4pm; boarding daily 24 hours

GOLDEN BONE PET RESORT

Just a stone's throw from the East End neighborhoods of Shadyside and East Liberty, Golden Bone Pet Resort seems to be the favored kennel among discerning dog owners in the city. Decent kennels are never cheap, of course, but Golden Bone offers an exceptional value, and it also does double duty as a grooming spot—you'll find bathing and other grooming rates at much better prices than at retail chains and other grooming businesses throughout the city. But assuming you're leaving Spot for an overnight stay, you'll be pleased to learn of the in-house amenities, which include air conditioning, in-floor heat, two large outdoor exercise areas with a wading pool, and around-the-clock care and security. Nervous pet owners interested in touring the facilities may do so Monday-Saturday 1pm-3pm, and will be pleased to know that live streaming video is available for many services. Golden Bone owners Marci and David Anderson live right across the street and have spent over two decades in the business while also rescuing greyhounds. Boarding rates per day are $16 for cats, $28-38 for dogs; grooming costs $35-45 cats, $22-70 dogs.

MAP 6: 6890 5th Ave., 412/661-7001, www.goldenbonepetresort.com; Mon.-Fri. 7am-7pm, Sat. 9am-5pm, Sun. 2pm-4pm

SHOPPING DISTRICTS AND CENTERS

BAKERY SQUARE

Located on a stretch of Penn Avenue in East Liberty that was once home to a bustling Nabisco plant, Bakery Square is a self-described "lifestyle center" and certainly Pittsburgh's new "it" place to work, shop, dine, and play. The $130 million facility is home to a huge LA Fitness facility, as well as retail shops like Anthropologie, Coffee Tree Roasters, and Free People. Even Google's recently relocated Pittsburgh offices are here, as are other tech-related efforts from the University of Pittsburgh and others. Budding makers can find inspiration and assistance at TechShop, a popular community workshop space and prototyping studio. And while the new center's architecture certainly could have been a bit more inspired, it is nevertheless one of a growing number of LEED-certified green

Make It Yourself

You don't have to be a life-long resident to realize that Pittsburgh is still very much a town of makers, regardless of the thousands of industry and manufacturing jobs that left the city in previous decades. The "can-do" spirit is still very much evident in Pittsburgh, from its vibrant arts and crafts community to its more entrepreneurial manufacturers and IT start-ups and, of course, in all the businesses that cater to the region's creative and hardworking ways.

Perhaps not surprisingly then, a number of makers labs—and even a rapid prototyping studio—have popped up in town to provide even more resources to crafty local citizens. Pittsburgh's maker community has since grown so robust that the city now even hosts its own annual **Maker Faire** (www.pghmakerfaire.com).

Garfield's Penn Avenue Arts Corridor is home to **Assemble** (5125 Penn Ave., Garfield, Tues.-Fri. 4pm-7pm, Sat. noon-4pm, www.assemblepgh.org), a nonprofit space that brings together makers of all ages and backgrounds. Assemble offers workshops, talks, gallery shows, and learning parties focused on teaching "STEAM" subjects (science, technology, engineering, art, and math).

Hack Pittsburgh (1936 5th Ave., www.hackpittsburgh.org) is a members-based workshop where area residents share skills and jointly undertake any number of creative projects. Members have a wide variety of backgrounds, from computer programming and engineering to fine arts and hobby crafting. The space is also open to the public every Friday for presentations, talks, demonstrations, and workshops.

The community workshop and rapid prototyping studio known as **TechShop** (192 Bakery Square Blvd., 412/345-7182, www.techshop.ws) is a newer addition to Pittsburgh maker scene. The space is loaded with high-end tools, computers, rapid prototyping equipment, and software. It operates with the noble mission of making the tools of innovation, including 3D printing, available to everyone. Hundreds of classes and workshops are available each month.

Kids can also get in on the creative and making action at **Makeshop** (10 Children's Way, 412/322-5058, www.makeshoppgh.com), a mini-studio inside the **Children's Museum of Pittsburgh** (www.pittsburghkids.org). Makeshop offers hands-on activities in woodworking, circuitry, sewing, animation, and assembly.

A new Carnegie Library initiative called **The Labs @ CLP** (thelabs@carnegielibrary.org) hosts a variety of maker workshops for kids in grades 6-12. Maker labs are currently offered at the Oakland (Main), Allegheny (North Side), Southside, and East Library branches of the **Carnegie Library of Pittsburgh** (www.clpgh.org).

developments in the city—there's even designated parking available for hybrid cars. But don't make the mistake of getting too excited when you spot the small bike-share station near Bakery Square's entrance; it's unfortunately only available to Google and CMU employees. There's a Marriott SpringHill Suites on-site, and since commercial developments are sprouting up all over the immediate area, including a location directly across the street, there's no telling what else will be here by the time you arrive.

MAP 6: 6425 Penn Ave., 412/683-3810, www.bakery-square.com

EASTSIDE

Although it's technically referred to as "a retail development connecting Shadyside and East Liberty," Eastside really isn't a cohesive shopping center in the traditional sense. In reality, it's an ever-expanding and constantly morphing collection of smaller retail developments that first got underway after the controversial demolition of East Liberty's high-rise apartment towers. To put it plainly, the Eastside retail area is a picture-perfect example of gentrification in action. And yet the fact remains that this formerly rough-around-the-edges area is quickly becoming a very pleasant place to shop and dine.

Roughly bordered by a Whole Foods Market (5880 Centre Ave.) on its southwest end and an enormous Target (6231 Penn Ave.) on its northeast end, the primary Eastside shopping center is home to a handful of trendy restaurants and a few chain stores, including PetSmart, Walgreens, and Starbucks. The surrounding East Liberty area is also home to popular bars, restaurants, and boutiques. And thanks to a new covered walkway attached to the upper level of the Eastside parking garage, it's finally possible to stroll over to Shadyside's Ellsworth Avenue business district, where art galleries and more bars and restaurants are located. An Aldi discount supermarket (5631 Baum Blvd.) and a Trader Joe's (6343 Penn Ave.) are both relatively nearby.

MAP 6: 5966 Penn Circle S., 412/391-7171, www.shopeastside.net

Greater Pittsburgh **Map 7**

BOOKS AND MUSIC

ARKHAM GIFT SHOPPE

The owner of Arkham had two decades of retail comic store experience before branching out on his own to open this store. This is a true comic-lover's dream store, where offerings include everything from action figures and T-shirts to graphic novels and both new and old comic titles. Naturally, a comic subscription service is available for hardcore collectors. And Arkham is a wonderful place to simply hang out and chew the fat with the shopkeepers. A few miles west of Hartwood Acres Park, Arkham is a bit of a hike from Downtown, but it's definitely worth the drive.

MAP 7: 3973 Rte. 8 (Wm. Flynn Hwy.), Allison Park, 412/486-3140, www.arkhamgiftshoppe.com; Wed. noon-8pm, Thurs.-Fri. 1pm-8pm, Sat. noon-7pm, Sun. noon-5pm

MYSTERY LOVERS BOOKSHOP

This Raven Award-winning shop just a few miles east of the city has been an Oakmont community staple since first opening its doors in 1990, and has welcomed countless touring mystery writers over the years. One of the largest specialty mystery book shops in the country, Mystery Lovers is also known for hosting several book clubs, and for regularly offering intimate catered dinners with popular authors. Various readings, lectures, and workshops take place throughout the year.

MAP 7: 514 Allegheny River Blvd., Oakmont, 412/828-4877, www.mysterylovers.com; Mon.-Sat. 10am-5pm, Sun. noon-4pm

CLOTHING AND ACCESSORIES

MOOP

While the handmade unisex bag designer and manufacturer known as Moop doesn't have a standard retail location, its Main Street studio is always abuzz, and the company welcomes appointments for tours and product viewing. Sample designs hang on a rack at the front of the studio, making it simple to have a look for yourself. And the staffers are always happy to explain exactly what goes into making their well-designed and beautifully crafted bags. Available in several styles and solid fashionable colors, the aesthetic of Moop's bags is a very clean and minimalistic one. And while some of the bags are most certainly designed for women, Moop's backpacks, messenger bags, and letter and porter bags make a wonderfully hip and utilitarian alternative to the classic leather briefcase for men. If you do stop by for a visit, make sure not to miss Moop's adorable studio cat, Clyde.

MAP 7: 406 S. Main St., Pittsburgh, 412/489-5477, www.moopshop.com; call or email to schedule an appointment

HEALTH AND BEAUTY

ESSPA KOZMETIKA ORGANIC SKINCARE

Well worth braving the 10-minute drive from town, Aspinwall's ESSpa Kozmetika has been named the city's best day spa for every year since 2005 by handfuls of local publications. The facials, treatments, and peels are offered, but so too are manicures and pedicures, make-up and lash extension applications, massages, mud body wraps and salt scrubs, traditional waxing, and the latest pain-free hair removal service. Working on-site is one of Pittsburgh's premiere plastic surgeons, the Harvard-trained Dr. J. Peter Rubin, who provides cosmetic surgery consultations in addition to Botox, collagen, and Restylane injections.

MAP 7: 17 Brilliant Ave., Aspinwall, 412/782-3888, www.esspa.net; Mon. 10am-5pm, Tues.-Sat. 9am-8pm, Sun. 11am-5pm; spa packages $150-600

SEWICKLEY SPA

Very high-end but not the least bit pretentious, Sewickley Spa is the absolute epitome of relaxation and peacefulness. Year after year, in fact, a good number of spa enthusiasts and trade publications claim it to be among the Greater Pittsburgh area's very best spas. The atmosphere is more or less in tune with what you'd expect at any high-quality spa, yet with Victorian-inspired finishing touches and details that complete the picture perfectly: waterfalls, comfy plush chairs, and changing rooms with trays of fruit and pastries. If that's not convincing enough, consider that a total of 112 ultimate spa treatments are offered. There's a good reason women and men both can be spotted here: There's something for everyone.

MAP 7: 337 Beaver St., Sewickley, 412/741-4240, www.sewickleyspa.com; daily 8:30am-6:30pm; packages and treatments $15-160

HOME DECOR AND FURNISHINGS

FRESH HEIRLOOMS

Formerly located in the heart of Lawrenceville, Fresh Heirlooms is the sort of store you'd expect to discover if *ReadyMade* magazine, say, morphed itself into a retail establishment. In other words, the shop offers handmade items created from reclaimed and repurposed materials. Most products are designed and made in-house by the shop's owner and her family, all of whom are skilled craftspeople committed to making high-quality products that will stand the test of time. The store also stocks creations by local salvage artists and offers design consultations; the artisans will even create custom work from your own furnishings and products. While it's now located outside the city in New Kensington, the shop and the classes and workshops they host are well worth the trip.

MAP 7: 887 5th Ave., New Kensington, 412/512-5098, www.freshheirlooms.com; Sat.-Sun. 10am-2pm, Mon.-Fri. by appointment

SHOPPING DISTRICTS AND CENTERS

THE GALLERIA OF MT. LEBANON

An upscale if slightly small indoor shopping mall deep in the South Hills, the Galleria is home to treasured retailers, many of which have no other locations in the city. To name just a few, you'll find Anthropologie, Pottery Barn Kids, A Pea in the Pod, Crabtree & Evelyn, Godiva Chocolatier, and Restoration Hardware, as well as a movie theater and a decent food court. As far as malls go, the Galleria is almost never terribly noisy or crowded, with the exception of the holiday shopping season, of course.

MAP 7: 1500 Washington Rd., Pittsburgh, 412/561-4000, www.galleriapgh.com; Mon.-Sat. 10am-9pm, Sun. noon-5pm

THE WATERFRONT

Perched along the Monongahela River in between Squirrel Hill and Munhall, The Waterfront is an enormous outdoor shopping center on the former site of U.S. Steel's Homestead Steel Works plant. Roughly a dozen of the mill's smoke stacks were preserved as something of an homage; they can be seen and even touched at the complex's southwest corner, next to a LongHorn Steakhouse restaurant on 5th Avenue. Try to arrive at the Waterfront by traveling from Squirrel Hill through Greenfield and then crossing the Homestead High Level Bridge, also known as the Homestead Grays Bridge, as the view of the river and of Homestead beyond is spectacular.

You'll find just about everything you'd expect in a traditional suburban shopping center, including an AMC Theaters cinema with stadium seating, dozens of eateries, a Giant Eagle grocery store, an enormous Lowe's hardware store, Macy's, Barnes & Noble, Target, Costco, Starbucks, a gas station, multiple specialty stores, and much more. Travelers can now stay overnight at the Waterfront, as a Hampton Inn & Suites location, a Courtyard Marriott, and a Holiday Inn Express are all on-site.

MAP 7: 149 W. Bridge St., Homestead, 412/476-8889, www.waterfrontpgh.com; Mon.-Sat. 10am-9pm, Sun. noon-6pm

VINTAGE AND ANTIQUES

THRIFTIQUE

Run by the same organization that operates the upscale Designer Days Boutique in Shadyside, Thriftique is the thrift and consignment store to visit if you're looking for slightly cheaper and more mainstream or "mall" brands: Gap, Banana Republic, Express, Chico, Ann Taylor, and Talbots, for example. Essentially, Thriftique is a better edited Goodwill. Its greatest asset, however, is probably its size; the store is simply enormous, and aside from men's, women's, and children's clothing and shoes, you'll find everything from furniture to housewares and from books to toys. Donations are accepted Monday through Friday 10am-4:30pm and on weekends by appointment only.

MAP 7: 7400 Church St., Swissvale, 412/271-0544, www.thriftiquepgh.com; Mon.-Fri. 10am-6pm, Sat. 9am-4pm

Hotels

Look for ★ to find recommended hotels.

HIGHLIGHTS

★ **Best Luxury Hotel:** You'll pay dearly for a room at the **Fairmont Pittsburgh,** but you won't find anything finer within the Golden Triangle (page 275).

★ **Best Room with a View:** Ask for a room on one of the top two floors of the **Renaissance Pittsburgh Hotel,** and you'll be able to take in a ball game from the comfort of your mattress. Make sure your room faces the Allegheny River (page 276).

★ **Best Urban Bed-and-Breakfast:** Situated within easy walking distance of all the North Shore's tourist attractions, including Rivers Casino and the Carnegie Science Center, **The Parador** is a Caribbean-flavored mega-B&B that'll transport you straight to the tropics (page 279).

★ **Most Historic Boutique Hotel:** Originally a Benedictine monastery, **The Priory,** built in 1888, is still home to Edwardian-era antiques and naturally elegant woodwork (page 279).

★ **Best Hidden Hostel:** Even most locals aren't aware that Pittsburgh has its very own hostel, the tiny **Hot Metal Lofts,** operated by a faith-based community (page 284).

★ **Best Historic Renovation:** Only at **Mansions on Fifth** can visitors bed down in a turn-of-the-century manse that was once home to Henry Clay Frick's attorney. It's listed on the National Register of Historic Places, and it boasts both an art gallery and a wine cellar (page 286).

★ **Best Long-Term Stay:** Check into one of the contemporary apartment-style options at **Shadyside Inn All Suites Hotel** and you might wonder if you haven't just discovered the bachelor or bachelorette pad of your dreams (page 286).

PRICE KEY

$ Less than $150 per night
$$ $150–250 per night
$$$ More than $250 per night

When it comes time to find a place to stay in Pittsburgh, the good news is that this city has more than enough hotel rooms to house just about any guest for nearly any length of time. Visit during a large convention or around the holidays, or even at the beginning or end of a college school year, and you're practically assured of finding some sort of vacancy somewhere. Yet it's an unfortunate fact that the variety of accommodation options leaves quite a bit to be desired. You'll find in abundance mostly corporate-style and chain hotels, most of them pricey. Hotels and guesthouses in Pittsburgh also tend to be clustered together in only a handful of neighborhoods, which means you're limited in terms of where in the city you'll stay. Backpackers and budget travelers will be disheartened to learn that hosteling options in Pittsburgh are limited.

But don't trade in your air ticket for a round-trip to Cleveland just yet; there *is* good news in the Steel City lodging scene, most of it revolving around the town's especially quaint bed-and-breakfasts. Visit just about any bed-and-breakfast in the city, in fact, and chances are you'll be pleasantly surprised to find such refined and sophisticated interiors in a town most popularly known for its grittiness and blue-collar history. Do keep in mind, however, that since most bed-and-breakfasts have a very limited number of rooms, advance reservations are highly recommended, even in the off-season.

CHOOSING A HOTEL

For any Pittsburgh visitors who've come to study or work at a college or area hospital, the university district of Oakland is the obvious choice. It has a decent number of hotels along with a fair amount of variety. Two Oakland hotels, for instance, offer full suites, and one offers a substantial discount to students.

Just a bit farther east is Shadyside, a relaxed and leafy neighborhood where both the homes and the commercial district are upscale. You'll find a number of bed-and-breakfasts; there's also a decent chain hotel directly across the street from Shadyside Hospital.

Downtown Pittsburgh, however, is where the majority of the town's tourists and business travelers call it a night. As is the case in most midsize downtowns, pricey chain hotels are the order of the day. Many Downtown hotels, however, offer a decent mix of telecommuting accessories and on-site eateries, making a weekend in the Golden Triangle as productive as it is entertaining.

Most guidebooks to the region encourage the shoestring traveler to investigate the many chain hotel options near the airport, and while that advice is certainly useful in theory, it does little good for anyone arriving by bus or train, not to mention anyone without the use of a private vehicle. The artistic-minded Bloomfield inn known as **EdenHouse** (4069-71 Liberty Ave., 412/654-7057, www.edenhouseshortstay.com) is currently the city's most affordable lodging, with weekly stays going for as low as $60 a night.

If you'd prefer to stay a bit outside the city, visit www.pittsburghbnb.com, which contains a list of inns and bed-and-breakfasts throughout the Greater Pittsburgh area and its surrounding countryside. The nationwide website www.bedandbreakfast.com is also useful.

For a more comprehensive listing of hotels and motels, cabins, campgrounds, bed-and-breakfasts, and resorts, visit the very informative www.visitpa.com. Also helpful for accommodation listings—as well as information about regional events—is www.visitpittsburgh.com.

The rates in this chapter are based on double occupancy in the high season (summer).

Downtown

Map 1

Downtown Pittsburgh is small enough that its entire distance can easily be covered on foot, so when choosing a hotel, there's really not much of a need to consider *where* in Downtown it's located. Rest assured that shopping, theaters, and restaurants will always be just a brief walk or taxi ride away.

CAMBRIA SUITES PITTSBURGH AT CONSOL ENERGY CENTER $$

A contemporary all-suite hotel just steps from the city's newest arena, Cambria Suites Pittsburgh ($159-239) is now the lodging option of choice for anyone attending an event at the CONSOL Energy Center. The 142 rooms are all nonsmoking, and a few even come complete with kitchenettes, hot tubs, and wet bars—not to mention killer city-skyline views. And although Cambria Suites is a chain hotel, it's decked out to resemble an independent boutique; the rooms, lobby, and social areas all convey something of a warm, Pottery Barn aesthetic. There's also a 24-hour fitness center and free Wi-Fi throughout, and a complimentary downtown shuttle service is included.

MAP 1: 1320 Centre Ave., 412/381-6687, www.cambriasuitespittsburgh.com

COURTYARD BY MARRIOTT PITTSBURGH DOWNTOWN $$

Conveniently tucked just outside Downtown's busiest streets, this still relatively new boutique-style hotel ($209-289) can't be beat, location-wise—it's practically within shouting distance of both the Convention Center and the August Wilson Center. The property itself sits inside four renovated historical buildings and features vaulted ceilings and a landscaped atrium. Right next door is the popular **Sonoma Grille,** a contemporary American restaurant with a fantastic wine list. **Bistro 922 Penn,** known for its phenomenal selection of Belgian beer, is just down the street.

MAP 1: 945 Penn Ave., 412/434-5551, www.marriott.com/pitcy

★ FAIRMONT PITTSBURGH $$$

Talk about a welcome reception: With its sleek and minimalist European vibe and its dramatically modern atmosphere, the Fairmont Hotel chain's first Pittsburgh location embodies nearly everything that has been lacking for so long in the city's luxury hotel scene. In the heart of Downtown's Cultural District, the 185 rooms ($212-1,200) feature floor-to-ceiling windows—many with stunning views—and all the standard trappings of a high-end boutique hotel, including iPod stations, brand-name toiletries, and a

lushly luxurious collection of the sort of furniture you might expect to see in an Ikea showroom. Guests at this LEED Gold-certified hotel are afforded access to the fitness center downstairs. There's also a popular on-site Asian restaurant, **Habitat,** and a lounge, **Andy's Wine Bar,** where live jazz can often be enjoyed.
MAP 1: 510 Market St., 412/772-8800 or 888/270-6647, www.fairmont.com/pittsburgh

OMNI WILLIAM PENN $$$

Prior to the arrival of the nearby Fairmont Pittsburgh, the Omni William Penn ($229-429) was known for many decades as the city's premiere luxury hotel; it's been welcoming well-heeled guests (including Lawrence Welk and John F. Kennedy) since 1916. Luckily, it's possible to experience the grandeur even if you're not a registered guest: Simply sink into one of the massive lobby's deep couches and gaze upon the many chandeliers and the baby grand. Or, wander into the attached Starbucks, the **Tap Room** (an English-style ale house), or the **Palm Court,** a restaurant known for its exquisite cocktails. Guests who've become used to modern boutique-style hotels will find the rooms a bit dated and uninspired, although there's definitely something to be said for the kitschy, old-world elegance of the place.
MAP 1: 530 William Penn Pl., 412/281-7100, www.omnihotels.com/pittsburgh

PITTSBURGH MARRIOTT CITY CENTER $$

Although not necessarily the most conveniently located hotel for those doing daily business anywhere in the heart of Downtown, the Pittsburgh Marriott City Center ($209-279) is especially well located for anyone who's come to town specifically to attend an event at the new CONSOL Energy Center; it sits almost directly next door. This hotel was renovated in 2012. Celebrity watchers staying here may even get the chance to spot their favorite star; band members and other performers appearing at the CONSOL Center often bunk here because of its obvious convenience. Guest rooms are meticulously decorated, from the HD flat-screen TVs to the LED reading lights, and a well-equipped business center is on-site. Just downstairs is a Starbucks and the **Steelhead Brasserie and Wine Bar,** a popular contemporary American eatery. There's also an indoor pool and a fitness center.
MAP 1: 112 Washington Pl., 412/471-4000 or 888/456-6600, www.marriott.com/pitdt

★ RENAISSANCE PITTSBURGH HOTEL $$$

Although owned by the Marriott organization, the Renaissance Pittsburgh Hotel ($179-429) is designed to look and feel like a stylish and creatively detailed boutique hotel. With its old-world European theme, it's one of the very few choices in Downtown for anyone interested in lodging that lacks the cookie-cutter corporate feel. Guest rooms, although outfitted with all the conveniences one would find in any Marriott, are smartly decorated as well, and the restaurant, **Braddock's American Brasserie,** is a locally celebrated European and American fusion spot with an impressive cocktail menu. A small bar, **Braddock's Street Side Grill,** has a decent craft beer selection. Baseball fans bunking here should request a room with a PNC Park view.

MAP 1: 107 6th St., 412/562-1200, www.renaissancepittsburghpa.com

WESTIN CONVENTION CENTER PITTSBURGH $$$

As the name cleverly suggests, the Westin Convention Center Pittsburgh ($339-469) is an ideal lodging choice for any out-of-towner planning to attend an event at the David L. Lawrence Convention Center. In fact, an enclosed skywalk connects the two buildings. The Westin is also home to the **Original Fish Market,** a fantastic seafood eatery with one of the city's best sushi bars. There's a 9,000-square-foot fitness center with full gym facilities, including a sauna, a lap pool, free weights, and aerobic and spin classes. Rooms are some of the Downtown area's largest; each one has a view of the central business district. A complimentary shuttle offers transportation within a one-mile radius of the hotel. Dogs under 50 pounds are welcome.

MAP 1: 1000 Penn Ave., 412/281-3700 or 888/627-7053, www.westinpittsburgh.com

WYNDHAM GRAND PITTSBURGH DOWNTOWN $$$

Directly across the street from the entrance to Point State Park, the Wyndham Grand Pittsburgh Downtown ($284-369) is the latest name of the property that for decades was known for as Hilton Pittsburgh. This is still one of the largest hotels in the city; all 712 rooms boast a phenomenal city view, some gazing out over the park and the three rivers beyond. There are also 72 suites, and the 17,280-square-foot ballroom is unlike anything else in the city. If you like your hotels monster-sized and you're not staying at the Omni William Penn, this is definitely your spot. The Wyndham Grand is also within walking distance of all the major North Shore attractions, including the sports stadiums.

MAP 1: 600 Commonwealth Pl., 412/391-4600, www.wyndham.com/pittsburgh

North Side

Map 1

Thanks in large part to all the recent development around the North Shore, the North Side has lately experienced something of a mini-hotel boom. If you're here to take in a Steelers or Pirates game, you shouldn't have much trouble securing a bed, although advance reservations are still a good idea in this area. When it comes to bed-and-breakfasts, however, travelers are absolutely spoiled with choices. There are scores of bed-and-breakfasts in the area, and every last one is creatively decorated and overflowing with character. Crossing one of the bridges to Downtown on foot is simple, not to mention a perfect way to get a great view of the city skyline. Yet with all there is to do on the North Side, you could easily spend a long weekend without ever leaving the neighborhood.

HYATT PLACE PITTSBURGH–NORTH SHORE $$

Although it's now the third hotel within shouting distance of PNC Park (a Marriott SpringHill Suites and a Residence Inn both sit on the field's northeast corner), there's much more to recommend about the city's new Hyatt Place ($139-164) property than its convenient-to-the-ballpark location. The gorgeous contemporary interiors are decidedly boutique-esque, featuring 42-inch HD TVs, minimalist furnishings, and soft lighting. Other amenities include oversized sleeper-sofas, a mini-fridge, and all the trappings of a top-notch business hotel: free Wi-Fi, a 24-hour fitness center, and a 24-hour business center.

MAP 1: 260 North Shore Dr., 412/321-3000, www.pittsburghnorthshore.place.hyatt.com

THE INN ON THE MEXICAN WAR STREETS $$

Without a doubt, this inn ($129-179) is the city's best all-around bed-and-breakfast. It boasts eight individually and uniquely decorated rooms and suites, a front porch shaded by stone arches and columns, a gorgeous lobby complete with a baby grand piano, and off-street parking; you just couldn't ask for a lovelier locale. This bed-and-breakfast is gay-owned, gay-friendly, and is patronized largely by gay men and lesbians. Heterosexuals are more than welcome, of course. A phenomenal contemporary American restaurant, **Acanthus,** is romantically located in a carriage house behind the inn. All rooms feature free Wi-Fi, TVs, and DVD players.

MAP 1: 604 W. North Ave., 412/231-6544, www.innonthemexicanwarstreets.com

★ THE PARADOR $$

Owned and operated by a Pittsburgher who spent time in Florida and was subsequently influenced by that state's tropical flavor, the Parador ($150-200) is a Caribbean-themed bed-and-breakfast situated in the unlikely locale of Allegheny West, just up the hill from the Carnegie Science Center. Previously known as the 8,000-square-foot Rhodes Mansion, which was built in 1870, the Parador's many suites and common areas seem to stretch on forever. Each room is decorated and detailed to suggest a different tropical flower, and the lavish 2,000-square-foot ballroom, with its incredibly ornate back bar mirror, must be seen to be believed. The inn's roomy backyard was recently transformed into a beach-themed tropical garden; there's also free Wi-Fi and a library for business meetings.

MAP 1: 939 Western Ave., 412/231-4800 or 888/540-1443, www.theparadorinn.com

★ THE PRIORY $$

A 42-room European-style boutique hotel within walking distance of all the North Side's major attractions, the Priory ($185-295) is a restored 19th-century Benedictine rectory that has been welcoming and harboring guests for more than two decades now. Dozens of local and national publications have sung its praises over the years, which shouldn't come as much of a surprise considering its timeless Victorian charm, its truly friendly and personalized service, and a lovely outdoor courtyard. A $2.7 million addition in 2011 features a fitness room, a business center, and a tiny pub known as the Monks' Bar, so the Priory is also a wise option for the traveling businessperson looking for something a bit more intimate than the average chain hotel. Complimentary Wi-Fi and a shuttle service are also available.

MAP 1: 614 Pressley St., 412/231-3338, www.thepriory.com

RESIDENCE INN NORTH SHORE $$

As with each of the Marriott's hugely popular Residence Inn locations, this addition to the tourist-friendly North Shore features comfortably roomy suites with kitchenettes and separate working and sleeping areas ($189-279). Thanks to the contemporary furniture, decor, and lighting, though, the rooms feel much more like well-appointed studio apartments than actual hotel suites. And yet the real prize is the hotel's location: You'd be hard-pressed to find a spot more conveniently situated to Downtown Pittsburgh without actually being downtown. And while on-site parking will set you back $19 daily (off-site parking is $22 daily), the hotel is within easy walking distance of both Heinz Field and PNC Park, as well as a host of recently opened bars and restaurants and the world-renowned Andy Warhol Museum. Pets are allowed for a nonrefundable $100 fee.

MAP 1: 574 W. General Robinson St., 412/321-2099 or 800/228-9290, www.marriott.com/pitrn

Oakland

Map 2

Oakland is the city's university district, and as such it's naturally home to chain hotels that do a booming business at the beginning and end of every school year. (Book well in advance if you'll be staying in this neighborhood during the end of August, the beginning of September, the end of April, or the start of May.) Oakland is also a good alternative to Downtown—you'll be surrounded by all the urban amenities, and both Downtown and the culture-packed neighborhoods of the East End can be easily reached by a quick taxi or bus ride.

HAMPTON INN UNIVERSITY CENTER $$

Although South Oakland's Hampton Inn ($139-229) is perfectly located for anyone visiting Magee-Womens Hospital, Carlow College, or the Pittsburgh Playhouse, it should be noted that because of its slightly hidden location in a somewhat confusing part of the city, out-of-towners arriving in their own vehicles will likely find themselves turned around unless they've been given very detailed directions. On the bright side, the Hampton Inn quite often has rooms available when the rest of Oakland is booked solid (at the beginning and end of college semesters, for instance). And although the 132 guest rooms are relatively plain, a daily hot breakfast, Wi-Fi, and a three-mile radius shuttle service are included. A fitness center and business center are on-site. Pets up to 50 pounds are welcome, and parking is $14 daily.

MAP 2: 3315 Hamlet St., 412/329-4969, http://hamptoninn.hilton.com

HILTON GARDEN INN PITTSBURGH UNIVERSITY PLACE $$

Previously known as the Wyndham Garden Hotel, this South Oakland mainstay ($161-269) received a much-needed contemporary makeover after its renaming in 2013. The location of this eight-floor hotel on the neighborhood's western border puts it within convenient reach of Carlow College, Magee-Womens Hospital, UPMC Presbyterian and Montefiore hospitals, and the Primary Care Center of Children's Hospital. On-site you'll find a restaurant, free Wi-Fi, a 24-hour business center, and a decent fitness center

Family House

In late 1983, a small group of doctors and influential community leaders in Pittsburgh took notice of a troubling trend taking place in the waiting rooms and hallways of the city's many hospitals: Out-of-town family members of patients undergoing long-term treatment for serious illnesses were sleeping in corridors and plastic chairs for days on end. Sometimes weeks on end. Determined to do something about it, the group formed a nonprofit organization and eventually raised enough money to refurbish an old mansion near the city's main hospital complex. Families of patients with life-threatening illnesses, and in some cases the patients themselves, were welcomed to temporarily move into the mansion at a very reasonable cost. A communal kitchen was built to cut down on the prohibitive expense of eating every single meal at a restaurant.

The popularity of **Family House** (412/647-7777, www.familyhouse.org), as the group called its accommodation, soon outgrew the confines of that first mansion. Today the organization has rooms and suites at four separate locales: in North Oakland (514 N. Neville St.), South Oakland (233 McKee Pl.), Shadyside (5245 Centre Ave.), and Central Oakland (116 Thackeray Ave.). All houses offer free shuttles to West Penn Hospital and most UPMC hospitals, as well as libraries, fitness rooms, on-site laundry facilities, TV lounges, free Wi-Fi, cable TV in each room, private phone lines and voice mail in each room, 24-hour security, and most important of all, a warm and caring family environment at affordable rates.

Single rooms, for instance, are $45 per day, while double rooms cost $60 per day and four-person suites are charged at $75 per day. For more information or to request a room, call or visit the Family House website.

with free weights. The bad news: Unless you want to shell out $18 a pop for valet service, you're on your own when it comes to parking.

MAP 2: 3454 Forbes Ave., 412/683-2040, www.hiltongardeninn.hilton.com

QUALITY INN UNIVERSITY CENTER $

It's perhaps a bit ironic that with a name like Quality Inn ($87-129), most travelers staying the night wouldn't necessarily expect to experience much quality at all. Yet all things considered, this particular location is actually rather nice. It's no boutique hotel, of course, but the rooms and beds are fairly large, and most come complete with small balconies. (Perfect for smokers who've checked into a nonsmoking room.) The hotel's real benefit, though, is its location: The Quality Inn is deeper in South Oakland than any other hotel, so parents visiting college students who live in the neighborhood will be well positioned, even if they've arrived without a car. A workout room and free wired Internet access are available. Extra bonus points: Parking is free, and there's a Panera Bread on the ground floor.

MAP 2: 3401 Boulevard of the Allies, 412/683-6100, www.qualityinn.com/hotel-pittsburgh-pennsylvania-PA369

clockwise from top left: Westin Convention Center Pittsburgh; Omni William Penn; Courtyard by Marriott Pittsburgh Downtown

RESIDENCE INN PITTSBURGH UNIVERSITY/ MEDICAL CENTER $$

Located in a rather odd stretch of North Oakland, the Residence Inn Marriott ($169-279) may seem like an impossibly inconvenient place to stay for visitors who've arrived without private vehicles. But the truth is that as the only hotel in the immediate area, it's perfectly positioned for anyone visiting North Oakland-based friends or family, and a shuttle service to and from central Oakland is complimentary for guests. As for the digs themselves, this is Oakland's only all-suite hotel; rooms come complete with a refrigerator, microwave, dishwasher, and a full stove and oven. There's also free Wi-Fi, a complimentary grocery shopping service, and an indoor pool and fitness center. On-site parking is available for $15 daily.

MAP 2: 3896 Bigelow Blvd., 412/621-2200 or 800/513-8766, http://marriott.com/property/propertypage/PITRO

WYNDHAM PITTSBURGH UNIVERSITY CENTER $$

Formerly a Holiday Inn Select location, the Wyndham Hotel Group's newly renovated home in Oakland ($183-249) offers 251 guest rooms with ergonomic work stations and free Wi-Fi, while amenities include an indoor pool and fitness center, a casual on-site restaurant, and a complimentary shuttle service. Location-wise, this is a smart choice for travelers needing to stay in Oakland but who would otherwise prefer not to be polluted by the noise and unsightliness of the urban jungle. Very near to both the Cathedral of Learning and Heinz Chapel, the hotel sits a few buildings in from busy 5th Avenue. The formerly drab rooms were brightened considerably following the property's handover to Wyndham.

MAP 2: 100 Lytton Ave., 412/682-6200, www.wyndham.com

South Side

Map 3

Most Pittsburghers think of the South Side as one of our town's most sinful and eclectic neighborhoods. Bars and clubs are everywhere, so if you've come to Pittsburgh primarily to play, sleeping on the South Side makes good sense. For additional advice about what to see, do, and eat in the area, visit www.southsidepittsburgh.com and www.southsideworks.com.

HOLIDAY INN EXPRESS HOTEL & SUITES $$

Just off East Carson Street but on the far opposite side of the neighborhood from SouthSide Works, the Holiday Inn Express ($181-229) is frequently booked full. Which isn't to say that it's a particularly unique place, although it is wonderfully located: Not only does it sit just a few blocks from the heart of the South Side

Flats, but its base near the 10th Street Bridge makes a walk into Downtown quite feasible. Guest rooms with free Wi-Fi and work desks are certainly comfortable enough, having been renovated in early 2012. A free shuttle will take you to Steelers, Pirates, and Penguins games, or to Rivers Casino on the North Shore. There's also an indoor pool and a fitness center. Parking is $14 daily.

MAP 3: 20 S. 10th St., 412/488-1130, www.hiexpress.com/pittsburghpa

★ HOT METAL LOFTS $

Owned and operated by something of an alternative and nondenominational church known as the Hot Metal Bridge Faith Community, the Hot Metal Lofts ($35) is indeed a youth hostel—complete with a few bunks and a communal dining area—and one that almost no one in Pittsburgh seems to be aware of. That's probably because the hostel primarily houses religious travelers who are participating in mission experiences with the church. Nevertheless, Hot Metal Lofts does open its door to all and sundry, and yet potential guests should probably expect to encounter at least some preaching and proselytizing during their stay. Reservations need to be made at least three weeks in advance. Groups pay an incredibly reasonable flat rate of $50.

MAP 3: 2700 Jane St., 412/481-4010, www.hotmetallofts.com

HYATT HOUSE PITTSBURGH SOUTH SIDE $$

Opened in 2013, this extended-stay hotel ($169-239) is tucked conveniently behind the SouthSide Works shopping center and features all the amenities you might expect from an upscale apartment complex, including a spacious outdoor grilling area with a view of the Monongahela River, laundry facilities, a fitness center and mini-market that are both open around the clock, a complimentary grocery shopping service, a free full-breakfast buffet, an indoor pool, free Wi-Fi, and more. Even the standard suites come with fully equipped kitchens and separate living and sleeping areas decked out in contemporary decor. Assuming you need long-term digs and can afford the bill, you won't do much better than Hyatt House within the city limits.

MAP 3: 2795 S. Water St., 412/390-2477, www.pittsburghsouthside.house.hyatt.com

MORNING GLORY INN $$

A bed-and-breakfast so subtly concealed on a residential street that even most locals don't realize it's there, the peacefully relaxing

Morning Glory Inn ($155-450) is the absolute antithesis of the hard-partying neighborhood it calls home. A lovingly restored 1862 Victorian, this is the South Side's only independent lodging. And trimmed as it is with antiques, period fireplaces, a cozy two-level "Attic Suite," and a wildly popular back garden area where wedding receptions are held most weekends, it's also one of Pittsburgh's better bed-and-breakfasts. Do bear in mind, however, that neither Downtown nor Oakland is within walking distance, regardless of the claims made on Morning Glory's website.

MAP 3: 2119 Sarah St., 412/431-1707, www.gloryinn.com

SHERATON HOTEL STATION SQUARE $$$

Should you find yourself booked into the Sheraton Hotel Station Square ($289-415), you may feel somewhat isolated from town. But assuming the weather is nice, reaching the business district is actually quite pleasant—just take a five-minute walk across the Smithfield Street Bridge. The Monongahela Incline leading to Mount Washington is also nearby. And unlike most chain hotels in the city, this one is smartly designed and boasts a beautifully modern lobby. The guest rooms are nicely understated, and on-site you'll find a fitness room, a pool, a contemporary American restaurant, and a cozy bar in the lobby of a six-story atrium.

MAP 3: 300 W. Station Square Dr., 412/261-2000 or 888/627-7029, www.sheratonstationsquare.com

SPRINGHILL SUITES PITTSBURGH SOUTHSIDE WORKS $$

Sitting smack-dab in the center of one of the city's best shopping centers—SouthSide Works—and within easy walking distance of East Carson Street's many amenities, the SpringHill Suites ($149-289) hotel is home to the sort of rooms that actually do feel a bit like home. Each suite, for instance, comes with a microwave, a fridge, and a wet bar. There's also free Wi-Fi, and the fitness center has a whirlpool, of all things. The hotel's inventively futuristic design and decor—which seem to have taken more than a few hints from the W Hotels chain—make this property truly unusual. The SpringHill Suites may be corporate-owned, but its modern design and layout easily compares with the hippest of boutique hotels. To avoid late-night noise coming from the nearby train tracks, request a room facing away from the Monongahela River.

MAP 3: 2950 S. Water St., 412/488-8003, www.springhillsuites.com/pitss

Shadyside

Map 4

The bed-and-breakfasts in Shadyside are all within walking distance of Walnut Street and Ellsworth Avenue, which is where the vast majority of the neighborhood's shopping, dining, and entertainment options can be found. If you're in town to visit one of the colleges or universities, walking is certainly an option, although you might prefer using a rental car or taxi to get there and back. Most of the bigger East End hospitals are also relatively close by.

THE INN ON NEGLEY $$

A restored period home built in the latter part of the 19th century, the Inn on Negley ($180-300) is a wonderfully quaint bed-and-breakfast tucked away in an upscale residential neighborhood. The eight individual rooms and suites, as well as the inn itself, are professionally decorated with antiques and period furniture; the overall style is a nicely done mixture of country charm and European sophistication. Each room comes with an imported down comforter and either a jetted shower system or whirlpool tub in the bathroom.

MAP 4: 714 S. Negley Ave., 412/661-0631, www.innsonnegley.com

★ MANSIONS ON FIFTH $$$

Guests of Mansions on Fifth ($230-650), a truly elegant and luxurious hotel that was renovated in 2012, have the unique opportunity to live as the city's most powerful industrialists and financiers once did. In the early 1900s, this stretch of 5th Avenue was known as "Millionaires Row," and the Mansions on Fifth comprise the former homesteads of the McCook and Reed families, built in the Elizabethan revivalist and Tudor styles. The 22 historical rooms and suites range from quite standard to gorgeously opulent. Some have second-level lofts and oversized bathrooms, while others are more reminiscent of an average boutique hotel. There's an impressive art gallery and even a wine cellar, and amenities include yoga classes and in-room massages.

MAP 4: 5105 5th Ave., 412/381-5105 or 800/465-9550, www.mansionsonfifth.com

★ SHADYSIDE INN ALL SUITES HOTEL $$

There's certainly nothing else quite like this in Shadyside—an all-suite hotel ($169-309) offering fully furnished one-bedroom, two-bedroom, and studio apartment-style lodging. With hardwood floors and widescreen HD TVs, the furnishings are contemporary enough. There's also free Wi-Fi and off-street parking, and its enviable location is just steps from the neighborhood's business district.

clockwise from top left: Hot Metal Lofts; a stained glass window in Mansions on Fifth; The Priory

Concierge and housekeeping services are available, as is a free shuttle van service. Some of the units allow pets.

MAP 4: 5405 5th Ave., 412/441-4444, www.shadysideinn.com

SUNNYLEDGE BOUTIQUE HOTEL $$

A historic landmark built in 1886, the Sunnyledge Boutique Hotel ($139-275) is one of the East End's most gorgeous bed-and-breakfast choices. Original oak paneling and fixtures are found throughout, and each of the eight guest rooms is decorated in its own unique and truly elegant Victorian style. Rooms come complete with whirlpool tub, minibar, and cable TV. A library, an exercise room, and a 24-hour concierge service are also available to guests. Sunnyledge features a five-star restaurant known as the **Tea Room** and a martini bar referred to as the **Club Room.**

MAP 4: 5124 5th Ave., 412/683-5014, www.sunnyledge.com

Bloomfield and Lawrenceville

Map 6

Conveniently located between the upscale shopping district of Shadyside and artsy, up-and-coming Lawrenceville, the Italian district of Bloomfield doesn't offer much in the way of lodging. Bloomfield is nevertheless one of the city's most authentic neighborhoods, and it's not far from the university and hospital district of Oakland.

COURTYARD MARRIOTT $$

The Courtyard Marriott ($199-239) sits right on the Shadyside/Bloomfield border, and it's the best choice for anyone visiting patients at the nearby Shadyside Hospital or the UPMC Hillman Cancer Center. It's also conveniently located for anyone visiting family or friends in Bloomfield or Friendship, and it isn't terribly far from North Oakland or East Liberty. The guest rooms, while clean and comfortable enough, aren't much to write home about, although there is free Wi-Fi, and a small indoor swimming pool and a Starbucks are on-site. A parking lot open only to guests is another bonus, although you'll be charged $18 daily for the privilege. A complimentary shuttle service travels through Shadyside, Oakland, and Bloomfield.

MAP 6: 5308 Liberty Ave., 412/683-3113, www.courtyardshadyside.com

EDENHOUSE $

Not necessarily a hotel and not quite a bed-and-breakfast, EdenHouse ($60-175) is a distinctive first for Pittsburgh. A short-term residence owned by two working artists, this creatively outfitted home is available for weekly and monthly rentals. (Shorter stays can sometimes be negotiated.) And because it's in a residential neighborhood, EdenHouse is an ideal choice for travelers interested in experiencing Pittsburgh just as a local would. Accommodation options include the 1,200-square-foot Loft, which sleeps six and features a Jacuzzi and a rooftop garden; the 700-square-foot Apartment, complete with a stove and dishwasher; and the Studio, an efficiency apartment with cable TV, Wi-Fi, and a kitchenette. The gorgeous interiors have something of a Pottery Barn vibe while also retaining a sophisticated artistic sensibility. And EdenHouse's location in the city's East End is simply unbeatable.

MAP 6: 4069-71 Liberty Ave., 412/621-1698, www.edenhouseshortstay.com

NOT ANOTHER HOSTEL $

As its name suggests, Not Another Hostel isn't really a hostel in the traditional sense. While it does have the expected communal areas, bunk beds, and international vibe, it's inside a private home, making the experience of staying there more akin to couch-surfing. What's more, the hostel operates on a donation-only model: You can pay the owners what you think your stay is worth, or you can pay them nothing. The only catch: NAH doesn't publicly share its address; however, it's within easy walking distance of Children's Hospital. To secure a bunk, you'll need to call or email (using a contact form on the hostel's website) 24 hours or less in advance of your stay to receive confirmation. Please call only between the hours of 9am and 9pm. The owners operate a second NAH location in Cincinnati, Ohio.

MAP 6: Near Penn Ave. and Main St., Lawrenceville, 412/667-8362, www.notanotherhostel.org

East Liberty and Garfield **Map 6**

Until very recently, East Liberty was gang-inflicted and synonymous with danger. Retail growth and creeping gentrification have changed the area to a great degree, although it's still wise to keep your wits about you after dark. The area is full of galleries and boundary-pushing restaurants and boutiques.

FRIENDSHIP SUITES $

Although technically located in the Friendship/Garfield area, Friendship Suites ($109-175) has a wonderfully convenient (and quietly residential) East End location, less than two miles from the university and hospital district of Oakland, as well as the Shadyside shopping district. This is essentially a B&B (minus the breakfast),

Hotel Chatter

This fair city has always been home to more than its fair share of chain hotels, generally built for and marketed to the middle-class business traveler. But if you happen to be in the market for a hip, creatively designed boutique inn or a shoestring-budget backpackers hostel, there aren't a lot of options.

That's probably why hotel development gossip has always been a bit of a masochistic parlor game among the city's cultured classes. Stick around long enough, in fact, and you're bound to hear the story about the W Hotel that's coming to East Liberty (not true), or the one about the youth hostel that's being built on the South Side (mostly true).

Then again, Pittsburgh's cultural quotient has been on the rise for some time now, and there are some pretty interesting commercial developments in town that weren't around even five years ago. So some of the lodging options covered here may finally be open for business by the time you purchase this guidebook. Then again, maybe not.

ACE HOTEL

According to the East Liberty neighborhood's redevelopment corporation, the long-rumored plan to bring the uber-hip ACE Hotel chain to Pittsburgh's ever-changing East End is finally beginning to see the light of day. Current plans call for a long-vacant YMCA building to be converted into a 63-room branch of the boutique hotel, which first opened in Seattle. The ACE, assuming it opens, will also be home to its own restaurant and a ballroom (120 S. Whitfield St., East Liberty, www.acehotel.com).

HOTEL INDIGO PITTSBURGH

If there's one hotel project on this list with the best chance of being included in the next edition of *Moon Pittsburgh,* it's the 137-room Hotel Indigo slated for development in East Liberty. After all, the property already has a mixed-use development—Indigo Square—named after it. Incidentally, Hotel Indigo locations are boutique hotels in the same way Blue Moon is a craft beer. They're corporate-owned, in other words, but they're close enough to the real thing to pass muster (Broad St., East Liberty, www.ihg.com/hotelindigo).

HOTEL MONACO

Planned for the future of the historical beaux-arts structure known as the James H. Reed Building, which sits across from Mellon Square at the corner of 6th Avenue and William Penn Way, is a 247-room outpost of the flashy Hotel Monaco. Owned and operated by the San Francisco-based Kimpton Hotel & Restaurant Group, which essentially pioneered the boutique hotel concept, Pittsburgh's Hotel Monaco is currently looking at an opening date sometime in late 2014 (35 6th Ave., Downtown, www.kimptonhotels.com).

PITTSBURGH HOSTEL PROJECT

The long-vacant 10,000-square-foot space sitting atop the South Side's Beehive Coffeehouse is the intended home of the Pittsburgh Hostel Project (PHP), which will house between 60 and 70 beds on its two floors, a kitchen, a dining area and common area, and nightly rates of $25-75. As of this writing, PHP director Anne Marie Toccket is in the process of rehabbing the future much-anticipated hostel (1327 E. Carson St., South Side, www.pittsburghhostel.org).

with spacious, apartment-like suites inside a lovely Victorian brick home. And although the proprietor doesn't live on-site, he prides himself on top-notch customer service and is always just a phone call away. Street parking is rarely a problem, and significant discounts are offered for weekly and monthly stays.

MAP 6: 301 Stratford Ave., 412/392-1935, www.friendshipsuites.com

SPRINGHILL SUITES PITTSBURGH BAKERY SQUARE $$

With a fresh and modernist interior design, this 110-room Marriott ($189-239) is within East Liberty's much-ballyhooed Bakery Square development, a mixed-use area where upscale retail meshes with corporate office space, including the new Google headquarters. Guests are afforded free use of the adjacent LA Fitness location, which can be reached via an enclosed walkway. Then again, considering all the mod-cons made available—free parking, free Wi-Fi, flat-screen TVs, a heated pool, and suites featuring refrigerators, microwaves, and separate living and work spaces—you may find it difficult to so much as leave the comfy confines of your room.

MAP 6: 134 Bakery Square Blvd., 412/362-8600, www.marriottspringhillpittsburghhotel.com

Greater Pittsburgh

Map 7

Pittsburgh's suburban areas are home to small clusters of hotels, the majority of them—such as those in Monroeville, Green Tree, the area on and around McKnight Road in the North Hills, and the sprawling area around the Pittsburgh International Airport—designed to serve business travelers. Monroeville, it's worth noting, has a surplus of hotels suited for just about any budget, and some are among the cheapest you'll find anywhere in Pittsburgh. You can probably guess what those hotels are most often used for, however; check in at your own risk.

Assuming you've arrived in Pittsburgh with your own vehicle, staying at either of the bed-and-breakfasts listed is a smart compromise between small-town living and the big city.

For detailed information about the dozens of hotels located near the airport, point your browser to www.visitpittsburgh.com/sleep and then choose the "West/Airport" location in the search field.

ARBORS BED & BREAKFAST $$

A 19th-century farmhouse nestled into a wooded and relatively obscure corner of the North Side, Arbors Bed & Breakfast ($95-255) is just minutes from the North Side's commercial district by car. Two rooms and one suite are available; all three are decked out in a fairly traditional "county inn" style, and all come with cable TV and a VCR. Just off the small downstairs kitchen is a sunroom; with its in-floor radiant heat and hot tub, it's undoubtedly the B&B's best feature. The management is particularly friendly and quick to offer sightseeing, nightlife, and dining recommendations. Guests desiring complete privacy can even rent out the entire facility for $425 per night or $800 for the weekend.

MAP 7: 745 Maginn Ave., Pittsburgh, 412/231-4643, www.arborsbnb.com

DOONE'S INN AT OAKMONT $$$

The Inn at Oakmont ($215-350), as it was formerly known, is your smartest bed-and-breakfast option if you'd like to be far from an urban neighborhood but still relatively close to Downtown Pittsburgh via car. The eight guest rooms and one suite are all equipped with Wi-Fi and a "sleep machine" programmed with, say, tropical noises or ambient sounds. A public golf course sits just across the street, and as an added bonus, the charming town of Oakmont is ideal for an afternoon or evening stroll and a bit of window-shopping.

MAP 7: 300 Rte. 909, Verona, 412/828-0410, www.theinnatoakmont.com

DOUBLETREE BY HILTON HOTEL PITTSBURGH–MONROEVILLE CONVENTION CENTER $$

Formerly a somewhat disappointing and run-down Radisson Hotel, this Doubletree ($129-239) location (just off the Pennsylvania Turnpike) has literally been renovated from the inside out, and it shows: The interiors are modern and even a touch trendy, which isn't a feature you're likely to find at most other Monroeville-area hotels. Along with the standard pool, hot tub, and fitness center, you'll find Wi-Fi in the rooms and throughout the hotel's public areas. There's also a decent wine bar and a small bistro-style restaurant. Parking is free, and pets up to 25 pounds are allowed with a nonrefundable $50 deposit. You'll definitely need a car to travel around the Monroeville area, however, which is essentially an endless outdoor strip mall filled with chain restaurants and big-box stores. The Monroeville Convention Center, however, sits just across the street.

MAP 7: 101 Mall Blvd., Monroeville, 412/373-7300, www.doubletree.hilton

HILTON GARDEN INN PITTSBURGH/SOUTHPOINTE $$

Situated a good 20 miles south of the city in the Washington/Canonsburg area, this is the hotel *par excellence* ($119-239) for business travelers needing to stay within shouting distance of the South Hills suburbs; Upper St. Clair, McMurray, Mount Lebanon, and Bridgeville are all nearby. Amenities include a 24-hour business center, a small outdoor garden area with a gazebo, a fitness center with a swimming pool and whirlpool, and a grand ballroom that can easily fit 1,000. The rooms and suites are perfectly clean and accommodating, but they're fairly standard in terms of style and design. Forty-two suites are available, and parking and Wi-Fi are both free.

MAP 7: 1000 Corporate Dr., Canonsburg, 724/743-5000, http://hiltongardeninn.hilton.com

HYATT REGENCY PITTSBURGH INTERNATIONAL AIRPORT $$

Every decent-size airport in the country is surrounded by hotels that serve the sort of traveler who, for whatever reason, doesn't actually need to enter the urban center of the city she's just flown into. For those travelers, the Hyatt Regency ($119-209) offers an especially convenient solution: Thanks to an enclosed walkway attaching the hotel to the airport, lodgers can go from baggage claim to check-in without ever leaving the building. The interior, designed to resemble a modern boutique hotel, is equally impressive: You'll find detailed and tasteful touches almost everywhere, from the warmly accented lobby to the fitness center. The hotel is ADA compliant, and pets are allowed. At $25 daily, however, parking is pricey.

MAP 7: 1111 Airport Blvd., 724/899-1234 or 800/233-1234, http://pittsburghairport.hyatt.com

Excursions

As any serious grid-hopper would most likely admit, sometimes the best part about visiting a city is waving goodbye. After all, in order to gain proper perspective on a place, first you've got to gain some distance. And even those with an unending love of the concrete jungle occasionally need to escape its reach.

Even if you're only planning on being in Pittsburgh for a week or two, I'd still encourage you to consider at least a brief day trip, if not a slightly longer weekend adventure. And while it's probably something of a widespread assumption that the further reaches of Western Pennsylvania don't have much to offer the average traveler, the exact opposite, in fact, is true.

Globetrotters the world over have long been visiting the state's Laurel Highlands, and for good reason: Not only does world-famous architecture coexist with the quiet beauty of wooded nature, but regular ol' fun can be had as well, especially along the banks of the almost-unpronounceable Youghiogheny (pronounced yaw-ki-GAY-nee) River, where some of Pennsylvania's wildest tubing and rafting takes place.

And while art, history, and railroad museums seem to exist in every last nook and cranny of this corner of the world, it's quite likely that you'll experience much more in locales with less institutional flavor: In a booth at a backwoods diner, for instance, where the apple pie and the eccentric locals remind you more of *Twin Peaks* than "America the Beautiful." Or maybe in front of the

Look for ★ to find recommended excursions.

HIGHLIGHTS

★ **Boldest Ode to Local Ingenuity:** The Big Mac sandwich was invented by a McDonald's franchise owner in the mid-1960s. The **Big Mac Museum Restaurant** is, naturally, the place to show your due respect (page 299).

★ **Best Residential Architecture:** Still regarded as one of the finest examples of American residential architecture, **Fallingwater** is quite possibly the most gorgeous—and the most photogenic—of Frank Lloyd Wright's works of utilitarian art (page 301).

★ **Best Retro Amusement Park: Idlewild Park** isn't necessarily the place to visit for death-defying roller coasters. But for a quaintly thrill-packed weekend afternoon, it can't be beat. Bring your "bathing costume" for a trip to **SoakZone,** the on-site water park (page 303).

★ **Best River Rafting:** Whether you're looking to master some of the country's most vicious Class V white-water rapids or would prefer to float lazily along a slow river in a giant inner tube, you'll find scores of outfitters along the banks of the Youghiogheny in **Ohiopyle State Park** (page 305).

★ **Best Landmark:** A must-see sight for rail fans the world over, the **Horseshoe Curve National Historic Landmark** is a 220-degree curve outside Altoona at the Kittanning Gap. Even today, it's considered an absolutely masterful feat of modern engineering (page 312).

★ **Classiest Tribute to a Local Tragedy:** No matter what's on your itinerary, an afternoon at the somber but impressive **Johnstown Flood Museum** is a must. The flood is still considered one of the country's worst natural disasters (page 312).

★ **Best State Park:** With its Old Mill and its covered bridge, the forested **McConnell's Mill State Park** in Portersville is as picturesque as it is welcoming to adventurists (page 318).

★ **Best Blast from the Past:** Just a short drive from Downtown Pittsburgh, **Old Economy Village** is the former home of the somewhat bizarre yet fiscally ingenious Harmony Society. The village gives some of the best clues as to how the society lived and worked (page 319).

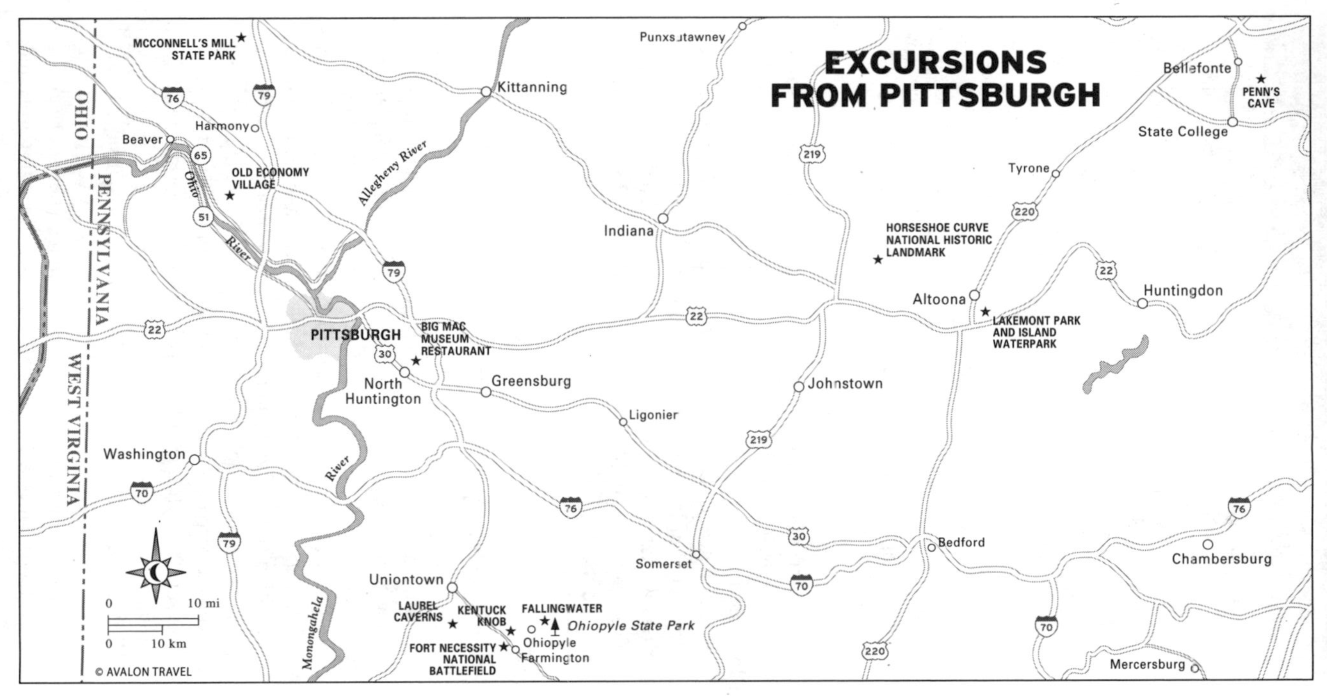
EXCURSIONS FROM PITTSBURGH
MCCONNELL'S MILL STATE PARK
Punxsutawney
Bellefonte
PENN'S CAVE
State College
Kittanning
Harmony
Beaver
OHIO
PENNSYLVANIA
WEST VIRGINIA
OLD ECONOMY VILLAGE
Ohio River
Allegheny River
Tyrone
Indiana
HORSESHOE CURVE NATIONAL HISTORIC LANDMARK
Altoona
LAKEMONT PARK AND ISLAND WATERPARK
Huntingdon
PITTSBURGH
BIG MAC MUSEUM RESTAURANT
North Huntington
Greensburg
Johnstown
Ligonier
Washington
Monongahela River
Uniontown
LAUREL CAVERNS
KENTUCK KNOB
FALLINGWATER
Ohiopyle State Park
Ohiopyle
FORT NECESSITY NATIONAL BATTLEFIELD
Farmington
Somerset
Bedford
Chambersburg
Mercersburg
0 10 mi
0 10 km
© AVALON TRAVEL

The Jimmy Stewart Museum

The city of Indiana is a pretty good distance to travel for just one museum, but for hardcore Jimmy Stewart fans, the pilgrimage will be more than worth your while. The now-deceased star of the silver screen grew up in Indiana, and the town boasts a statue of his likeness as well as the **Jimmy Stewart Museum** (835 Philadelphia St., Indiana, 724/349-6112 or 800/835-4669, www.jimmy.org, Mon.-Sat. 10am-4pm, Sun. noon-4pm, admission $7 adult, $6 senior, $5 child), which can be found inside the Indiana library and next to its city hall.

The museum contains all manner of movie memorabilia pertaining to Stewart's life, including posters and film clips. There's also a decent gift shop. Don't miss the separate room dedicated to the Stewart family history in Western Pennsylvania—Jimmy Stewart's kin, apparently, have lived in and around the Indiana area since the time of the Civil War.

While at the museum, ask for directions to Jimmy's boyhood home, which remains a private residence. Also ask for directions to the former location of J. M. Stewart & Sons Hardware, Jimmy's father's store, where he worked as a boy.

shelves at an out-of-the-way thrift store, where a stack of ultra-rare vinyl records are waiting for you in a wooden bin and priced at a dollar each.

But ultimately, it doesn't much matter which way you explore the outer reaches of Pittsburgh or how you decide to have fun. What matters is that you've simply gotten out there. You've explored. You've tried something new. And when the novelty of the rural areas and the tiny little towns begins to wear thin, you know what to do, right? (Hint: Sometimes the best part about visiting the country is waving goodbye.)

PLANNING YOUR TIME

Because Pennsylvania is such a large and sprawling state, it's wise to consult a decent map before simply heading out on the highway. The Keystone State is packed with quaint rural areas, small towns that modern time seems to have forgotten, and still-pristine wilderness areas. But it's also heavy with industrial detritus and drab four-lane highways. So do yourself a favor and take the time to sit down with a friendly guesthouse or bed-and-breakfast owner, or a decent state guidebook, before setting out. For comprehensive state and day-trip info, I recommend *Moon Pennsylvania,* by Anna Dubrovsky, *Pennsylvania Off the Beaten Path,* by Christine O'Toole, and *Pennsylvania Curiosities,* by Clark DeLeon.

Visitors without a lot of time to spare should consider heading toward the nearby Laurel Highlands. Not only can the area be reached quickly by car from Pittsburgh (about an hour's drive), but it also offers a wide variety of popular activities, from protected wilderness areas to amusement parks to world-famous works of architecture.

Those with a bit more time on their hands might also consider heading north to the Lake Erie area. Aside from the grandeur of the Great Lake itself, Erie is home to the seven-mile-long peninsula known as Presque Isle State Park. Along the way, interesting little towns and unique shopping opportunities are not far from I-79.

Laurel Highlands

The Laurel Highlands region contains a wealth of diverse activities. A family of four with differing interests may need to visit four separate sites to keep everyone happy, but for what it's worth, you'll probably find all four of them here. The area's most popular tourist attraction is Frank Lloyd Wright's Fallingwater, but if you're planning to visit the house during a quick day trip, consider leaving a little earlier and mixing in a few side activities along the way.

A massive archive of area activities can be found on the website of the **Laurel Highlands Visitors Bureau** (120 E. Main St., Ligonier, 724/238-5661 or 800/333-5661, www.laurelhighlands.org).

SIGHTS

★ Big Mac Museum Restaurant

Pittsburgh boosters are quite fond of reminding out-of-towners that McDonald's iconic Big Mac sandwich was invented in the region (by franchise owner Jim Delligatti in 1965). The **Big Mac Museum Restaurant** (9061 U.S. 30, North Huntingdon, 724/863-9837, www.bigmacmuseum.com, Mon.-Fri. 4:30am-midnight, Sat. 4:30am-1am, Sun. 5:30am-11pm) is positive proof of that very fact. And aside from bowing down at the altar of the famous sandwich, you can also sink your teeth into one, as this site actually is a working McDonald's restaurant. You'll find a life-sized bust of Delligatti himself, a ridiculously huge (and unnervingly lifelike) Big Mac statue, and classic McDonald's memorabilia. Whether you're a junk food junkie or a pop culture obsessive, you'll get a kick out of this over-the-top homage to the two all-beef patties. (Take Exit 67 off the Pennsylvania Turnpike.)

Bushy Run Battlefield

Named after a small area stream of the same name, the events that took place in the summer of 1763 at **Bushy Run Battlefield** (1253 Bushy Run Rd., Jeannette, 724/527-5584, www.bushyrunbattlefield.com, Wed.-Sun. 9am-5pm, admission $5 adult, $3 child) were certainly nothing fun. While pressing west in an effort to relieve the soldiers who'd been defending Fort Pitt (the present-day Point State

clockwise from top left: SoakZone; Big Mac Museum Restaurant; the Flight 93 National Memorial

Park), a British army was ambushed by Native Americans. As is always the case with turf wars, much blood was spilled on both sides.

The 250th anniversary of the battle at Bushy Run occurred in 2013, so what better time than now—especially given our own country's current conflicts—to remind yourself and perhaps your family that history always repeats itself? Aside from being the Keystone State's only recognized Native American battlefield, Bushy Run offers live battle reenactments, troop encampments, a visitors center, and guided tours of the battlefield itself.

Compass Inn Museum

At **Compass Inn Museum** (1382 Rte. 30 E., Laughlintown, 724/238-4983, www.compassinn.com, Tues.-Sat. 11am-4pm, Sun. 1pm-5pm, admission $9 adult, $6 child), a restored 1799 stagecoach stop, guided tours given by docents in period costume share the story of how life was lived in the early 1800s, with a specific focus on transportation. This particular stagecoach stop was an inn, and on the grounds are three reconstructed outbuildings, including a blacksmith shop and a barn. Inside the barn visitors will see and learn about the Conestoga wagon and the standard stagecoach. The 90-minute tour also includes a stop at a reconstructed cookhouse, complete with a beehive oven. Gifts and period reproductions are available at the on-site country store, and hour-long candlelight tours are offered November through mid-December.

★ Fallingwater

Declared by architects and critics worldwide as one of the most stunning private structures ever built in the United States, Frank Lloyd Wright's **Fallingwater** (Rte. 381, Mill Run, 724/329-8501, www.fallingwater.org, Thurs.-Tues. 10am-4pm, admission $23 adult, $17 child) is an absolute must-see for anyone visiting Pittsburgh who also has access to a car. Considering that a mere 90-minute drive from Downtown will get you there, this makes for a fantastic day trip no matter what the season.

Designed in 1935 for the Kaufmann family, who at the time owned one of Pittsburgh's most profitable department store companies, Fallingwater is quite possibly the finest example of Wright's praiseworthy architectural philosophy, which he referred to as "organic architecture": Wright was a staunch believer in the concept that art and nature could coexist peacefully, so when Edgar J. Kaufmann asked for his house to be built next to a favorite waterfall in Mill Run, Wright instead designed it to rest *above* the falls. To see the house from its left or right side is equally stunning; Wright cleverly built the boxy sandstone shapes and cantilevered levels directly into the sloping earth.

After serving its initial purpose for 26 years (the house was used as a weekend getaway), Fallingwater opened to the public in 1963. Notably, it remains the only important Wright structure in the area open to the public with both its furniture and artwork intact. (Wright was legendary for wishing to control the interior look and layout of the homes he designed.)

Besides regular tours, visitors may choose an in-depth tour ($65 pp) or a sunset tour ($110 pp). Adjacent to the Fallingwater grounds is the 5,000-acre **Bear Run Nature Reserve**—great for hiking and bird-watching. And Frank Lloyd Wright's **Kentuck Knob** (www.kentuckknob.com)—another innovatively designed residence—is only seven miles away.

Flight 93 National Memorial

Regardless of anyone's personal opinion about what exactly happened, or who exactly was responsible, for the events that took place in this country on September 11, 2001, the fact remains that a great many innocent people lost their lives on that day. And while the World Trade Center in New York City was certainly the most tragic of the three sites affected, there were victims in Southwestern Pennsylvania as well: the 40 passengers and crew members who were traveling aboard United Airlines Flight 93, which crashed into an open field in Somerset County. The permanent **Flight 93 National Memorial** (6424 Lincoln Hwy., Stoystown, 814/893-6322, www.nps.gov/flni, www.honorflight93.org, summer daily 9am-7pm, winter daily 9am-5pm, free) pays homage to them all.

A 2.5-mile access road leads to a one-mile ring road, which itself encircles a field adjacent to the crash site, where the passengers and crew now rest in peace. The memorial includes a tasteful and minimalistic white marble wall, on which all 40 names are engraved. Thousands of personal items left behind by visitors as tributes can be viewed along a 40-foot fence, which was erected specifically to display the mementos. The 150-acre Field of Honor, meanwhile, which covers one-half mile of land in diameter, links the entire site. Plans are currently in place to erect 40 memorial groves, as well as a visitor and education center.

Fort Ligonier

Built by the British for protection during the French and Indian War, the historical interest in **Fort Ligonier** (200 S. Market St., intersection of U.S. 30 and PA Route 711, Ligonier, 724/238-9701, www.fortligonier.org, mid-Apr. to mid-Nov. Mon.-Sat. 10am-4:30pm, Sun. noon-4:30pm, admission adult $10, child $6) is largely due to its seeming impenetrability: During its eight years of existence, the fort's walls were somehow never penetrated.

A full eight acres of the original fort site have been preserved and can be toured today. There's also an impressive museum featuring a French and Indian War art gallery, and a rare collection of pistols once owned by George Washington.

Fort Necessity National Battlefield

If you've already visited the Fort Pitt Museum in Pittsburgh's Point State Park, you may be encouraged to stop by **Fort Necessity National Battlefield** (1 Washington Pkwy., Farmington, 724/329-5512, www.nps.gov/fone, daily 9am-5pm, admission $5 adult, children 15 and under are free), where the French and Indian War of 1754 first rang out. To start, stop by the battlefield's **visitor center** for a current schedule of activities and to view a short film, *Road to Necessity,* which summarizes the bloody events that took place here. Interactive museum exhibits briefly explain the war as well.

Next, follow a short path to an area known as **Great Meadow.** Nestled into the shadow of the Allegheny Mountains, this is a site of serious historical proportions, as the war actually began here. Visitors feeling a bit restless may want to explore the five miles of hiking trails that surround the site, while history buffs might prefer the seven-mile side trip to **Jumonville Glen** (open daily 9am-4pm, free with paid admission to Fort Necessity National Battle Field), where George Washington met the French face to face for the very first time.

Ohiopyle State Park, Fallingwater, and Laurel Caverns are all nearby.

★ Idlewild Park and SoakZone

Originally constructed in 1878, **Idlewild Park** (Rte. 30 East, Ligonier, 724/238-3666, www.idlewild.com, June-Aug. daily 10:30am-8pm, $36.99 general admission, $27.99 senior, free child 2 and under) during its salad days wasn't much more than a recreational campground with picnic tables and an artificially constructed lake. As the mid-20th century approached, however, Idlewild began attempting to transform itself into an honest-to-goodness amusement park. That plan didn't fully come to fruition until 1983, when the Kennywood Park Corporation bought the company out.

Today, the park consists of seven theme areas, including Olde Idlewild, where the Ferris wheel, the merry-go-round, and other similarly quaint attractions are located, and **SoakZone,** a water park with various slides and pools. The five remaining areas, including Mister Rogers' Neighborhood of Make-Believe and Story Book Forest, are considerably tame, and clearly aimed more toward the youngest of guests rather than teenaged coaster fans or anyone seeking thrill rides.

Kentuck Knob

Although it's certainly less visited than Fallingwater, **Kentuck Knob**

(723 Kentuck Rd., Chalk Hill, 724/329-8501, www.kentuckknob.com, Apr.-Oct. Sun.-Tues. and Thurs.-Sat. 10am-4pm, Wed. noon-4pm, Nov. Sun.-Tues. and Thurs.-Sat. 10am-3pm, Wed. noon-3pm, tours $20 adult, $14 child) is nonetheless a fascinating and truly unique example of Frank Lloyd Wright's architectural genius. Exploring both structures during a day trip from Pittsburgh is definitely possible. Aside from the standard admission tour, brunch tours, sculpture garden tours, and in-depth tours are also available.

Wright was 86 years old when he designed Kentuck Knob for a family who'd visited Fallingwater a number of times and greatly admired it. Alternatively known as "Hagan House" and "The Child of Fallingwater," Kentuck Knob was constructed according to the specifications of a style Wright referred to as "Usonian," which had no attics or basements and was intended to keep building and utility costs low. Derived partly from Wright's Prairie-style homes, the Usonians were relatively small, one-story structures with flat roofs. Kentuck fits that descriptor well, although it also features a number of surprising 60-degree angles; the house was built on a hexagonal grid. (Pay attention while wandering around the house, as the hexagonal theme is repeated throughout.)

Laurel Caverns

Fifty miles south of Pittsburgh near Uniontown, 435-acre **Laurel Caverns Geological Park** (200 Caverns Park Rd., Farmington, 724/438-3003 or 800/515-4150, www.laurelcaverns.com, May-Oct. daily 9am-5pm, tours $12 adult, $10 child) offers a wealth of family-style activities, including 55-minute guided tours of the sandstone caverns, as well as much more strenuous caving exploration tours lasting as long as three hours. Before or after taking a tour of the caverns, visitors can pay $35 to rappel three times off a 45-foot-high cliff. And for a mere $6 per person there's Kavernputt, an 18-hole miniature golf course inside a 10,000-square-foot artificial cave. Gemstone panning, meanwhile, will set you back $6.

Originally called Laurel Hill Cave, and then Dulaney's Cave, Laurel Caverns is the largest cave in the state of Pennsylvania. It's also the 16th-longest developed cave in the United States; there are 2.8 miles of passages for visitors to safely explore. According to local historians and anthropologists, the caverns have been explored since the late 1700s and were once used by Native Americans as protection from enemies and the natural elements.

Because the temperature inside the caverns remains steady at about 55°F year-round, visitors are encouraged to bring sweaters or light jackets even on warm summer days.

Lincoln Highway Experience Museum

Any serious aficionado of roadside Americana knows that the

Steelers Training Camp

Serious football fans passing through the Laurel Highlands in midsummer should absolutely visit the **Pittsburgh Steelers Training Camp,** which has been held at **Saint Vincent College** (300 Fraser Purchase Rd., Latrobe, 724/537-4560, www.stvincent.edu, free) since 1968.

The six-time Super Bowl champs show up at some point in mid-July, and the camp, one of the most fan-friendly in the NFL, lasts for roughly one month. Practices open to the public tend to run 3pm-5pm daily. (Morning practices are off-limits.) The training schedule is neither finalized nor made public until a few weeks prior to the camp's start, so keep an eye on the Steelers website (www.steelers.com) for details.

If you're planning on bringing little ones, consider enrolling them in **The Steelers Experience,** a kid-friendly program that takes place during the Steelers afternoon practices, on a field adjacent to the Steelers themselves. Players, coaches, and other team employees host games, exhibits, and simulated practice sessions for kids. Check the website or call the college for more information.

Saint Vincent is also home to the **Fred Rogers Center** (300 Fraser Purchase Rd., Latrobe, 724/805-2750, www.fredrogerscenter.org), where visitors can stop by the multimedia **Fred Rogers Exhibit,** an interactive display designed for both adults and children.

Lincoln Highway, which was formally dedicated on Halloween, 1913, was our country's first coast-to-coast highway. Most visitors to the Laurel Highlands, however, aren't aware that the historic highway traverses the area. Those who'd care to educate themselves should pay a visit to the **Lincoln Highway Experience Museum** (3435 U.S. 30 East, Latrobe, 724/879-4241, www.lhhc.org/lhexperience.asp, Mon.-Fri. 9am-4pm, admission $4 adult), perhaps the kitschiest tourist attraction in all of Southwestern Pennsylvania.

A brief documentary about the highway is one of the museum's highlights, but don't miss the gift shop, where crafts by area artisans mix with books, collectible items, and goofy pop-culture trinkets. Best of all, the price of admission includes a copy of the 60-page *Lincoln Highway Driving Guide.* But if you'd prefer to simply tour the highway on your lonesome, explore the website at www.lhhc.org (click the "LH Tour" tab), where self-guided trip suggestions abound.

★ Ohiopyle State Park

Encompassing just over 19,000 forested acres, **Ohiopyle** (724/329-8591, www.dcnr.state.pa.us) provides standard state park activities: biking, trekking, horseback riding, fishing, and even hunting. But without a doubt, the vast majority of Pittsburghers who come here have something else in mind: a white-water boating or white-water rafting trip on the ever-popular Youghiogheny ("yaw-ki-GAY-nee") River.

clockwise from top left: Fort Necessity visitor center; rafting in Ohiopyle State Park; Fallingwater

Soar Like a Bird

Visitors to the Laurel Highlands who happen to have an adventurous streak will likely be pleased to learn that the quickly growing trend of ziplining has recently reached the area. At the **Adventure Center at Nemacolin Woodlands Resort** (1001 Lafayette Dr., Farmington, 724/329-8555, www.nemacolin.com), a high-altitude obstacle course known as the **Fatbird Canopy Tour** ($90-100 pp) is your destination. The three ziplines are some of the longest in the state.

The **Ohiopyle Zip Line Adventure Park** (4 Sherman St., Ohiopyle, 724/329-8531, www.laurelhighlands.com/activities/Zipline, $15-39 pp) is another option. Two levels of difficulty allow children as young as four to participate. While not nearly as death-defying as the aforementioned Fatbird Canopy, the 200-foot Ohiopyle zipline experience involves a similar up-in-the-air jungle gym complete with spider-web netting, wooden logs, and rickety bridges.

Finally, there's the **Canopy Tour & Zip Line Course** at **Seven Springs Mountain Resort** (777 Waterwheel Dr., Seven Springs, 814/352-7777, www.7springs.com, $47 pp). The nearly 2,000 feet of ziplines include the **Screaming Hawk Zipline,** which allows adrenaline junkies to pause briefly on a series of swaying wooden towers, some of them standing 350 feet in the air. This one ain't for the squeamish, folks.

There are all sorts of reasons why Pennsylvanians love the Yough (pronounced "yock"), but the diversity of the river is certainly at the top of the list. Beginners can easily float down the Lower Yough's Class II rapids, while at the same time, some of the country's most experienced rafters can challenge themselves in the Class IV and V rapids of the Upper Yough, where some of the finest white-water rafting on the entire East Coast takes place. Numerous outfitters in the area rent equipment and offer tours for all levels.

Camping at Ohiopyle is a possibility—visit the park's website for detailed information and a campground map. Wooden camping cottages that sleep five people are also available.

What's more, Ohiopyle doesn't empty out during the winter months. Snowmobiling, cross-country skiing, and sledding all take place.

Saint Vincent Gristmill

Built in 1854 by the same community of Benedictine monks who continue to grind grain here today, **Saint Vincent Gristmill** (300 Fraser Purchase Rd., Latrobe, 724/537-0304, www.saintvincentgristmill.com, Mon.-Sat. 9am-4pm, free) offers a rare opportunity to experience a religious tradition that isn't often made public. The Gristmill General Store sells hard-crusted breads baked by the monks, jams, flour, bread mix, and more. An on-site museum contains exhibits and screens a video of the milling process, while the **Gristmill Coffeehouse** (Mon.-Thurs. 8am-9pm, Fri.-Sat. 8am-5pm) offers free Wi-Fi. A viewing area offers the opportunity to watch the monks at work, but because the grinding schedule varies, it's not always possible to catch the brothers in action.

Westmoreland Museum of American Art

One of only three museums in the state that focus exclusively on American art, the **Westmoreland Museum of American Art** (temporary location at 4764 State Road 30, Greensburg, 724/837-1500, www.wmuseumaa.org, Wed.-Fri. noon-7pm, Sat.-Sun. 10am-5pm, free) has been welcoming visitors to Greensburg ever since 1959. Especially in its first two decades, the curatorial team managed to build a rather impressive collection of work by American masters, including paintings by Winslow Homer, Mary Cassatt, and John Singer Sargent.

Along with various paintings and portraiture, items kept in the permanent collection include sculpture, toys, works on paper (such as lithographs and etchings), and decorative arts, which include jugs, cupboards, and other largely utilitarian pieces.

Families visiting the museum might enjoy spending time at KidSpace, a hands-on interactive room where children can make their own creations while surrounded by pieces from the museum's folk art collection.

Due to an expansion and renovation project, the museum is currently residing at a temporary location. In the spring of 2015, the collection will return to the permanent building (221 N. Main St., Greensburg).

RESTAURANTS

Located in downtown Ligonier, the **Ligonier Tavern** (137 W. Main St., Ligonier, 724/238-4831, www.ligoniertavern.com, Mon.-Thurs. 11:30am-9pm, Fri.-Sat. 11:30am-10pm, Sun. noon-8pm, $17-24) has three separately designed dining rooms inside a beautifully detailed turn-of-the-20th-century Victorian house. Cuisine is fairly casual and leans toward American and seafood. Sandwiches, salads, pasta, and chicken entrées are all popular. If the weather is nice, diners can choose to sit outside on the house's second-floor patio. A bakery offers a wide selection of fantastic cakes.

With a name like **Ruthie's Diner** (1850 U.S. 30, Ligonier, 724/238-9930, daily 6am-9pm, $7-11), you can probably guess the sort of food that's on offer: burgers, sandwiches, and cups of black coffee, for the most part. This is the perfect place to make a pit stop if you're in the midst of road-tripping and searching for the heart of America, or some such romantic notion. And as any local will surely tell you, Ruthie's also serves one of the finest breakfasts in town. Not terribly healthy, of course, but delicious and protein-packed just the same.

Adjacent to the Great Allegheny Passage (GAP) at the West Newton Trailhead is **The Trailside** (108 W. Main St., West Newtown, 724/872-5171, www.thetrailside.com, daily 11am-11pm, $6-10), a casual American-bistro-style eatery serving sandwiches, burgers, and salads. Ask for a table on the outdoor deck, which overlooks the GAP trail and the Youghiogheny River. Free Wi-Fi is available, and a pub offers a decent selection of craft beers.

HOTELS

Home to one of only six Frank Lloyd Wright homes in the country in which visitors can actually stay the night, the most sought-after accommodation at **Polymath Park Resort** (1 Usonian Dr., Acme, 877/833-7829, www.polymathpark.com) is known as **Duncan House** ($399). It's a minimalist Usonian-style structure, and visitors must rent the entire home, which is actually a bargain when you consider it sleeps six. Other structures on the resort that can be rented include the **Blum House** ($299), with its geometric windows and roof lines, and the **Balter House** ($299); both were designed by Wright's apprentice, Peter Berndtson. For those who'd rather bunk elsewhere, tours of the resort ($22 pp) take place Sunday through Friday at 11:30am, 12:30pm, and 1:30pm.

Roughly a 20-minute drive from Fallingwater is the **Lodge at Chalk Hill** (2920 National Pike, Rte. 40 East, Chalk Hill, 724/438-8880 or 800/833-4283, www.thelodgeatchalkhill.com, $70-200), a recently renovated lakeside lodge and mountain retreat situated on 37 acres of land. Visitors to Ohiopyle, Fort Necessity, Laurel Caverns, and the Christian W. Klay Winery (www.cwklaywinery.com) will all find their destinations within an easy drive of the lodge.

Along Route 40 in Farmington, the historical **Stone House Inn** (3023 National Pike, Farmington, 724/329-8876, www.stonehouse-inn.com, $99-209) sits a mere two miles from the Fort Necessity Battlefield. Fallingwater, Kentuck Knob, and Ohiopyle are also close. One of the first inns to open along the National Road, Stone House Inn has been lodging and feeding travelers since 1822. There are seven Victorian-style bed-and-breakfast suites on-site, as well as six modern rooms in the New Zeigler Wing that come complete with whirlpool tub, contemporary furnishings, and other modern conveniences.

A four-star luxury resort, **Nemacolin Woodlands Resort** (1001 LaFayette Dr., Farmington, 724/329-8555 or 866/344-6957, www.nemacolin.com, $319-2,999) is so lovely that you may decide not to leave the grounds at all. Visitors and guests can indulge in golfing, luxurious spa packages, casual or fine dining, and a wide variety of adventure or cultural-recreation activities. Lodgers have a choice of six different accommodation options, including a boutique hotel, a classic European-style hotel, a lodge, and a townhouse. Nightly rates are steep but well worth the unique experience.

Not far from Seven Springs Mountain Resort is the **Historic Log Cabin Inn** (191 Main St., Donegal, 724/771-9131, www.historiclog-cabininn.com, $149-349), which was built sometime around 1750 and truly is just as fun as it sounds. It's said to have the largest logs in the county, and you'll even find a potbelly stove and a natural log staircase. Supposedly, George Washington once spent the night.

Backpackers and GAP cyclists requiring affordable lodging will be pleased to learn of **The Hostel on Main** (506 Main St., Rockwood, 814/926-4546, www.hostelonmain.com, $22-50), in a historical building that was renovated in 2009. It offers three private rooms, a standard dorm with bunk beds, and bicycle storage and racks.

PRACTICALITIES

Visitors Center

The **Laurel Highlands Visitor Bureau** is in Ligonier (120 E. Main St., 724/238-5661 or 800/333-5661, www.laurelhighlands.org; Mon.-Fri. 9am-5pm). Information for Fayette, Somerset, and Westmoreland Counties can be collected at the bureau, or you can simply gather the info online.

Media

The region's largest newspaper is Greensburg's right-leaning ***Tribune-Review*** (www.triblive.com), a daily that also publishes a Pittsburgh-specific edition. The daily ***Herald-Standard*** (www.heraldstandard.com), headquartered in Uniontown, covers Fayette County, while Somerset County is covered by the ***Daily American*** (www.dailyamerican.com) newspaper. Johnstown's largest newspaper is the ***Tribune-Democrat*** (www.tribune-democrat.com).

Getting There

The majority of the Laurel Highlands' major attractions can be accessed by heading east out of the city on U.S. 30. Yet since the region is so large, drivers will probably want to have an updated road atlas on hand. Rand McNally's oversized *The Road Atlas* is probably the country's most popular; it can be purchased at most major bookstores and also includes driving maps of Canada and Mexico.

Greyhound buses (800/231-2222, www.greyhound.com) regularly travel to cities within the Laurel Highlands region.

A one-way **Amtrak train** ride (412/471-6172 or 800/872-7245, www.amtrak.com) from Pittsburgh to Greensburg will set you back $10-20.

The **Arnold Palmer Regional Airport** (www.palmerairport.com) serves the Greater Greensburg area.

Getting Around

For the most part, visitors to Laurel Highlands should arrive with a car or other private vehicle. Contact information for travel and transportation options can be found on the website of the **Laurel Highlands Visitors Bureau** (www.laurelhighlands.org), including companies that offer organized tours of the area.

Visitors to Greensburg can visit the website of the **Westmoreland County Transit Authority** (www.westmorelandtransit.com) for schedule and fare information.

Altoona, State College, and Johnstown

Even if you're a longtime Pittsburgh resident who knows the Steel City inside and out, if you haven't yet explored much of Johnstown, you may very well find yourself surprised at the fairly large number of activities and sights of interest the town offers. And Johnstown's a simple drive, too: If you're headed east toward the Westmoreland Museum of Art or Idlewild, you're halfway there.

Not much farther northeast is Altoona, which is something of an international meeting point for rail fans. (The Railroaders Memorial Museum and the Horseshoe Curve Historic Landmark are both there.) Continue onward to State College, the home of Penn State University. It's a perfectly quaint college town and also home to small museums and interesting cave sites, many of which can be explored during guided tours.

SIGHTS

Frank & Sylvia Pasquerilla Heritage Discovery Center

Included with the price of admission to the Johnstown Flood Museum is admission to the **Frank & Sylvia Pasquerilla Heritage Discovery Center** (201 6th Ave., Johnston, 814/539-1889 or 888/222-1889, www.jaha.org/DiscoveryCenter/virtualtour.html, daily 10am-5pm, admission $8 adult, $7 senior, $6 student). It tells the stories of the thousands of southern and eastern European immigrants who flocked to Johnstown during the last two decades of the 1800s and the first decade of the 1900s.

You'll learn what life was like in Johnstown for a Slovakian butcher, a Russian shopkeeper, and a Hungarian goose farmer, to name just a few. Through an interactive video display, visitors will also view the experience of immigrants being questioned at Ellis Island, and they'll learn about the conditions in Europe that led many to seek a new life elsewhere in the first place.

Other exhibits at the museum show what life was like in the steel mills where many immigrants toiled, while a theater exhibition includes interviews with both the children and grandchildren of the immigrants.

★ Horseshoe Curve National Historic Landmark

A longtime favorite of hardcore rail fans who journey to Altoona to visit the Railroaders Memorial Museum is the **Horseshoe Curve National Historic Landmark** (visitors center at 40th St. and Burgoon Rd., Altoona, 814/941-7960, www.railroadcity.com, Mon.-Sat. 10am-4pm, Sun. 11am-4pm, admission $6 or free with admission to Railroaders Memorial Museum). A legendary railroad curve located about six miles west of Altoona at the Kittanning Gap, the rail's extreme bend is, in fact, shaped like a horseshoe. Its 220-degree arc was designed by J. Edgar Thomson; it opened to trains in 1854 as a way to significantly reduce the travel time from one end of Pennsylvania to the other. The arc was necessary because of the summit of the Allegheny Mountains, which the track was designed to skirt. Designated as a National Historic Landmark in 1966, the curve has been a successful tourist attraction for decades.

Stop by the visitors center first, where displays illustrate the construction of the curve. The center also features a gift shop packed with items of interest to the rail fan. From there, guests can ride a funicular railway up to the train tracks, or they can choose to hike up the stairway instead.

★ Johnstown Flood Museum

The **Johnstown Flood Museum** (304 Washington St., Johnstown, 814/539-1889 or 888/222-1889, www.jaha.org/FloodMuseum/oklahoma.html, daily 10am-5pm, admission $8 adult, $7 senior, $6 student) documents a massive flooding catastrophe that took place in that city on May 31, 1889, and in which 2,209 people perished. The causes of the disaster were a neglected dam and a massive storm.

Those who stop at this especially well-developed museum will have the chance to view artifacts and documents relating to the greatest tragedy ever to befall the city of Johnstown, including a 26-minute Academy Award-winning documentary film that recreates the flood by using archival photos. Also on-site is a relief-map model that uses lights and sound effects to illustrate the flood's path through the Conemaugh Valley. Particularly moving—even disturbing—is the museum's collection of personal artifacts that were recovered after the flood, including a set of keys belonging to a telegraph operator who warned of the dam's impending danger. Also part of the permanent exhibit is an original, renovated "Oklahoma House." Although they were originally designed for Oklahoma Territory homesteaders, the prefab houses, which measured either

Flood City Music Festival

Should you happen to find yourself in the Pittsburgh area over Labor Day weekend, and should you happen to be a fan of Americana and roots music—blues, zydeco, folk, jazz, and R&B, for instance—you're in luck. That's when the **Flood City Music Festival** (www.floodcitymusic.com, $25-30) takes place at **People's Natural Gas Park** (90 Johns St., Johnstown), which can be found just across the river from Point Stadium and beside the Cambria Iron Company National Historic Landmark.

Throughout the three days of the festival, which was formerly known as the Johnstown FolkFest, concertgoers can expect to hear roughly 70 hours of live music by bands both world-famous and nearly unknown. Past performers have included Los Lobos, Sleepy LaBeef, The Smithereens, Sharon Jones and the Dap-Kings, Brave Combo, Robert Cray Band, Big Sandy & His Fly-Rite Boys, Robbie Fulks, Southern Culture on the Skids, Buckwheat Zydeco, and R. L. Burnside. Check the festival's webpage for information about accommodations and driving directions. Free parking is generally available—signs will be posted—and free shuttle buses frequently travel back and forth between parking lots and the festival grounds.

Insider tip: The town's legendary **Inclined Plane** operates free of charge throughout the festival's three days.

10 by 20 feet or 16 by 24 feet, were also used to shelter refugees of the Johnstown flood.

Visitors can also request information about a downtown Johnstown walking tour, on which many historical buildings that survived the flood can be seen. More information about the tour and a map of the downtown area can be found on the museum's website.

Johnstown Inclined Plane

Known as the world's steepest vehicular inclined plane, the cable cars of the **Johnstown Incline** (711 Edgehill Dr., Johnstown, 814/536-1816, www.inclinedplane.org, Apr.-Sept. Mon.-Thurs. 8am-10pm, Fri. 8am-11pm, Sat. 9am-11pm, Sun. 9am-10pm, tickets $2.25 one way, $4 round-trip) travel 896.5 feet up the side of Yoder Hill—which has a grade of 70.9 percent—to reach an elevation of 1,693.5 feet. Built by the Cambria Iron Company in 1890 and 1891, the incline was designed specifically so that residents of the hilltop community known as Westmont could easily transport their horses and wagons from ground level to home and back again.

However, on March 1, 1936, the incline served a distinctly different role when, once again, the city suffered a flood. Nearly 4,000 area residents were lifted to dry, higher ground via the incline. The cable cars served the same emergency purpose again on June 20, 1977, during the city's most recent flood.

Visitors to the incline, which was built by Samuel Diescher, the engineer also responsible for building Pittsburgh's Duquesne and Monongahela Inclines, can walk out onto an extended observation deck that offers a rather lovely view of the Johnstown area. A visitors center displays archival photographs of the city and its numerous floods, and from the center's lobby it's possible to view the massive machinery of the incline in action. The **James Wolfe Sculpture Trail** is directly behind the incline.

Lakemont Park and Island Waterpark

Although it first welcomed visitors in 1894 as a trolley park, and then in 1899 as a full-fledged amusement park, **Lakemont Park** (700 Park Ave., Altoona, 800/434-8006, www.lakemontparkfun.com, call for hours, admission Wed.-Fri. $5, Sat.-Sun. $9.95) isn't a particularly large attraction. The few rides include two roller coasters and a go-kart track. Also on-site and included with the price of admission is **Island Waterpark,** complete with slides and pools. Visitors are welcome to enjoy the park's 18-hole miniature golf course and its arcade.

Historically speaking, Lakemont holds two particularly interesting claims to fame: Not only is it the eighth-oldest amusement park in the country, but it's also home to the historical Leap-The-Dips coaster, a wooden ride built in 1902 that is the world's oldest. The figure-eight style design makes for a fairly slow and gentle ride. The coaster was given its due respect back in 1996, when it was awarded National Historic Landmark status.

Penn's Cave

Known as the country's only all-water cavern, **Penn's Cave** (222 Penns Cave Rd., Centre Hall, 814/364-1664, www.pennscave.com, call or visit website for hours, cavern tours $16.95 adult, $8.95 child) is a particularly unique local site. Because the caverns are literally flooded, guided one-hour tours are given by motorboat. Along the way, visitors will see stalagmites, stalactites, and limestone corridors, and trout can often be seen jumping high above the water. (Look out for the stalagmite that bears a striking resemblance to the Statue of Liberty.)

Penn's Cave also offers a 90-minute wildlife, farm, and nature tour ($19.95 adult, $11.95 child), during which safari buses shuttle visitors throughout the area's 1,500 acres of preserved forests and fields. Mountain lions, wolves, bison, black bears, and wild mustangs are just some of the animals you may encounter. The new **Prospector Pete's Miners Maze** ($5.95 adult, $2.95 child) is a 4,800-square-foot maze full of twists and turns; it's especially popular with kids.

Railroaders Memorial Museum

One of Western Pennsylvania's most popular railroading attractions, the **Railroaders Memorial Museum** (1300 9th Ave., Altoona, 814/946-0834, www.railroadcity.com, Mon.-Sat. 9am-5pm, Sun. 11am-4pm, admission $10 adult, $9 child, $8 senior) was designed specifically to honor the American railroaders who have contributed significantly to the country's culture and industry. And it makes good sense that the site is located in Altoona: Not only has the city long been known as an important epicenter of rail activity, but the Horseshoe Curve National Historic Site and the Staple Bend Tunnel (the country's first railroad tunnel) are both nearby. (Admission to the Horseshoe Curve is included.)

Built in 1998, the museum uses a mixture of interactive displays, video presentations, and exhibits to tell the cultural and social story of those who worked in the industry. In other words, the major emphasis is not on the wheels and tracks that moved the industry forward, but rather on the people who worked on and alongside the rails throughout the 1920s. And because the light-and-sound exhibits are fairly advanced, the museum feels much more like a place to play than simply a place to drearily read placards and gaze at dusty models.

RESTAURANTS

Conveniently located in Somerset, **The Summit Diner** (791 N. Center Ave., Somerset, 814/445-7154, daily 5am-10pm, $7-14) is a 24-hour greasy spoon with surprisingly good food. You'll find it open for business literally every day of the year. The menu is filled with American standards, and the hotcakes are a local favorite. All the meat is cut and served right in the restaurant's own kitchen.

A third-generation family-owned and -operated establishment, **Mel's Restaurant and Bar** (127 W. Patriot St., Somerset, 814/445-9841, www.somersetcounty.com/mels, daily 9am-2am, $3-11) is the sort of honky-tonk café where one might expect to find a preponderance of gentlemen sporting cowboy hats and chewing tobacco. The menu is a low-budget selection of cheeseburgers, hot dogs, and sloppy joes, and don't be surprised if yours is served on a paper plate. Mel's also boasts a 240-square-foot dance floor, live music on the weekend, and a pool table.

HOTELS

Tucked away in the Allegheny Mountain Range near Blue Knob is the **Majestic World Lodge and Retreat** (679 Memory Ln., Portage, 814/693-0189 or 877/365-6972, www.majesticworldlodge.com, $95 and up), a family-owned and -operated lodge 3,000 feet up in the Alleghenies—one of the highest elevations in the state. The lodge itself is a converted, historical barn where guests can gaze out at an elk herd from the comfort of a covered wooden deck. The grounds are absolutely gorgeous, and incidentally, the snowy winter season is a particularly picturesque time of the year to visit. In spring, the grounds are covered with a carpet of lovely wildflowers.

All rooms are uniquely designed; rustic types will feel especially at home amongst the patchwork quilts and incredibly creative headboards fashioned from antler horns and cedar logs. The inn offers hunts for elk, red stags, whitetails, buffalo, fallow deer, and rams.

Nearby attractions include the historical **Bedford Village** (220 Sawblade Rd., Bedford, 814/623-1156, www.oldbedfordvillage.com, admission adults $10, senior $9, student $5, daily 9am-5pm) and the numerous sights and museums of Johnstown. The home field of the **Altoona Curve** (1000 Park Ave., 814/943-5400, www.altoonacurve.com), a minor league baseball club, is roughly a 35-minute drive away.

One of the most gorgeous and unusual places to spend the night in Somerset County, the **Stone Ridge Bed & Breakfast** (2825 Carpenters Park Rd., Davidsville, 814/288-3931, www.stoneridgebb.com, $130-175 d) is essentially an A-frame lodge that guests have all to themselves. The grounds couldn't be more romantic—especially during winter. The A-frame comes complete with a stone fireplace, two bedrooms, and two decks, one with a grill. A hot tub is available for use year-round, and the especially rustic surroundings are home to numerous animals, including wild turkey and deer. Blue Knob, Seven Springs Mountain Resort, and Hidden Valley are all relatively close, and downtown Johnstown is only seven miles away.

Bunking at **Schantz Haus** (687 E. Campus Ave., Davidsville, 814/479-2494, $65-80), a bed-and-breakfast that sits on 120 acres of farm land, is a good call for visitors who'd like to add a little rural adventure to their accommodations. It sits on a working dairy farm, and guests can milk cows or bottle-feed a calf.

PRACTICALITIES

Tourist Offices

The **Central Pennsylvania Convention & Visitors Bureau** (800 E. Park Ave., State College, Mon.-Fri. 7:30am-6pm, Sat.-Sun. 9am-6pm, 814/231-1400 or 800/358-5466, www.visitpennstate.org) services State College and offers resources for outdoor adventures and cultural and sporting events.

The Altoona section of the **Official Tourism Website of the State of Pennsylvania** (www.visitpa.com/cities/altoona) is a good resource, along with the **Altoona Visitors Bureau** website (www.explorealtoona.com).

Those headed to Johnstown should check out the **Greater Johnstown/Cambria County Convention & Visitors Bureau** (111 Roosevelt Blvd., Ste. A, Johnstown, 814/536-7993 or 800/237-8590, www.visitjohnstownpa.com, Mon.-Fri. 8am-5pm, Sat.-Sun. 11am-3pm), in particular for information on seasonal events, such as the city's annual **PolkaFest** (www.visitjohnstownpa.com/polkafest).

Media

The daily ***Tribune-Democrat*** (www.tribune-democrat.com) is the best-known newspaper covering the Johnstown area, while ***Johnstown Magazine*** (www.johnstownmag.com) digs deeper into the culture and lifestyles of the region. Pick up a copy of the ***Centre Daily Times*** (www.centredaily.com) newspaper for daily news about the Central Pennsylvania area. ***State College Magazine*** (www.statecollegemagazine.com) celebrates the region in all its glossy, four-color glory. The daily ***Altoona Mirror*** (www.altoonamirror.com) covers both Altoona and State College.

Getting There

From Pittsburgh, a drive to either Altoona, State College, or Johnstown will require a trip on U.S. 22. Those headed to Johnstown will eventually go south on Route 219, while explorers venturing up to Altoona or State College will use Route 220.

Greyhound buses leave the Downtown Pittsburgh depot multiple times a day for State College. Buses leave twice a day each for Johnstown and Altoona.

Amtrak trains service Altoona.

University Park Airport (www.universityparkairport.com) is right in State College and offers flights to major hubs, including Philadelphia, Detroit, and Washington/Dulles.

Getting Around

Public transport in the State College area is handled by CATA, the **Centre Area Transportation Authority.** Visit www.catabus.com for schedules and a downloadable PDF of the most recent Ride Guide. To order a taxi in the area, call **AA Taxi** (814/231-8294).

The **Cambria County Transit Authority** (www.camtranbus.com) is responsible for public transportation in Johnstown; when in Altoona use **AMTRAN** (www.amtran.org). For 24-hour **taxi service** in either Cambria or Somerset County, call 814/535-4584 or 814/539-1584.

Beaver County and Butler County

The counties of Beaver and Butler sit just north of the city of Pittsburgh and are quite often considered a part of Pittsburgh, especially by the counties' own residents. Old Economy Village and the Harmony Historic District are the big tourism draws—at both sites you can observe the unique and alternative ways of living practiced by the now-nonexistent Harmony Society.

For more extensive information, spend some time on the counties' official tourism sites, www.visitbeavercounty.com and www.visitbutlercounty.com.

SIGHTS

Harmony Historic District and Harmony Museum

Founded in 1804 and now a National Landmark District, the **Harmony Historic District** is a relatively small but engaging area where examples of both Harmonist and Mennonite lifestyles can be seen and studied. This walkable area is where the **Harmony Museum** (218 Mercer St., Harmony, 724/452-7341, www.harmonymuseum.org, Tues.-Sun. 1pm-4pm, admission $7 adult, $6 senior, $3 child) can be found. At the museum you'll see an example of a communal Harmonist room; also on-site is a Harmonist wine cellar, accessible by way of a stone-cut staircase. The museum also owns a small collection of Native American artifacts that were discovered in the area.

Other structures of interest in the district include the **Wagner-Bentel House,** which is a brick duplex that was constructed by the Harmonists for two sisters and their families, and the reconstructed **Henry Denis Ziegler log house,** which sits directly across the street from the museum and is made of hand-hewn oak logs.

★ McConnell's Mill State Park

Encompassing 2,546 acres of the Slippery Rock Creek Gorge, **McConnell's Mill State Park** (via I-79 near the intersection of U.S. 19 and U.S. 422, Portersville, 724/368-8811, www.dcnr.state.pa.us, open daily sunrise-sunset, free) is named after a logging mill built to channel the creek's water, as well as the water's power. The park has long been a favorite day trip for those living in Pittsburgh's northern suburbs, but considering that it's less than 40 miles from Downtown, it also makes for a worthwhile excursion for city visitors in need of a quick wilderness break.

There are any number of activities to keep you occupied once inside the park. You're almost certain to see rock climbers, especially if you venture toward Rim Road's climbing area, which sits on the other side of the creek from the Old Mill (where an emergency phone is also located). Head to the intersection of Breakneck Bridge Road and Cheeseman Road to reach the advanced climbing area. White-water rafting and kayaking are also big, and with seven miles of trails, it would be simple to pass half a day simply exploring the pristine, forested splendor of the region.

The **McConnell's Mill Heritage Festival** takes place during the third or fourth weekend of September. The operational era of the Old Mill (1852-1928) is celebrated during the festival, and visitors can enjoy activities such as corn-grinding demonstrations and old-time musical entertainment.

To reach the park from Downtown, take I-79 to U.S. 19 (Exit 28). Look for signs pointing toward McConnell's Mill Road, where you'll find the park sitting roughly 1,000 feet north of the U.S. 19 and U.S. 422 intersection. From mid-May through the end of October, 45-minute interpretive tours of the **Historic Gristmill** (1761 McConnells Mill Rd., Portersville, 724/368-9320, Fri.-Sun. 11am-4pm, free) take place.

★ Old Economy Village

Formerly the home of the 19th-century communal Christian group known as the Harmony Society, the village of Economy, known in its current restored form as **Old Economy Village** (270 16th St., Ambridge, 724/266-4500, www.oldeconomyvillage.org, Tues.-Sat. 10am-5pm, Sun. noon-5pm, admission $10 adult, $9 senior, $6 child), was in its day widely recognized as a God-fearing and stoically hard-working place.

The Harmonists fled Germany in the late 1700s due to persecution from the Lutheran Church and went on to purchase 3,000 acres of land in Pennsylvania's Butler County. After moving to Indiana and then returning to Pennsylvania, they settled here; their curious sect is today regarded as one of the country's most successful experiments in economics and alternative living. Completely regardless of gender, the Harmonists shared all manner of village tasks; they also produced everything needed for survival within the confines of the village. And although the society lasted for more than a century, no Harmonists remain today. Why not? The society's members were all unmarried, and none believed in the concept of procreation. Oops.

Nonetheless, the Harmony Society's history and the Old Economy Village site both make for fascinating studies. Village visitors will have the opportunity to see the society's community kitchen, its cabinet shop and blacksmith shop, a granary, the Economy Post Office, and more.

Grove City Premium Outlets

About an hour's drive from Downtown Pittsburgh, **Premium Outlets** (1911 Leesburg Grove City Rd., Grove City, 724/748-4770, www.premiumoutlets.com, Mon.-Sat. 10am-9pm, Sun. 10am-7pm) is an almost ridiculously large outlet mall—it covers so much ground, in fact, you may have to return for a second visit in order to see it all. There are 130 brand-name outlet stores, including American Eagle, Ann Taylor, Banana Republic, BCBG Max Azria, Brooks Brothers, Calvin Klein, Coach, Gap Outlet, Guess, J.Crew, Nike, and Polo Ralph Lauren. Also available are housewares, home furnishings, children's apparel, lingerie, and luggage. To book a group tour of 15 or more, visit the website.

RESTAURANTS

The locally beloved and admired **Restaurant ECHO** (1740 Rte. 228, Cranberry Township, 724/779-3246, www.restaurantecho.com, Mon.-Fri. 11:30am-2pm and 5pm-midnight, Sat. 5pm-midnight, Sun. 4pm-9pm, $10-29) was previously known only as a world-class fine-dining spot serving European-influenced New American cuisine at eye-popping prices. The restaurant's newly opened **ECHO Bistro,** however, features casual fare, dozens of beer choices, and a genuinely affordable lunch menu.

A self-described beanery, eatery, brewery, and community center, the **North Country Brewing Company** (141 S. Main St., Slippery Rock, 724/794-2337, www.northcountrybrewing.com, Mon.-Thurs. 11am-11pm, Fri.-Sat. 11am-midnight, Sun. 11am-10pm, $8-23) is close to McConnell's Mill State Park. The on-site brewery is phenomenal, the weekly specials often include wild game, and the creatively built sandwiches and burgers are exactly what you'd expect to find in a college town: mouthwatering and especially large. Check the website for live music schedules.

If your itinerary includes a quick side-trip to the Mars town square in Butler County, where a **UFO-style flying saucer** (Brickyard Rd., Mars) makes for a fantastic photo-op, you might also want to pop into the **Mars Brew House** (502 Pittsburgh St., Mars, 724/625-2555, www.marsbrewhouse.com, Mon.-Sat. 8am-5pm, $2-7) for a quick pick-me-up. No, the Brew House isn't an alien abduction site; it's a friendly and cozy coffee shop offering sandwiches and salads alongside the standard espresso drinks and teas. Live acoustic music performances happen Saturday noon-2pm.

HOTELS

Particularly popular with golfers, **Conley Resort** (740 Pittsburgh Rd., Butler, 800/344-7303, www.conleyresort.com, $84 and up) offers all guests a complimentary breakfast as well as use of the on-site waterpark, which consists of two slides, a pool, a sauna, a hot tub, and a replica of a pirate ship with its own water cannon. Guests also receive a discount at the resort's golf course. Rooms are nothing to shout about but are certainly clean and comfy enough. And since Conley is such a spacious place, it's also a popular spot for business meetings and conferences.

Located on a 175-acre farm in the Butler County town of Renfrew is the **Heather Hill Bed and Breakfast** (268 Rader Scholl Rd., Renfrew, 724/538-5168, www.heatherhillbnb.com, $85-140), where the farm animals range from Peruvian Paso horses to Hereford cattle. The renovated 1821 farmhouse includes four bedrooms, a game room, three wood-burning stoves, and a large country-style kitchen.

Family-run and just five minutes from Beaver's shopping district, **Willows Inn** (1830 Midland Beaver Rd., Industry, 724/643-4500 or 866/660-4501, www.willowsinnpa.com, $65 and up) has 30 recently remodeled rooms, free wireless access, and famously delicious smorgasbords. It also has a banquet hall and a pub onsite. Penn State's Beaver campus is a 10-minute drive away, and both Geneva College and Old Economy Village are 20 minutes away.

PRACTICALITIES

Tourist Offices

The **Beaver County Recreation & Tourism Department,** in the Bradys Run Recreation Facility (121 Bradys Run Rd., Beaver Falls, 800/342-8192, www.visitbeavercounty.com, Mon.-Fri. 8:30am-4:30pm), offers information on attractions, seasonal events, lodging, and other amenities.

The **Butler County Tourism & Convention Bureau** (310 E. Grandview Ave., Zelienople, 724/234-4619 or 866/856-8444, www.visitbutlercounty.com, Mon.-Fri. 8:30am-4:30pm) provides information on cultural events, sports, local history, and much more.

Media

The ***Butler Eagle*** (www.butlereagle.com) is a major daily newspaper serving the residents of Butler County. While in Beaver County, pick up the daily ***Beaver County Times*** (www.timesonline.com).

Getting There

Driving to both Beaver and Butler Counties from Downtown Pittsburgh is a breeze: Simply take U.S. 22 west to U.S. 30 west to reach Beaver. For Butler, head out of the city on I-279 north, which turns into I-79 north. Pittsburgh's Yellow Cab drivers will be all too happy to shuttle you anywhere within the two counties, but be sure to ask about any extra fees you might accrue by traveling outside Allegheny County.

Getting Around

The **Beaver County Transit Authority** (724/728-8600, www.bcta.com) is responsible for operating the region's bus service; schedules, maps, and more can be found its website. For information about travels in and around Butler County, visit the website of **The Bus** (www.butlertransitauthority.com), or call 724/283-1783. Information about various **limousine and taxi services** in Butler County can be found at www.visitbutlercounty.com. Or, call the **National Taxi Directory** (www.1800taxicab.com) toll-free at 800/TAXI-CAB (800/829-4222) for further information. The NTD offers telephone numbers of the nearest taxi companies based on the phone number you're calling from.

Background

The Setting

Because of the three rivers that wind and wend their way throughout all stretches of the city, and also because of the small hills and deep valleys that seem to appear out of nowhere in this region, Pittsburgh is well known as an often difficult-to-traverse part of the country. Yet it's also known as a deeply beautiful place. Much of Southwestern Pennsylvania, as well as much of suburban Pittsburgh, is heavily forested; many regions are blanketed with strong trees and wildlife.

Within Pittsburgh's inner-city limits, the story is much different. The majority of the neighborhoods where tourists will find themselves are quite urban, and many of the most interesting East End areas are surrounded by low-income neighborhoods.

GEOGRAPHY AND CLIMATE

Pittsburgh is located in the southwest corner of the state of Pennsylvania, where it sits near the foothills of the Allegheny Mountains. The city sits 696 feet above sea level.

In total, Pittsburgh consists of 58.3 square miles, with 55.6 square miles consisting of landmass and 2.7 square miles consisting of water. In other words, approximately 4.75 percent of the City of Pittsburgh is water.

The city sits on a landmass known as the Allegheny Plateau; this is the area where the city's three rivers—the Allegheny, the Monongahela, and the Ohio—come together at the westernmost tip of the Downtown Pittsburgh area, which is also known as the Golden Triangle.

Pittsburgh is an especially hilly city, and while it has a continental climate with four seasons, it's also a relatively rainy and snowy place, with approximately 37 inches of rain annually and 43 inches of snow annually.

Pittsburgh's temperature varies widely throughout the year, with the winter months of December, January, and February averaging a low temperature of a chilly 22°F and the summer months of June, July, and August averaging a high temperature of a rather steamy (and often humid) 82.6°F.

ENVIRONMENTAL ISSUES

Because of the many industrial factories and steel-producing mills that dotted the Pittsburgh cityscape for roughly 150 years, it was inevitable that the town would eventually suffer from the effects of environmental pollution. In fact, during much of the 20th century, the entirety of Pittsburgh was so smoke- and soot-covered that visitors nicknamed it "The Smoky City"; still very much a part of

Steel City lore are stories of businessmen leaving the confines of their Downtown offices during the lunch break and returning an hour later to find their white shirts turned dark gray. As a result of the pollution, an alarmingly large number of Pittsburghers living within the city limits at the time suffered from respiratory illnesses. But thanks to the steadfast efforts of one of the city's most popular mayors, David Lawrence, things began to change for the better during the 1950s, as smoke control became a leading local issue.

And although Pittsburgh has a good distance to travel before it becomes a leading national light in the area of environmental pollution control (emissions from public buses are still a heated issue, for instance), many changes have been made for the better. The locally based Green Building Alliance (www.gbapgh.org) is a nonprofit organization concerned with integrating environmentally responsible design into new area construction. Pittsburgh can now claim the world's first LEED-certified convention center, the David L. Lawrence Convention Center, and the country's first LEED-certified dormitory, Carnegie Mellon University's Stever House (formerly New House Residence Hall). In fact, Western Pennsylvania today is home to more than 500 professionals with LEED credentials.

History

It's something of a little-known fact that Pittsburgh's history is very much intertwined with that of our nation's first president, George Washington, who first visited the area in 1753. Then a 21-year-old major, Washington surveyed the land at the junction of the Allegheny and Monongahela Rivers (the current location of Point State Park) and wrote that it was "extremely well suited for a Fort; as it has the absolute Command of both Rivers."

Perhaps not surprisingly, the French were also impressed by the city's strategic location at the fork of the three rivers. In 1754, they managed to drive Washington's Virginia militia away, and then built a fort on the site themselves. It was named Fort Duquesne. Four years passed, and the British, led by General John Forbes, defeated the French and reclaimed the fort, which was first rebuilt and then renamed. (The wily French had burned the fort to the ground before fleeing.) The new site became known as Fort Pitt, after William Pitt, the English prime minister. On the first day of December, General Forbes named the camp at Fort Duquesne "Pittsburgh."

In 1787, roughly a decade after a heated dispute between the states of Virginia and Pennsylvania, both of whom wanted to claim Pittsburgh as their own, the Pittsburgh Academy was founded in a small log cabin; it would eventually become the University of Pittsburgh. (The cabin can still be visited on Pitt's campus to this day; it sits near the corner of Forbes Avenue and Bigelow Boulevard.)

Clearly, the Pittsburgh of the late 18th century was becoming an outpost to reckon with; the weekly *Pittsburgh Gazette,* the first newspaper to exist west of the Alleghenies, had seen its first issue the year prior. In 1816, Pittsburgh was finally incorporated as a city. By 1820, Pittsburgh's population was just north of 7,000 souls. A decade later, it had grown to more than 12,500.

Pittsburgh had its first experience with major tragedy in 1845, when a fire destroyed roughly a third of the city and left about 12,000 people homeless. Less than a decade later, Pittsburgh's reputation as the "Smoky City" began to grow: The Jones & Laughlin Steel Corporation was founded in 1853. The Clinton iron furnace opened in 1859. And then in 1864, at the age of 29, Andrew Carnegie decided to join the iron business. A Scotsman, he soon became known as the richest man in America. In 1889 he dedicated the region's first Carnegie Library, which still operates in Braddock, and in 1900 he founded the Carnegie Technical School, now known as Carnegie Mellon University.

A true city of industry, Pittsburgh continued cranking through a series of milestones for the next 50 years: The first World Series was played here in 1903; the first motion picture house opened here in 1905; the country's first commercial radio station broadcast from here in 1920. For all its successes, however, Pittsburgh's reputation as an unpleasant place to visit managed to precede it. At the time, the town was known as one of the most polluted cities in America; streetlights were often kept on throughout the day. That all began to change in 1946, though, when Mayor David Lawrence kicked off the city's first official Renaissance, an urban renewal plan that eventually stripped Pittsburgh of its Smoky City image and transformed it into the epicenter of medicine, education, technology, and culture that it is today. One of the city's biggest triumphs came in 1953, when Dr. Jonas Salk discovered the polio vaccine at the University of Pittsburgh.

Although its population has been in steady decline for decades, Pittsburgh continues to march on as a top-ranked metropolis, and in both 1985 and 2007 it was named "America's Most Livable City" by Rand-McNally's *Places Rated Almanac.* That honor was repeated in 2009 by *The Economist,* and again in 2010 by *Forbes.*

In 1989, the city elected its first female mayor, the much-loved Sophie Masloff. And then in 2006, another victory: The Pittsburgh Steelers, whose successful 1970s franchise resulted in the town becoming known as the City of Champions, managed to regain a touch of their former glory by winning a fifth Super Bowl. Just three years later, the Steelers tumbled into the history books by grabbing an unprecedented sixth Super Bowl win.

PITTSBURGH TODAY

No one can deny that Pittsburgh made giant leaps in its effort to become a world-class city during the urban redevelopment process known as Renaissance II. Officially begun in 1980, this was when the city saw construction of Three Rivers Stadium and a bevy of downtown skyscrapers and shopping centers, including USX Tower, Mellon Bank Tower, Oxford Centre, and PPG Place. Pittsburgh's intention was to transform itself from a city of industry into a tech, medicine, and education hub. This was all well and good, until along came the disaster known as Renaissance III.

Led by then-mayor Tom Murphy, RIII was centered on redeveloping and revitalizing the city's downtown core, especially the area around Market Square. Pittsburghers weren't fond of Murphy's plan, which was to drive out decades-old retailers and bring in big-box chains, and ultimately the scheme failed. Before long, the abandoned Fifth and Forbes Corridor, as the area is known, was filled with empty storefronts.

As if that weren't enough, Pittsburgh in the early part of the 21st century has been feeling the burn of a serious image crisis, during which many of the town's young and creative types have left in search of brighter opportunity and better jobs elsewhere. Attempting to halt this flow, a group of corporate and civic leaders in 2002 and 2003 created the Image Gap Committee. Soon, the city had burned through roughly $200,000 in grant money to acquire a new motto, a Pittsburgh font, and even a city-specific color scheme. The so-called Pittsburgh Regional Branding Initiative was widely mocked, and the city's image didn't seem to have improved much as a result.

That all began to change in late 2006, however, when the newly elected mayor, Bob O'Connor, unexpectedly died as a result of cancer and was replaced by Luke Ravenstahl, who'd been serving as City Council president. At the time, Ravenstahl was just 26 years old—the youngest mayor in the city's history, by a long shot. Naturally, Ravenstahl's entrée to Pittsburgh politics attracted a good deal of media attention, both locally and nationally, and not all of it was positive. Ravenstahl was widely mocked, for instance, after appearing on the *Late Show with David Letterman,* during which he spoke in a pronounced Pittsburgh accent. And yet while his mayoral run certainly had its controversial moments, the general consensus among average Pittsburghers seems to be that Ravenstahl did a decent job for the city, by and large.

Pittsburgh's current economic stability, for instance, is a particularly strong indicator that the city has at least begun the process

The Best, the Worst, and Everything in Between

You may have heard of Pittsburgh's notable civic commendation, which, interestingly enough, came in the form of a 2012 article in *National Geographic Traveler* magazine.

The article in question was the magazine's annual roundup known as "Top 25 Places"—the 25 locales across the globe considered by *Nat Geo*'s editors to be the year's most desirable and of-the-moment travel destinations. Tucked in between such exotic destinations as Sri Lanka and Croatia was the Steel City itself. To say that local hearts were aflutter would be putting it mildly.

In fact, for a midsized town that most outsiders—and even some locals—tend to think of as unremarkable at best, Pittsburgh seems to have quite an uncanny knack for popping up on such lists. Then again, the city has also had more than its fair share of egg-on-face moments where the mainstream media is concerned. Here's a brief list of some of the other national yardsticks by which Pittsburgh has been measured.

- **America's worst bicycling city:** *Bicycling Magazine*, 1990
- **America's worst city for singles:** *Forbes*, 2004
- **America's eighth drunkest city:** *Forbes*, 2006
- **Most livable city in America:** Rand-McNally's *Places Rated Almanac*, 2007
- **America's 25th fittest city:** *Men's Health*, 2009
- **America's third-worst hair city:** TotalBeauty.com, 2009
- **Most livable city in America:** *Forbes*, 2010
- **America's 10th dirtiest city:** *Forbes*, 2010
- **Twentieth prettiest city in the world:** Huffington Post, 2010
- **America's 28th best bicycling city:** *Bicycling Magazine*, 2010
- **Third worst-dressed city in America:** *GQ*, 2011
- **America's second-best city for moms:** The Daily Beast, 2011
- **America's eighth-best city for single mothers:** Zillow.com, 2011
- **America's sixth vainest city:** *Men's Health*, 2012
- **America's fourth most-literate city:** Central Connecticut State University, 2012
- **One of the country's 10 best cities for older singles:** AARP, 2012
- **America's eighth most-polluted city:** American Lung Association, 2013
- **America's best city for retirement:** NerdWallet.com, 2013

of getting itself back on track. In fact, quite unlike most other North American metropolitan areas, Pittsburgh has managed to remain economically strong throughout the Great Recession of the 2000s. Jobs have been lost here at a much slower rate than in other cities of similar size, and the housing market has actually improved over the past few years.

In 2009, Pittsburgh became the subject of nationwide curiosity once again when President Barack Obama and the White House choose the city to host the G20 summit, a meeting of political and financial world leaders. According to the president, the inspirational story of Pittsburgh's economic recovery was a major reason why the city was recommended as a host. Its national reputation as a leader in ecological building practices apparently didn't hurt either, and in fact the summit was held at the David L. Lawrence Convention Center, one of the largest LEED-certified buildings in the world.

All in all, the future is looking decidedly bright for Pittsburgh today. It's a city that recently celebrated its 250th anniversary, and where major construction and urban revitalization projects seem to be popping up quicker than ever. As usual, the future of the city of Pittsburgh can probably best be expressed with one lone punctuation symbol: a question mark.

Government and Economy

GOVERNMENT

Although Pittsburgh was a serious Republican stronghold in the years prior to the Great Depression, the city and its surrounding Allegheny County have largely supported Democratic politicians and ideals in the decades since. The city's support of Democrats initially came about in the 1930s, when immigration to the area was in full bloom, largely due to the huge need for unskilled laborers to populate the area's mills. Indeed, President Franklin Delano Roosevelt's Works Progress Administration proved so popular with the city's largely Eastern European immigrant population that voting Democrat essentially became expected of members of Pittsburgh's working class. Today, that tradition continues, and in Allegheny County there are roughly 2.25 registered Democratic voters for every registered Republican.

ECONOMY

Pittsburgh first became an economic powerhouse in the mid-1800s, thanks to the efforts of Scottish immigrant Andrew Carnegie and others involved in the city's iron, steel, and glass industries. The American steel industry suffered a massive collapse in the early 1980s, however, as production began moving to more affordable plants overseas. Displaying the most admirable side of its entrepreneurial and hardworking nature, Pittsburgh steadfastly refused to wither away and took immediate and massive strides to reinvent itself. The city today owes its economic strength to a diverse mixture of health care, education, technology, and biotechnology. Finance and tourism also play important roles.

The University of Pittsburgh Medical Center (UPMC) is by far the region's largest employer, with some 27,000 employees in Allegheny County alone. West Penn Allegheny Health System and the University of Pittsburgh both employ approximately 10,000 area residents each. Nonetheless, Pittsburgh continues to lead the country in population decline. Although the city claimed 677,000 residents in 1950, today fewer than 312,000 remain. This likely has much to do with Allegheny County's current per capita income, which rests at $26,140.

A number of Fortune 500 and Fortune 1,000 companies continue to be headquartered in Pittsburgh, including Alcoa, PPG Industries, and Allegheny Technologies. Other well-known mega-companies headquartered in Pittsburgh include American Eagle Outfitters, Bayer Corporation, Westinghouse Electric, and 84 Lumber. At the time of writing, the future of Pittsburgh's long-beloved H.J. Heinz Company was unclear; in early 2013 it was acquired for $23 billion by Warren Buffet's Berkshire Hathaway and the private equity firm 3G Capital.

Health Care

It simply isn't possible to overstate the contribution of the University of Pittsburgh Medical Center to the local economy. Easily the largest employer in Western Pennsylvania, UPMC is also responsible for much of the area's construction boom; the organization spends roughly $250 million annually on construction activity. And because of the patients, families of patients, and investment dollars it attracts from around the county, UPMC estimates that every dollar it spends generates $1.25 for the region itself. Considering that UPMC's annual budget stretches just past $5 billion, it goes without saying that the center's contribution is invaluable for the Southwestern Pennsylvania region.

West Penn Allegheny Health System, the region's second-most important economic leader in the health-care industry, consists of Allegheny General Hospital, West Penn Hospital, Canonsburg General Hospital, and other regional hospitals.

Education

Referred to by some civic boosters as the College City, the greater Pittsburgh area is home to 33 colleges and universities, the most prominent being the University of Pittsburgh, Carnegie Mellon University, and Duquesne University. Economically, Pitt is the area's powerhouse; the school pours more than $350 million annually into area businesses whose goods and services keep the behemoth afloat. The university's annual payroll exceeds $530 million, and

Pitt is responsible for roughly $200 million in government revenues, such as real estate and sales taxes, each year.

More than 135,000 college and university students matriculate at a Pittsburgh area school each year. Some schools, such as Carlow University, Chatham College, the Art Institute of Pittsburgh, Point Park University, and Robert Morris University, sit right within the city limits. Other schools, such as Seton Hill University, Slippery Rock University, Indiana University of Pennsylvania, and Washington & Jefferson College, are spread throughout the southwestern region of the state.

More information can be found on the website of the Pittsburgh Council on Higher Education (www.pchepa.org) and at www.thecollegecity.com.

Technology and Biotechnology

Pittsburgh's tech and biotech industries are much larger and more developed than even most locals realize. Carnegie Mellon University continues to take giant strides in the fields of robotics and software engineering; the school's Software Engineering Institute (a federally funded research and development center) spent upward of $43 million in 2003.

Organizations such as the Pittsburgh Lifesciences Greenhouses (a joint venture between Pitt and CMU) have been instrumental in positioning Southwestern Pennsylvania as a bioscience, nanobiotechnology, and robotics leader. Researchers study neurological disorders, tissue engineering, and drug discovery, among other biotechnology developments.

To stay abreast of local tech news and information, check out the website of the Pittsburgh Technology Council (www.pghtech.org).

People and Culture

POPULATION

In 2010, the U.S. Census Bureau listed the population of Pittsburgh as 305,704. That figure represents a whopping population decline from 2000, when the census counted a total of 334,563 Pittsburgh residents. Currently, women and senior citizens are well represented in Pittsburgh; the population is nearly 52 percent female, and persons over the age of 65 make up 13.8 percent of the population. Twenty-six percent of Pittsburgh's population is black or African American, while the local population of Hawaiians and other Pacific Islanders is so small that the group failed to rate on the census report. Just over 68 percent of all Pittsburghers are white or Caucasian.

Historically, Pittsburgh has welcomed immigrants since the mid-1700s, the majority being from southern and eastern European countries such as Italy and Poland. Pittsburgh saw its largest influx of European immigration during the end of the 19th century and the beginning of the 20th. The majority came in search of work, having heard of Pittsburgh's reputation as an industrial powerhouse. Many of the smaller row houses (or "mill houses") that still stand today in Lawrenceville, the South Side Slopes, and other riverside neighborhoods were first occupied by these eastern European laborers.

A good number of early immigrants also came to Pittsburgh from Germany and Ireland. The North Side of Pittsburgh, originally a separate city known as Allegheny, is the region where the majority of the city's German immigrants settled, and in the East End neighborhood of Squirrel Hill, Hebrew and Yiddish are still widely spoken on the streets today.

THE ARTS

Probably because Pittsburgh has for so long been an industrial town with a deeply woven blue-collar temperament, many of the fine arts, performing arts, and visual arts haven't caught on here as quickly or successfully as in other metropolitan cities of equivalent size. And although Pittsburghers tend to vote Democratic, ours is something of a rural-influenced backwoods culture. Professional sports are hugely popular; a citywide passion for the Pittsburgh Steelers in particular seems to be the one cultural quirk that unites all Pittsburghers.

For the most part, Pittsburghers are a very proud people; regional pride is something you're likely to encounter over and over again during your stay. Unlike on the more recently developed West Coast, a large number of Pittsburgh residents have lived in the area their entire lives. In many cases, their parents have as well; grandparents of Pittsburghers in their late 20s and early 30s were quite often European immigrants. Many of those life-long Pittsburghers, especially those who grew up within the city limits and speak with an accent known as "Pittsburghese" (technically North Midland U.S. English) are referred to as "yinzers." This is generally considered a derogatory term, and shouldn't be used outside of familiar company. To learn about the unique Southwestern Pennsylvania accent, visit www.pittsburghspeech.com and www.pittsburghese.com.

Today, Pittsburgh's arts scene is slowly gaining both traction and national attention. The Pittsburgh Symphony Orchestra has long been noted as one of the nation's best. And due in large part to the city's extremely low cost of living, young artists and other creative types have been relocating to Pittsburgh—generally in the neighborhoods of the East End—from bigger and more expensive urban areas.

Arts, Crafts, and Folk Traditions

At the Smithsonian-affiliated **Senator John Heinz History Center** (www.pghhistory.org), scads of interesting facts about Western Pennsylvania's history and heritage can be investigated. The 200,000-square-foot museum includes exhibits about Pittsburgh's glass-making and wood-making history; examples of decorative metalwork from a locally based company are also displayed.

At the **Pittsburgh Glass Center** (www.pittsburghglasscenter.org), tours and demonstrations are given in the flame-working and glass-blowing rooms. Classes, private lessons, and studio rentals are available for further study.

At the Strip District's **Society for Contemporary Craft** (www.contemporarycraft.org), works of metal, wood, glass, clay, and fiber can be viewed. Pittsburgh artists are occasionally featured, although the majority of the works are created by non-mainstream artists from around the world.

Pittsburgh Center for the Arts (www.pittsburgharts.org) has frequently changing gallery rooms and a popular schedule of classes for both children and adults in ceramics, jewelry making, printmaking, bookbinding, creative writing, and more.

At **Artists Image Resource** (www.artistsimageresource.org) on the North Side, where silkscreens and other print works are displayed, anyone is welcome to use the studio's paints and supplies to silkscreen his or her own T-shirts, tote bags, or posters for a small fee. Open Studio nights and times change occasionally; contact 412/321-8664 or info@artistsimageresource.org for more information.

Particularly worthwhile is a day trip to the National Historic Landmark site of **Old Economy Village** (www.oldeconomyvillage.org), the former home of the 19th-century Harmony Society. You can tour the site and experience the Harmonists' lifestyle by participating in candle-making, bookbinding, and more.

Literature

Pittsburgh has long had a strong literary history, and, in fact, the University of Pittsburgh was the first institution of higher learning in the United States to offer a Master of Fine Arts degree in Creative Nonfiction. Pittsburgh author Lee Gutkind spearheads the program; he's also the founding editor of the literary journal *Creative Nonfiction,* which is headquartered in Shadyside.

Pitt's nationally regarded writing program has seen scores of well-known and widely published instructors; writers of note who've recently taught in the program include the hard-living fiction writer Chuck Kinder, who was one of Raymond Carver's best friends and, according to rumor, was the Pitt professor that the character in Michael Chabon's *Wonder Boys* is based on. (The street that Kinder's character lives on in the *Wonder Boys* film is South Atlantic Street in Friendship.) The poet Toi Derricotte was also a Pitt instructor, as was Faith Adiele, a nonfiction writer and the author of *Meeting Faith: The Forest Journals of a Black Buddhist Nun*. Current instructors of note include the poet Lynn Emanuel and the National Book Award winner Terrance Hayes.

Renowned poet Jack Gilbert (*Views of Jeopardy, Monolithos*) was born in Pittsburgh in 1925. Author David McCullough, who won the Pulitzer Prize for the masterful biography *John Adams,* is also a Pittsburgh native. And although he has since left town, author John Edgar Wideman (*Brothers and Keepers*) wrote highly regarded novels about African American life in the Pittsburgh neighborhood of Homewood. Pittsburgher Stewart O'Nan's novel *Everyday People* explored the hardscrabble life of African Americans living in the East End neighborhood of East Liberty.

Possibly better known than all the above combined are Pittsburghers Annie Dillard and Gertrude Stein. Dillard's *An American Childhood* examines the events of her childhood in 1950s Pittsburgh. Stein (*The Autobiography of Alice B. Toklas*) was a legendary feminist novelist and playwright who grew up on the city's North Side and eventually settled in Paris.

Music

Possibly Pittsburgh's most famous musician, historically speaking, was Stephen Collins Foster, who lived in Lawrenceville and is buried in Allegheny Cemetery. Foster was a singer, a song leader, and a composer whose first major success was "Oh! Susanna."

Pittsburgh has also produced its share of jazz legends. Although he was a native of Dayton, Ohio, Billy Strayhorn's music career officially began in Pittsburgh; today he's best known for composing the jazz staple "Take the A Train." The jazz pianist and composer Erroll Garner was born here in 1921; he went on to play with Charlie Parker, among others. Like Gertrude Stein, jazz drummer Kenny Clarke was born here but chose to settle in Paris. He's known as an important innovator of the bebop drumming style. Earl Hines was another well-known jazz pianist also born in Pittsburgh, as was Mary Lou Williams, who worked with Duke Ellington and Thelonious Monk.

Pittsburgh's most legendary jazz venue was the Hill District's Crawford Grill, which still stands today at 2141 Wylie Avenue. Throughout the 1930s, '40s, and '50s, Pittsburgh's Hill District (then known as "Little Harlem") and the Crawford Grill were both well known and respected in prominent African American social

Pittsburgh's Famous Faces

Regardless of its plain and simple "jus' folks" facade, the Steel City has cranked out an impressive roster of iconic celebrities in fields ranging from music and the visual arts to literature and theater. This is a list of superstars who were either born in the Pittsburgh area or lived and worked here for a significant length of time.

- **Actors and Hollywood players:** F. Murray Abraham, Steven Bochco, Dan Cortese, Ann B. Davis, Jeff Goldblum, Michael Keaton, Gene Kelly, Dennis Miller, Fred Rogers, George Romero, Tom Savini, Jimmy Stewart, Sharon Stone
- **Artists and writers:** Nellie Bly, Rachel Carson, Mary Cassatt, Willa Cather, Michael Chabon, Annie Dillard, Teeny Harris, Philip Pearlstein, Gertrude Stein, Bunny Yeager, Andy Warhol, August Wilson
- **Singers and musicians:** Christina Aguilera, Perry Como, Billy Eckstine, Stephen Foster, Erroll Garner, Wiz Khalifa, Henry Mancini, Bret Michaels, Mac Miller, Trent Reznor

circles. The jazz guitarist George Benson, in fact, was born and raised in the Hill District and later graduated from Schenley High School. The midcentury American doo-wop group known as the Del-Vikings, meanwhile, consisted of U.S. Air Force members who were stationed in Pittsburgh at the time of the group's founding.

Since the late 1970s, rock 'n' roll—especially the brand of rock now known as "classic rock"—has been favored in Pittsburgh. One of the area's most famous rockers is Joe Grushecky. As a longtime friend of Bruce Springsteen's, Grushecky has been known to bring the Boss to town—unannounced—to perform secret concerts at small clubs. Local musician Donny Iris was a pop and R&B superstar in his own right throughout the 1970s, and the Clarks, a rock group that still performs and records today, has managed to achieve national and even some international success. Bret Michaels, who fronted the world-famous hair-metal band Poison in the 1980s and early '90s and then went on to become something of a reality TV star, is also originally from the Pittsburgh area.

Of the city's more recent musical talent, the young rappers Mac Miller and Wiz Khalifa, along with electronic musician Girl Talk (Gregg Gillis), have seen the widest recognition outside Pittsburgh's borders. That is, unless you count Christina Aguilera, who grew up in Wexford. Other Pittsburgh-based bands of note include legendary punk outfits Aus-Rotten and Anti-Flag, the math-rock band Don Caballero, and the jam-band Rusted Root.

Television and Film

For a short while in the 1990s, thanks largely to the efforts of the Pittsburgh Film Office, it seemed as if Southwestern Pennsylvania was on its way to becoming a budget alternative to Hollywood.

Vancouver, British Columbia, seems to be claiming that honor for the time being, but movies and the occasional TV show continue to be filmed here with some regularity.

Certainly the city's proudest television accomplishment was the airing of *Mister Rogers' Neighborhood,* a genuine broadcasting treasure hosted by a true American icon, Fred Rogers, who passed away in February 2003. Produced for 33 years, it was the longest-running program ever aired by PBS.

A number of television shows have been set in Pittsburgh but filmed elsewhere, including *Mr. Belvedere,* which followed the trials and tribulations of an upper-middle-class Beaver Falls family; *My So Called Life,* a hugely popular teen drama that launched the careers of Claire Danes and Jared Leto; *Queer as Folk,* a Showtime series that followed the lives of a group of gay and lesbian friends who partied in the bars on Liberty Avenue; and *The Guardian,* a legal drama that alternated between real shots of Pittsburgh and fake shots filmed on a Culver City lot.

Pittsburgh's film history has been long and varied. Aside from the 1980s classic *Flashdance,* probably the most important movie filmed in the city remains George Romero's *Night of the Living Dead.* Much of the film, which Romero co-wrote with fellow Pittsburgher John Russo, was filmed in Evans City, which sits about 30 miles north of Pittsburgh in Butler County. Romero has since relocated to Toronto, although the famed makeup artist Tom Savini, who worked on Romero's *Dawn of the Dead* (a *Night of the Living Dead* sequel that was filmed inside the Monroeville Mall), still resides in the city.

Hollywood classics filmed in and around the Pittsburgh area in years past include *The Deer Hunter; Lorenzo's Oil;* and *The Silence of the Lambs,* a few scenes of which were shot in the Carnegie Museum of Natural History. More recent productions that have taken place locally include *The Dark Knight Rises; Out of the Furnace;* and *The Perks of Being a Wallflower,* which was based on the book of the same name by the Pittsburgh-raised author Stephen Chbosky, who also directed the film and wrote its screenplay.

To learn more about the city's film and television history and its current goings-on, visit the website of the Pittsburgh Film Office at www.pghfilm.org.

FESTIVALS AND EVENTS

Perhaps because so many pockets of Pittsburgh still preserve a proud small-town vibe, it's not unusual to see even the most plebeian of neighborhood parades, block parties, and ethnic-themed gatherings packed full of families, teenagers, or anyone else who happens to wander by. And should you choose to show up at one of Pittsburgh's annual citywide fests, you might wonder if maybe the entire town hasn't arrived. In particular, the Three Rivers Arts Festival, First Night Pittsburgh, and Light Up Night are absolute can't-miss events for any true local or, for that matter, any visitor interested in understanding what it means to live in the Steel City in the 21st century.

In other words, most festivals here are true community events, and not just excuses to swill cheap beer out of plastic cups (although if that's what you're looking for, you won't likely be disappointed).

The weeks between Memorial Day and Labor Day are a particularly active time for outdoor gatherings and organized events.

Winter

FIRST NIGHT PITTSBURGH

Yeah, I know: December 31 is actually the *last* night of the year, not the first. But hey, this is Pittsburgh; we're not exactly known for sweating the small stuff. Not that **First Night Pittsburgh** (Pittsburgh Cultural Trust, 803 Liberty Ave., 412/471-6070, www.firstnightpgh.com, free) is ever anything small. On the contrary, this is one of the most popular and packed events of the entire year, regardless of the fact that it's usually freezing cold outside. The party takes place in and around the Market Square and Cultural District areas of Downtown, and the celebration, naturally, is all about ringing in the New Year. The twist is that this party, parade, and overall people procession is family-friendly and alcohol-free (though you can sneak away for a drink in a nearby bar or restaurant that isn't participating in the festivities). Entertainment changes a bit from year to year but generally involves onstage music and dance, a street parade, copious food booths, and, at the end of the night, a spectacular fireworks display.

HANDMADE ARCADE

Pittsburgh's largest independent craft fair, **Handmade Arcade** (David L. Lawrence Convention Center, 1000 Ft. Duquesne Blvd., www.handmadearcade.com, free), held in December, started in 2004 and has been the city's favorite Etsy-style DIY marketplace for years. Independent crafters and offbeat artisans come from all over the city, the state, and even the country to display and sell everything from screen-printed T-shirts to hand-bound books and stationery to weird-o stuffed creatures, oddly unusual knitted accessories, buttons, badges, zines, and must-have home decor and kitchen accessories. To accommodate the many thousands who show up with cash in hand, the Handmade Arcade now takes place inside the convention center in Downtown. The Hands-on Handmade programs, which happen throughout the day, invite visitors to take part in mini-tutorials and crafting demos, perhaps transforming them into next year's artsy entrepreneurs. Early birds can pay a small fee (around $15) to receive a swag bag filled with coupons and handmade goodies.

LIGHT UP NIGHT

For Pittsburghers, **Light Up Night** (Pittsburgh Downtown Partnership, 412/566-4190, www.downtownpittsburgh.com, free, though $10 buttons are needed for access to some of the venues and events) signals the official start of the holiday season each November. Tens of thousands of people stream into Downtown for the occasion, which literally consists of lighting up the night; major department stores and small businesses alike line their facades with blinking holiday lights, and the city suddenly becomes a mini-Winter Wonderland. A few special exhibits are erected as well, including a massive Christmas tree near the Market Square fountain; the fountain becomes an outdoor ice skating rink during this time of year. Also festively lit up and worth a look is Station Square, which can easily be reached on foot by traversing the Smithfield Street Bridge.

PITT NATIONALITY ROOMS HOLIDAY TOURS

What better time to tour the Nationality Rooms at Pitt's Cathedral of Learning than the holiday season (November-January), when every room is fully decked out in each country's respective holiday style? Even if you've already toured the rooms, which are a series of fully functional classrooms designed and decorated to resemble classrooms from 26 separate nations, the **Pitt Nationality Rooms Holiday Tours** (Cathedral of Learning, University of Pittsburgh, corner of 5th Ave. and Bigelow Blvd., 412/624-6000, www.nationalityrooms.pitt.edu, self-guided tours free; guided tours $4 adult, $2 child) is still worth considering, especially if you're traveling with youngsters who might benefit from learning something about the international traditions of Christmas.

Spring

PITTSBURGH CRAFT BEER WEEK

Pittsburgh Craft Beer Week (events held at various bars and restaurants, www.pittsburghcraftbeerweek.com, cost varies by event) is a relative newcomer to the festival circuit, and one that has been growing along with the craft beer market in the area. Regional craft beers are showcased on tasting menus and often paired with complimentary small plates and snacks at numerous independently owned bars throughout the week. There are also meet-the-brewer events and various educational events related to the art of brewing. There are even special beers brewed exclusively for PCBW. The proceeds from many of the week's events often go to help support local charities and organizations. A word of warning: Many events sell out quickly, so do reserve yourself a place early if a particular event or venue recommends it.

PITTSBURGH FOLK FESTIVAL

Since 1956, the **Pittsburgh Folk Festival** (1000 Fort Duquesne Blvd., David L. Lawrence Convention Center, 412/565-6000 or 412/278-1267, www.pghfolkfest.org, $10 adult, $9 senior, $2 child 2-12, free kids under 2), which takes place in late April or early May, has presented an ideal opportunity to explore the cultural intricacies of more than two dozen nationalities, all without leaving Downtown. Ethnic food and entertainment are offered throughout the day, and visitors have the chance to practice ethnic dances or to simply shop for souvenirs in the international bazaar. Participating nationalities vary from year to year.

PITTSBURGH INTERNATIONAL CHILDREN'S FESTIVAL

For parents who aim to afford their children lots of wholesome learning and entertainment opportunities, but who can't possibly bear to suffer through another brain-numbing performance of *Barney on Ice,* the **Pittsburgh International Children's Festival** (West Park, 412/321-5520, www.pghkids.org, $8 per person per show; children under 2 years old are free but require a lap pass) may be just the thing. Each May, a weeklong showcase of professional theater companies from around the world is held, much to the delight of kids of all ages. Performances run the gamut from acrobatics to music and dance to comedy and drama.

ST. PATRICK'S DAY PARADE

Get this: Pittsburghers are so nuts about St. Paddy's Day that, depending on which day the holiday actually falls on, it's sometimes celebrated *twice.* It works like this: The **St. Patrick's Day Parade** (begins at Liberty Ave. and 11th St., www.pittsburghirish.org/parade, free) always takes place on a Saturday in March, so if St. Paddy's Day falls on a weekday, the parade will happen the Saturday *before* the actual holiday. Confused yet? Just remember this: In Pittsburgh, that means two excuses to party. And what a party it is. The parade, which begins as early as 10am and snakes through Downtown, is a fete of almost unbelievable proportions. Think floats, marching bands, and a very inebriated crowd (it's one of the few times of the year when drinking on public streets is tolerated if not encouraged). And no, you don't have to be Irish (or a connoisseur of green beer) to join in.

ANTHROCON

Should you stumble upon a prowling gang of grown adults, every last one of them dressed in an elaborate, head-to-toe cartoon animal costume, do not panic. They're members of a relatively unknown yet hugely passionate subculture known as "furries," and their largest annual convention, appropriately known as **Anthrocon** (David L. Lawrence Convention Center, 832/387-6771, www.anthrocon.org, $30 one-day membership, check website for other membership information), draws 5,000 to the Steel City each July. Furries are obsessed with anthropomorphic animals—animals, that is, with human characteristics, like Tony the Tiger or Sonic the Hedgehog. The Steel City has hosted these furry faithfuls since 2006, and is happy to have them. The non-profit organization Anthrocon, Inc. has donated more than $125,000 to various charity organizations since 1997, and in 2012 alone, Anthrocon estimates that its convention contributed more than $4 million to the Pittsburgh area economy.

Convention registration can be completed online; one-day memberships are $30, while access to the entire four-day shebang will run you anywhere from $50 to $250, depending on the number of special perks you'd like to enjoy during the event. You don't need to be a furry or arrive in costume to attend.

BIKEFEST

Organized annually by the politically active and nonprofit Bike Pittsburgh organization, which for years now has been working to transform Pittsburgh into a safe, friendly, and accessible place for cyclists, **BikeFest** (3410 Penn Ave., 412/325-4334, www.bikepgh.org/campaigns/bikefest, cost varies, most daytime events are free) is a phenomenal 10-day-long celebration of bicycle culture at its very best, with an emphasis on education and inclusiveness. Bike races, leisurely rides, bike scavenger hunts, bike polo games, bike workshops, and even bike-themed movie screenings and readings take place throughout the festival. And although the fest's specific events change slightly with each passing year, the city's ever-growing cycling community can always count on a phenomenal opening day kickoff party, featuring deejays, raffles, and a silent auction. BikeFest is held in August.

CINEMA IN THE PARK

When it comes to wholesome and affordable summer entertainment that's appropriate for the entire family, it's tough to beat the city's **Cinema in the Park** (various city parks, 412/422-6426, http://pittsburghpa.gov/citiparks/cinema-in-park, free), which offers an entire season's worth of free movies screened out-of-doors at seven different public parks. The films start as soon as the sun sets, and each park has a different screening schedule, making it theoretically possible to see a free movie each day of the week from June through August. Most locals enjoy the movies picnic-style, complete with blankets and coolers full of food. Alcohol, however, is strictly forbidden. Oakland's Schenley Park on Flagstaff Hill is probably the event's most popular location. Call or visit the website for park locations and detailed schedules.

FOURTH OF JULY FIREWORKS

Pittsburgh's celebration of Independence Day probably won't come across as anything outside the norm to those born and raised between sea and shining sea. The city's free celebration takes place at Point State Park; arrive early to secure a seat near the rivers. Blankets or portable chairs are suggested if you'll be staying awhile, and entertainment is generally provided by massive public address-style speakers blasting patriotic rock 'n' roll.

PEDAL PITTSBURGH

Since Pittsburgh has become a more bike friendly town in recent years, with its hills, valleys, bridges, waterways, and, yes, miles of bike trails, it's a simple fact that one of the best ways to experience the unique sights and landscape of the city is atop two wheels. And that's exactly why **Pedal Pittsburgh** (2730 Sidney St., 412/325-4334, www.pedalpittsburgh.org; $35 adults, $15 children), which, by the way, is a recreational ride and not a race, is so popular. More than 2,000 cyclists show up every August to take part in this celebration of the common bike, which involves a number of different rides that range from the simple and short to the lengthy and challenging. So whether you're a hardcore cyclist, a biking newbie, or even a child, you'll be able to participate at a comfortable pace. Departures happen in the early morning, while the Finish Line Festival, which includes food trucks and live entertainment, is scheduled during the middle of the day.

PENNSYLVANIA MICROBREWERS FEST

Craft brewers from all across Pennsylvania and beyond gather annually in June for the **Pennsylvania Microbrewers Fest** (800 Vinial St., 412/237-9402, www.pennbrew.com, $32), a celebration of obscure and creatively brewed beer. The event, which has been going strong since 1995, conveniently takes place at the North Side's Penn Brewery. Attendees are welcome to sample nearly unlimited quantities of roughly 100 different beers, from Belgian Ales to India Pale Ales to organic beers. A meal is included with the price of admission.

PITTSBURGH BLUES FESTIVAL

Not content to simply celebrate the blues, the **Pittsburgh Blues Festival** (412/460-2583, www.pghblues.com, $30-50), which takes place in July, is also a highly successful food drive that has raised funds for the Greater Pittsburgh Community Food Bank since 1995. Of course, most folks do come primarily for the music and no wonder: Nationally and internationally acclaimed artists perform throughout the weekend, and especially big-name acts take the stage every evening. The location of the festival changes every year, so be sure to call or visit the festival's website well in advance. The setup is always the same, however: Food vendors offer Southern-themed eats, a KidZone tent keeps the little ones amused, and hours upon hours of good ol' American blues fill the ears.

PITTSBURGH MARATHON

After its much-publicized five-year hiatus, during which the city lacked the funds to keep it operational, the hugely popular **Pittsburgh Marathon** (starts in Downtown Pittsburgh, 412/586-7785, www.pittsburghmarathon.com, $95-155) was finally brought back to life in 2009, thanks in large part to its new corporate sponsor, Dick's Sporting Goods. The city's especially hilly terrain, of course, makes the marathon, which takes place in May, a visual delight for those used to running races in much flatter cities; the course covers portions of the North Shore, the South Side, Oakland, Shadyside, and Bloomfield, and it also crosses each one of the city's three rivers. Less advanced runners also have the option of competing in a half-marathon; relay teams are also an option. There's also a kids' marathon for runners ages 5-14. The registration fees are $95-155; the lowest price listed is for early-bird registration, and prices increase as the marathon date approaches.

PITTSBURGH THREE RIVERS REGATTA

One of the city's most beloved summer events, the four-day-long **Three Rivers Regatta** (Point State Park, 412/875-4841, www.threeriversregatta.net, free) pays tribute to one of Pittsburgh's most valuable resources: its winding waterways. The festival takes place in July inside Downtown's Point State Park, and, naturally, many of the best events take place in the drink. Families can enjoy Grand Prix powerboat races, personal watercraft stunt shows, bass fishing, and even a boat demonstration by the U.S. Navy from the stadium-style seating that lines the Allegheny River. But fun stuff happens on land and in the air, too: hot-air-balloon rides, a dog Frisbee show, a U.S. Navy parachute team exhibition. There's even a concert series featuring marquee-level acts.

PITTSBURGH TRIATHLON AND ADVENTURE RACE

The **Pittsburgh Triathlon and Adventure Race** (33 Terminal Way, Ste. 333B, Friends of the Riverfront, 412/488-0212, www.friendsoftheriverfront.org), a serious physical endurance test involving water, cycle, and foot races, will undoubtedly be your only opportunity to swim in the fairly polluted Allegheny River without being considered completely out of your mind. But this isn't a contest to be taken lightly; the event, which takes place in August, begins with a 1.5K swim from the North Shore to the Roberto Clemente Bridge and back, and then a rigorous 40K bike ride along I-279, and finally a 10K run along the Allegheny River. In other words, don't bother entering unless you're in absolutely top physical shape. Observing the race is an event in itself, however, and there's always the **Adventure Race**—a light two-mile canoe paddle followed by a 3.2-mile run that takes place at the same time as the Pittsburgh Triathlon. This is a good option for people who are not physically fit enough to participate in the triathlon but are looking for a challenge nonetheless. The registration fees vary by race/event. An additional $10 USA Triathlon fee is required for each athlete.

PITTSBURGH VINTAGE GRAND PRIX

A 10-day festival of races, car shows, and motorsports events, the **Pittsburgh Vintage Grand Prix** (Schenley Park, www.pittsburghvintagegrandprix.com) features one of the finest vintage car shows of its kind in the country. Classic car enthusiasts—all amateur drivers—motor throughout the streets of leafy Schenley Park for 10 days each July. Motorists arrive in what will almost certainly be the most unusual assortment of vehicles you've ever seen in one setting; expect mint-condition antique and specialty vehicles from all over the world. Proceeds benefit Pittsburghers with disabilities, although all events are free for spectators.

PRIDEFEST AND PRIDE IN THE STREET

Originally organized by the Delta Foundation of Pittsburgh and taking place in the heart of the Golden Triangle, **PrideFest** and **Pride in the Street** (Liberty Ave., Downtown, 412/332-2800, www.pittsburghpride.org, Pride in the Street $25, PrideFest free) are two separate but related celebrations of gay life and culture that happen during the same weekend in June; the events culminate with the ever-popular **Pride Awareness March.** Both events are day-long affairs that happen out-of-doors on Liberty Avenue, where various deejays and gay-culture icons perform on stage. Other festival events range from spoken word performances to drag shows to carnival games. Food and drink vendors are also plentiful, and PrideFest features a beer garden that requires a separate $25 entrance fee.

Festival of Firsts

Each fall, the Pittsburgh Cultural Trust sets aside an inspiring four weeks to host the Pittsburgh International Festival of Firsts (www.pifof.org), a nonstop barrage of international art that has never before been seen in the United States. The event has quickly become known for its contemporary and eclectic mix of visual art exhibits, theater and dance productions, musical performances, and even genre-blurring acts like puppet shows and acrobatic ensembles.

The 2013 festival alone brought in artists from across Canada, Australia, France, Austria, Belgium, Switzerland, and Holland. Highlights included a 40-foot-tall rubber duck that floated and bobbed along the Ohio River.

Although future dates aren't yet set in stone, the festival is always held in the fall; for those with even the slightest interest in contemporary art, the festival is not to be missed. Tickets are $25 for performances, and many visual arts exhibits are free. Due to the festival's popularity, tickets often sell out quickly, and advance purchase is recommended. All tickets can be purchased at the Pittsburgh Cultural Trust's website, www.trustarts.org/events.

THREE RIVERS ARTS FESTIVAL

Pittsburgh simply wouldn't be the same without the much-loved **Three Rivers Arts Festival** (Point State Park and other Downtown locations, 412/281-8723, www.3riversartsfest.org, free), a two-week-long June celebration of live music, crafts, dance, performance, visual and contemporary art, and even a touch of carnival culture. It was founded in 1960 by a committee affiliated with the Carnegie Museum of Art, and portions of the festival take place at various locations throughout Downtown, although the bulk of the activity happens in and around Point State Park. Keep your eyes peeled for festival schedules, which include maps and free concert listings. You'll need to stroll the length of Downtown's Penn and Liberty Avenues to explore all the participating galleries, while vendors who arrive from around the country to hawk handicrafts cluster near the Hilton, just across the street from Point State Park and the never-ending row of food carts. Installations and a performance art shows can be found just inside the park.

Fall

DIA DE LOS MUERTOS FESTIVAL

Sponsored by the Pittsburgh Center for Creative Reuse (PCCR), the **Dia de los Muertos Festival** (various locations, www.pccr.org, cost varies by event) is a two-day affair that celebrates the Mexican Day of the Dead on November 1-2. Local galleries, restaurants, and bars have been known to get in on the action, and with a recent Sprout Fund grant, the festival is sure to continue growing. Festival activities start long before the actual events, however, as PCCR and other arts and community organizations host a solid month's worth of crafting workshops, covering everything from traditional papier-mâché masks to more general Mexican decor. If you're more inclined to create your festival decor alone, you can also stop by the fabulous **PCCR** shop (214 N. Lexington St., 412/473-010, Tues.-Sun. 11am-6pm), where you'll find a plethora of reusable craft materials and other unusual goods.

A FAIR IN THE PARK

A contemporary arts and crafts festival that has been organized by the Craftsmen's Guild of Pittsburgh since 1970, the three-day **A Fair in the Park** (Mellon Park, 412/370-0695, www.afairinthepark.org, free), held in September, has long been one of the Pittsburgh art community's most anticipated annual celebrations. More than 20,000 craft obsessives from Pittsburgh and beyond arrive each year to shop for handmade works of jewelry, glass, metal, clay, and much more. A packed-full schedule of activities and entertainment is also a big part of the fun: Glassblowers, metalsmiths, and sculptors can be observed in the act of creation, and a wide variety of musicians and performing artists set up shop as well. The popular I Made It! Market vendors are always in attendance, and the Children's Museum of Pittsburgh also sponsors a popular family and children's area, where the little ones can get their craft on, free of charge.

MEXICAN WAR STREETS HOUSE AND GARDEN TOUR

Neighborhood renovation is the theme of the decidedly upscale **Mexican War Streets House and Garden Tour** (412/323-9030, www.mexicanwarstreets.org, $18 in advance, $20 at the door) during September, when owners of gorgeously restored homes in Pittsburgh's Victorian-era district open their doors and allow complete strangers to tramp through their living rooms. Many homes you'll see along the tour are listed on the National Register of Historic Places. Even swankier is the black-tie pre-tour gala; it takes place in a different location each year. Visit the website for ticket and location information.

OKTOBERFEST

Although smaller Oktoberfest celebrations take place at a handful of brewpubs throughout Southwestern Pennsylvania every September, Pittsburghers on the hunt for the biggest and best party always head to the outdoor patio at **Penn Brewery** (412/237-9400, www.pennbrew.com, free). The event takes place over the length of two weekends, and the festivities follow the same schedule as Oktoberfest in Munich. And just as in Germany, the party is all about food, drink, music, and dance. Traditional German bands perform in both the outdoor tent and the restaurant. All manner of schnitzels and wursts are available, as is the brewery's special-edition Oktoberfest brew.

Within the city limits, Oktoberfest is also celebrated at **Hofbräuhaus Pittsburgh** (www.hofbrauhauspittsburgh.com) at SouthSide Works, where a portion of the event involves the crowing of Miss Oktoberfest.

For *serious* Oktoberfest fans willing to take a bit of a drive, the free-to-the-public **Pennsylvania Bavarian Oktoberfest** (www.paoktoberfest.com) in Canonsburg (about a 30-minute drive from Downtown) is known as one of the biggest celebrations of its type in the country. Call 724/745-1812 for more information.

PITTSBURGH IRISH FESTIVAL

Sandcastle's Riverplex waterpark is the site of the city's annual weekend celebration of the Emerald Isle, the **Pittsburgh Irish Festival** (1000 Sandcastle Dr., Riverplex at Sandcastle, Homestead, 412/422-1113, www.pghirishfest.org, Fri. $5; Sat. and Sun. $12 adult in advance or $14 adult at the gate, $8 student, senior, military, and police officers; ID card required for student, senior, military, and police discounts), which takes place in September. Many activities revolve around the main stage, where both traditional and contemporary Irish musicians perform daily. Celtic dancing, traditional musical instrument demonstrations, traditional Irish eats, and activities aimed specifically at children round out the long weekend. But do be aware that although the festival is advertised as family friendly, a good number of attendees tend to get inebriated.

PITTSBURGH NEW WORKS FESTIVAL

For thespians and theater buffs in the Steel City, no event compares with the **New Works Festival** (111 9th St., CAPA, 412/944-2639, www.pittsburghnewworks.org, most performances $15; unlimited festival passes $40; student and senior discounts available), an annual showcase of one-act plays that stretches over a four-week period in September and October. As is the case with most new-works festivals, an even mixture of comedy, drama, and highly experimental work is presented, and although some performances are the work of Southwestern Pennsylvania-based playwrights, playwrights from across the country are represented as well. Shows take place at locations around town. The main location of the festival is Pittsburgh's Creative and Performing Arts High School in Downtown.

RICHARD S. CALIGUIRI CITY OF PITTSBURGH GREAT RACE

When the Pittsburgh Marathon was temporarily canceled several years ago due to citywide financial troubles, the annual **Great Race** (starts at Frick Park, 412/255-2493, www.rungreatrace.com, registration fees $30 per runner; prices for additional race weekend events vary), held each September, was the city's sole opportunity for competitive foot racing. Now that the marathon is back and stronger than ever, the Great Race has once again taken something of a back seat, although it remains a decidedly serious sporting event that attracts pro athletes from all around the world. The contest consists of a 5K run and walk (about 8 miles), as well as a 10K run (about 16 miles). The run, which begins at Squirrel Hill's Frick Park and ends at Point State Park, Downtown, generally draws as many as 10,000 participants. But unless you're at the absolute height of your competitive game, don't count on coming home with a prize; Kenyan athletes almost always take top honors. Teams consisting of three to five runners are also welcome to compete.

THREE RIVERS FILM FESTIVAL

An annual presentation of the Pittsburgh Filmmakers family, the **Three Rivers Film Festival** (various locations, www.3rff.com, opening and closing night tickets $15, single tickets $10, Six-Pack Pass including admission to six films $50) is now a quarter of a century old. Documentaries, foreign films, locally produced shorts, and films that would otherwise never be screened in a market as small as Pittsburgh's are shown at three separate locations: the **Regent Square Theater** (1035 S. Braddock Ave., Edgewood), **Harris Theater** (809 Liberty Ave., Downtown), and **Melwood Screening Room** (477 Melwood Ave., Oakland). The festival takes place in November, and special events vary from year to year. Past festivals have featured Pere Ubu's live accompaniment to a Roger Corman film and a screening of nickelodeon films from the early 1900s.

Essentials

Getting There

Thanks to its easy-to-navigate Pittsburgh International Airport, its bus and train depots, and its convenient location on I-76 between Chicago and Philadelphia, you shouldn't expect any problems getting into or out of the Greater Pittsburgh area.

BY AIR

More than eight million travelers each year land at **Pittsburgh International Airport** (PIT, 412/472-5510 or 412/472-3525, www.pitairport.com), which offers 150 nonstop flights each day to 38 different destinations. Located 16 miles northwest of Downtown, PIT was one of the first American airports to construct a mammoth, mall-like shopping center on its premises. Along with a collection of more than 100 stores and restaurants, the airport boasts a full-service U.S. Post Office, a nondenominational chapel featuring a daily Roman Catholic mass, and six international gates. Be sure to look out for the gorgeous and appropriately titled Alexander Calder mobile, *Pittsburgh*.

Today, eight commercial air carriers serve Pittsburgh International, including Jet Blue (www.jetblue.com), which flies to New York's JFK and Boston's Logan International Airport. Other budget airlines serving PIT include AirTran (www.airtran.com) and Southwest (www.southwest.com). Air Canada, Delta, United, U.S. Airways, and American Airways currently serve Pittsburgh International as well.

Cheap public transport to and from the airport begins and ends with the **28X Airport Flyer** bus, a bargain at $3.75. The route begins at Carnegie Mellon University before making its way past the University of Pittsburgh, down 5th Avenue in Oakland, and into Downtown. Allow 45 minutes if traveling from Oakland or 30 minutes if traveling from Downtown. Contact the **Port Authority** (412/442-2000, www.portauthority.org) for scheduling information. Be aware that the first 28X bus of the day doesn't arrive at the airport until 5:14am, so the bus might not be a reliable option if you have an early morning flight. (For domestic flights, allow a minimum of 90 minutes to check in and get through security; allow two hours if you're flying internationally.) The final 28X of the day, which departs from the lower-level ground transportation area outside baggage claim (near Door 6), leaves at midnight.

A **Yellow Cab taxi** (412/321-8100) will take you to Pittsburgh International at any time of the day or night, but expect to pay around $50 from Downtown, not including a gratuity. Calling Yellow Cab well in advance and booking a taxi is highly recommended, as is booking much earlier than you actually need to:

Yellow Cabs in Pittsburgh have a nasty habit of not showing up when they say they will. Should your cab fail to arrive, you can usually find an active taxi rank outside most Downtown hotels at all hours of the day and night.

Your only other transport options to the airport, aside from booking a private car (look in the telephone book under "Airport Transportation" to explore that option), are the customer courtesy shuttles that run regularly from most Downtown hotels. Inquire at your hotel about this service.

PIT offers a long-term parking lot for travelers who need to leave their vehicles at the airport for days or weeks at a time, although two private companies offer much cheaper rates. **Charlie Brown's Airport Parking** (600 Flaugherty Run Rd., 412/262-4931, www.charliebrownsairportparking.com) charges $7 per day or $45 per week, although you'll first need to download and print out the discount coupon available on the website. The rates at **Globe Airport Parking** (412/264-4373 or 412/262-9130, www.globeparking.com) are exactly the same, and yes, you'll also need to print out the coupon available on this company's website to secure those low prices.

BY TRAIN

Pittsburgh's **Amtrak** station (412/471-6170, www.amtrak.com) is Downtown (1100 Liberty Ave.), directly across the street from the recently rebuilt Greyhound bus station and directly on the border of the Strip District. Trains depart daily for destinations throughout the United States and Canada, although fares on nondirect routes are generally higher than those offered by Greyhound. Trips on Amtrak also tend to take substantially longer than those on the bus—not necessarily a bad thing, as most American train routes pass through surroundings that highway travelers never get a chance to witness.

Popular destinations include Washington, D.C. ($49-143, 7.5 hours), Philadelphia ($55-132, 7.5 hours), and New York City ($73-174, 9 hours).

BY BUS

Directly across the street from the Amtrak station at Liberty Avenue and 11th Street, the newly rehabbed **Greyhound** depot (55 11th St., 800/231-2222, www.greyhound.com) features a striking cylindrical glass facade and a huge Greyhound sign, making it conveniently visible from probably a half dozen blocks away.

The double-decker coaches operated by the British company **Megabus** (www.megabus.com) offer significantly cheaper fares than those offered by Greyhound. They also feature electrical outlets and free onboard Wi-Fi and cleaner coaches. In Pittsburgh, Megabus picks up and drops off passengers outside the David L. Lawrence Convention Center, just north of the intersection of 10th Street and Penn Avenue. Coaches departing Pittsburgh travel to Philadelphia ($26 one-way); New York City ($49 one-way); Cleveland; Detroit; Washington, D.C.; and Morgantown (WV), among other destinations. Visit the Megabus website to buy tickets and to view scheduling and passenger information.

Getting Around

PUBLIC TRANSPORTATION

Port Authority Transit (412/422-2000, www.portauthority.org) operates buses, trains, and two inclines within Allegheny County. Bus, train, and incline rides are $2.50. Transfers cost an extra $1; they're generally good for three or four hours and can be used for one ride going in any direction.

The light rail system, known locally as the T, has four stops in Downtown, two on the North Shore, and another at Station Square. The train also travels through the suburbs of the South Hills; one line ends at South Hills Village Mall, while the other continues on to the town of Library. Riding within the Free Fare Zone, which includes any of the four Downtown stops and the two North Shore stops, is of course free. A ride to the end of the line—or for that matter, anywhere in Zone 2, which begins after the Washington Junction stop—costs $3.75 one-way.

The city's two remaining inclines travel up and down Mount Washington. The Monongahela Incline begins across the street from Station Square and discharges passengers on Grandview Avenue. The Duquesne Incline also ends on Grandview Avenue but roughly a mile to the west in the Duquesne Heights district. (This is where Mount Washington's most expensive restaurants are located.) Its street-level station is somewhat inconveniently located along a busy road. If you'd like to ride both inclines, your best bet is to take the Monongahela Incline from Station Square up to Mount Washington and then walk down Grandview Avenue to the Duquesne Incline. Take the Duquesne down to street level, where you can then walk across a pedestrian bridge to a parking lot. Head toward the river, where you'll find a footpath that conveniently leads back to Station Square.

Weekly and monthly transit passes can be purchased at the **Port Authority Downtown Service Center** (534 Smithfield St., 412/255-1356) or at most Giant Eagle grocery stores.

DRIVING

Because Pittsburgh's public transportation system is relatively reliable, getting by without a car can certainly be done. To fully explore the city's outer reaches, however, a car is a necessary accoutrement. Pittsburgh is a notoriously confusing city to navigate, however, so consider investing in a street atlas. Rand McNally's spiral-bound *Pittsburgh: Street Guide* is a good choice. Also be aware that most neighborhoods within the city limits require all drivers to display a neighborhood-specific parking sticker in their window. If you park without a sticker, you'll generally need to move your car within one hour to avoid a ticket.

Rental cars are available at various locations throughout the city. At the Pittsburgh International Airport, you'll find rental counters for **Budget** (800/527-0700, www.budget.com), **Dollar** (800/800-4000, www.dollarrentacar.com), **Hertz** (800/654-3131, www.hertz.com), and **Avis** (412/472-5200, www.avis.com) on the same level as baggage claim.

TAXIS

Yellow Cab (412/321-8100, www.pghyellowcab.com) is the city's solitary taxi company. Contrary to popular belief, cabs *can* be hailed in Pittsburgh, but only in certain parts of town (Downtown, the South Side, and Station Square are your best bets). If absolutely no cabs are around, try walking to the closest hotel; empty taxis often wait outside for potential passengers. During late-night hours and especially on the weekends, cabs converge en masse on the South Side and at Station Square.

BICYCLING

In 1990, a poll in *Bicycling* magazine ranked Pittsburgh among the 10 worst U.S. cities for cycling. But the city's biking landscape has seen radical changes over the past quarter-decade, thanks in large part to organizations like **Bike Pittsburgh** (188 43rd St., 412/325-4334, www.bike-pgh.org), a nonprofit cycling and advocacy group committed to making the city safer and more accessible for cyclists. With very few exceptions, Pittsburgh's roadways lack bicycle lanes, so take special care to travel safely on busy or crowded roads. To explore the further reaches of the city without the added stress of traffic, download a map of the **Three Rivers Heritage Trail** at www.friendsoftheriverfront.org. Urban cyclists, meanwhile, will surely want to download the beautifully designed *Pittsburgh Bike Map* available on Bike Pittsburgh's website.

Your First Stop in the City

For far too many years, our city's solitary visitors center was relegated to a cramped and rather underwhelming kiosk located on Downtown's Liberty Avenue. A few years back, however, Pittsburgh's tourism board opened the doors to a truly awe-inspiring welcome center on the ground floor of Fifth Avenue Place (120 5th Ave., 412/456-7800, www.fifthavenueplacepa.com), a Downtown skyscraper located a mere stone's throw from the original Liberty Avenue kiosk. Officially known as **Welcome Pittsburgh** (412/281-7711 or 877/568-3744, www.visitpittsburgh.com), it's the absolute final word on what to do and where to go during your time in the Steel City. The counter agents are pleasant and friendly, and the center doubles as a gift shop, selling everything from commemorative Heinz pickle pins to trendy Pittsburgh T-shirts.

If you're flying into town, you can also stop by the small VisitPittsburgh booth at the airport. You'll find it in the Landside Terminal near baggage claim. Other Welcome Pittsburgh mini-outposts can be found inside the gift shop of the Senator John Heinz History Center in the Strip District (1212 Smallman St., 412/454-6000, www.heinzhistorycenter.org) and at the top of the Duquesne Incline on Mount Washington (1197 W. Carson St.). And while you're there, don't forget to grab a copy of the annual *Official Visitors Guide,* which makes a wonderful companion to this very book.

ACCESSIBILITY

The Pittsburgh Transportation Group—owner of the city's Yellow Cab company and the SuperShuttle Airport Service—also operates a special service, **Freedom Coach,** for people in wheelchairs and the otherwise mobility impaired. The company's specially equipped Ford Windstar minivans have fold-down ramps and rear-entry access, a universal wheelchair tie-down system, and air conditioning with separate backseat controls. Curb-to-curb service is offered. For more information call 412/444-4444 or visit www.pghtrans.com.

VisitPittsburgh publishes a slim yet information-packed free brochure, ***Pittsburgh's Accessibility Guide,*** with details about local ADA-compliant businesses, assistive technology companies based in the area, and more. It can be accessed online at www.visitpittsburgh.com/access or picked up at the organization's main Welcome Center on the first floor of Fifth Avenue Place (120 5th Ave., Downtown, 412/281-7711).

Tips for Travelers

WEATHER

Depending on who you ask, the average annual rainfall in Pittsburgh is somewhere between 37 and 40 inches a year, which may or may not mean that the Steel City sees more precipitation than Seattle, an unfounded factoid that you'll likely hear over and over again during your stay. But one thing's for sure: Thanks to the hilly topography of the immediate area and the effect of Lake Erie, which sits about 125 miles to the north, Southwestern Pennsylvania is well known as a region with 12 months of wildly unpredictable weather. And what's more, Pittsburgh is not a particularly good place for the depressed: Roughly 200 days of cloud cover are clocked annually, which means the town once known as "Smoky City" remains one of the cloudiest places in America. (Juneau, Alaska, tops the list.)

Happily, however, we do experience four complete seasons in Western Pennsylvania. Summers get good and hot, with the temperature generally hanging between 70 and 80°F (although much hotter days are not uncommon). Winter temperatures settle in somewhere between 20 and 30°F. For detailed day-to-day weather system tracking, log on to the **Weather Channel** online (www.weather.com), or take a look at **WPXI**'s local online forecast (www.wpxi.com/weather).

HOURS

Generally speaking, Pittsburgh is a town that rolls up its sidewalks fairly early. Bars close at 2am, and if business is slow during the week, they may close earlier than that. (Thankfully, business is *never* slow in a Pittsburgh bar on the weekend.) If you're staying on the East End, or anywhere on the South Side, expect the streets to get particularly rowdy around 15 minutes before the bars close on weekend nights. The South Side's East Carson Street in particular can be a frightening place at 2am; fistfights and police cruisers are a not uncommon sight.

Restaurants, too, tend to call it a day fairly early in the evening. Unlike those in the fine-dining scenes in cities like Philadelphia, Chicago, and San Francisco, popular eateries in Pittsburgh stop serving as early as 10 or 10:30pm, even on weekends. Always call ahead if your evening has gotten off to a late start.

Like most financial districts, Downtown Pittsburgh becomes

something of a ghost town on weekends and by about 6pm on weekdays, assuming there are no parades, festivals, or art crawls taking place.

TIPPING

At restaurants, servers should be tipped 15 percent of the check for average service or 20 percent for exceptional service. At coffee shops, leave the barista a few coins for a simple drink, such as house coffee. (Or simply drop your change into the barista's tip jar.) If you're ordering a more complicated espresso-based drink, it's not uncommon to leave a dollar. A 15-20 percent tip is also appropriate for taxi drivers, as well as anyone else performing a service for you, such as a massage therapist, a hairdresser, or an attendant or manicurist at a spa or salon.

In hotel rooms, you'll often find an envelope with the name of your room's attendant written on the front. If exceptional service is important to you, be sure to leave anywhere from $2 to $10 a day, depending on the quality of the hotel itself. (Attendants at more expensive hotels expect larger tips, while attendants at budget hotels usually aren't tipped at all.) A hotel concierge should be tipped $5-10. If a particularly complicated or time-sensitive service was performed, tip accordingly.

At bars, a minimum tip of a dollar per drink is expected, unless you're ordering a round, in which case you could probably get away with a bit less. Bartenders in Pittsburgh's dive bars don't necessarily expect a dollar a drink, even if the bar in question is particularly popular. Tip well in these busy places, however, and you'll often find that your service improves.

SMOKING

As a result of the Clean Indoor Air Act, which was signed into law in mid-June 2008, smoking in most public places and workplaces is now banned throughout the entire Commonwealth of Pennsylvania. Still, the practice of smoking in Pittsburgh's public places continues on to some degree, thanks to various permissions and loopholes in the law. Casinos and private clubs, for instance, aren't affected by the ruling, and taverns can be exempted from the law if food sales make up 20 percent or less of their total gross sales.

The Commonwealth maintains an online list of every establishment in Pennsylvania that is legally exempt from the ban; to find it, visit www.portal.state.pa.us and search for "CIAA Exception Approvals."

Health and Safety

As North American urban areas go, Pittsburgh is a relatively safe place, and locals are almost always more than happy to help a lost, confused, or otherwise disoriented outsider. And while the city does claim a rather high number of dangerous, no-go areas, the majority of these neighborhoods are safe during the day, and most are in obscure enough locales that the average tourist has little chance of stumbling into them.

Neighborhoods in which you'd be wise to keep your wits about you include the North Side, assuming you're north of the Andy Warhol Museum or in the area surrounding the Mattress Factory. (The area known as the North Shore, where PNC Park, Heinz Field, and the Carnegie Science Center are located, is quite safe.) Also take care in the East End. While East Liberty is newly gentrifying and has much to offer visitors, it's still something of a downtrodden locale. Parts of deep Lawrenceville (near the Allegheny River) can be a bit rugged, as can parts of Garfield, including the stretch of the Penn Avenue Corridor between the Allegheny Cemetery and the entrance to East Liberty. When exploring the Penn Avenue Corridor, avoid entering the residential streets on the side of Penn Avenue that sits opposite the Bloomfield and Friendship neighborhoods.

The Hill District and Uptown should also be avoided after dark; should you find yourself at a CONSOL Energy Center event at night, take care to walk back in the direction of Downtown.

HOSPITALS AND PHARMACIES

The majority of Pittsburgh's hospitals and health-care centers are clustered within the university district of Oakland. These include **UPMC Presbyterian, UPMC Montefiore, Magee-Womens Hospital of UPMC, Western Psychiatric Institute and Clinic of UPMC,** and even **The Western PA School for the Blind** (www.wpsbc.org). For more information, visit www.upmc.com. The **Children's Hospital of Pittsburgh of UPMC** was formerly located in Oakland but now is in a colorful new Lawrenceville building (4401 Penn Ave., www.chp.edu).

UPMC Mercy is in between Oakland and Downtown in the Uptown neighborhood, while **Allegheny General Hospital** is in North Side and the **Western Pennsylvania Hospital** is found on Bloomfield's Liberty Avenue. Allegheny General and Western Penn, as it's known, are both part of the West Penn Allegheny Health System (www.wpahs.org).

The **UPMC Health Plan** is one of Western Pennsylvania's most popular and widely used insurance programs. For information, visit www.upmchealthplan.com. For detailed information about the effects of the Affordable Care Act on Pennsylvania citizens, visit www.pahealthoptions.com.

EMERGENCY SERVICES

To call the police, or for fire or medical emergencies, dial 911. For an electrical emergency, dial 412/393-7000. If you have a gas emergency in Pittsburgh, dial 412/442-3095. The Poison Information Center can be contacted at 412/681-6669 or 412/390-3300. For water and sewer emergencies in Pittsburgh, dial 412/255-2409. The toll-free number for PA Crime Stoppers is 800/472-8477. Dial Pittsburgh's nonemergency services phone number, 311, to access information about city government services and to report nonemergencies such as potholes.

Information and Services

MEDIA AND COMMUNICATION

Phones and Area Codes

On February 1, 1998, Pittsburgh gained a new area code, 724, for telephone numbers existing outside the city limits. The change affected nearly 1.5 million phone lines. The vast majority of those were outside Allegheny County, although a few areas within Allegheny County were affected as well.

Other counties using the 724 area code include Armstrong, Beaver, Butler, Fayette, Greene, Indiana, Lawrence, Mercer, Washington, and Westmoreland Counties, as well as parts of Clarion, Crawford, and Venango Counties. The vast majority of neighborhoods within Allegheny County, which includes the City of Pittsburgh, use the 412 area code. No matter where you're calling to or from, however, you'll always need to dial the appropriate area code before dialing the phone number.

Internet Services

All branches of the **Carnegie Library of Pittsburgh** (412/622-3114, www.clpgh.org) offer free Internet access; a library card is required to get online. Visitors from out of town or abroad can request a temporary library card by showing a state-issued driver's license or a valid passport. The main branch of the Carnegie Library in Oakland conveniently offers free wireless service on its first and second floors. Wireless access is also available at cafés around town, including all **Crazy Mocha** locations (www.crazymocha.com) and all **Panera Bread** locations (www.panerabread.com). Most major hotels offer free high-speed wireless as well, as does the Pittsburgh International Airport.

Important Contact Information

SERVICES

- **Lawyer Referral Service:** 412/261-5555, www.acbalrs.org
- **Neighborhood Legal Services Association:** 412/255-6700 or 866/761-6572, www.nlsa.us
- **Non-emergency city services:** 311, www.pittsburghpa.gov/311
- **Pittsburgh Parking Authority:** 412/560-7275, www.pittsburghparking.com
- **Pittsburgh Public Schools:** 412/622-7920 or 412/622-3500, www.pps.k12.pa.us

TRANSPORTATION

- **Amtrak (train):** 412/471-6172 or 800/872-7245, www.amtrak.com
- **Greyhound (bus):** 412/392-6504 or 800/231-2222, www.greyhound.com
- **Pittsburgh International Airport:** 412/472-3525, www.pitairport.com
- **Port Authority Transit (regional bus and subway):** 412/442-2000, www.portauthority.org
- **Yellow Cab Taxi:** 412/321-8100, www.pghyellowcab.com

UTILITIES

- **Comcast Cable:** 412/447-1987 or 866/922-0069, www.comcast.com
- **Duquesne Light (electricity):** 888/393-7100 for customer service or 888/393-7000 for emergencies, www.duquesnelight.com
- **Equitable Gas:** 800/654-6335 for customer service or 800/253-3928 for emergencies, www.equitablegas.com

Mail and Messenger Services

The **United States Postal Service** maintains post offices in almost every Pittsburgh neighborhood; visit www.usps.com to search for a specific location or call 800/275-8777. Both **UPS** (800/742-5877, www.ups.com) and **FedEx** (800/463-3339, www.fedex.com) are handy for sending overnight packages or international shipping; call or go online to find the nearest location. For post office box rentals, **The UPS Store** (1739 E. Carson St., 412/381-7755, www.theupsstorelocal.com/1080) offers a reliable alternative to the USPS, with 24-hour mailbox access and a slew of other products and services available, such as copying, packaging, and shipping.

All three of Pittsburgh's bike messenger companies also deliver by car, should you need something picked up or delivered to a location that isn't within realistic cycling distance. The city's largest service is **Jet Messenger** (412/471-4722, www.jetrush.com). Your other choices are **American Expediting Company** (412/321-4546, www.amexpediting.com) and **Quick Messenger** (412/481-5000).

Magazines and Newspapers

Pittsburgh's two daily newspapers include the left-leaning ***Pittsburgh Post-Gazette*** (www.post-gazette.com) and the conservative ***Pittsburgh Tribune-Review*** (www.triblive.com). The city's solitary alternative newsweekly, ***Pittsburgh City Paper*** (www.pghcitypaper.com), is useful for its arts and entertainment listings, as well as for its well-reported news and feature stories.

Other area newspapers include ***Pittsburgh Business Times*** (www.bizjournals.com/pittsburgh), which is closely watched by the city's white-collar crowd; ***New Pittsburgh Courier*** (www.newpittsburghcourieronline.com), a weekly focusing primarily on African-American news and events; ***Pittsburgh Catholic*** (www.pittsburghcatholic.org), which serves Western Pennsylvania's considerable Catholic population and, tellingly enough, boasts the city's largest circulation; and ***Out*** (www.outonline.com), a gay and lesbian paper serving the tristate area.

Pittsburgh Magazine (www.pittsburghmagazine.com) is the area's best monthly; it offers feature stories as well as local arts, food, and travel information. Other area magazines with heavy concentrations of arts and culture coverage include ***Pittsburgh Quarterly*** (www.pittsburghquarterly.com) and ***Whirl*** (www.whirlmagazine.com), the latter of which is filled largely with photos of local celebrities flitting about at high-society fundraisers.

Table Magazine (www.tablemagazine.com) is a quarterly publication dedicated to the Southwestern Pennsylvania food scene; ***Edible Allegheny*** (www.ediblecommunities.com/allegheny) also covers the Greater Pittsburgh area food scene, with an emphasis on organic foods and sustainable farming practices.

Pittsburgh TEQ is a high-quality business-to-business magazine serving the area's entrepreneurial tech communities; it's published bimonthly by the Pittsburgh Technology Council. Nationally distributed bicycle magazines published in the Pittsburgh area include ***Dirt Rag*** (www.dirtragmag.com), ***Bicycle Times*** (www.bicycletimesmag.com), and ***Urban Velo*** (www.urbanvelo.org).

Pittsburgh has a healthy independent publishing scene. ***Creative Nonfiction*** (www.creativenonfiction.org) is a highly respected journal published by Pitt instructor Lee Gutkind, who was instrumental in establishing the literary journalism genre of the same name. **The New Yinzer** (www.newyinzer.com) is an online literary journal featuring fiction, poetry, and experimental prose; special print issues are occasionally published. ***Cafe Racer*** (www.caferacermag.com) is a hip motorcycle-culture magazine published by former *Tribune-Review* columnist Mike Seate.

Radio and TV

Affiliates of every major network exist in Pittsburgh. The city's **PBS** station, **WQED** (www.wqed.org), holds the distinction of being the first community-owned station in the country. **PCTV21** (www.pctv21.org) is Pittsburgh's public access station.

The city has a multitude of radio stations; check About.com's list at www.pittsburgh.about.com/od/radio, or stream local stations online at www.tunein.com/radio/Pittsburgh-r100023.

Some of the more popular area stations include **WESA 90.5 FM** (Pittsburgh's NPR affiliate); **WQED 89.3 FM** (classical and public radio); **WYEP 91.3 FM** (community-supported adult alternative); **WDVE 102.5 FM** (hard rock and classic rock); **3WS 94.5 FM** (oldies and classic hits); **WTAE 1250 AM** (local news and sports); **Y108 FM** (country); **KDKA 1020 AM** (news and talk); and **WRCT 88.3 FM** (free-form independent music from Carnegie Mellon).

PUBLIC LIBRARIES

Enter a public library anywhere in the city of Pittsburgh, and you're not only entering a sacred monument to learning and growth, you're also passing through an important chapter, so to speak, of Pittsburgh's history.

The Scottish industrialist and philanthropist Andrew Carnegie was responsible for the creation of every last library in Pittsburgh, as he was for many other free libraries across the United States and even throughout the world. Without Carnegie's impetus to share the gift of education with the working-class employees of his steel mills, the free library as we know it today likely wouldn't exist. It is worth noting, however, that not all of Carnegie's employees, who saw their wages lowered so that library construction could go forward, saw fit to return the love. Said one such steel worker in Margaret Byington's *Homestead: The Households of a Mill Town:* "We'd rather they hadn't cut our wages and let us spend the money for ourselves. What use has a man who works 12 hours a day for a library, anyway?"

Good point. Nonetheless, the Carnegie Library system today is a thing of wonder. To find the branch nearest you, visit www.clpgh.org.

Carnegie Library of Pittsburgh Main (4400 Forbes Ave., 412/622-3114) is in Oakland, directly across from Pitt's Hillman Library; the lovely Schenley Plaza separates the two. Following an extensive renovation, this main branch features free high-speed Wi-Fi on its first and second floors, a magazine room, an outdoor reading deck, and a Crazy Mocha café. The main branch also offers a career services center, an art and music room with an extensive collection of CDs, DVDs, and books on tape, and a superb magazine and newspaper collection.

The **Squirrel Hill** branch of the Carnegie Library (5801 Forbes Ave., 412/422-9650) was the lucky recipient of a $4.7 million modernist renovation. The Arthur Lubetz and Associates architecture firm responsible for the redesign is currently scheduled to take part in revitalizing every library in the Carnegie system. The **Downtown** (612 Smithfield St., 412/281-7141) and **Homewood** (7101 Hamilton Ave., 412/731-3080) locations were also renovated in years past. Other library branches can be found in **East Liberty** (130 S. Whitfield St., 412/363-8232), **Mount Washington** (315 Grandview Ave., 412/381-3380), **Lawrenceville** (279 Fisk St., 412/682-3668), and the **South Side** (2205 E. Carson St., 412/431-0505). Visit www.clpgh.org or any city library location to view a map of the entire 20-branch system.

PLACES OF WORSHIP

Because Pittsburgh is so heavy with Italian and eastern European immigrants, Catholicism is practically omnipresent. If it's a Catholic chapel you're after, you won't need to look too terribly hard. In fact, in some neighborhoods (including Bloomfield, where the first edition of this book was partially written), the ringing of church bells can still be heard throughout the day. To plug more effectively into the local scene, pick up a copy of the ***Pittsburgh Catholic*** (800/392-4670, www.pittsburghcatholic.org) at just about any chapel, or take a look at the website of the **Roman Catholic Diocese of Pittsburgh** at www.diopitt.org.

The East End neighborhood of Squirrel Hill is one of the largest Jewish neighborhoods on the East Coast; you'll find nearly two dozen synagogues. **Beth Shalom** (5915 Beacon St., www.bethshalompgh.org) is one of the neighborhood's most popular. Visit the Pittsburgh page at **JewishGen KehilaLinks** (http://kehilalinks.jewishgen.org) for a fairly comprehensive list of synagogues in Squirrel Hill and beyond.

The **Jewish Community Center** (5738 Forbes Ave., 412/521-8010, www.jccpgh.org) is at the corner of Forbes and Murray Avenues in Squirrel Hill. Often referred to by locals as the JCC, it holds a fitness center, art classes for children and adults, theater and musical performances, and much more, including the **American Jewish Museum,** which is the solitary museum in the western part of Pennsylvania devoted solely to the exploration of Jewish history and culture. And yes, all races, religions, and creeds are welcome at the JCC.

Pittsburgh is also home to the **Sri Venkateswara Temple** (1230 S. McCully Dr., Penn Hills, 412/373-3380, www.svtemple.org), one of the oldest Hindu temples in the country. The Hare Krishna community of **New Vrindaban** (304/843-1600, www.newvrindaban.com) is located about an hour's drive from Pittsburgh in Moundsville,

West Virginia. Call or visit the community's website for detailed directions.

Buddhists in the Pittsburgh area congregate at Sewickley's **Zen Center of Pittsburgh** (124 Willow Ridge Rd., Sewickley, 412/741-1262, www.deepspringzen.org), a Soto Zen temple with a resident priest. **City Dharma** (http://citydharma.wordpress.com) is an affiliate of the Zen Center; the organization regularly holds meditation events at the Church of the Redeemer (5700 Forbes Ave., Squirrel Hill, next to St. Edmund's Academy). Visit the City Dharma website for an up-to-date event schedule. **Stillpoint** (137 41st St., www.stillpointzen.org) is a Soto Zen practice community that gathers regularly in Lawrenceville.

Muslims in Pittsburgh are well served by the mosque at the **Islamic Center of Pittsburgh** (4100 Bigelow Blvd., 412/682-5555, www.icp-pgh.org), conveniently located in North Oakland and within easy walking distance of all Oakland universities.

In Pittsburgh, even the tattooed and pierced set has a church to serve their specific needs. Supported by both the United Methodist Church and the Presbyterian Church, **The Hot Metal Bridge Faith Community** (2700 Jane St., 412/481-4010, www.hotmetalbridge.com, Sun. gatherings at 9:30am and 11:30am) is something of a nondenominational community geared toward people who tend to find standard church services too, well, *standard*. They offer a children's ministry, a youth ministry, and a homeless ministry; they also operate a community kitchen on the South Side known as The Table.

To view a brief listing of city and suburban churches, visit www.greaterpittsburgh.com/html/sgp97.html.

MAJOR BANKS

The Pittsburgh area's two largest financial service organizations are **PNC Bank** (www.pncbank.com) and **Citizens Bank** (www.citizensbank.com); the latter bought out the Pittsburgh-headquartered Mellon Bank back in 2001. Both PNC and Citizens have branch locations and automatic teller machines (ATMs) in all reaches of the city.

Dollar Bank (www.dollarbank.com) is another area bank with numerous locations; the bank's no-fee and no-minimum checking accounts are a popular draw. **Mars National Bank** (www.marsbank.com), meanwhile, has multiple branches in the North Hills suburbs. And headquartered in the small Western Pennsylvania town of Hermitage is the **First National Bank** (www.fnb-online.com). With over 200 locations in Western Pennsylvania and northeastern Ohio, F.N.B. is currently the eighth-largest bank in the Pittsburgh region.

First Niagara Bank (www.fnfg.com) became the most recent addition to the city's banking community when it purchased 57 National City branches from PNC. Currently headquartered in Buffalo, New York, the company also sponsors the outdoor Burgettstown concert venue known as the First Niagara Pavilion, which was formerly known as the Post-Gazette Pavilion and, before that, the Coca-Cola Star Lake Amphitheater.

Most major banks can handle foreign currency exchanges even for customers without an account, but be prepared to pay a substantial service charge. Also, be aware that many Pittsburghers still refer to ATMs as "MAC" machines. This is a stubborn holdover from the days of Mellon Bank, which referred to its ATMs as "money access machines."

RELOCATION

If you're thinking about the possibility of making the Greater Pittsburgh area your permanent home, do yourself a favor and spend some time on the comprehensive and educational website of **Imagine Pittsburgh** (www.imaginepittsburgh.com). There you'll find business resources and demographic information about the area, as well as a cost-of-living calculator, housing advice, and lots of useful information about life in the region.

Other resource-rich sites worth visiting include those of the **Greater Pittsburgh Chamber of Commerce** (www.greaterpittsburghchamberofcommerce.com), the **Pittsburgh Regional Alliance** (www.pittsburghregion.com), and the **Pittsburgh Downtown Partnership** (www.downtownpittsburgh.com). Also useful is www.pittsburghcityliving.com.

Finding a Job

To search the current listings of jobs offered by the City of Pittsburgh, visit the city's site at www.pittsburghpa.gov.

The Pittsburgh Career Connector (http://pghcareerconnector.com) provides job-seeking info for those with interest or experience in the business or technology fields.

Other useful online search engines include www.careerbuilder.com, www.monster.com, and http://pittsburgh.craigslist.org.

The University of Pittsburgh Medical Center has long been one of the city's largest employers. To access its online list of regularly updated open positions, visit http://jobs.upmc.com.

The *Pittsburgh Post-Gazette*, the *Pittsburgh Tribune-Review*, and the *Pittsburgh City Paper* all carry job listings.

Coworking

Coworking (the practice of numerous individuals, many of whom are self-employed or work as freelancers, getting together to work in a shared office environment) is a growing international trend that Pittsburgh has embraced with speed and tenacity. Aside from the fact that working solo in a home office is often lonely, the coworking philosophy revolves around the idea that creative types thrive when surrounded by their own kind. If you're a self-employed entrepreneurial type thinking of putting down roots in a new city, you could certainly do worse than Pittsburgh—especially if you have any sort of a tech or programming background.

To learn more about the local coworking process, visit www.pittsburghcoworking.com. These currently active spaces all offer monthly memberships:

THE BEAUTY SHOPPE

Many beauty shoppers, as members here are known, are professionals working for small, creative arts-based organizations. This was the first coworking space to open in the city, and its location at the nexus of the East End's newest commercial developments can't be beat. Memberships start at $100 per month, or $50 monthly for students (6101 Penn Ave., Suite 201, East Liberty, www.thebeautyshoppe.org).

BRUNO WORKS

Located in the Bruno Building atop Downtown's ToonSeum, the two-floor Bruno Works bills itself as a "work space for tiny little start-ups." There's a dedicated photography area, a conference room, and plenty of communal office and art supplies. Unconventional learning events happen monthly as part of Bruno's Community Creative School. Memberships start at $75 per month (945 Liberty Ave., Unit 600, Downtown, 412/434-7080, www.brunoworkspgh.com).

CATAPULT PGH

Although it's largely home to self-employed creative types—writers, designers, entrepreneurs, and de-

Housing

The University of Pittsburgh provides a wonderful service through its **Housing Resource Center.** Apartment listings, roommate matching services, sublets, and housing guides can be accessed even by nonstudents at the center's Off Campus Living website (www.ocl.pitt.edu). The same site also includes information about purchasing a home in Pittsburgh, finding the best housing insurance for your needs, and picking the right neighborhood. There's even information about local hotels and bed-and-breakfasts, should you find yourself temporarily without a roof over your head. To access the site's very useful list of emergency and nonemergency contact information, visit www.ocl.pitt.edu/important-numbers-and-addresses.

velopers, for instance—Catapult emphasizes strength among community, and members often share the progress of their projects and may even collaborate. The vibe is decidedly laid-back, and during a monthly event known as Show 'n' Tell, nonmember speakers discuss their own current projects and business ideas. Memberships start at $50 per month (4327 Butler St., Lawrenceville, 412/407-3327, www.catapultpgh.org).

THE HARDWARE STORE

With a focus mainly on video and media production, The Hardware Store is not entirely unlike the offices of a public television station, say. There's a podcasting studio, a media production suite, a state-of-the-art audio studio, and even a green screen. The space's Allentown location, it's worth noting, is a bit out of the way and slightly inconvenient to access. Memberships are $150 monthly (744 E. Warrington Ave., Allentown, www.meetup.com/Events-at-the-Hardware-Store).

REVV OAKLAND

Designed for early-stage tech startups, the 5,000-square-foot Revv space is beautifully designed, and it even offers private office rentals. Community events happen regularly, and professional services, including legal, tax, and accounting, are also offered. Memberships begin at $100 monthly, or $500 monthly for a private office (122 Meyran Ave., Oakland, 412/944-2499, www.revvoakland.com).

STARTUPTOWN

Quite unlike the average coworking space, the StartUptown office is actually a century-old renovated home that also boasts 10,000 square feet of commercial space. Partly because of its location inside the Pittsburgh Central Keystone Innovation Zone, most tenants are affiliated with small startups. Solo-flying freelancers, however, are also welcome. Contact StartUptown directly for information about monthly membership rates, which vary according to members' needs (1936 5th Ave., Uptown, 412/644-0123, www.startuptown.org).

Many Pittsburghers interested in renting, subletting, or finding a prospective roommate do a brisk business on Craigslist. The local site can be accessed at http://pittsburgh.craigslist.org. You might also scan the bulletin boards and message boards throughout the Pitt and CMU campuses; housing notices are often posted there.

Agencies involved in the renting and selling of homes are located in a number of Pittsburgh neighborhoods, especially Shadyside and Squirrel Hill. One particularly popular agency, **Franklin West** (272 Shady Ave., Shadyside, 412/661-1151, www.franklinwest.com), specializes in contemporary apartments and townhouses.

Resources

Suggested Reading

Bell, Thomas. *Out of this Furnace.* University of Pittsburgh Press, 1976. An emotionally wrenching story that tells of the trials and tribulations of three generations of a Slovakian family who immigrated to America and ended up working in the Braddock steel mills.

Chabon, Michael. *The Mysteries of Pittsburgh.* Harper Perennial, 1989. Chabon is a graduate of the University of Pittsburgh and a former employee of the long-lived but now shuttered Jay's Bookstall; *Mysteries* was his first novel and also the book that was meant to catapult his rising star into the stratosphere. It didn't happen exactly that way, but this is nonetheless an incredible read about the existential and sexual dilemmas of a group of young adults passing their first summer after college.

Creative Nonfiction Foundation. *Pittsburgh in Words.* Creative Nonfiction, 2008. Published in celebration of the city's 250th anniversary, this magazine-like publication (which was produced by *Creative Nonfiction,* a local literary journal) features true stories by writers attempting to share and explain the true essence of the Steel City.

Dillard, Annie. *An American Childhood.* Harper Perennial, 1988. Dillard ponders her 1950s Pittsburgh childhood in this classic book about growing up, seeing the world anew, and the unavoidable pain of slowly becoming an adult.

Lorant, Stefan. *Pittsburgh: The Story of an American City.* The Derrydale Press, 1999. Based on decades of tireless research, this heavy, hardcover coffee-table book tells nearly every last facet of the city's story, from the battles of the mid-1750s to the 1990s. Incredibly detailed and packed with dozens of gorgeous photos, *Pittsburgh* reset the standard for historical and cultural books about cities when it was first published in the 1970s.

Musson, Robert A. *Brewing in Greater Pittsburgh.* Arcadia Publishing, 2012. As part of the *Images of America* series, Musson's volume documents

Pittsburgh's surprisingly active 250-year history as a beer-brewing town. The book features more than 200 historical photographs.

O'Nan, Stewart. *Everyday People.* Grove Press, 2001. A fictional tale about gangs, drugs, and the life of hard knocks in East Liberty, a still economically disadvantaged neighborhood that is nevertheless growing more gentrified each year.

Orr, C. Prentiss, Abby Mendelson, and Tripp Clarke. *Pittsburgh Born, Pittsburgh Bred.* Senator John Heinz History Center, 2008. Experience a touch of Steel City pride as you thumb through this engaging coffee-table book, which contains the stories of "500 of the more famous people who have called Pittsburgh home."

Toker, Franklin. *Pittsburgh: A New Portrait.* University of Pittsburgh Press, 2009. A stunningly ambitious look at Pittsburgh as a timeless American city, this heavy volume has now replaced Stefan Lorant's legendary *Pittsburgh* book as the definitive final word on the Steel City, from its earliest days to modern times.

Wideman, John Edgar. *Brothers and Keepers.* Holt, Rinehart, and Winston, 1984. One of the most popular books from this Pittsburgh-based writer, who long chronicled life in the Homewood ghetto. In *Brothers and Keepers,* Wideman waxes poetic about the differences between his life, heavy with learning and culture, and the life of his brother, who is serving a life sentence in jail.

Wilson, August. *Fences.* Samuel French, Inc., 1986. Probably the most legendary play ever penned by Hill District native August Wilson. The story, for which Wilson was awarded the Pulitzer Prize, concerns the struggle of Troy Maxson, a proud black man who can't quite get a grasp on the quickly changing world of the 1960s.

Internet Resources

INFORMATION AND EVENTS

About.com

www.pittsburgh.about.com

A solid online destination for keeping abreast of upcoming events and local news, About's Pittsburgh site also boasts info about finding a job, finding a home, and finding fun things to do with the family.

Carnegie Library of Pittsburgh
www.carnegielibrary.org
The Carnegie Library's website is an absolutely indispensable research site for scholars of all things Pittsburgh. Click the Tools & Research tab at the top of the homepage, and then choose the Pittsburgh link. There, you'll be directed to a wonderfully detailed collection of Pittsburgh data, be it cultural, historical, or just about anything else.

City of Pittsburgh
www.pittsburghpa.gov
The official City of Pittsburgh site provides information about city parks, tourism, road closures, and city-sponsored events. New residents in particular should explore the site's Resources and City Directory pages.

The College City
www.thecollegecity.com
Particularly useful for its fantastic collection of local links, this site should also be the first stop for any college student interested in area schools. It's also a useful site for new residents and tourists looking to discover the city's youthful and active opportunities.

Global Pittsburgh
www.globalpittsburgh.org
This wonderfully useful site is concerned with connecting Pittsburgh's various international communities. Visitors or new residents from abroad can search for job opportunities, new friends and activities, and information about immigration.

Imagine Pittsburgh
www.imaginepittsburgh.com
Launched as part of a three-year, $3 million marketing campaign to increase awareness of the Pittsburgh area's numerous achievements and its nearly unlimited possibility for growth, this site does a wonderful job of explaining why Pittsburgh is such a unique place. You'll also find links to the helpful tourism sites of 11 surrounding counties.

Pittsburghese
www.pittsburghese.com
This is a hilariously good-natured guide to one of North America's most curious regional dialects, Pittsburghese. It includes a glossary, a translator, an audio quiz—even Pittsburghese calisthenics. (Believe me, yinz are gonna need it.)

Venture Outdoors
www.ventureoutdoors.org
Local nonprofit organization Venture Outdoors is responsible for a surprisingly large percentage of the activities that take place on Pittsburgh's rivers. Check this site for a bevy of outdoorsy recreation opportunities.

VisitPittsburgh
www.visitpittsburgh.com
The Greater Pittsburgh Convention & Visitors Bureau site is where you'll find all the necessary information to plan a vacation or business trip to the Steel City. Essentially a mini online guidebook, VisitPittsburgh also allows visitors to book hotel and vacation packages. Particularly useful are the suggested itineraries for those interested in taking day trips to the nearby counties and countryside.

NEWS

New Pittsburgh Courier
www.newpittsburghcourieronline.com
The online version of the weekly newspaper geared toward the city's African American community.

Pittsburgh Business Times
www.bizjournals.com/pittsburgh
This local edition of the nationwide *Business Times*, a weekly newspaper, is a must-read for local entrepreneurs and corporate types.

Pittsburgh Catholic
www.pittsburghcatholic.org
This widely read weekly newspaper is published by the Diocese of Pittsburgh. It boasts the largest circulation of any paper in the region.

Pittsburgh City Paper
www.pghcitypaper.com
The city's solitary alternative newsweekly maintains a huge online archive of feature stories. The website is also indispensable for its comprehensive event listings and many restaurant reviews.

Pittsburgh Indymedia
www.pittsburgh.indymedia.org
This community-based media site is filled with regional news, most with a heavily liberal bias. Pittsburgh's activism community is surprisingly large, and this is where many of them congregate.

Information about upcoming protests and antiwar marches can be found here.

***Pittsburgh* Magazine**
www.pittsburghmagazine.com
The website of Pittsburgh's regional monthly magazine offers a wealth of feature stories, an extensive events calendar, thoughtful dining reviews, and more.

Pittsburgh Post-Gazette* and *Pittsburgh Tribune-Review
www.post-gazette.com
www.triblive.com
Find up-to-the-minute local and national news at the websites of Pittsburgh's two daily newspapers, the liberal and more critically acclaimed *Post-Gazette* and the conservative *Tribune-Review,* which publishes a handful of smaller community papers under its Trib Total Media banner.

Pop City
www.popcitymedia.com
This weekly online magazine documents the Pittsburgh experience primarily for the young and active crowd. Tech, lifestyle, and entrepreneurial news is featured.

BLOGS

Behind the Steel Curtain
www.behindthesteelcurtain.com
Pittsburgh is home to an untold number of Steelers fan blogs, and this is one of the very finest.

Boring Pittsburgh
www.boringpittsburgh.com
In its role as an enthusiastic cheerleader for the city, Boring Pittsburgh covers cool and quirky happenings and other events.

I Heart Pgh
www.iheartpgh.com
This is a quirky, well-edited, and frequently updated listing of events, especially those with a focus on the arts.

Pittsburgh Bloggers
www.pghbloggers.org
A blog about local blogs, it's useful largely because of its incredibly extensive collection of links.

Steeltown Anthem

www.steeltownanthem.com

This is an art, design, and architecture blog with a distinctive *Dwell* magazine sensibility.

Yinzperation

www.yinzperation.com

Inspired by a challenge to meet new Pittsburghers, Yinzperation is a clever interview-style blog that introduces readers to some of the city's unique personalities.

Index

F

G

H

IJ

KL

M

NO

P

QR

S

T

UVWXYZ

Restaurants Index

Nightlife Index

Shops Index

Hotels Index

Photo Credits

Title Page: ceiling of Pittsburgh's Amtrak Station © VisitPittsburgh; page 2 (top) Pittsburgh skyline with fireworks © VisitPittsburgh, (bottom) strolling along the Allegheny River © Dan Eldridge; page 18 (top left) Andy Warhol Bridge (7th Street Bridge) © Dan Eldridge, (top right) Pan sculpture and the Cathedral of Learning at University of Pittsburgh © Dan Eldridge, (bottom) Pittsburgh Pirates' game © VisitPittsburgh; page 3 Duquesne Incline © VisitPittsburgh; page 21 © National Aviary; page 22 © VisitPittsburgh; page 23 © Martha Rial; page 24 © Sean Pavone/123rf.com; page 25 © VisitPittsburgh; page 26 courtesy of Center for PostNatural History; page 26 (top) © TJ Ladner, (bottom) © VisitPittsburgh; page 28 © Matt Stroud; page 29 (top) fountain at PPG Place © VisitPittsburgh, (bottom) © tupungato/123rf.com; page 37 (top left) courtesy of PNC Legacy Project, (top right) © Dan Eldridge, (bottom) © August Wilson Center; page 47 (top left) © Dan Eldridge, (top right) © VisitPittsburgh, (bottom) © VisitPittsburgh; page 52 all © VisitPittsburgh; page 60 (top left) © VisitPittsburgh, (top right) © Steven Heap/123rf.com, (bottom) © VisitPittsburgh; page 66 all © VisitPittsburgh; page 69 © Gino Santa Maria/123rf.com; page 75 (top left) © VisitPittsburgh, (top right) © VisitPittsburgh, (bottom) © Dan Eldridge; page 77 © flickr.com/travis_warren123; page 85 (top) Meat & Potatoes © TJ Ladner, (bottom) meal at Franktuary © Sarah VanTassel; page 92 (top left) © Dan Eldridge, (top right) © TJ Ladner, (bottom) © Dan Eldridge; page 96 © Kamil Macniak/123rf.com; page 99 all © Dan Eldridge; page 102 © Dan Eldridge; page 107 all © Dan Eldridge; page 112 (top left) © Dan Eldridge, (top right) © VisitPittsburgh, (bottom) © Dan Eldridge; page 122 all © Dan Eldridge; page 132 (top) Franktuary © Sarah VanTassel, (bottom) Tiffany MacIsaac and Kyle Bailey of Washington DC's Birch and Barley join Cure's Justin Severino, photo © Adam Milliron; page 139 (top left) © Dan Eldridge, (top right) © Dan Eldridge, (bottom) © Laura Petrilla; page 142 (top) Church Brew Works © VisitPittsburgh, (bottom) Spin Bartini © Dan Eldridge; page 153 all © Dan Eldridge; page 166 (top left) © Dan Eldridge, (top right) © VisitPittsburgh, (bottom) © Dan Eldridge; page 169 (top) Benedum Center © Dan Eldridge, (bottom) Harris Theater © Dan Eldridge; 170 Arcade Comedy Theater © Dan Eldridge; page 175 (top left) © Dan Eldridge, (top right) © Dan Eldridge, (bottom) © VisitPittsburgh; page 182 all © Dan Eldridge; page 192 (top) Pittsburgh Pirates' game © Richard Kane/123rf.com, (bottom) © Martha Rial; page 194 Kayak Pittsburgh © VisitPittsburgh; page 196 © Dan Eldridge; page 203 © Dan Eldridge; page 206 (top left) © Ron Notarius/VisitPittsburgh, (top right) © Dan Eldridge, (bottom) © VisitPittsburgh; page 208 © Dan Eldridge; page 228 (top) © Wildcard, (bottom) © Dan Eldridge; page 232 © Dan Eldridge; page 242 (top left) © Dan Eldridge, (top right) © Bryan Heller, (bottom) © Petagogy; page 261 all © Dan Eldridge; page 271 (top) © Dan Eldridge, (bottom) Mansions on Fifth © Melody Farrin; page 272 bunkbeds at Hot Metal Lofts © Mike Holohan; page 282 (top left) © VisitPittsburgh, (top right) © VisitPittsburgh, (bottom) © Dan Eldridge; page 287 (top left) © Mike Holohan, (top right) © Annie O'Neill, (bottom) © VisitPittsburgh; page 294 (top) biking at Ohiopyle State Park photo courtesy of Laurel Highlands Visitors Bureau, (bottom) horse-drawn carriage ride at Nemacolin Woodlands Resort photo courtesy of Laurel Highlands Visitors Bureau; page 300 all courtesy of Laurel Highlands Visitors Bureau; page 306 (top left and top right) courtesy of Laurel Highlands Visitors Bureau, (bottom) courtesy of Western Pennsylvania Conservancy; page 323 (top) © Visions Of America LLC, (bottom) the Waterfront shopping center on the former site of U.S. Steel's Homestead Steel Works plant © Dan Eldridge; page 348 all © Dan Eldridge

Acknowledgments

Ah, the Acknowledgments page—so many wonderfully thoughtful people to thank, and such a small space in which to do so. As was the case with the first and second editions of this guide, my fiancée, Carrie Ann, wins the prize of my largest and most sincere bundle of gratitude. As usual, Carrie went far above and beyond the call of duty, assisting not only with massive amounts of research, but with writing and editing as well. In fact, were it not for the time and effort she put into this edition, you probably wouldn't be reading it. Thank you so much, babe. It's impossible to overstate how much poorer my life would be without you in it.

Thanks so much to Kris and Doug Richard, who housed and fed me in beautiful Baden during my research-and-photography excursion. Thanks also to Stella and Ray Voegel for allowing me to tool around Pittsburgh in the Jetta—especially since you had to deal with an extra dose of insanity from you-know-who as a result. (I still feel bad about that.)

Thanks to Nurse Jen, who filled me in on all sorts of unusual dining tips while we waited to board our respective planes at Chicago-Midway. You definitely helped set the tone for a great trip, Jen. Thanks to Tania Grubbs of the (very cool) PNC Legacy Project, who reminded me—after many years of being away—just what it is that makes Pittsburgh such a uniquely special place. (It's the people, and especially their infectious and undying enthusiasm for the city.) Thank you to the wonderful employees of Visit Pittsburgh, the city's tourism bureau. The information Visit Pittsburgh provides—both freely and in abundance—goes a long way toward making the *Moon Pittsburgh* guides as useful as they are.

And a huge thanks to you, my readers, for spending your hard-earned money on this book. I only hope you'll find it worthwhile, and that it will show you a side of Pittsburgh you might otherwise never know exists. If you'd like to contact me regarding *Moon Pittsburgh*—or anything else, for that matter—send a tweet to @YoungPioneers. Enjoy Pittsburgh!